BIOGRAPHICAL CONCORDANCE OF THE NEW TESTAMENT

BIOGRAPHICAL CONCORDANCE OF THE NEW TESTAMENT

MADISON DALE COOK

LOIZEAUX BROTHERS
Neptune, New Jersey

B. McCALL BARBOUR
28 GEORGE IV BRIDGE
EDINBURGH EH1 1ES, SCOTLAND

FIRST EDITION, JANUARY 1985

Library of Congress Cataloging in Publication Data

Cook, Madison Dale, 1943-
  Biographical concordance of the New Testament

  Includes index.
  1. Bible.   N.T.—Biography—Concordances.   I. Title.
BS2305.C58 1984   225.9'22   84-7164
ISBN 0-87213-089-4

EXPLANATORY MARKS

* = actions or activities of the disciples and/or apostles as a "group"
♀ = female
[ ] = enclose the pronunciation of the name, followed by the meaning of the name

The following abbreviations for the books of the Bible are used:

Gen	= Genesis	Nah	= Nahum
Exod	= Exodus	Habk	= Habakkuk
Lev	= Leviticus	Zeph	= Zephaniah
Num	= Numbers	Hag	= Haggai
Deut	= Deuteronomy	Zech	= Zechariah
Josh	= Joshua	Mal	= Malachi
Judg	= Judges	Matt	= Matthew
Ruth	= Ruth	Mark	= Mark
1Sam	= 1 Samuel	Luke	= Luke
2Sam	= 2 Samuel	John	= John
1Kng	= 1 Kings	Acts	= The Acts
2Kng	= 2 Kings	Rom	= Romans
1Chr	= 1 Chronicles	1Cor	= 1 Corinthians
2Chr	= 2 Chronicles	2Cor	= 2 Corinthians
Ezra	= Ezra	Gal	= Galatians
Neh	= Nehemiah	Eph	= Ephesians
Esth	= Esther	Phil	= Philippians
Job	= Job	Col	= Colossians
Ps	= Psalms	1The	= 1 Thessalonians
Prov	= Proverbs	2The	= 2 Thessalonians
Eccl	= Ecclesiastes	1Tim	= 1 Timothy
SS	= Song of Solomon	2Tim	= 2 Timothy
Isa	= Isaiah	Tit	= Titus
Jer	= Jeremiah	Phle	= Philemon
Lam	= Lamentations	Heb	= Hebrews
Ezek	= Ezekiel	Jas	= James
Dan	= Daniel	1Pet	= 1 Peter
Hos	= Hosea	2Pet	= 2 Peter
Joel	= Joel	1Joh	= 1 John
Amos	= Amos	2Joh	= 2 John
Obad	= Obadiah	3Joh	= 3 John
Jona	= Jonah	Jude	= Jude
Mic	= Micah	Rev	= Revelation

COMPARATIVE INDEX

The following index specifies those characters who are recorded in one testament under another name or that of another spelling from that name given in the other testament. Such instances often occur due to a change in alliteration from the original languages into the English.

Those entries followed by an * indicate a probable relationship although not completely affirmed.

Old Testament	New Testament	Old Testament	New Testament
Abijam	Abia	Kish	Cis
Abram	Abraham	Korah	Core
Ahaz	Achaz	Mahalaleel	Maleleel
Azaliah*	Esli	Manasseh	Manasses
Asher	Aser	Melchizedek	Melchisedec
Balak	Balac	Methuselah	Mathusala
Barachiah	Berechias	Nahor	Nachor
Belteshazzar	Daniel	Naphtali	Nephthalim
Beor	Bosor	Noah	Noah; Noe
Boaz	Booz	Peleg	Phalec
Coniah	Jechonias	Pharez	Phares
Eber*	Heber	Perez	Phares
Elijah	Elias	Rahab	Rachab; Rahab
Elisha	Eliseus	Rahel	Rachel
Hagar	Agar	Rebekah	Rebecca
Hamor	Emmor	Rehoboam	Roboam
Henoch	Enoch	Reu*	Ragau
Hezekiah	Ezekias	Salah	Sala
Hezron	Esrom	Salma	Salmon
Hosea	Osee	Sarai	Sara; Sarah
Isaiah	Esaias	Serug	Saruch
Israel	Jacob	Shealtiel	Salathiel
Jeconiah	Jechonias	Shelah	Sala
Jehoiachin	Jechonias	Shem	Sem
Jehoshaphat	Josaphat	Sheth	Seth
Jephthah	Jephthae	Shimei*	Semei
Jerubbaal	Gideon	Tamar	Thamar
Jerubbesheth	Gideon	Terah	Thara
Jeshua	Jesus	Uriah	Urias
Jonah	Jonas	Uzziah	Ozias
Joshua	Jesus	Zebulun	Zabulon
Josiah	Josias	Zechariah	Zacharias
Judah	Juda; Judas	Zerah	Zara
Kenan	Cainan	Zerubbabel	Zorobabel

INTRODUCTION

The study of biographies, especially those of Bible characters, is a fascinating, interesting, and enlightening experience.

This work is one suited to a biographical vein. The original idea was to include in a concordance fashion every individual listed by name in the New Testament and every reference of a biographical nature about that individual. However, the selection of traits and events of a biographical nature is often quite arbitrary. One should note that differences of opinion occur among scholars relative to the very identity of various Biblical characters and much more so relative to their specific activities. The reader may find instances where specific items may be of significance to the author as biographical, yet to the reader the items have no such bearing. Consequently, the judgment of the author of necessity must prevail since individual consultation with every reader is impossible if yet even desirable because many disagreements and disputations would be certain to arise. In those rare instances where the reader may take issue with the traits presented, the effect, nevertheless, will be to spur him to deeper levels of study and Biblical introspection.

This study seeks to provide a biographical concordance that differs much from any other similar works concerning Bible characters. No attempt has been made to provide for an exact rendering of wording for each entry, but rather a short synopsis of the "meaning" of the entry in question is often provided. Likewise, no attempt has been made to produce a completely exhaustive work but to provide a basic working manual representative of the author's views, opinions, and interpretations of the New Testament text as recorded in the King James version of the Holy Scriptures, incorporating a fundamental, conservative position.

Only those "human beings" mentioned in the actual text of the New Testament are included. Extraterrestrial beings such as Michael the archangel, the angel Gabriel, and Satan, for example, are purposely excluded. In like fashion, no attempt has been made to chronicle the life of Jesus Christ in this work since that is a study in itself.

The reference number placed at the front of each entry is the beginning point of each reference. Occasionally, a reference enclosed in parenthesis will follow an entry. This indicates that the particular reference in question continues from the point of original reference (the reference number at the beginning of the line) through the verse indicated by the parenthesis at the ending of the reference.

Frequently, the reader is confronted by a reference to a passage accompanied by an asterisk (*). The asterisk refers the reader to those actions and activities of the collective "group" of disciples and/or apostles and does not necessarily infer that the reference is directly applicable to the individual in question.

For the reader's convenience, the pronunciation and the meaning of each entry is enclosed in brackets immediately following the individual's name. When more than one person by the same name appears in the text, only one reference to that name is provided, accompanied by numbered entries identifying each of these personalities.

A

AARON [a'-ur-un = enlightened; illumined]
First high priest of Israel, son of Amram (father) and Jochebed (mother), brother of Moses and Miriam, had four sons who were priests (Nadab, Abihu, Eleazar, and Ithamar); accompanied Moses before Pharoah, and introduced idol worship for Israel in the absence of Moses at Mt. Sinai.(see also Exod 4—40; Lev 1—24; Num 1—33; Deut 9, 10, 32)

Luke	1: 5	Elisabeth (wife of Zacharias) was of his lineage
Acts	7:40	asked by the Israelites to make them gods to go before them
Heb	5: 4	called of God (to the priesthood as a high priest)
	7:11	had an order (priesthood)
	9: 4	his rod budded
	9: 4	his rod was contained in the ark of the covenant

ABEL [a'-bel = vanity]
Second son of Adam and Eve, by faith offered an acceptable (blood) sacrifice from his flock before the Lord, and was murdered by his brother Cain.(See also Gen 4)

Matt	23:35	a righteous man
	23:35	his righteous blood would be upon the scribes and Pharisees
Luke	11:51	his blood would be required of this generation
Heb	11: 4	by faith offered unto God a more excellent sacrifice than Cain
	11: 4	was righteous
	11: 4	God testified of his gifts
	11: 4	being dead, yet speaketh by faith
	11:13	died in faith, not having received the promises, but was persuaded of them and embraced them
	11:13	confessed that he was a stranger and pilgrim on the earth
	11:16	desired a better country
	11:16	God is not ashamed to be called his God
	11:16	God hath prepared for him a city
	11:39	had obtained a good report through faith
	11:39	received not the promise
Heb	12:24	Jesus' blood being sprinkled, speaketh better things than his shed blood
1Joh	3:12	slain by his brother (Cain)
	3:12	his works were righteous

ABIA [ab-i'-ah = Jehovah is my father]
1. Also called Abijam in the Old Testament, a son of Roboam (Rehoboam) king of Judah; father of Asa, and an ancestor of Joseph (husband of Mary, of whom was born Jesus). (See also 1Kng 14,15; 1Chr 3)

Matt	1: 7	begotten by Roboam

Matt	1: 7	begat Asa

2. A priest having an order in the tabernacle service. Zacharias (father of John the Baptist) was of his order.

Luke	1: 5	Zacharias was a priest of his course (division or group)

ABIATHAR [ab-i'-uth-ur = father of superfluity; father of a remnant]
A high priest who fled to David in the cave of Adullam for refuge, one of a group of conspirators who conferred with Adonijah and endeavored to make him king instead of Solomon, and replaced as high priest by Zadok. (See also 1Sam 22, 23; 2Sam 15; 1Kng 1, 2, 4; 1Chr 15, 18, 24, 27)

Mark	2:26	the high priest (in the days of David)

ABIUD [a-bi'-ud = father of honor]
Son of Zorobabel and father of Eliakim and ancestor of Joseph (husband of Mary, of whom was born Jesus).

Matt	1:13	begotten by Zorobabel
	1:13	begat Eliakim

ABRAHAM [a'bra-ham = father of a multitude]
The father of the Jewish nation, name was changed from Abram, a man of faith, received a covenant from the Lord; following the death of his father Terah, sojourned to Canaan where his wife, Sarah (also his half-sister) gave birth to a son Isaac, when Abraham was 99 years of age; and the father of Ishmael by Hagar, his wife's handmaid. (See also Gen 17—50; Exod 2—4; Lev 26; Deut 6, 9, 30, 34)

Matt	1: 1	Jesus Christ was of his lineage
	1: 2	begat Isaac
	1:17	fourteen generations from him to David
	3: 9	claimed by Pharisees and Sadducees as father
	8:11	will be seated with many from the east and west, and with Isaac and Jacob in the kingdom of Heaven
	22:32	God was his God
Mark	12:26	God is his God
Luke	1:55	spoken to by the Lord
	1:55	one of the fathers of Israel
	1:55	had seed
	1:73	God had sworn him an oath
	1:73	father of Israel
	3: 8	was claimed to be father of many
	3:34	father of Isaac
	3:34	son of Thara
	13:16	an infirmed woman who was healed by Jesus was his daughter (of his lineage)
	13:28	will be present in the kingdom of God
	16:22	the beggar (Lazarus) having died, was carried by the angels into his bosom (figurative for paradise)

ABRAHAM *(continued)*

Luke 16:23 seen by the rich man (who was in hell) with Lazarus (in his bosom)
16:24 called "father" by the rich man who asked that he in mercy would send Lazarus with water to cool his tongue
16:25 explained the condition of the eternal state to the rich man
16:27 called "father" by the rich man
16:30 called "father" by the rich man
16:31 explained man's hardness of heart
19: 9 Zacchaeus was his son (of his lineage)
20:37 the Lord was his God
20:37 recognized the same God as Moses

John 8:33 the Jews claimed to be his seed
8:37 Jesus stated that the Jews were his seed
8:39 claimed as father by the Jews
8:39 his children would do his works
8:40 never sought to kill one who told the truth
8:52 is dead
8:53 claimed as father by the Jews
8:53 is dead
8:56 recognized as father of the Jews by Jesus
8:56 rejoiced to see Jesus' day, saw it, and was glad
8:57 Jews questioned his being seen by Jesus
8:58 before he was, Jesus was

Acts 3:13 a father of Israel
3:13 God was his God
3:25 restatement of the covenant God made with him
7: 2 God appeared to him
7: 2 claimed as father of the Jewish nation
7: 2 lived in Mesopotamia before he dwelt in Charran (Haran)
7: 3 told by God to get out of his own country and from his kindred, and to go to a land which he would show him
7: 4 left the land of the Chaldeans and dwelt in Charran (Haran)
7: 4 his father died
7: 4 moved on to the promised land
7: 5 was given no inheritance in the land by the Lord, yet was promised that he and his seed after him would receive it for a possession
7: 5 as yet had no child
7: 6 would have seed
7: 8 was given the covenant of circumcision
7: 8 begat Isaac and circumcised him the eighth day
7:16 bought a sepulchre of the sons of Emmor
7:17 God had sworn a promise to him
7:32 father of Moses

Acts 7:32 God was his God
13:26 children were born of his stock (lineage)

Rom 4: 1 father (of the Jews) pertaining to the flesh
4: 3 believed God and was counted righteous
4: 9 faith was reckoned to him for righteousness when he was in uncircumcision (4:10)
4:11 received the sign of circumcision
4:11 had faith yet being uncircumcised
4:11 father of all them that believe
4:12 father of circumcision to those who are of the circumcision and to those who have his faith
4:12 spiritual father of those who believe
4:12 had faith being yet uncircumcised
4:13 received the promise that he should be the heir of the world through the righteousness of faith
4:16 had faith
4:16 father of us all
4:17 father of many nations
4:17 believed before God
4:18 against hope he believed in hope
4:18 father of many nations
4:18 was promised seed
4:19 was not weak in faith
4:19 considered not his own body dead at an hundred years of age
4:19 considered not the deadness of Sarah's womb
4:20 staggered not at the promise of God through unbelief
4:20 was strong in faith, giving glory to God
4:21 was fully persuaded that what God had promised, He was able also to perform
4:22 his faith was imputed to him for righteousness
4:23 it (righteousness) was imputed to him
9: 7 had seed
9: 7 had seed who were not (considered) his children
9: 7 in Isaac would his seed be called
11: 1 Paul was of his seed

Gal 3: 6 believed God and it was accounted to him for righteousness
3: 7 they which are of faith are his children
3: 8 all nations were to be blessed in him
3: 9 faithful and blessed with those of the faith
3:14 the blessing given to him came on the Gentiles through Jesus Christ
3:16 promises made to him and his seed (who is Christ)
3:18 given the inheritance by promise not by the law
3:29 those that are Christ's are his seed

12

ABRAHAM *(continued)*

Gal	4:22	had two sons, one by a bondmaid and the other by a freewoman (4:26)
Heb	2:16	Jesus took of Himself his (Abraham's) seed
	6:13	God made promise to him
	6:14	was to be blessed and multiplied by God
	6:15	after he had patiently endured, obtained the promise
	7: 1	met by Melchisedec when returning from the slaughter of the kings
	7: 1	blessed by Melchisedec
	7: 2	gave a tenth part (tithe) of all to Melchisedec
	7: 4	the patriarch
	7: 4	gave the tenth (tithe) of the spoils to Melchisedec
	7: 5	the sons of Levi came out of his loins
	7: 6	Melchisedec's descent is not counted from his descent
	7: 6	paid tithes to Melchisedec
	7: 6	blessed by Melchisedec
	7: 6	had the promises (of God)
	7: 7	less than Melchisedec who blessed him
	7: 9	Levi tithes (to Melchisedec) in (through) him
	7:10	Levi was yet in his loins when he met Melchisedec
	11: 8	by faith, when called to go out into another place, obeyed, not knowing whither he went
	11: 8	was to receive an inheritance
	11: 9	by faith sojourned in the land of promise dwelling in tabernacles with Isaac and Jacob
	11: 9	heir of the promise
	11:10	looked for a city which hath foundations, whose builder and maker is God
	11:12	from him, being as good as dead, sprang as many people as the stars of the sky and as the sand of the sea
	11:13	died in faith, not having received the promises, but was persuaded of them and embraced them
	11:13	confessed that he was a stranger and pilgrim on the earth
	11:16	desired a better country
	11:16	God is not ashamed to be called his God
	11:16	God hath prepared for him a city
	11:17	by faith when he was tried, offered up Isaac
	11:17	had received the promise (of God)
	11:17	offered up his only begotten son (Isaac)
	11:18	in Isaac his seed would be called
	11:19	accounted that God was able to raise up Isaac from the dead
	11:19	received him (Isaac) in a figure
Heb	11:39	had obtained a good report through faith
	11:39	received not the promise
Jas	2:21	called father of the Jews
	2:21	justified by works
	2:21	offered Isaac his son upon the altar
	2:22	faith wrought with his works, and by works his faith was made perfect
	2:23	believed God and it was imputed unto him for righteousness
	2:23	called the friend of God
1Pet	3: 6	was obeyed by Sarah
	3: 6	called lord by Sarah

ACHAICUS [a-kai'-icus = belonging to Achaia; wailing]
A believer who ministered to the needs of the apostle Paul.

1Cor	16:17	had gone to Paul (along with Stephanas and Fortunatus)
	16:17	supplied Paul's needs (which the Corinthian church had failed to do)
	16:18	had refreshed Paul's spirit and that of the Corinthian church

ACHAZ [a'-kaz = he holds]
The Old Testament Ahaz, son of Joatham and father of Ezekias, and one of the kings of Judah. (See also 2Kng 15—23; 2Chr 27—29; Isa 1, 7, 14, 38)

Matt	1: 9	begotten by Joatham
	1: 9	begat Ezekias

ACHIM [a'-kim = woes; without winter]
Son of Sadoc, father of Eliud, and an ancestor of Joseph (husband of Mary, of whom was born Jesus).

Matt	1:14	begotten of Sadoc
	1:14	begat Eliud

ADAM [ad'um = of the ground]
The first man and a direct creation of God, husband of Eve, father of Cain, Abel, and Seth (among others); and because of his sin of partaking of the forbidden fruit in the Garden of Eden, sin (the sin nature) and death were imputed to all his progeny. (See also Gen 2—5)

Luke	3:38	father of Seth
	3:38	son of God
Rom	5:12	by him sin entered into the world
	5:14	death reigned from him to Moses
	5:14	transgressed
	5:14	the figure of Him that was to come
	5:15	through his offense many be dead
	5:16	sinned
	5:16	by him the judgment was to condemnation
	5:17	by his offense death reigned
	5:18	by his offense judgment came upon all men to condemnation
	5:19	by his disobedience many were made sinners

13

ADAM *(continued)*

1Cor	15:22	in him all die
	15:45	the first man
	15:45	was made a living soul
	15:47	the first man
	15:47	is of the earth, earthy
	15:48	as he is earthy such are they also that are earthy
	15:49	all men bear his image (earthy)
1Tim	2:13	first formed
	2:14	not deceived
Jude	:14	seven generations before Enoch

ADDI [ad'-di = ornament of God]
An ancestor of Jesus (apparently through the line of Mary, Jesus' mother), son of Cosam, and father of Melchi.

| Luke | 3:28 | father of Melchi |
| | 3:28 | son of Cosam |

AENEAS [e'-ne-as = praise]
A man of Lydda who had been bedfast eight years of the palsy, and healed by Peter.

Acts	9:32	dwelt at Lydda (9:33)
	9:33	found in Lydda by Peter
	9:33	had been eight years in bed sick of the palsy
	9:34	healed in the name of Jesus Christ and arose immediately
	9:35	was seen by those who dwelt in Lydda and Saron

AGABUS [ag'-a-bus = meaning uncertain]
A prophet who had come from Jerusalem to Antioch, prophesied of a coming world-wide famine, and later prophesied of Paul's imprisonment at Jerusalem.

Acts	11:27	a prophet (11:28)
	11:27	being from Jerusalem, came to Antioch (11:28)
	11:28	stood up and signified by the spirit that there should be great dearth (famine) throughout all the world
	21:10	came down from Judea
	21:10	a prophet
	21:11	came unto Paul and his company
	21:11	took Paul's girdle, bound his own hands and feet, and prophesied by the Holy Ghost this would happen to Paul should he go to Jerusalem

AGAR ♀ [a'-gar = to flee]
Old Testament Hagar, Egyptian handmaid of Sarah (Abraham's wife), who bore Ishmael. (See also Gen 16, 21, 25)

Gal	4:22	bondwoman who bore Abraham a son
	4:24	bore children for bondage
	4:30	bondwoman
	4:30	Scripture demanded that she and her son be cast out
	4:30	her son would not be heir with the son of the freewoman
	4:31	believers are not her children

AGRIPPA [ag-rip'-pah = horse-hunter]
1. Herod I [her'-od = heroic]
Grandson of Herod the Great, a king placed over Judea by the Romans, responsible for the death of the apostle James, accepted praise of men as a god, was eaten of worms, and died.

Acts	12: 1	the king
	12: 1	stretched forth his hand to vex certain of the church
	12: 2	killed James the brother of John with the sword
	12: 3	saw that the death of James pleased the Jews
	12: 3	proceeded to take Peter
	12: 4	apprehended Peter, put him in prison, and delivered him to four quaternions of soldiers to keep him
	12: 4	intended after Easter to bring Peter forth to the people
	12: 6	would have brought forth Peter
	12:11	God had delivered Peter out of his hand
	12:19	had sought Peter and found him not
	12:19	examined the keepers and commanded that they should be put to death
	12:19	left Judea and went to abide at Caesarea
	12:20	was highly displeased with them of Tyre and Sidon
	12:20	they of Tyre and Sidon came to him desiring peace
	12:20	his chamberlain was Blastus
	12:20	his country nourished the country of Tyre and Sidon
	12:21	on an appointed day, arrayed in royal apparel, sat upon his throne and made an oration unto the people
	12:22	the people proclaimed his voice was that of a god, and not of a man
	12:23	was smitten of an angel of the Lord because he gave not God the glory
	12:23	was eaten of worms
	12:23	gave up the ghost (died)

2. Herod II [her'-od = heroic]
Son of Herod Agrippa I, great-grandson of Herod the Great, lived in an incestuous relationship with his sister Bernice, and was witnessed to by Paul. (Acts 26)

Acts	25:13	king
	25:13	accompanied by Bernice
	25:13	came to Caesarea to salute Festus
	25:14	stayed many days (in Caesarea)
	25:14	the king
	25:22	declared he would hear Paul himself
	25:22	his desire granted by Festus
	25:23	came (along with Bernice) with great pomp and entered into the place of hearing, with the chief captains and principal men of the city
	25:24	king

14

AGRIPPA *(continued)*

Acts	25:24	informed of Paul by Festus
	25:24	saw Paul
	25:26	Paul brought before him in order that Festus might have something to write unto Augustus (concerning Paul's appeal)
	25:26	king
	26: 1	permitted Paul to speak for himself (in his own defense) (26:2)
	26: 2	king
	26: 3	known of Paul to be expert in all customs and questions among the Jews
	26: 3	besought by Paul to patiently hear him
	26: 7	king
	26: 8	thought it incredible that God should raise the dead
	26:13	king
	26:19	king
	26:26	king
	26:26	knew that none of these things Paul had spoken were hidden from him
	26:27	king
	26:27	believed the prophets
	26:28	almost persuaded to be a Christian
	26:30	rose up, went aside and talked with the others that Paul had done nothing worthy of death or of bonds (26:31)
	26:32	speaking to Festus said Paul might have been set at liberty if he had not appealed unto Caesar

ALEXANDER [al-ex-an'-dur = helper of man]
1. Son of Simon (the Cyrenian) who was compelled to carry Jesus' cross, and brother of Rufus. (Possibly identical with #3)

| Mark | 15:21 | son of Simon (a Cyrenian) |
| | 15:21 | brother of Rufus |

2. Kindred of the high priest and member of the examining council at Jerusalem concerning the apostles.

Acts	4: 6	kindred of the high priest
	4: 6	part of the committee at Jerusalem which examined Peter and John (4:7)
	4: 8	ruler of the people
	4: 8	elder of Israel
	4:15	conferred with the council concerning Peter and John, and could not deny the miracle (4:16)
	4:18	as part of the council, commanded Peter and John not to speak at all or teach in the name of Jesus
	4:21	further threatening Peter and John, let them go, finding nothing how to punish them

3. A Jew who was drawn out of the multitude at the uproar in Ephesus. (Possibly identical with #1)

Acts	19:33	drawn out of the multitude (at Ephesus)
	19:33	put forth by the Jews
	19:33	beckoned with the hand and would have made defense unto the people
	19:34	a Jew

4. A man made shipwreck by blasphemy and delivered unto Satan by Paul. (Possibly identical with #5)

| 1Tim | 1:19 | made shipwreck (1:20) |
| | 1:20 | delivered unto Satan by Paul, to learn not to blaspheme |

5. A coppersmith who did Paul much evil. (Possibly identical with #4)

2Tim	4:14	a coppersmith
	4:14	did Paul much evil
	4:14	would be rewarded according to his works
	4:15	had greatly withstood Paul's words

ALPHAEUS [al-fe'us = leader; chief]
1. Father of James the apostle. Some conjecture that he may also have been the husband of Mary the mother of Jesus after Joseph's death, which would make his son James (the apostle) identical with James the half-brother of Jesus. (Possibly identical with Cleophas)

Matt	10: 3	father of James (the apostle)
Mark	3:18	father of James (the apostle)
Luke	6:15	father of James (the apostle)
Acts	1:13	his son (James) was with the apostles in the upper room

2. Father of Levi (Matthew). (May be identical with #1)

| Mark | 2:14 | father of Levi (Matthew) |

AMINADAB [a-min'-a-dab] = my people is willing]
Son of Aram, father of Naasson, and ancestor of Jesus.

Matt	1: 4	begotten by Aram
	1: 4	begat Naasson
Luke	3:32	father of Naasson (3:33)
	3:33	son of Aram

AMON [a'-mon = workman]
Son of Manasses, father of Josias, and ancestor of Jesus.

| Matt | 1:10 | begotten by Manasses |
| | 1:10 | begat Josias |

AMOS [a'-mos = burden bearer]
An ancestor of Jesus, father of Mattathias, and son of Naum.

| Luke | 3:25 | father of Mattathias |
| | 3:25 | son of Naum |

AMPLIAS [am'-ple-as = enlarged]
Beloved of the apostle Paul and probably lived at Rome.

| Rom | 16: 8 | greeted by Paul |
| | 16: 8 | beloved in the Lord (of Paul) |

ANANIAS [an-an-i'-us = Jehovah is gracious]
1. A participant at the Jerusalem church, who, along with his wife, Sapphira, lied to the Holy Spirit concerning the sale of their property and, consequently, was struck down in death.

Acts	5: 1	a man
	5: 1	husband of Sapphira
	5: 1	together with his wife, sold a possession and kept back part of the price (5:2)
	5: 2	his wife was privy to the deal
	5: 2	brought a certain part (of the price) and laid it at the apostles' feet
	5: 3	Satan had filled his heart to lie to the Holy Ghost
	5: 3	kept back part of the price of the land
	5: 4	had conceived wickedness in his heart, to lie unto God
	5: 5	hearing (Simon) Peter's words, fell down and gave up the ghost
	5: 6	was wound up, carried out and buried
	5: 7	had a wife (who did not know he was dead)
	5: 9	had agreed together (with his wife) to tempt the Spirit of the Lord
	5: 9	had been buried
	5:10	his wife was buried next to him

2. A disciple at Damascus who was instructed by the Lord in a vision to go to Saul (Paul) and heal him of his blindness.

Acts	9:10	a disciple at Damascus
	9:10	spoke with the Lord in a vision (9:16)
	9:11	told to arise and inquire in the house of Judas for Saul of Tarsus
	9:12	was the object of a vision of Saul (Paul)
	9:13	had heard of the evil done of Saul (Paul) to the saints at Jerusalem
	9:13	made excuses for not following God's command (9:14)
	9:15	told by the Lord to go his way
	9:17	entered the house of Judas
	9:17	obeyed the Lord and ministered unto the needs of Saul (Paul)
	9:17	put his hand on Saul (Paul) that he might receive his sight and be filled with the Holy Spirit
	9:17	was first to call Saul (Paul) "brother"
	22:12	a devout man according to the law
	22:12	had a good report of all the Jews which dwelt in Damascus
	22:13	stood before Paul and instructed him to receive his sight
	22:13	was looked upon by Paul
	22:14	instructed Paul in his appointed ministry (22:16)

3. Jewish high priest at Jerusalem whom the apostle Paul unwittingly reviled and who plotted with others to take the life of Paul.

Acts	23: 2	the high priest
	23: 2	ordered those that stood by Paul to smite him on the mouth
	23: 3	called a "whited wall" by Paul
	23: 3	judged Paul after the law and commanded Paul to be smitten contrary to the law
	23: 4	the high priest
	23:14	conspired with others to kill Paul (23:15)
	23:30	given commandment by Claudius Lysias to say before Felix what he had against Paul
	24: 1	the high priest
	24: 1	after five days descended with the elders (to Caesarea)
	24: 1	accompanied by Tertullus
	25: 2	informed Festus against Paul
	25: 3	desired favor against Paul, that Festus would send him to Jerusalem
	25: 3	plotted to lay wait in the way to kill Paul

ANDREW [an'drew = manly]
One of the twelve apostles, a fisherman of Bethsaida, the son of Jona, the brother of Simon Peter whom Andrew brought to Jesus, and originally, a disciple of John the Baptist.

Matt	4:18	seen (while fishing with Peter) by Jesus on Sea of Galilee
	4:18	fisherman
	4:18	brother of Simon Peter
	4:19	called by Jesus and straightway left his net and followed Him (4:20)
	8:23*	followed Jesus into a ship
	8:25*	came to and awoke Jesus and asked Him to save the disciples, for they were perishing
	8:26*	fearful
	8:26*	of little faith
	8:27*	marveled at Jesus
	9:10*	sat at meat with Jesus along with publicans and sinners
	9:14*	fasted not
	9:19*	followed Jesus
	9:37*	instructed to pray that the Lord would send forth laborers into His harvest (9:38)
	10: 1*	was called unto Jesus
	10: 1	one of the twelve disciples
	10: 1*	given power to cast out unclean spirits
	10: 1*	given power to heal all manner of sickness and disease
	10: 2	one of the twelve apostles
	10: 2	brother of Simon Peter (also an apostle)
	10: 5	one of the twelve (apostles)
	10: 5*	commanded to go neither to the Gentiles, nor into any city of the Samaritans
	10: 6*	sent forth by Jesus to the lost sheep of the house of Israel

ANDREW *(continued)*

Matt 10: 7* commanded by Jesus to preach "the kingdom of heaven is at hand"

10: 8* commanded to heal the sick, cleanse the lepers, raise the dead, cast out devils (demons)

10: 8* had freely received

10: 9* was to provide neither gold, nor silver, nor brass, nor scrip, neither two coats, neither shoes, nor staves (for himself) (10:10)

10:11* in every city or town, was to inquire who was worthy, and to abide with them

10:12* was to salute each house he entered

10:13* his peace was to come upon each worthy house, but return to him if unworthy

10:14* was to shake off the dust of his feet therein, when not received or heard by a house or city

10:16* sent forth (by Jesus) as a sheep in the midst of wolves

10:16* was to be wise as a serpent and harmless as a dove

10:17* would be delivered to the councils, scourged in synagogues, and brought before governors and kings for (Jesus') sake (10:18)

10:19* was to take no thought concerning what he would speak when delivered up, for the Spirit of his Father would speak in him (10:20)

12: 1* was an hungered and plucked corn in the field and ate

12: 2* accused by the Pharisees of acting unlawfully on the Sabbath day

12:49* called mother and brethren of Jesus

13:10* questioned Jesus about His use of parables

13:11* was given unto him to know the mysteries of the kingdom of Heaven

13:16* saw and heard (spiritually)

13:17* had seen and heard (spiritually)

13:18* had the parable of the sower explained by Jesus (13:23)

13:36* had the parable of the wheat and tares explained by Jesus (13:43)

13:51* claimed to have understood all these things (parables)

14:15* came to Jesus and requested Him to send the multitude away

14:16* instructed by Jesus to feed the multitude

14:17* requested by Jesus to bring the five loaves and two fishes to Him (14:18)

14:19* given the blessed loaves by Jesus

14:20* distributed the loaves to the multitude

14:20* took up of the fragments that remained twelve baskets full

14:22* constrained by Jesus to get into a ship and go before Him unto the ship and go before Him unto the other side (of Sea of Galilee)

Matt 14:24* his ship was tossed with waves

14:25* approached by Jesus (walking on the sea)

14:26* saw Jesus walking on the water (Sea of Galilee) and was afraid

14:27* told by Jesus to be of good cheer and not be afraid

14:33* being in the ship, worshiped Jesus, claiming Him to be the Son of God

14:34* came into the land of Gennesaret

15: 2* accused by the scribes and Pharisees of transgressing the tradition of the elders by not washing his hands when he ate bread

15:12* came to Jesus, informed Him that the Pharisees were offended at His saying

15:23* came and besought Jesus to send away her that cried after him

15:32* was called (unto Jesus)

15:34* had seven loaves and a few little fishes

15:36* given the loaves and fishes (by Jesus)

15:36* gave the loaves and fishes to the multitude

15:37* took up of the broken meat that was left seven baskets full

16: 5* was come to the other side and had forgotten to take bread

16: 6* told to beware of the leaven of the Pharisees and Sadducees

16: 7* reasoned with the other disciples over Jesus' words

16: 7 had taken no bread

16: 8* of little faith

16: 8* reasoned with other disciples (concerning the lack of bread)

16: 9* took up baskets (of fragments)

16:10* took up baskets (of fragments)

16:11* did not understand Jesus' words concerning the leaven (doctrine) of the Pharisees and Sadducees

16:12* understood how that Jesus spake not of bread, but of the doctrine of the Pharisees and Sadducees

16:13* was in Caesarea Philippi

16:13* answered Jesus' question concerning His identity (16:14)

16:15* questioned as to his view of Jesus' identity

16:20* charged by Jesus to tell no man that He was Jesus the Christ

16:21* shown by Jesus the sufferings He must undergo

17:15* could not cure the lunatic boy (17:16)

17:19* asked Jesus why he could not cast out the devil (demon)

17:20* could not cast out the devil (demon) because of unbelief

17:22* abode in Galilee

17:23* was exceedingly sorry

ANDREW *(continued)*

Matt 17:24* came to Capernaum
18: 1* asked Jesus who is the greatest in the kingdom of Heaven
19:13* rebuked those who brought children to Jesus
19:14* rebuked in turn by Jesus
19:25* exceedingly amazed at Jesus' answer to the rich young ruler and asked who could be saved
19:27* had forsaken all and followed Jesus
19:28* had followed Jesus
19:28* promised by Jesus to sit upon the twelve thrones judging the twelve tribes of Israel
20:17* going up to Jerusalem, taken apart and foretold by Jesus of His betrayal, crucifixion, and resurrection (20:19)
20:24* was moved with indignation towards James and John because of their request of Jesus
20:29* departed from Jericho (for Jerusalem)
21: 1* arrived in Bethphage and Mount of Olives
21:20* saw the withered fig tree and marveled
24: 1* came to Jesus to show Him the buildings of the temple
24: 2* Jesus spoke to him of coming destruction of the temple
24: 3* asked Jesus of the sign of His coming and the end of the world
26: 8* was indignant at the actions of the woman
26:10* had troubled the woman
26:17* asked Jesus where he should prepare for Him the Passover
26:19* did as Jesus had appointed and made ready the Passover
26:20* celebrated Passover with Jesus and the rest of the twelve
26:22* asked Jesus if he were the one to betray Him
26:26* while eating (the Passover) given the bread by Jesus
26:27* given the cup (by Jesus)
26:30* having sung a hymn went out into the Mount of Olives
26:31* Jesus predicted that he would be offended because of Him
26:35* claimed he would never deny Jesus, even though it meant death
26:36* came with Jesus to Gethsemane
26:36* instructed to sit and pray
26:40* fell asleep in the garden of Gethsemane
26:43* fell asleep again in the garden (of Gethsemane)
26:45* told to sleep on now and take his rest
26:46* told to arise and go (with Jesus)
26:56* forsook Jesus and fled

Matt 28:13* would be accused of stealing Jesus' body by night
28:16* went into Galilee into place (mountain) appointed
28:17* saw Jesus and worshiped Him
28:19* given the great commission (28:20)
28:20* Jesus would always be with him, even unto the end of the world

Mark 1:16 seen by Jesus casting a net into the sea
1:16 brother of Simon (Peter)
1:16 a fisherman
1:17 told by Jesus to follow Him and become a fisher of men
1:18 forsook his nets and followed Jesus
1:21 went into Capernaum with Jesus
1:29 had been at the synagogue at Capernaum
1:29 he and his brother entered their house, along with Jesus, James, and John
1:29 lived in Capernaum
1:31 ministered unto by Peter's wife's mother
1:36 followed Jesus to His solitary place of prayer (1:37)
2:15 sat at meat with Jesus, Levi (Matthew), and many publicans and sinners
2:18 did not fast as the disciples of John (Baptist) and Pharisees did
2:23 plucked ears of corn in the cornfields on the Sabbath day
3: 7 withdrew from the synagogue with Jesus to the sea
3:14* ordained by Jesus (to be with Him)
3:14* would be sent forth to preach (by Jesus)
3:15* would be given power by Jesus to heal sickness and to cast out devils (demons)
3:18* a disciple of Jesus (one of the twelve)
3:20* could not eat bread with Jesus because of the multitude
4:10* asked Jesus about the parable of the sower
4:11* was given to know the mystery of the kingdom of God
4:33* had many parables taught him by Jesus
4:34* when alone, with the rest of the twelve, had all things expounded by Jesus
4:36* sent away the multitude
4:36* with the rest of the twelve, took Jesus to the other side of the sea
4:38* in fear, awakened Jesus in the midst of the storm
4:40* was fearful and had no faith
4:41* feared exceedingly
4:41* questioned among the other disciples as to what manner of man Jesus was that even the wind and

ANDREW *(continued)*

the sea obeyed Him

Mark 5: 1* went with Jesus across the sea of Galilee to the country of the Gadarenes

6: 1* followed Jesus into His own country

6: 7* sent forth two by two (by Jesus)

6: 7* given power over unclean spirits

6: 8* commanded to take nothing on his journey except a staff, and to be shod with sandals and only one coat (6:9)

6:12* went out, and preached that men should repent

6:13* cast out many devils (demons) and anointed with oil many that were sick, and healed them

6:30* an apostle

6:30* gathered together unto Jesus to report what he had done and taught

6:31* had no leisure so much as to eat

6:32* departed privately with Jesus into a desert place by ship

6:36* asked Jesus to send away the multitude into the villages to buy themselves bread

6:37* told by Jesus to give food to the multitude

6:37* asked Jesus if he should go and buy bread to feed the people

6:38* when asked by Jesus the available provisions, reported five loaves and two fishes

6:39* made the people sit down by hundreds and fifties (6:40)

6:41* given the food blessed by Jesus to distribute to the crowd

6:43* took up twelve baskets full of fragments and of the fishes

6:45* constrained by Jesus to get into the ship and go to the other side unto Bethsaida

6:47* was alone (with the other disciples) in the ship in the midst of the sea

6:48* toiled in rowing the ship for the winds were contrary

6:48* Jesus came unto him in about the fourth watch of the night walking upon the sea

6:49* saw Jesus walking upon the sea and cried out for he supposed it had been a spirit

6:50* saw Jesus and was troubled but admonished by Him to fear not

6:51* was amazed beyond measure and wondered that the wind ceased as Jesus entered the ship

6:52* because of his hardened heart, had forgotten about the miracle of the loaves

6:53* came into the land of Gennesaret

6:54* got out of the ship

7: 5* walked not according to the traditions of the elders (ate bread with unwashed hands)

Mark 8: 5* informed Jesus of the seven loaves

8: 6* set the loaves before the people

8: 7* receiving the blessed fishes from Jesus, set them before the people

8: 8* gathered seven baskets of fragments

8:18* entered into a ship with Jesus and went into Dalmanutha

8:13* entered into the ship again with Jesus, departed to the other side

8:14* had forgotten to take bread, and had only one loaf in the ship

8:16* had no bread

8:17* having seen the miracles, still did not understand as his heart was possibly yet hardened

8:19* took up twelve baskets full of fragments at the feeding of the five thousand

8:20* took up seven baskets full of fragments at the feeding of the four thousand

8:27* went into the towns of Caesarea Philippi with Jesus

8:27* responded to Jesus' question concerning His identity with "John the Baptist, Elias, and one of the prophets" (8:28)

8:30* charged to tell no man that Jesus was the Christ

8:31* taught by Jesus of the things concerning Himself

9:14* questioned by the scribes

9:18* could not cast out a dumb spirit

9:30* passed through Galilee

9:32* did not understand the words of Jesus, but was afraid to ask

9:33* came to Capernaum

9:33* disputed with the other disciples on the way to Capernaum as to whom should be the greatest (9:34)

9:38* forbade a man from casting out devils (demons) in Jesus' name, because he did not follow Him

10:13* rebuked those who brought young children to Jesus that He should teach them

10:14* rebuked in turn by Jesus

10:24* astonished at the words of Jesus concerning those with riches

10:26* astonished at Jesus' words

10:28* had left all and followed Jesus

10:32* went up to Jerusalem with Jesus and was amazed and afraid

10:41 was much displeased with James and John

10:46* went to Jericho

10:46* went out of Jericho with Jesus

11: 1* came nigh to Jerusalem, unto Bethphage and Bethany, at the Mount of Olives

11:11* went to Bethany with Jesus and

19

ANDREW *(continued)*

stayed until the morrow (11:12)

Mark 11:14* heard Jesus curse the fig tree
11:15* returned to Jerusalem with Jesus
11:19* went out of Jerusalem (10:20)
11:20* witnessed the fig tree dried up from the roots
11:27* came again to Jerusalem
13: 3 sat upon the Mount of Olives
13: 3 asked Jesus privately concerning the sign when all things shall be fulfilled (13:4)
13: 5 cautioned, by Jesus, not to be deceived
14:12* asked Jesus where they should go and prepare the Passover
14:17* in the evening of the first day of unleavened bread, went with Jesus to the upper room
14:18* sat and ate together with Jesus
14:19* began to be sorrowful over Jesus' statement of betrayal and ask, "Is it I?"
14:20* dipped with Jesus in the dish
14:22* ate the Passover with Jesus
14:23* drank of the communion cup
14:26* sang a hymn and went out to the Mount of Olives
14:31* exclaimed that even if it meant death, he would not deny Him
14:32* went to Gethsemane and was told to sit there while Jesus prayed
14:50* forsook Jesus and fled
16:10* mourned and wept
16:11* believed not Mary Magdalene's account
16:14* Jesus appeared unto him as he sat at meat (with the other disciples)
16:14* upbraided by Jesus for his unbelief and hardness of heart, because he believed not them which had seen Him after He was risen
16:15* commissioned to go into all the world and preach the gospel to every creature
16:20* went forth and preached everywhere, with signs following

Luke 4:38* ministered unto by Peter's wife's mother (4:39)
5:30* murmured against by scribes and Pharisees
5:30* ate and drank with publicans and sinners
5:33* ate and drank instead of fasting
6: 1* plucked ears of corn and ate (rubbing them in his hands) on the Sabbath
6: 2* claimed (by the Pharisees) to be doing that which was not lawful to do on the sabbath days
6:13* chosen as one of the twelve
6:13* also called (named) an apostle
6:14* an apostle
6:14* brother of Simon Peter
6:17* came down from the mountain with Jesus and stood in the plain

Luke 8: 1* went throughout every city and village with Jesus
8: 9* questioned Jesus concerning a parable
8:10* unto him it was given to know the mysteries of the kingdom of God
8:22* went into a ship with Jesus and launched forth for the other side
8:23* the boat, filled with water, put him in jeopardy
8:24* called Jesus "Master"
8:24* came to Jesus and awakened Him during the storm
8:25* asked by Jesus concerning his faith
8:25* was afraid and wondered concerning Jesus' power over the elements
8:26* arrived at the country of the Gadarenes (Gadara)
9: 1* given power and authority over all devils (demons) and to cure diseases
9: 2* sent by Jesus to preach the kingdom of God and to heal the sick
9: 3* was to take neither staves, nor scrip, neither bread, neither money, neither have two coats
9: 4* was to abide in whatever house he entered
9: 6* went through the towns, preaching the gospel, and healing everywhere
9:10* returned and told Jesus all he had done
9:10* went privately with Jesus into a desert place belonging to the city called Bethsaida
9:12* requested that Jesus send away the multitude so that they might go into the towns and lodge and get victuals (food)
9:13* had only five loaves and two fishes, but was requested by Jesus to give food to the multitude
9:14* made the multitude sit down in companies by fifties (9:15)
9:16* gave the blessed loaves and fish unto the multitude
9:17* took up twelve baskets of fragments
9:18* was alone with Jesus (and the rest of the twelve)
9:18* in response to Jesus' question as to His identity, responded, "John the Baptist, Elias, and one of the prophets risen again" (9:19)
9:20 straitly charged and commanded to tell no man that Jesus is the Christ (9:21)
9:40* could not cast the spirit (demon) out of boy
9:45* feared to ask Jesus concerning His teaching
9:46* reasoned with the other disciples as to which of them should be greatest
9:49* forbade a man from casting out

ANDREW *(continued)*

		devils (demons) in Jesus' name because he followed not with the disciples
Luke	10:24*	saw and heard what many prophets and kings had desired to experience
	12: 1*	warned by Jesus to beware of the leaven of Pharisees
	12: 4*	friend of Jesus
	17: 5*	asked Jesus to increase his faith
	18:15*	rebuked those who brought infants to Jesus
	18:16*	rebuked, in turn, by Jesus
	18:28*	had left all and followed Jesus
	18:31*	taken unto Jesus and instructed of things to come (18:33)
	18:34*	understood none of these teachings of Jesus
	19:29*	with Jesus, came nigh to Bethphage and Bethany at the Mount of Olives
	19:37*	rejoiced and praised God with a loud voice (19:38)
	22:14*	sat down with Jesus (in the upper room for the Passover)
	22:14*	was called an apostle
	22:15*	Jesus truly desired his presence in eating the Passover
	22:19*	partook of the first Lord's Supper (22:20)
	22:23*	inquired among the disciples as to which of them would betray Jesus
	22:24*	a strife existed among the disciples as to which one should be accounted the greatest
	22:28*	had continued with Jesus in His temptations
	22:29*	was appointed a kingdom (that he might eat and drink at Jesus' table in His kingdom and sit on thrones judging the twelve tribes of Israel) (22:30)
	22:35*	had lacked nothing
	22:36*	told to prepare (for his new task)
	22:39*	followed Jesus to the Mount of Olives
	22:40*	told to pray that he enter not into temptation
	22:45*	found sleeping for sorrow (by Jesus)
	22:46*	told to rise and pray, lest he enter into temptation
	22:49*	perceiving the forthcoming events, asked Jesus if he should use his sword
	24: 9*	was told all things concerning the resurrection by Mary Magdalene, Joanna, Mary the mother of James, and the other women (24:10)
	24:10*	an apostle
	24:11*	the words of the women seemed as idle tales and he believed them not
	24:33*	being gathered together (with the other disciples) Cleopas found him and declared that the Lord was

		risen indeed and had appeared to Simon (24:34)
Luke	24:36*	Jesus appeared unto him (after the resurrection) but he was terrified and affrighted, and supposed he had seen a spirit (24:37)
	24:38*	asked by Jesus why he was troubled and why thoughts arose in his heart
	24:40*	was shown Jesus' hands and feet
	24:41*	believed not yet for joy, and wondered
	24:42*	gave Jesus a piece of a broiled fish and of an honeycomb
	24:45*	his understanding was opened by Jesus that he might understand the scriptures
	24:46*	was witness of these things (24:48)
	24:49*	told to tarry in Jerusalem until he was endued with power from on high
	24:50*	led by Jesus out as far as to Bethany and was blessed of Him
	24:52*	worshiped Jesus and returned to Jerusalem with great joy
	24:53*	was continually in the temple, praising and blessing God
John	1:35	a disciple of John the Baptist
	1:38	seen by Jesus while following Him
	1:38	called Jesus "Rabbi"
	1:39	came and saw where Jesus dwelt and abode with Him that day
	1:40	heard John speak and followed Him
	1:40	brother of Simon Peter
	1:41	found his brother Simon (Peter) and told him of finding the Messiah
	1:42	brought Simon (Peter) to Jesus
	1:42	the son of Jona
	1:44	of Bethsaida
	2: 2*	called to the marriage in Cana in Galilee
	2:11*	believed on Jesus
	2:12*	went to Capernaum and continued there not many days
	2:17*	remembered that it was written of Him, "the zeal of thine house hath eaten me up"
	2:22*	after the resurrection, remembered Jesus' words and believed the Scriptures, and the words Jesus had said
	3:22*	came into the land of Judea with Jesus and tarried there with Him
	4: 2*	did baptize
	4: 8*	had gone away unto the city to buy meat
	4:27*	came unto Jesus and marveled that He talked with the Samaritan woman, yet did not question Him
	4:31*	called Jesus "Master"
	4:31*	implored Jesus to eat
	4:33*	questioned among the disciples if Jesus had been brought food to eat
	4:38*	had been sent to reap where he had

ANDREW *(continued)*

		not labored, and had entered into others' labors
John	6: 3*	went up into a mountain and sat with Jesus
	6: 8*	a disciple of Jesus
	6: 8*	brother of Simon Peter
	6: 9*	informed Jesus of the lad with five loaves and two fishes
	6:10*	instructed by Jesus to have the multitude sit down
	6:11*	distributed the loaves and fishes to the multitude
	6:13*	gathered twelve baskets of fragments
	6:16*	went down to the sea, entered a ship and went toward Capernaum (6:17)
	6:19*	after rowing twenty-five to thirty furlongs, saw Jesus walking on the sea and was afraid
	6:20*	told not to be afraid
	6:21*	willingly received Him into the ship
	6:22*	was entered into the only boat there
	6:22*	was apart from Jesus in the boat alone (with the other disciples)
	6:67*	asked, by Jesus, if he would also go away
	6:69*	believed and was sure that Jesus was the Christ, the Son of the living God
	6:70*	chosen as one of the twelve
	9: 2*	questioned Jesus concerning the man born blind
	11: 8*	called Jesus "Master"
	11:11*	friend of Lazarus
	11:54*	continued with Jesus at Ephraim
	12:16*	understood not, at first, the events of the triumphal entry of Jesus
	12:16*	after Jesus' glorification, remembered that these events had been written of Jesus, and had been done unto Him
	12:22*	told by Philip that certain Greeks desired to see Jesus
	12:22*	along with Philip, told Jesus that certain Greeks sought to see Him
	13: 5*	feet washed by Jesus
	13:12*	had his feet washed by Jesus
	13:13*	called Jesus "Master" and "Lord"
	13:14*	had his feet washed by Jesus
	13:14*	told, by Jesus, that he ought to wash one another's feet
	13:15*	had been given an example that he should do as Jesus had done to him
	13:18*	was known and chosen of Jesus
	13:21*	when told that one of them would betray Jesus, looked on the others, doubting of whom He spoke (13:22)
	13:28*	knew not for what intent Jesus spoke these words to Judas Iscariot
	13:34*	given a new commandment to love one another

John	13:34*	given a new commandment to love one another
	13:34*	loved of Jesus
	13:35*	love one to another was a mark that he was a true disciple of Jesus
	14:25*	was with Jesus
	14:26*	would be instructed by the Holy Spirit in all things
	14:26*	the words Jesus had spoken would be brought to his remembrance
	14:27*	Jesus' peace was given to him and left with him
	14:31*	was told to arise and go with Jesus
	15: 3*	was clean through the Word
	15: 9*	loved of Jesus
	15:12*	commanded to love one another
	15:12*	loved of Jesus
	15:16*	chosen of Jesus, and ordained of Him to go and bring forth fruit, and that his fruit should remain
	15:17*	commanded to love one another
	15:19*	not of the world
	15:19*	chosen out of the world by Jesus
	15:19*	hated of the world
	15:27*	would bear witness, because he had been with Jesus from the beginning
	16: 4*	was with Jesus
	16: 6*	sorrow had filled his heart
	16:12*	could not bear the words of Jesus
	16:22*	presently had sorrow
	16:24*	had asked nothing of the Father in Jesus' name
	16:27*	loved of the Father
	16:27*	loved Jesus, and believed that He came from God
	16:29*	could now understand plainly Jesus' words
	16:30*	was sure that Jesus knew all things
	16:30*	believed that Jesus came forth from God
	18: 1*	went with Jesus over the brook Cedron and entered into a garden (Gethsemane)
	18: 2*	often resorted there with Jesus
	20:18*	told by Mary Magdalene that she had seen the Lord and that He had spoken unto her
	20:19*	while assembled together (with the other disciples) with the doors shut for fear of the Jews, Jesus appeared in the midst
	20:20*	saw Jesus' hands and side and was glad
	20:21*	sent by Jesus and given His peace
	20:22*	breathed on by Jesus and received the Holy Ghost
	20:25*	told Thomas that he had seen the Lord
	20:25*	informed by Thomas that he would not believe without specific conditions being met
	20:26*	the doors being shut again, Jesus appeared the second time to him and the apostles

ANDREW *(continued)*

John 20:30* many other signs were done in his presence which are not written (in this book)

Acts 1: 2* had been given commandments by Jesus (through the Holy Ghost)

1: 2* chosen by Jesus

1: 3* was shown Jesus alive after His passion

1: 3* spoken to by Jesus of the things pertaining to the kingdom of God

1: 3* saw Jesus forty days

1: 4* commanded, by Jesus, not to depart from Jerusalem, but to wait for the promise of the Father

1: 5* would be baptized with the Holy Ghost

1: 6* questioned Jesus concerning the restoration of the kingdom to Israel

1: 7* was not to know the times or the seasons which the Father had put in His own power

1: 8* after receiving the Holy Spirit, would receive power and would witness unto Jesus Christ throughout the earth

1: 9* beheld as Jesus was taken up into Heaven at His ascension

1:10* was joined by two men in white apparel while he looked steadfastly toward Heaven

1:11* a man of Galilee

1:11* was gazing up into Heaven

1:11* Jesus was taken up from him into Heaven

1:11* was told that Jesus would come in like manner as he had seen Him go into Heaven

1:12* returned to Jerusalem and went into an upper room (1:13)

1:14* continued in prayer and supplication with the women, Mary the mother of Jesus, and with His brethren

1:21* was with the Lord Jesus at various times

1:24* prayed concerning the ordination of one to be a witness of Jesus' resurrection

1:26* gave forth his lot (concerning Judas Iscariot's successor)

2: 1* present at the day of Pentecost

2: 2* while sitting in the house, cloven tongues like as of fire sat upon him, he was filled with the Holy Ghost and spoke with other tongues (2:4)

2: 6* his speech confounded the multitude because every man heard in his own language

2: 7* a Galilean

2:13* mocked by some who claimed him as full of new wine

2:14* stood with (Simon) Peter

2:15* was not drunk

Acts 2:32* was a witness to the resurrection of Jesus

2:37* asked by the multitude on day of Pentecost what they should do

2:42* many continued steadfastly in his doctrine and fellowship

2:43* many wonders and signs were done by him

4:33* with great power gave witness of the resurrection of the Lord Jesus

4:33* great grace was upon him

4:35* the price of possessions sold by Christians was laid at his feet

4:35* distributed to every man (of the Christian community) as he had need

4:36* gave Joses a surname of Barnabas

4:37* Joses's money was laid at his feet

5: 2* the gift of Ananias and Sapphira was laid at his feet

5:12* by his hands were many signs and wonders wrought among the people

5:12* was with one accord with the others in Solomon's porch

5:13* no man durst join himself to him (the apostles)

5:13* was magnified of the people

5:16* healed the multitude of sicknesses and unclean spirits

5:18* placed in the common prison by the high priest and Sadducees

5:19* released from prison by the angel of the Lord and told to go, stand, and speak in the temple (5:20)

5:21* entered into the temple early in the morning and taught

5:22* was not found in the prison

5:25* was standing in the temple and teaching the people

5:26* brought without violence and set before the council (5:27)

5:27* questioned by the high priest (5:28)

5:28* had been commanded not to teach in this (Jesus') name

5:28* had filled Jerusalem with his doctrine and had (seemingly) intended to bring Jesus' blood upon his accusers

5:29* believed that he ought to obey God rather than men

5:32* witness of God (and of His works)

5:33* Jewish leaders took counsel to slay him

5:34* put a little space from the Sanhedrin (for their deliberation)

5:40* called back before the council, beaten, commanded not to speak in the name of Jesus, and let go

5:41* departed from the council rejoicing that he was counted worthy to suffer shame for His name

5:42* daily in the temple and in every house, ceased not to teach and preach Jesus Christ

ANDREW *(continued)*

Acts 6: 2* called the multitude together and stated it was not reasonable that he should leave the Word of God and serve tables
6: 3* instructed that seven men of honest report be chosen to be appointed to serve tables
6: 4* determined to give himself continually to prayer and to the ministry of the Word
6: 6* the chosen seven were set before him, for whom he prayed and laid his hands on them
8: 1* remained in Jerusalem in the midst of great persecution
8:14* was in Jerusalem
8:14* hearing that Samaria had received the Word of God, sent Peter and John to Samaria
9:27* Saul (Paul) was brought to him by Barnabas and he was informed of Saul's (Paul's) conversion experience and his bold preaching at Damascus
9:28* was accompanied by Saul (Paul) in coming in and going out at Jerusalem
10:39* was witness of all things Jesus did both in the land of the Jews and in Jerusalem
10:41* a witness, chosen before of God
10:41* ate and drank with Jesus after His resurrection
10:42* commanded by Jesus to preach unto the people, and testified that it was Jesus which was ordained of God to be the Judge of quick and dead
11: 1* was in Judea
11: 1* heard that the Gentiles had also received the Word of God
11:15* the Holy Ghost fell on him at the beginning (Pentecost)
13:31* saw Jesus many days
13:31* came up with Jesus from Galilee to Jerusalem
13:31* was His (Jesus') witness unto the people
15: 2* Paul, Barnabas, and others were sent by the church at Antioch to consult with him over the matter of circumcision
15: 4* received Paul, Barnabas, and the others from Antioch
15: 6* came together (with elders) to consider the matter (of circumcision)
15: 8* given the Holy Ghost
15: 9* God made no difference between him and a Gentile
15:10* was not able to bear the yoke
15:22* acting with the elders, sent chosen men back to Antioch with Paul and Barnabas

15:23* acting with the elders and brethren, wrote letters of instruction to the Gentiles at Antioch, Syria, and Cilicia
15:24* gave no commandment that Gentile believers must be circumcised and keep the law
15:25* considered it good, being assembled, to send chosen men unto the believers
15:25* loved Barnabas and Paul
15:27* sent Judas and Silas to the Gentile believers
15:33* Judas (Barsabas) and Silas returned unto him
16: 4* with the elders, ordained decrees
16: 4* was at Jerusalem
Rom 16: 7* Andronicus and Junia were well known to him
1Cor 4: 9* Paul thought God had set him (and the apostles) forth last, as it were appointed to death
4: 9* made a spectacle unto the world, to the angels, and to men
4:10* a fool for Christ's sake
4:10* weak, despised
4:11* hungered, thirsted, was naked, was buffeted, and had no certain dwelling place
4:12* labored, working with his own hands
4:12* being reviled, he blessed; being persecuted, he suffered it; being defamed, he entreated (4:13)
4:13* made as the filth of the world, and the offscouring of all things
9: 5* had power to lead about a sister, a wife
15: 5* had seen the risen Lord
15: 7* the risen Lord was seen of him
15:11* preached
Rev 21:14* name inscribed in the twelve foundations of the new Jerusalem
21:14* an apostle of the Lamb

ANDRONICUS [an-dro-ni'-cus = conqueror; victory of man]
A kinsman and fellow prisoner of Paul and Junia and saved before Paul.

Rom 16: 7 saluted by Paul
16: 7 kinsman of Paul (and Junia)
16: 7 fellow prisoner of Paul and Junia
16: 7 of note (well-known among the apostles)
16: 7 was in Christ (saved) before Paul was

ANNA ♀ [an'-nah = grace]; a prophetess
An aged prophetess, daughter of Phanuel, of the tribe of Asher, widowed 84 years, continually served night and day in the temple at Jerusalem, present at the presentation of Jesus by His parents, and claimed Him to be the Messiah.

Luke 2:36 a prophetess
2:36 the daughter of Phanuel

ANNA *(continued)*

Luke	2:36	of the tribe of Aser (Asher)
	2:36	of a great age
	2:36	had lived with an husband seven years from her virginity
	2:37	was a widow of about fourscore and four years
	2:37	departed not from the temple, but served God with fastings and prayers night and day
	2:38	gave thanks upon seeing the child Jesus
	2:38	spake of Jesus to all that looked for redemption in Jerusalem

ANNAS [an'-nas = grace of Jehovah]
A Sadducee, a high priest of the Jews, son of Seth, placed in office by Quirinius the governor of Syria in 7 A.D., removed from office by Valerius Gratus in 15 A.D., father-in-law of Caiaphas, and seems to have been a very influential, powerful, and wealthy man.

Matt	20:18	Jesus would be betrayed unto him
	20:18	would condemn Jesus to death
	20:19	would deliver Jesus to the Gentiles
	21:15	was sore displeased upon seeing the wonderful things Jesus did, and hearing the people cry "Hosanna to the Son of David"
	21:16	questioned Jesus concerning the statement of the multitude
	21:17	left by Jesus
	21:23	questioned Jesus by what authority He acted and who gave Him this authority
	21:24	questioned in turn by Jesus concerning the baptism of John (21:25)
	21:25	reasoned with the other chief priests and elders concerning Jesus' question of the baptism of John (21:26)
	21:27	would not answer Jesus' question, and was likewise not answered by Jesus
	21:31	answered Jesus' question concerning the parable
	21:31	Jesus prophesied that the publicans and harlots go into the kingdom of God before him
	21:32	believed not John (the Baptist)
	21:32	repented not (in order to believe)
	21:45	perceived that Jesus had spoken of him (in the parable)
	21:46	sought to lay hands on Jesus but feared the multitude
	26: 3	assembled with the chief priests and scribes and elders of the people unto the palace of Caiaphas
	26: 4	consulted to take Jesus by subtlety and kill him
	26:14	approached by Judas (Iscariot) and covenanted with him for the delivery (betrayal) of Jesus for thirty pieces of silver (26:15)

Matt	26:47	(had sent) a great multitude with swords and staves, along with Judas to take Jesus
	26:59	with the other priests, elders, and all the council, sought false witnesses against Jesus
	26:60	found no false witnesses against Jesus
	27: 1	when morning was come, took counsel against Jesus to put Him to death
	27: 2	having bound Jesus, led Him away and delivered Him to Pilate
	27: 3	the thirty pieces of silver were returned to him and the other chief priests and elders by Judas
	27: 6	took the thirty pieces of silver, took counsel, and bought the potter's field to bury strangers in (27:7)
	27:12	accused Jesus (before Pilate)
	27:20	persuaded the multitude that they should ask Barabbas, and destroy Jesus
	27:41	mocked Jesus saying He saved others, but Himself He could not save (27:42)
	27:42	stated he would believe Jesus if He were to come down from the cross
	27:62	went to Pilate and requested the sepulchre be made sure until the third day (27:64)
	27:63	called Jesus a deceiver
	27:65	told by Pilate they had a watch, and to go and make it as sure as they could
	27:66	went and made the sepulchre sure, sealing the stone and setting a watch
	28:11	was shown by some of the watch, all the things that were done
	28:12	gave large money unto the soldiers instructing them to say His disciples came by night and stole Him away while they slept (28:13)
	28:14	promised to persuade the governor and secure the soldiers
Mark	8:31	would reject Jesus
	10:33	Jesus would be delivered unto him
	10:33	would condemn Jesus to death and deliver Him to the Gentiles
	11:18	heard that Jesus cleansed the temple and sought how they (he) might destroy Him
	11:18	feared Jesus, because all the people were astonished at His doctrine
	11:27	came to Jesus in the temple and inquired as to His authority for His actions (11:28)
	11:29	answered by Jesus that if he answered Jesus' question, his question would be answered
	11:30	questioned by Jesus
	11:31	reasoned with the others as to the effects of various possible answers to Jesus' question (11:32)

ANNAS *(continued)*

Mark 11:32 feared the people
11:33 answered that they (he) could not tell the aswer to Jesus' question
11:33 was informed by Jesus that He would not answer their (his) question
12: 1 spoken unto by Jesus by parables
12:12 sought to lay hold on Jesus because they (he) knew He had spoken the parable against them (the chief priests)
12:12 feared the people
12:12 left Him and went his way
12:13 sent certain of the Pharisees and the Herodians (to Jesus) to catch Him in His words
14: 1 sought how to take Jesus by craft, and put Him to death
14:10 approached by Judas Iscariot to betray Jesus unto them
14:11 hearing Judas's proposal, was glad and promised to give him money
14:43 had sent a great multitude with swords and staves with Judas (to take Jesus)
14:53 was assembled with all the chief priests, elders, and scribes
14:55 sought for witnesses against Jesus to put Him to death, and found none
14:64 condemned Jesus to be guilty of death
15: 1 straightway in the morning, held a consultation with the elders, scribes, and the whole council
15: 1 bound Jesus and carried Him away, and delivered Him to Pilate
15: 3 accused Jesus of many things (before Pilate)
15: 4 witnessed many things against Jesus
15:10 (Pilate knew) he had delivered Jesus for envy
15:11 moved the people that Pilate should release Barabbas unto them
15:31 mocking, said that He saved others; Himself He cannot save (15:32)

Luke 3: 1 contemporary of Tiberius Caesar, and Herod, Philip and Lysanias (tetrarchs) and Pontius Pilate (3:2)
3: 2 ruled along with Caiaphas
3: 2 one of the high priests
9:22 Jesus prophesied he would reject Him
19:47 sought to destroy Jesus, and could not find what he might do (19:48)
20: 1 together with the other chief priests, scribes, and elders, came upon Jesus
20: 2 asked Jesus by what authority He acted and who gave Him this authority
20: 3 questioned in turn by Jesus, concerning the baptism of John (20:4)

Luke 20: 5 reasoned with the others concerning the various possible answers to Jesus' question (20:6)
20: 7 answered Jesus that he could not tell the answer to His question
20: 8 informed by Jesus that He likewise would not answer His question
20:19 the same hour sought to lay hands on Jesus for he perceived that He had spoken the parable against him
20:19 feared the people
20:20 watched Jesus
20:20 sent forth spies that they might deliver Him unto the power and authority of the governor
22: 2 sought how he might kill Jesus
22: 2 feared the people
22: 4 communed with Judas Iscariot concerning the betrayal of Jesus
22: 5 was glad (concerning the betrayal of Jesus) and covenanted to give Judas money
22:52 asked by Jesus if he came out as against a thief with swords and staves
22:53 daily being with Jesus in the temple, had not stretched forth his hand against Him
22:53 this was his hour
22:66 as soon as it was day, led Jesus into the council
22:67 asked Jesus plainly if He were the Christ
22:67 told by Jesus that if He told him, he would not believe
22:68 told by Jesus he would not answer Him, nor let Him go
22:70 asked Jesus if He were the Son of God
22:71 questioned concerning the need of further witnesses, as he had heard of Jesus' own mouth
23: 1 led Jesus unto Pilate
23: 2 (falsely) accused Jesus of perverting the nation and forbidding to give tribute to Ceasar
23: 4 told by Pilate that he found no fault in Jesus
23: 5 was more fierce, saying that Jesus stirred up the people teaching throughout all Jewry
23:13 stood and vehemently accused Jesus (before Herod)
23:13 called together by Pilate along with the rulers and the people, and told that he had found no fault in Jesus of those things of which he had accused Him (23:14)
23:23 his voice (among others) prevailed (before Pilate)
24:20 delivered Jesus to be condemned to death, and crucified Him

John 7:32 sent officers to take Jesus
7:45 officers returned to him without Jesus

ANNAS *(continued)*

John 7:48   had not believed on Jesus
11:47   gathered with a council to decide what to do with Jesus
11:48   feared that Jesus, if left alone, would cause the Romans to come and take away his place and the nation
11:53   from that day took council to put Him to death
11:57   gave a commandment that if any man knew where He was, he should show it, that they might take Him
12:10   consulted to put Lazarus also to death
18: 3   had presented a band of men and officers to Judas (Iscariot, to take Jesus)
18:13   Jesus led first to him
18:13   father-in-law of Caiaphas
18:24   sent Jesus bound unto Caiaphas
19: 6   seeing Jesus, cried out for His crucifixion
19: 6   told by Pilate to take Him (himself) and crucify Him
19:11   had the greater sin than Pilate
19:15   claimed to have no king but Caesar
19:21   endeavored to correct Pilate concerning the title given to Jesus

Acts 4: 1   came upon Peter and John, for teaching the people (4:2)
4: 2   grieved that Peter and John taught the people and preached through Jesus the resurrection from the dead
4: 3   laid hands on Peter and John, and put them in hold (prison) unto the next day
4: 6   the high priest
4: 6   had kindred
4: 6   part of the committee at Jerusalem which examined Peter and John (4:7)
4: 8   ruler of the people
4: 8   elder of Israel
4:13   marveled when he saw the boldness of Peter and John and perceived that they were unlearned and ignorant men
4:13   took knowledge of them (Peter and John) that they had been with Jesus
4:14   beholding the man which was healed, standing with them, could say nothing against it (the miracle)
4:15   conferred with the council (alone) concerning Peter and John and could not deny the miracle (4:16)
4:18   as part of the council commanded Peter and John not to speak at all or teach in the name of Jesus
4:21   further threatening Peter and John, let them go, finding nothing how to punish them
5:17   a Sadducee

Acts 5:17   rose up, filled with indignation
5:18   laid hands on the apostles and put them in the common prison
5:21   called the council together and sent to the prison to have them (the apostles) brought
5:24   hearing these things (the escape of the apostles from the prison) doubted of them whereunto this would grow
5:25   was told that the apostles were standing in the temple teaching the people
5:27   questioned the apostles concerning their activities (5:28)
5:28   stated that the apostles intended to bring Jesus' blood upon them (the Jewish leaders)
5:30   (had part with them who) slew Jesus, and hanged (Him) on a tree
5:33   hearing Peter's words, was cut to the heart and took counsel to slay the apostles
5:40   agreed to the words of Gamaliel
5:40   called the apostles, beat them, commanded them not to speak in the name of Jesus, and let them go
9: 1   approached by Saul (Paul) for letters to Damascus to bind men and women believers and return them to Jerusalem (9:2)
9:14   had given authority to Saul (Paul) to bind all that call on the name of Jesus
13:27   knew not Jesus nor the voices of the prophets
13:27   condemned Jesus
13:28   found no cause of death in Jesus, yet desired that He be slain
22: 5   bore witness of Paul's former actions
22: 5   granted letters to Paul to bring bound to Jerusalem for punishment, those that followed Christ
22:30   commanded to appear before the chief captain (a Roman) concerning Paul
26:10   had given authority to Paul to shut up in prison, the saints of God
26:12   gave authority and commission to Paul to go into Damascus

ANTIPAS [an'-tip-as = against father; against all]
1. Herod [her'-od = heroic]
An abbreviation of the name Antipater, tetrarch of Galilee and Perea, son of Herod the Great by Malthace, brother of Archaleas, had John the Baptist beheaded because of his oath to Herodias' daughter, and judge before Jesus.

Matt 14: 1   the tetrarch
14: 1   heard of the fame of Jesus
14: 2   had servants
14: 2   claimed that Jesus was John the Baptist risen from the dead

ANTIPAS (*continued*)

Matt	14: 3	had laid hold on, bound, and put John the Baptist in prison for Herodias's sake
	14: 3	brother of Philip
	14: 4	told by John the Baptist that it was not lawful to have Herodias (as his wife)
	14: 5	wanted to execute John the Baptist but feared the multitude
	14: 6	pleased by the dancing of Herodias's daughter on his birthday
	14: 7	promised with an oath to give Herodias's daughter whatsoever she would ask
	14: 8	was asked for the head of John the Baptist in a charger
	14: 9	the king
	14: 9	was sorry
	14: 9	for his oath's sake and to save face, commanded that John the Baptist's head be given Herodias's daughter
	14:10	sent and beheaded John in the prison (14:11)
Mark	6:14	the king
	6:14	heard of Jesus
	6:14	believed Jesus was John the Baptist risen from the dead
	6:16	declared Jesus to be John (the Baptist) whom he had beheaded, risen from the dead
	6:17	had sent for John (the Baptist) and bound him in prison for Herodias's sake
	6:17	brother of Philip (husband of Herodias)
	6:17	had married Herodias, his brother Philip's wife
	6:18	told by John (the Baptist) that it was not lawful to have his brother's wife
	6:20	feared John (the Baptist), observed him, and heard him gladly
	6:21	on his birthday made a supper to his lords, high captains, and chief estates of Galilee
	6:22	was pleased by the dancing of Herodias's daughter and promised her her wish
	6:23	swore his offer of Herodias's daughter's wish to the half of his kingdom
	6:24	Herodias's daughter, upon advice of her mother, asked him for the head of John the Baptist in a charger (6:25)
	6:26	was exceeding sorry, but for his oath's sake and to save face would not reject her wish
	6:27	immediately sent an executioner to bring the head of John the Baptist
	8:15	Jesus spoke of his leaven (sin)
Luke	3: 1	contemporary of Tiberius Caesar, and Pontius Pilate, Philip and

		Lysanias (tetarch) and Annas and Caiaphas (high priests) (3:2)
Luke	3: 1	tetrarch of Galilee
	3: 1	brother of Philip
	3:19	the tetrarch
	3:19	reproved by John the Baptist for Herodias his brother Philip's wife, and for all the evils which he had done
	3:20	shut up John (the Baptist) in prison
	8: 3	Chuza was his steward
	9: 7	heard of all the works of Jesus
	9: 7	the tetrarch
	9: 7	perplexed because it was said of some that John (the Baptist) was risen from the dead, or that Elias had appeared or that one of the old prophets was risen again (9:8)
	9: 9	had beheaded John (the Baptist)
	9: 9	heard much of Jesus and desired to see Him
	13:31	some Pharisees tried to persuade Jesus that he (Herod) would kill Him
	13:32	called a fox by Jesus
	23: 7	Galilee was under his jurisdiction
	23: 7	Jesus was sent to him
	23: 7	was at Jerusalem at the time of the Passover
	23: 8	was exceedingly glad when he saw Jesus and hoped to see some miracle done by Him
	23: 8	had desired to see Jesus for a long season because he had heard many things of Him
	23: 9	questioned Jesus with many words, but received no answer
	23:11	had men of war
	23:11	set Jesus at nought, mocked Him, arrayed Him in a gorgeous robe, and sent Him back to Pilate
	23:12	he and Pilate the same day were made friends whereas before they were at enmity
	23:14	having examined Jesus, found no fault in Him concerning their accusations
	23:15	had been sent Jesus by Pilate
Acts	4:27	had gathered with others against Jesus (to do the predetermined will of God) (4:28)
	13: 1	the tetrarch
	13: 1	had been brought up with Manaen

2. An abbreviation of the name Antipater and a faithful martyr at Pergamos.

Rev.	2:13	Christ's faithful martyr
	2:13	slain among those of Pergamos

APELLES [a-pel'-leze = called; without receptacle (hide)]
A Christian of Rome whom, according to Paul, was "approved in Christ" and to whom Paul sent his greetings.

Rom	16:10	was to be saluted by Paul
	16:10	approved in Christ

APOLLOS [ap-ol'-los = a destroyer]
Short for Apollonius, a Jew of Alexandria, an
eloquent man who was mighty in the scriptures,
but who required additional instruction from
Aquila and Priscilla in the Word, and a convincing
speaker and preacher to the Jews.

Acts	18:24	a Jew
	18:24	born at Alexandria
	18:24	eloquent, and mighty in the scriptures
	18:25	came to Ephesus
	18:25	was instructed in the way of the Lord
	18:25	being fervent in spirit, spake and taught diligently the things of the Lord, knowing only the baptism of John
	18:26	began to speak boldly in the synagogue
	18:26	taken unto Aquila and Priscilla and had the way of God expounded unto him more perfectly
	18:27	was disposed to pass into Achaia
	18:27	the disciples in Achaia were exhorted to receive him
	18:27	when he was come, helped them much which had believed through grace
	18:28	mightily convinced the Jews, publicly, from the scriptures that Jesus was Christ
	19: 1	was at Corinth
1Cor	1:12	some of the Corinthian believers claimed to be (followers) of him
	3: 4	some Corinthian believers said they were (followers) of him
	3: 5	a minister (by whom the Corinthians believed)
	3: 6	watered (the gospel in the hearts of the Corinthians)
	3:22	was the believers' (possession)
	4: 1	the minister of Christ
	4: 1	the steward of the mysteries of God
	4: 6	Paul, in a figure, had transferred to himself and Apollos the faults of others (for instructional purposes)
	16:12	a (Christian) brother of Paul
	16:12	his will was not at all to come to Corinth at that time
	16:12	would come to Corinth when he had a convenient time
Tit	3:13	Paul asked Titus to bring him when he came to Nicopolis to be with Paul

APPHIA ♀ [af'-fee-ah = a name expressive of
endearment; dear one]
A Christian woman of Colosse, beloved of Paul,
a recipient of the book of Philemon, probably the
wife of Philemon, and mother of Archippus, and
she was stoned during the reign of Nero.

| Phle | : 2 | co-recipient, with Philemon and Archippus, of letter of Philemon |
| | : 2 | beloved of Paul and Timothy |

AQUILA [ac-quil'-ah = eagle; immovable]
A Jew of Pontus, forced to leave Rome and went
to Corinth, a tentmaker, and along with his wife
Priscilla instructed Apollos more fully in the word
of God.

Acts	18: 2	found by Paul, who came unto him and Priscilla
	18: 2	a Jew
	18: 2	born in Pontus, but lately came from Italy
	18: 2	husband of Priscilla
	18: 3	Paul abode with him (and his wife)
	18: 3	a tentmaker by occupation, as was Paul
	18:18	sailed to Syria with Paul and Priscilla
	18:19	left at Ephesus by Paul, with his wife Priscilla
	18:26	hearing Apollos, took him unto him (and Priscilla) and expounded the way of God more perfectly
Rom	16: 3	was to be greeted (along with Priscilla) by the Roman church for Paul
	16: 3	helper of Paul in Christ Jesus
	16: 4	for Paul's life had laid down his neck
	16: 4	given thanks by Paul and all the churches of the Gentiles
	16: 5	the church met in his (and Priscilla's) house
1Cor	16:19	saluted the Corinthian church
	16:19	the church met in his house (and Priscilla's)
2Tim	4:19	was to be saluted by Timothy, for Paul

ARAM [a'-ram = high, exalted]
Son of Shamer and of the tribe of Asher. (See also
1Chr 7)

Matt	1: 3	begat by Esrom
	1: 4	begat Aminadab
Luke	3:33	father of Aminadab
	3:33	son of Esrom

ARCHELAUS [ar-ke-la'-us = people's chief]
A son of Herod the Great by Malthace; elder
brother of Antipas; ruler of Idumea, Judea, and
Samaria; and deposed in 6 A.D.

| Matt | 2:22 | son of Herod (the Great) |
| | 2:22 | reigned in place of his father (in Judea) |

ARCHIPPUS [ar-kip'-pus = chief groom]
Fellow soldier of Paul, a Christian of Colosse,
mentioned as a recipient of Paul's letter to Philemon, and probably the son of Philemon and
Apphia.

Col	4:17	was to be told (by Paul through the Colossians) to take heed to the ministry which he had received in the Lord, and fulfill it
Phle	: 2	corecipient, with Philemon and Apphia, of the letter of Philemon
	: 2	fellow soldier with Paul and Timothy

29

ARETAS [ar'e-tas = pleasing]
A ruler (king) over Damascus and possibly the
father-in-law of Herod the tetrarch.

2Cor 11:32 the king
       11:32 over the governor (of Damascus)

ARISTARCUS [ar-is-tar'-cus = the best ruler]
A man of Macedonia and a native of Thessalonica,
a traveling companion and fellow prisoner of Paul,
and taken along with Gaius at the riot in Ephesus.

Acts 19:29 was caught and was rushed into
             the theater (at Ephesus)
      19:29 of Macedonia
      19:29 Paul's companion in travel
      19:37 neither a robber of churches, nor a
             blasphemer (of Diana)
      20: 4 of the Thessalonians
      20: 4 accompanied Paul into Asia
      20: 5 went before and tarried for Paul
             (and Luke) at Troas
      20: 6 abode seven days with Paul (and
             Luke) at Troas
      20:13 going before by ship, sailed unto
             Assos
      20:14 met Paul at Assos, took him in, and
             came to Mitylene
      20:15 sailed over against Chios, next day
             arrived at Samos, tarried at Trogyl-
             lium, and next day came to Miletus
      20:34 Paul's hand had ministered unto
             his necessities
      27: 2 entered into a ship (with Paul and
             Luke) of Adramyttium and
             launched, meaning to sail by the
             coast of Asia
      27: 2 a Macedonian of Thessalonica
      27: 3 the next day touched at Sidon
      27: 4 launched from Sidon and sailed
             under Cyprus, because the winds
             were contrary
      27: 5 sailed over the sea of Cilicia and
             Pamphylia, and came to Myra
      27: 6 put on a ship of Alexandria sailing
             into Italy
      27: 7 sailed slowly many days, scarcely
             coming against Cnidus, not being
             suffered of the wind
      27: 7 sailed under Crete, over against
             Salmone, and came to the fair ha-
             vens, near the city of Lasea (27:8)
      27:13 sailed close by Crete
      27:16 ran under the island of Clauda
      27:16 had much work to come by the boat
      27:18 exceedingly tossed with a tempest
      27:19 cast out, with his own hands, the
             tackling of the ship
      27:20 saw neither sun nor stars in many
             days, and all hope that they should
             be saved was taken away
      27:27 had been driven up and down
             Adria fourteen nights
      27:33 besought by Paul to take meat
      27:33 had tarried and continued fasting
             fourteen days

Acts 27:34 was prayed to take some meat for
             his health
      27:34 not one hair would fall from his
             head
      27:36 was of good cheer and took meat
      27:37 was one of 276 passengers in the ship
      27:44 escaped safely to land
      28: 1 had escaped to the island of Melita
      28: 2 was shown no little kindness (by
             the people of Melita)
      28: 2 received because of the present rain
             and cold
      28: 7 received by Publius and lodged
             three days courteously
      28:10 honored with many honors
      28:10 when he departed, was laden with
             such things as were necessary
      28:11 after three months departed in a
             ship of Alexandria
      28:12 landed at Syracuse and tarried
             three days
      28:13 sailed on to Rhegium and thence
             to Puteoli
      28:14 found brethren (at Puteoli) and
             was desired to tarry with them
             seven days
      28:14 went toward Rome
      28:15 met by the brethren at Appii
             Forum and The Three Taverns
      28:16 came to Rome
Col   4:10 a fellow prisoner of Paul
       4:10 saluted the church at Colosse
       4:11 a Jewish fellow worker who had
             been a comfort to Paul
Phle   :24   fellow laborer with Paul
       :24   Paul requested Philemon to salute
             him

ARISTOBULUS [a-ris-to-bu'-lus = the best
counsellor]
A citizen of Rome, whose household was greeted
by Paul.

Rom 16:10 those of his household saluted of
            Paul

ARPHAXAD [ar-fax'-ad = I shall fail as the
breast]
A son of Shem. (See also Gen 10—11)

Luke   3:36 father of Cainan
       3:36 son of Sem (Shem)

ARTEMAS [ar'-te-mas = whole, sound]
A companion of Paul whom he thought to send
to Titus.

Tit   3:12 possibly sent by Paul to Titus

ASA [a'-sah = physician]
A king of Judah, responsive to the need of ridding
the kingdom of idolatry, Son of Abijam and great-
grandson of Solomon, diseased in his feet in his
old age, reigned forty plus years, and buried in
Jerusalem. (See also 1Kng 15,16, 22; 2Chr 14—17,
20, 21)

ASA *(continued)*

Matt 1: 7 begotten of Abia
 1: 8 begat Josaphat

ASER [a'-sur = happy]
Old Testament Asher, a patriarch, the eighth son
of Jacob (by Zilpah, the handmaid of Leah),
father of four sons and one daughter, and father
of the tribe which bears his name. (See also Gen
30, 35, 46, 49; Exod 1; Num 26; Josh 17)

Matt 1: 2 begat by Jacob
Luke 2:36 Anna the prophetess and Phanuel
 her father were of his tribe
John 4:12 drank at the well (Jacob's)
 4:12 a child of Jacob
Acts 7: 8 begat by Jacob
 7: 8 one of the patriarchs
 7: 9 one of the patriarchs
 7: 9 moved with envy, sold Joseph into
 Egypt
 7:11 found no sustenance
 7:12 sent by Jacob to Egypt for corn
 7:13 on his second visit (to Egypt),
 Joseph was made known to him
 7:13 was made known unto Pharaoh
 7:15 went down into Egypt and died
 7:16 was carried into Sychem and was
 laid in the sepulcher that Abraham
 bought
Rev 7: 6 twelve thousand sealed of his tribe
 21:12 his name is inscribed upon the
 gates of the new Jerusalem
 21:12 a child of Israel (Jacob)

ASYNCRITUS [a-sin'-cri-tus = incomparable]
A Christian at Rome and saluted by Paul.

Rom 16:14 saluted by Paul
 16:14 was with other brethren

AUGUSTUS [aw-gus'-tus = sacred, kingly];
really only a title, not a proper name
1. The Roman emperor at the time of the birth of
Christ, whose real name was Caius Octavius
Caepias; a relative of Julias Caesar; born in 63
B.C.; and decreed that all the world should be
taxed.

Luke 2: 1 decreed that all the world should
 be taxed
 2: 1 contemporary of Cyrenius, governor of Syria (2:2)
2. Probably a reference to Nero, another emperor
of Rome who was reigning at the time of the death
of Paul.

Acts 25:21 Paul had appealed to be reserved
 unto his hearing
 25:25 Paul had appealed unto him
 25:25 Festus had determined to send Paul
 to him
 25:26 Paul was brought before Agrippa
 in order that Festus might have
 somewhat to write unto him (concerning Paul's appeal)

AZOR [a'zor = helper]
Son of Eliakim, father of Sadoc, and ancestor of
Jesus.

Matt 1:13 begotten of Eliakim
 1:14 begat Sadoc

B

BALAAM [ba'-la-am = lord of the people; con-
founding the people]
A prophet, son of Beor, lived at Pethor of
Mesopotamia, spoken to by a donkey or beast of
burden in an audible voice, offered a bribe to
pronounce a curse upon Israel but forbidden of
the Lord and instead pronounced a blessing. (See
also Num 22—24, 31; Deut 23; Josh 13, 24)

2Pet 2:15 the son of Bosor
 2:15 evil men follow his way
 2:15 loved the wages of unrighteousness
 2:16 rebuked for his iniquity
 2:16 a dumb ass speaking with man's
 voice forbade his madness
Jude :11 people in Jude's day were greedily
 running after his error for reward
Rev 2:14 some of Pergamos held his doctrine
 2:14 taught Balac to cast a stumblingblock before the children of Israel,
 to eat things sacrificed to idols, and
 to commit fornication

BALAC [ba'-lak = waster]
Old Testament Balak, son of Zippor and a king
of Moab, and endeavored to persuade Balaam to
pronounce a curse upon Israel. (See also Num
22—24)

Rev 2:14 taught by Balaam to cast a
 stumblingblock before the children
 of Israel, to eat things sacrificed unto
 idols, and to commit fornication

BARABBAS [ba-rab'-bas = father's son]
A robber, murderer, notable prisoner who had
made insurrection, and released by Pontius Pilate
in preference to Jesus Christ at the passover in
Jerusalem.

Matt 27:16 a notable prisoner
 27:17 was offered to the people along
 with Jesus, for release
 27:20 chief priests and elders persuaded
 the multitude to ask for him instead
 of Jesus
 27:21 people asked for his release
 27:26 released by Pilate
Mark 15: 7 a prisoner
 15: 7 lay bound with them that had made
 insurrection with him
 15: 7 a murderer

BARABBAS *(continued)*

Mark 15:11 his release was requested by the multitude
    15:15 released by Pilate
Luke 23:18 the multitude cried for his release instead of Jesus' release
    23:19 was in prison for sedition and murder
    23:25 released unto the people at their desire
    23:25 had been cast into prison for sedition and murder
John 18:40 his release desired by the Jews (instead of Jesus')
    18:40 a robber
Acts 3:14 a murderer

BARACHIAS [bar'-ak-i'-as = Jehovah blesses]
Old Testament Berechiah, father of Zechariah, and slain between the temple and the altar. (See also Zech 1)

Matt 23:35 father of Zacharias

BARAK [ba'-rak = lightning]
A son of Abinoam of the tribe of Naphtali, a military leader who lead Israel to victory against the Canaanites (led by Sisera), and an associate of Deborah. (See also Judg 4—5)

Heb 11:32 acted by faith (11:33)
    11:39 had obtained a good report through faith
    11:39 received not the promise

BAR-JESUS [bar-je'-sus = son of Joshua]— see ELYMAS

BAR-JONA [bar-jo'-nah = son of a dove]— see SIMON PETER

BARNABAS [bar'na-bas = son of consolation]
Originally Joses but given the name Barnabas (son of exhortation) by the apostles, a Levite from Cyprus, designated an apostle, probably a cousin of John Mark with whom he traveled in missionary endeavors, separated unto the work by the Holy Spirit and sent out by the Church at Antioch, and a traveling companion of Paul on the first missionary journey (after a sharp contention they parted ways).

Acts 9:27 took Saul (Paul) to the apostles and declared unto them his conversion experience and his bold preaching at Damascus
    11:22 was sent of the church at Jerusalem as far as to Antioch
    11:23 seeing the grace of God, was glad, and exhorted them all, that with purpose of heart they would cleave unto the Lord
    11:24 a good man
    11:24 full of the Holy Ghost and faith
    11:25 departed to Tarsus to seek Saul (Paul)

found Saul (Paul) and brought him to Antioch
Acts 11:26 a whole year assembled with the church and taught much people
    11:29 along with Saul (Paul) carried the relief to the elders from the brethren in Judea (11:30)
    12:25 along with Saul (Paul) returned to Jerusalem when he had fulfilled his ministry
    12:25 took John Mark with him and Saul (Paul) to Jerusalem
    13: 1 was in the church at Antioch
    13: 1 a prophet and teacher
    13: 2 ministered to the Lord and fasted
    13: 2 the Holy Spirit required he be separated (along with Paul) unto the work to which He had called him
    13: 3 fasted and prayed
    13: 3 the prophets and teachers laid their hands on him and sent him away
    13: 4 sent forth by the Holy Ghost
    13: 4 departed with Saul (Paul) (and John) unto Seleucia and thence sailed to Cyprus
    13: 5 at Salamis preached the word of God in the synagogues
    13: 5 had John (Mark) to his minister (as an assistant)
    13: 6 on the isle of Paphos found Bar-jesus (Elymas) with Sergius Paulus
    13: 8 withstood by Bar-jesus (Elymas)
    13:13 left Paphos with Saul (Paul) and John Mark, and came to Perga in Pamphylia
    13:13 John (Mark) left him and returned to Jerusalem
    13:14 departed from Perga and came to Antioch in Pisidia
    13:14 entered the synagogue on the sabbath day and sat down
    13:15 invited to speak, by the rulers of the synagogue
    13:32 declared the good tidings that God had fulfilled His promise in raising up Jesus (13:33)
    13:43 many followed him and Saul (Paul) being persuaded to continue in the grace of God
    13:46 waxed bold, rebuked the Jews, and turned to the ministry to the Gentiles
    13:47 the Lord commanded that He had set them (him and Saul) to be a light of the Gentiles
    13:50 the Jews raised persecution against him and Saul (Paul) and expelled them out of their coasts
    13:51 shook off the dust of his feet against them (of Antioch in Pisidia), and came to Iconium
    14: 1 entered the synagogue in Iconium
    14: 1 so spake that a great multitude believed

BARNABAS *(continued)*

Acts 14: 3   abode a long time in Iconium speaking boldly in the Lord

14: 3   granted of the Lord, that signs and wonders might be done by his hands

14: 4   part of the city followed him and Saul (Paul)

14: 4   called an apostle

14: 5   object of an assault by both Jews and Gentiles to despitefully use him and stone him

14: 6   fled to Lystra, Derbe and the surrounding region

14: 7   preached the gospel

14:11   people of Lystra thought he and Saul (Paul) to be gods

14:12   was called Jupiter (a god)

14:13   hearing the people would have sacrificed unto him, rent his clothes and ran in among the people (14:14)

14:14   called an apostle

14:15   man of like passions as the people of Lystra, who preached unto them the living God

14:18   scarcely restrained the people from doing sacrifice unto him

14:20   next day departed with Saul (Paul) to Derbe

14:21   preached the gospel and taught many in Derbe

14:21   returned to Lystra, Iconium, and Antioch confirming the souls of the disciples and exhorting them to continue in the faith (14:22)

14:23   ordained elders in every church

14:23   prayed with fasting

14:23   commended them to the Lord

14:24   passed throughout Pisidia and came to Pamphylia

14:25   having preached the word in Perga, went down into Attalia

14:26   sailed to Antioch from whence he had been commended to the grace of God

14:26   had fulfilled his work (his mission)

14:27   gathered the church together and rehearsed all that God had done with him (and Paul)

14:28   abode a long time with the disciples (at Antioch)

15: 2   along with Paul, had no small dissension and disputation with those teaching false doctrine

15: 2   the church (at Antioch) sent him (among others) to Jerusalem unto the apostles and the elders about this question (of circumcision)

15: 3   being brought on his way by the church, passed through Phenice and Samaria

15: 3   declared the conversion of the Gentiles, causing great joy

Acts 15: 4   came to Jerusalem, was received of the church, the apostles, and elders, and declared all things God had done with him

15:12   given audience by the counsel at Jerusalem and declared what miracles and signs God had wrought among the Gentiles by him (and Paul)

15:13   held his peace

15:22   Judas (Barsabas) and Silas were sent with him and Paul back to the Gentiles at Antioch

15:25   beloved of the apostles, elders, and brethren of the Jerusalem church

15:26   had hazarded his life for the name of our Lord Jesus Christ

15:30   dismissed, came to Antioch, gathered the multitude together, and delivered the epistle

15:35   continued in Antioch teaching and preaching the word of the Lord

15:36   asked by Paul to accompany him on a return missionary visit to every city where they had preached

15:37   determined to take John Mark along

15:39   his contention with Paul (over John Mark) was so sharp that they parted company

15:39   took Mark and sailed unto Cyprus

1Cor 9: 6   had the power (right) to forbear working

Gal 2: 1   went to Jerusalem with Paul and Titus

2: 9   given right hands of fellowship by James, Cephas, and John that he might be sent to the heathen

2:13   carried away with the dissimulation of the circumcision

Col 4:10   uncle of Marcus (Mark; John Mark)

BARSABAS [bar-sab'-as = son of the host]
1. Joseph—see JOSEPH (surnamed JUSTUS BARSABAS)
2. Judas—see JUDAS (BARSABAS)

BARTHOLOMEW [bar-thol'-o-mew = son of Tolmai]
A disciple and apostle of Jesus, one of the twelve, and possibly identical with Nathanael

Matt 8:23*   followed Jesus into a ship

8:25*   came to and awoke Jesus, and asked Him to save the disciples, for they were perishing

8:26*   fearful

8:26*   of little faith

8:27*   marveled at Jesus

9:10*   sat at meat with Jesus, along with publicans and sinners

9:14*   fasted not

9:19*   followed Jesus

BARTHOLOMEW *(continued)*

Matt 9:37* instructed to pray that the Lord would send forth laborers into His harvest (9:38)

10: 1* was called unto Jesus

10: 1 one of the twelve disciples (of Jesus)

10: 1* given power to cast out unclean spirits

10: 1* given power to heal all manner of sickness and disease

10: 3 one of the twelve apostles

10: 5 one of the twelve (apostles)

10: 5* commanded to go neither to the Gentiles, nor into any city of the Samaritans

10: 6* sent forth by Jesus to the lost sheep of the house of Israel

10: 7* commanded by Jesus to preach "the kingdom of heaven is at hand"

10: 8* commanded to heal the sick, cleanse the lepers, raise the dead, cast out devils (demons)

10: 8* had freely received

10: 9* was to provide neither gold, nor silver, nor brass, nor scrip, neither two coats, neither shoes, nor staves (for himself) (10:10)

10:11* in every city or town, was to inquire who was worthy, and to abide with them

10:12* was to salute each house he entered

10:13* his peace was to come upon each worthy house, but return to him if unworthy

10:14* was to shake off the dust of his feet therein, when not received or heard by a house or city

10:16* sent forth (by Jesus) as a sheep in the midst of wolves

10:16* was to be wise as a serpent and harmless as a dove

10:17* would be delivered to the councils, scourged in the synagogues, and brought before governors and kings for (Jesus') sake (10:18)

10:19* was to take no thought concerning what he would speak when delivered up, for the Spirit of his Father would speak in him (10:20)

12: 1* was an hungered and plucked corn in the field and ate

12: 2* accused by the Pharisees of acting unlawfully on the Sabbath day

12:49* called mother and brethren by Jesus

13:10* questioned Jesus about His use of parables

13:11* was given unto him to know the mysteries of the kingdom of Heaven

13:16* saw and heard (spiritually)

13:17* had seen and heard (spiritually)

13:18* had the parable of the sower explained by Jesus (13:23)

13:36* had the parable of the wheat and tares explained by Jesus (13:43)

13:51* claimed to have understood all these things (parables)

Matt 14:15* came to Jesus and requested Him to send the multitude away

14:16* instructed by Jesus to feed the multitude

14:17* requested by Jesus to bring the five loaves and two fishes to Him (14:18)

14:19* given the blessed loaves by Jesus

14:19* distributed the loaves to the multitude

14:20* took up the fragments that remained twelve baskets full

14:22* constrained by Jesus to get into a ship and to go before Him unto the other side (of the Sea of Galilee)

14:24* his ship was tossed with waves

14:25* approached by Jesus (walking on the sea)

14:26* saw Jesus walking on the water (Sea of Galilee) and was afraid

14:27* told by Jesus to be of good cheer and not be afraid

14:33* being in the ship, worshiped Jesus, claiming Him to be the Son of God

14:34* came into the land of Gennesaret

15: 2* accused, by the scribes and Pharisees, of transgressing the tradition of the elders by not washing his hands when he ate bread

15:12* came to Jesus, informing Him that the Pharisees were offended at His saying

15:23* came and besought Jesus to send away her that cried after him

15:32* was called (unto Jesus)

15:34* had seven loaves and a few little fishes

15:36* given the loaves and fishes (by Jesus)

15:36* gave the loaves and fishes to the multitude

15:37* took up of the broken meat that was left seven baskets full

16: 5* was come to the other side and had forgotten to take bread

16: 6* told to beware of the leaven of the Pharisees and Sadducees

16: 7* reasoned with the other disciples over Jesus' words

16: 7* had taken no bread

16: 8* of little faith

16: 8* reasoned with the other disciples (concerning the lack of bread)

16: 9* took up baskets (of fragments)

16:10* took up baskets (of fragments)

16:11* did not understand Jesus' words concerning the leaven (doctrine) of the Pharisees and Sadducees

16:12* understood how that Jesus spoke not of bread, but of the doctrine of the Pharisees and Sadducees

16:13* was in Caesarea Phillippi

16:13* answered Jesus' question concerning His identity (16:14)

16:15* questioned as to his view of Jesus' identity

BARTHOLOMEW *(continued)*

Matt 16:20* charged by Jesus to tell no man that He was Jesus the Christ

16:21* shown by Jesus the sufferings He must undergo

17:15* could not cure the lunatic boy (17:16)

17:19* asked Jesus why he could not cast out the devil (demon)

17:20* could not cast out the devil (demon) because of unbelief

17:22* abode in Galilee

17:23* was exceedingly sorry

17:24* came to Capernaum

18: 1* asked Jesus who is the greatest in the kingdom of Heaven

19:13* rebuked those who brought children to Jesus

19:14* rebuked in turn by Jesus

19:25* exceedingly amazed at Jesus' answer to the rich young ruler and asked who could be saved

19:27* had forsaken all and followed Jesus

19:28* had followed Jesus

19:28* promised by Jesus to sit upon the twelve thrones judging the twelve tribes of Israel

20:17* going up to Jerusalem, taken apart and foretold by Jesus of His betrayal, crucifixion, and resurrection (20:19)

20:24* was moved with indignation towards James and John because of their request of Jesus

20:29* departed from Jericho (for Jerusalem)

21: 1* arrived in Bethphage and Mount of Olives

21:20* saw the withered fig tree and marveled

24: 1* came to Jesus to show Him the buildings of the temple

24: 2* Jesus spoke to him of coming destruction of the temple

24: 3* asked Jesus of the sign of His coming and of the end of the world

26:8* was indignant at the actions of the woman

26:10* had troubled the woman

26:17* asked Jesus where he should prepare for Him the Passover

26:19* did as Jesus had appointed and made ready the Passover

26:20* celebrated Passover with Jesus and the rest of the twelve

26:22* asked Jesus if he were the one to betray Him

26:26* while eating (the Passover) given the bread by Jesus

26:27* given the cup (by Jesus)

26:30* having sung a hymn, went out into the Mount of Olives

26:31* Jesus predicted that he would be offended because of Him

Matt 26:35* claimed he would never deny Jesus, even though it meant death

26:36* came with Jesus to Gethsemane

26:36* instructed to sit and pray

26:40* fell asleep in the garden of Gethsemane

26:43 fell asleep again in the garden (of Gethsemane)

26:45* told to sleep on now and take his rest

26:46* told to arise and go (with Jesus)

26:56* forsook Jesus and fled

28:13* would be accused of stealing Jesus' body by night

28:16* went into Galilee into the place (mountain) appointed

28:17* saw Jesus and worshiped Him

28:19* given the great commission (28:20)

28:20* Jesus would always be with him, even unto the end of the world

Mark 3:14* ordained by Jesus (to be with Him)

3:14* would be sent forth to preach (by Jesus)

3:15* would be given power by Jesus to heal sicknesses and cast out devils (demons)

3:18* a disciple of Jesus (one of the twelve)

3:20* could not eat bread with Jesus because of the multitude

4:10* asked Jesus about the parable of the sower

4:11* was given to know the mystery of the kingdom of God

4:33* had many parables taught him by Jesus

4:34* when alone, with the rest of the twelve, had all things expounded by Jesus

4:36* sent away the multitude

4:36* with the rest of the twelve, took Jesus to the other side of the sea

4:38* in fear, awakened Jesus in the midst of the storm

4:40* was fearful and had no faith

4:41* feared exceedingly

4:41* questioned among the other disciples as to what manner of man Jesus was that even the wind and the sea obeyed Him

5: 1* went with Jesus across the sea of Galilee to the country of the Gadarenes

6: 1* followed Jesus into His own country

6: 7* sent forth two by two (by Jesus)

6: 7* given power over unclean spirits

6: 8* commanded to take nothing on his journey except a staff, and to be shod with sandals and only one coat (6:9)

6:12* went out, and preached that men should repent

6:13* cast out many devils (demons) and

35

BARTHOLOMEW *(continued)*

anointed with oil many that were sick, and healed them

Mark 6:30* an apostle

6:30* gathered together unto Jesus to report what he had done and taught

6:31* had no leisure so much as to eat

6:32* departed privately with Jesus into a desert place by ship

6:36* asked Jesus to send away the multitude into the villages to buy themselves bread

6:37* told by Jesus to give food to the multitude

6:37* asked Jesus if he should go and buy bread to feed the people

6:38* when asked by Jesus the available provisions, reported five loaves and two fishes

6:39* made the people sit down by hundreds and by fifties (6:40)

6:41* given the food blessed by Jesus to distribute to the crowd

6:43* took up twelve baskets full of fragments and of the fishes

6:45* constrained by Jesus to get into the ship and go to the other side unto Bethsaida

6:47* was alone (with the other disciples) in the ship in the midst of the sea

6:48* toiled in rowing the ship for the winds were contrary

6:48* Jesus came unto him in about the fourth watch of the night walking upon the sea

6:49* saw Jesus walking upon the sea and cried out for he supposed it had been a spirit

6:50* saw Jesus and was troubled but admonished by Him to fear not

6:51* was amazed beyond measure and wondered that the wind ceased as Jesus entered the ship

6:52* because of his hardness of heart, had forgotten about the miracle of the loaves

6:53* came into the land of Gennesaret

6:54* got out of the ship

7: 5* walked not according to the traditions of the elders (ate bread with unwashed hands)

8: 5* informed Jesus of the seven loaves

8: 6* set the loaves before the people

8: 7* receiving the blessed fishes from Jesus, set them before the people

8: 8* gathered seven baskets of fragments

8:10* entered into a ship with Jesus and went into Dalmanutha

8:13* entered into the ship again with Jesus, departed to the other side

8:14* had forgotten to take bread, and had only one loaf in the ship

8:16* had no bread

Mark 8:17* having seen the miracles, still did not understand as his heart was possibly yet hardened

8:19* took up twelve baskets full of fragments at the feeding of the five thousand

8:20* took up seven baskets full of fragments at the feeding of the four thousand

8:27* went into the towns of Caesarea Philippi with Jesus

8:27* responded to Jesus' question concerning His identity with "John the Baptist, Elias, and one of the prophets" (8:28)

8:30* charged to tell no man that Jesus was the Christ

8:31* taught by Jesus of the things concerning Himself

9:14* questioned by the scribes

9:18* could not cast out a dumb spirit

9:30* passed through Galilee

9:32* did not understand the words of Jesus, but was afraid to ask

9:33* came to Capernaum

9:33* disputed with the other disciples on the way to Capernaum as to whom should be the greatest (9:34)

9:38* forbade a man from casting out devils (demons) in Jesus' name, because he did not follow Him

10:13* rebuked those who brought young children to Jesus that He should touch them

10:14* rebuked, in turn, by Jesus

10:24* astonished at the words of Jesus concerning those with riches

10:26* astonished at Jesus' words

10:28* had left all and followed Jesus

10:32* went up to Jerusalem with Jesus and was amazed and afraid

10:41 was much displeased with James and John

10:46* went to Jericho

10:46* went out of Jericho with Jesus

11: 1* came nigh to Jerusalem, unto Bethphage and Bethany, at the Mount of Olives

11:11* went to Bethany with Jesus and stayed until the morrow (11:12)

11:14* heard Jesus curse the fig tree

11:15* returned to Jerusalem with Jesus

11:19* went out of Jerusalem (10:20)

11:20* witnessed the fig tree dried up from the roots

11:27* came again to Jerusalem

14:12 asked Jesus where they should go and prepare the Passover

14:17* in the evening of the first day of unleavened bread, went with Jesus to the upper room

14:18* sat and ate together with Jesus

14:19* began to be sorrowful over Jesus' statement of betrayal and to ask,

BARTHOLOMEW (*continued*)
  "Is it I?"

Mark 14:20* dipped with Jesus in the dish
      14:22* ate the Passover with Jesus
      14:23* drank of the communion cup
      14:26* sang a hymn and went out to the Mount of Olives
      14:31* exclaimed that even if it meant death, he would not deny Him
      14:32* went to Gethsemane and was told to sit there while Jesus prayed
      14:50* forsook Jesus and fled
      16:10* mourned and wept
      16:11* believed not Mary Magdalene's account
      16:14* Jesus appeared unto him as he sat at meat (with the other disciples)
      16:14* upbraided by Jesus for his unbelief and hardness of heart, because he believed not them which had seen Him after He was risen
      16:15* commissioned to go into all the world and preach the gospel to every creature
      16:20* went forth and preached everywhere, with signs following

Luke   6: 1* plucked ears of corn and ate (rubbing them in his hands) on the Sabbath
       6: 2* claimed (by the Pharisees) to be doing that which was not lawful to do on the Sabbath days
       6:13* chosen as one of the twelve
       6:13* also called (named) an apostle
       6:14 an apostle
       6:17* came down from the mountain with Jesus and stood in the plain
       8: 1* went throughout every city and village with Jesus
       8: 9* questioned Jesus concerning a parable
       8:10* unto him it was given to know the mysteries of the kingdom of God
       8:22* went into a ship with Jesus and launched forth for the other side
       8:23* the boat, filled with water, put him in jeopardy
       8:24* called Jesus "Master"
       8:24* came to Jesus and awakened Him during the storm
       8:25* asked by Jesus concerning his faith
       8:25* was afraid and wondered concerning Jesus' power over the elements
       8:26* arrived at the country of the Gadarenes (Gadara)
       9: 1* given power and authority over all devils (demons) and to cure diseases
       9: 2* sent by Jesus to preach the kingdom of God and to heal the sick
       9: 3* was to take neither staves, nor scrip, neither bread, neither money, neither have two coats
       9: 4* was to abide in whatever house he entered

Luke   9: 6* went through the towns, preaching the gospel, and healing everywhere
       9:10* returned and told Jesus all he had done
       9:10* went privately with Jesus into a desert place belonging to the city called Bethsaida
       9:12* requested that Jesus send away the multitude so that they might go into the towns and lodge and get victuals (food)
       9:13* had only five loaves and two fishes, but was requested by Jesus to give food to the multitude
       9:14* made the multitude sit down in companies by fifties (9:15)
       9:16* gave the blessed loaves and fish unto the multitude
       9:17* took up twelve baskets of fragments
       9:18* was alone with Jesus (and the rest of the twelve)
       9:18* in response to Jesus' question as to His identity, responded, "John the Baptist, Elias, and one of the prophets risen again" (9:19)
       9:20* straitly charged and commanded to tell no man that He is the Christ (9:21)
       9:40* could not cast the spirit (demon) out of the boy
       9:45* feared to ask Jesus concerning His teaching
       9:46* reasoned with the other disciples as to which of them should be greatest
       9:49* forbade a man from casting out devils (demons) in Jesus' name because he followed not with the disciples
      10:24* saw and heard what many prophets and kings had desired to experience
      12: 1* warned by Jesus to beware of the leaven of the Pharisees
      12: 4* friend of Jesus
      17: 5* asked Jesus to increase his faith
      18:15* rebuked those who brought infants to Jesus
      18:16* rebuked, in turn, by Jesus
      18:28* had left all and followed Jesus
      18:31* taken unto Jesus and instructed of things to come (18:33)
      18:34* understood none of these teachings of Jesus
      19:29* with Jesus, came nigh to Bethphage and Bethany at the Mount of Olives
      19:37* rejoiced and praised God with a loud voice (19:38)
      22:14* sat down with Jesus (in the upper room for the Passover)
      22:14* was called an apostle
      22:15* Jesus truly desired his presence in eating the Passover
      22:19* partook of the first Lord's Supper (22:20)

BARTHOLOMEW *(continued)*

Luke 22:23* inquired among the disciples as to which of them would betray Jesus

22:24* a strife existed among him and the other disciples as to which one should be accounted the greatest

22:28* had continued with Jesus in His temptations

22:29* was appointed a kingdom (that he might eat and drink at Jesus' table in His kingdom and sit on thrones judging the twelve tribes of Israel) (22:30)

22:35* had lacked nothing

22:36* told to prepare (for his new task)

22:39* followed Jesus to the Mount of Olives

22:40* told to pray that he enter not into temptation

22:45* found sleeping for sorrow (by Jesus)

22:46* told to rise and pray, lest he enter into temptation

22:49* perceiving the forthcoming events, asked Jesus if he should use his sword

24: 9* was told all things concerning the resurrection by Mary Magdalene, Joanna, Mary the mother of James, and the other women (24:10)

24:10* an apostle

24:11* the words of the women seemed to him as idle tales and he believed them not

24:33* being together (with the other disciples) Cleopas found him and declared that the Lord was risen and had appeared to Simon (24:34)

24:36* Jesus appeared unto him (after the resurrection) but he was terrified and affrighted and supposed he had seen a spirit (24:34)

24:38* asked by Jesus why he was troubled and why thoughts arose in his heart

24:40* was shown Jesus' hands and feet

24:41* believed not yet for joy, and wondered

24:42* gave Jesus a piece of broiled fish and of an honeycomb

24:45* his understanding was opened by Jesus that he might understand the scriptures

24:46* was witness of these things (24:48)

24:49* told to tarry in Jerusalem until he was endued with power from on high

24:50* led by Jesus out as far as to Bethany and was blessed of Him

24:52* worshiped Jesus and returned to Jerusalem with great joy

24:53* was continually in the temple, praising and blessing God

John   2: 2* called to the marriage in Cana of Galilee

John   2:12* went to Capernaum and continued there not many days

2:17* remembered that it was written of Him, "the zeal of thine house hath eaten me up"

2:22* after the resurrection, remembered Jesus' words and believed the Scriptures, and the words Jesus had said

3:22* came into the land of Judea with Jesus and tarried there with Him

4: 2* did baptize

4: 8* had gone away unto the city to buy meat

4:27* came unto Jesus and marveled that He talked with the Samaritan woman, yet did not question Him

4:31* called Jesus "Master"

4:31* implored Jesus to eat

4:33* questioned among the disciples if Jesus had been brought food to eat

4:35* told to look on the fields for they were white already to harvest

4:38* had been sent to reap where he had not labored, and had entered into others' labors

6: 3* went up into a mountain and sat with Jesus

6:10* instructed by Jesus to have the multitude sit down

6:11* distributed the loaves and fishes to the multitude

6:13* gathered twelve baskets of fragments

6:16* went down to the sea, entered a ship and went toward Capernaum (6:17)

6:19* after rowing twenty-five to thirty furlongs, saw Jesus walking on the sea and was afraid

6:20* told not to be afraid

6:21* willingly received Him into the ship

6:22* was entered into the only boat there

6:22* was apart from Jesus in the boat alone (with the other disciples)

6:67* asked, by Jesus, if he would also go away

6:69* believed and was sure that Jesus was the Christ, the Son of the living God

6:70* chosen as one of the twelve

9: 2* questioned Jesus concerning the man born blind

11: 8* called Jesus "Master"

11:11* friend of Lazarus

11:54* continued with Jesus at Ephraim

12:16* understood not, at first, the events of the triumphal entry of Jesus

12:16* after Jesus' glorification, remembered that these events had been written of Jesus, and had been done unto Him

13: 5* feet washed by Jesus

13:12* had his feet washed by Jesus

BARTHOLOMEW (*continued*)

John   13:13* called Jesus "Master" and "Lord"

13:14* had his feet washed by Jesus

13:14* told, by Jesus, that he ought to wash one another's feet

13:15* had been given an example that he should do as Jesus had done to him

13:18* was known and chosen of Jesus

13:21* when told that one of them would betray Jesus, he looked on the others, doubting of whom He spoke (13:22)

13:28* knew not for what intent Jesus spoke these words to Judas Iscariot

13:34* given a new commandment to love one another

13:34* loved of Jesus

13:35* love one to another was a mark that he was a true disciple of Jesus

14:25* was with Jesus

14:26* would be instructed by the Holy Spirit in all things

14:26* the words Jesus had spoken would be brought to his remembrance

14:27* Jesus' peace was given to him and left with him

14:31* was told to arise and go with Jesus

15: 3* was clean through the Word

15: 9* loved of Jesus

15:12* commanded to love one another

15:12* loved of Jesus

15:16* chosen of Jesus, and ordained of Him to go and bring forth fruit, and that his fruit should remain

15:17* commanded to love one another

15:19* not of the world

15:19* chosen out of the world, by Jesus

15:19* hated of the world

15:27* would bear witness, because he had been with Jesus from the beginning

16: 4* was with Jesus

16: 6* sorrow had filled his heart

16:12* could not bear the words of Jesus

16:22* presently had sorrow

16:24* had asked nothing of the Father in Jesus' name

16:27* loved of the Father

16:27* loved Jesus, and believed that He came from God

16:29* could now understand plainly Jesus' words

16:30* was sure that Jesus knew all things

16:30* believed that Jesus came forth from God

18: 1* went with Jesus over the brook Cedron and entered into a garden (Gethsemane)

18: 2* often resorted there with Jesus

20:18* told by Mary Magdalene that she had seen the Lord and that He had spoken unto her

20:19* while assembled together (with the other disciples) with the doors shut for fear of the Jews, Jesus appeared in the midst

John   20:20* saw Jesus' hands and side and was glad

20:21* sent by Jesus and given His peace

20:22* breathed on by Jesus and received the Holy Ghost

20:25* told Thomas that he had seen the Lord

20:25* informed by Thomas that he would not believe without specific conditions being met

20:26* the doors being shut again, Jesus appeared the second time to him and the apostles

20:30* many other signs were done in his presence which are not written (in this book)

Acts   1: 2* had been given commandments by Jesus (through the Holy Ghost)

1: 2* chosen by Jesus

1: 3* was shown Jesus alive after His passion

1: 3* spoken to by Jesus of the things pertaining to the kingdom of God

1: 3* saw Jesus forty days

1: 4* commanded, by Jesus, not to depart from Jerusalem, but to wait for the promise of the Father

1: 5* would be baptized with the Holy Ghost

1: 6* questioned Jesus concerning the restoration of the kingdom to Israel

1: 7* was not to know the times or the seasons which the Father had put in His own power

1: 8* after receiving the Holy Spirit, would receive power and would witness unto Jesus Christ throughout the earth

1: 9* beheld as Jesus was taken up into Heaven at His ascension

1:10* was joined by two men in white apparel while he looked steadfastly toward Heaven

1:11* a man of Galilee

1:11* was gazing up into Heaven

1:11* Jesus was taken up from him into Heaven

1:11* was told that Jesus would come in like manner as he had seen Him go into Heaven

1:12* returned to Jerusalem and went into an upper room (1:13)

1:14* continued in prayer and supplication with the women, Mary the mother of Jesus, and with His brethren

1:21* was with the Lord Jesus at various times

1:24* prayed concerning the ordination of one to be a witness of Jesus' resurrection

1:26* gave forth his lot (concerning Judas Iscariot's successor)

2: 1* present at the day of Pentecost

Acts 2: 2* while sitting in the house, cloven tongues like as of fire sat upon him, he was filled with the Holy Ghost and spoke with other tongues (2:4)

2: 6* his speech confounded the multitude because every man heard in his own language

2: 7* a Galilean

2:13* mocked by some who claimed him as full of new wine

2:14* stood with (Simon) Peter

2:15* was not drunk

2:32* was a witness to the resurrection of Jesus

2:37* asked by the multitude on the day of Pentecost what they should do

2:42* many continued steadfastly in his doctrine and fellowship

2:43* many wonders and signs were done by him

4:33* with great power gave witness of the resurrection of the Lord Jesus

4:33* great grace was upon him

4:35* the price of possessions sold by Christians was laid at his feet

4:35* distributed to every man (of the Christian community) as he had need

4:36* gave Joses a surname of Barnabas

4:37* Joses's money was laid at his feet

5: 2* the gift of Ananias and Sapphira was laid at his feet

5:12* by his hands were many signs and wonders wrought among the people

5:12* was with one accord with the others in Solomon's porch

5:13* no man durst join himself to him (the apostles)

5:13* was magnified of the people

5:16* healed the multitude of sicknesses and unclean spirits

5:18* placed in the common prison by the high priest and Sadducees

5:19* released from prison by the angel of the Lord and told to go, stand, and speak in the temple (5:20)

5:21* entered into the temple early in the morning and taught

5:22* was not found in the prison

5:25* was standing in the temple and teaching the people

5:26* brought without violence and set before the council (5:27)

5:27* questioned by the high priest (5:28)

5:28* had been commanded not to teach in this (Jesus') name

5:28* had filled Jerusalem with his doctrine and had (seemingly) intended to bring Jesus' blood upon his accusers

5:29* believed that he ought to obey God rather than men

Acts 5:32* witness of God (and of His works)

5:33* Jewish leaders took council to slay him

5:34* put a little space from the Sanhedrin (for their deliberation)

5:40* called back before the council, beaten, commanded not to speak in the name of Jesus, and let go

5:41* departed from the council rejoicing that he was counted worthy to suffer shame for His name

5:42* daily in the temple and in every house, ceased not to teach and preach Jesus Christ

6: 2* called the multitude together and stated it was not reasonable that he should leave the Word of God and serve tables

6: 3* instructed that seven men of honest report be chosen to be appointed to serve tables

6: 4* determined to give himself continually to prayer and to the ministry of the Word

6: 6* the chosen seven were set before him, for whom he prayed and laid his hands on them

8: 1* remained in Jerusalem in the midst of great persecution

8:14* was in Jerusalem

8:14* hearing that Samaria had received the Word of God, sent Peter and John to Samaria

9:27* Saul (Paul) was brought to him by Barnabas and he was informed of Saul's (Paul's) conversion experience and his bold preaching at Damascus

9:28* was accompanied by Saul (Paul) in coming in and going out at Jerusalem

10:39* was witness of all things Jesus did both in the land of the Jews and in Jerusalem

10:41* a witness chosen before of God

10:41* ate and drank with Jesus after His resurrection

10:42* commanded by Jesus to preach unto the people, and testified that it was Jesus which was ordained of God to be the Judge of quick and dead

11: 1* was in Judea

11: 1* heard that the Gentiles had also received the Word of God

11:15* the Holy Ghost fell on him at the beginning (Pentecost)

13:31* saw Jesus many days

13:31* came up with Jesus from Galilee to Jerusalem

13:31* was His (Jesus') witness unto the people

15: 2* Paul, Barnabas, and others were sent by the church at Antioch to

BARTHOLOMEW *(continued)*

consult with him over the matter of circumcision

Acts 15: 4* received Paul, Barnabas, and the others from Antioch

15: 6* came together (with the elders) to consider the matter (of circumcision)

15: 8* given the Holy Ghost

15: 9* God made no difference between him and a Gentile

15:10* was not able to bear the yoke

15:22* acting with the elders, sent chosen men back to Antioch with Paul and Barnabas

15:23* acting with the elders and brethren, wrote letters of instruction to the Gentiles at Antioch, Syria, and Cilicia

15:24* gave no commandment that Gentile believers must be circumcised and keep the law

15:25* considered it good, being assembled, to send chosen men unto the believers

15:25* loved Barnabas and Paul

15:27* sent Judas and Silas to the Gentile believers

15:33* Judas (Barsabas) and Silas returned unto him

16: 4* with the elders, ordained decrees

16: 4* was at Jerusalem

Rom 16: 7* Andronicus and Junia were well known to him

1Cor 4: 9* Paul thought God had set him (and the apostles) forth last, as it were appointed to death

4: 9* made a spectacle unto the world, to the angels, and to men

4:10* a fool for Christ's sake

4:10* weak, despised

4:11* hungered, thirsted, was naked, was buffeted, and had no certain dwelling place

4:12* labored, working with his own hands

4:12* being reviled, he blessed; being persecuted, he suffered it; being defamed, he entreated (4:13)

4:13* made as the filth of the world, and the offscouring of all things

9: 5* had power to lead about a sister, a wife

15: 5* had seen the risen Lord

15: 7* the risen Lord was seen of him

15:11* preached

Rev 21:14* name inscribed in the twelve foundations of the New Jerusalem

21:14* an apostle of the Lamb

BARTIMAEUS [bar-ti-me'-us = son of Timaeus]
A blind beggar healed by Jesus at Jericho.

Matt 20:29 lived in Jericho

20:30 a blind man

Matt 20:30 sat by the wayside

20:30 heard that Jesus passed by and calling Him Lord, cried out to Him for mercy

20:31 rebuked by the multitude (that he should hold his peace)

20:31 cried the more, asking Jesus for mercy

20:32 called for by Jesus and asked his desire

20:33 asked that his eyes might be opened

20:34 received the compassion of Jesus, who touched his eyes

20:34 immediately received sight and followed Jesus

Mark 10:46 lived at Jericho

10:46 son of Timaeus

10:46 blind

10:46 sat by the highway side begging

10:47 heard it was Jesus, and began to cry out for mercy

10:48 charged to hold his peace, but cried the more

10:49 was called to Jesus

10:49 blind

10:50 cast away his garment, rose, and came to Jesus

10:51 asked by Jesus of his desire

10:51 blind

10:51 asked Jesus that he might receive his sight

10:52 his faith made him whole

10:52 immediately received his sight

10:52 followed Jesus

Luke 18:35 lived at Jericho

18:35 was blind

18:35 sat by the wayside begging

18:36 heard the multitude pass by and asked what it meant and was told that Jesus of Nazareth passeth by (18:37)

18:38 cried out unto Jesus for mercy

18:39 rebuked by those present to hold his peace, but cried out much more for mercy

18:40 commanded by Jesus to be brought to Him

18:41 asked by Jesus of his desire, he requested that he might receive his sight

18:42 received his sight

18:42 his faith had saved him

18:43 immediately received his sight, and followed Jesus, glorifying God

BENJAMIN [ben'-ja-min = son of the right hand]
The youngest of the patriarchs, the second son of Jacob by Rachel (who died in childbirth), named Benoni (son of my sorrow) by his mother but changed to Benjamin (son of my right hand) by his father, born in Canaan near Bethlehem, only full brother of Joseph, and the father of the tribe bearing his name. (See also Gen 35, 42—46,49; Deut 33)

41

BENJAMIN *(continued)*

Matt	1: 2	begotten of Jacob
John	4:12	drank of the well (Jacob's)
	4:12	a child of Jacob
Acts	7: 8	begat by Jacob
	7: 8	one of the patriarchs
	7:11	found no sustenance
	7:13	on the second visit (to Egypt), Joseph was made known to him
	7:13	was made known unto Pharaoh
	7:15	went down into Egypt and died
	7:16	was carried into Sychem and was laid in the sepulcher that Abraham bought
	13:21	(King) Saul was of his tribe
	13:21	Cis (King Saul's father) was of his tribe
Rom	11: 1	Paul was of his tribe
Rev	7: 8	twelve thousand sealed of his tribe
	21:12	his name is inscribed upon the gates of the New Jerusalem
	21:12	a child of Israel (Jacob)

BERNICE ♀ [bur-ni'-see = victorious]
Daughter of Herod Agrippa I, sister of Agrippa II, with whom she lived in an incestuous relationship.

Acts	25:13	accompanied King Agrippa to Caesarea to salute Festus
	25:14	stayed many days (in Caesarea)
Acts	25:23	came (along with Agrippa) with great pomp and entered into the place of hearing with the chief captains and principal men of the city
	26:30	rose up, went aside and discussed with the others concerning Paul

BLASTUS [blas'-tus = a bud]
A chamberlain of Herod Agrippa I, and a friend of the people of Tyre and Sidon.

Acts	12:20	King Herod's chamberlain
	12:20	a friend of them of Tyre and Sidon

BOANERGES [bo-an-er'-jees = sons of thunder]

1. James — see JAMES (son of Zebedee)
2. John — see JOHN (son of Zebedee)

BOOZ [bo'-oz = fleetness]
Old Testament Boaz, a citizen and wealthy landowner of Bethlehem, kinsman of Elimelech, played the part of the kinsman redeemer and married Ruth (the Moabitess), father of Obed, grandfather of Jesse, great-grandfather of David, and an ancestor of Jesus.(See also Ruth 2—4)

Matt	1: 5	begotten of Salmon of Rachab (Rahab)
	1: 5	begat Obed of Ruth
Luke	3:32	father of Obed
	3:32	son of Salmon

BOSOR [bo'-sor = torch; lamp]
Old Testament Beor, father of Balaam the prophet. (See also Num 22, 24, 31; Deut 23;Josh 13, 24; Mic 6)

2Pet	2:15	father of Balaam

C

CAESAR [a title, not a proper name: See AUGUSTUS, CLAUDIUS: TIBERIUS]

CAIAPHAS [cah'-ya-fus = depression]
Surname or another name of Joseph, a high priest of Israel, son-in-law of Annas, presided at the trial of Jesus, and rent his garments (an unlawful act).

Matt	20:18	Jesus would be betrayed unto him
	20:18	would condemn Jesus to death
	20:19	would deliver Jesus to the Gentiles
	21:15	was sore displeased upon seeing the wonderful things Jesus did and hearing the people cry "Hosanna to the Son of David"
	21:16	questioned Jesus concerning the statements of the multitude
	21:17	left by Jesus
	21:23	questioned by what authority He acted and who gave Him this authority
	21:24	questioned in turn by Jesus concerning the baptism of John (21:25)
	21:25	reasoned with the other chief priests and elders concerning Jesus' question about the baptism of John (21:26)
	21:27	not answering Jesus' question, was likewise not answered by Jesus
	21:31	answered Jesus' question concerning the parables
	21:31	Jesus prophesied that the publicans and harlots would go into the kingdom of God before him
	21:32	believed not John (the Baptist)
	21:32	repented not (in order to believe)
	21:45	perceived that Jesus had spoken of them (him) in the parable
	21:46	sought to lay hands on Jesus, but feared the multitude
	26: 3	assembled at his palace with the chief priests, scribes, and elders of the people
	26: 3	the high priest
	26: 4	consulted to take Jesus by subtlety and kill Him
	26:14	approached by Judas Iscariot and convenanted with him for the delivery (betrayal) of Jesus for thirty pieces of silver (26:15)

CAIAPHAS *(continued)*

Matt 26:47 had sent a great multitude with swords and staves, along with Judas (Iscariot) to take Jesus

26:51 his servant Malchus's ear was cut off with a sword

26:57 Jesus brought from Garden of Gethsemane to his palace (26:58)

26:57 the high priest

26:58 Peter followed Jesus into his palace and sat with the servants

26:59 with the other chief priests, elders, and all the council, sought witnesses against Jesus, to put Him to death

26:60 found no false witnesses against Jesus

26:62 high priest

26:62 questioned Jesus concerning testimony of the false witnesses

26:63 adjured Jesus to tell whether He was the Christ, the Son of God

26:65 rent his clothes and accused Jesus of blasphemy

26:66 asked the council for their verdict

26:69 Peter sat outside his palace

27: 1 when morning was come, took counsel against Jesus to put Him to death

27: 2 having bound Jesus, led Him away and delivered Him to Pontius Pilate the governor.

27: 3 the thirty pieces of silver were returned to him by Judas

27: 6 took the thirty pieces of silver, took counsel, and bought the potter's field to bury strangers in (27:7)

27:12 accused Jesus (before Pilate)

27:20 persuaded the multitude that they should ask Barabbas, and destroy Jesus

27:41 mocked Jesus saying He saved others, but Himself He could not save (27:42)

27:42 stated he would believe Jesus if He were to come down from the cross

27:62 went to Pilate and requested the sepulcher be made sure until the third day (27:64)

27:63 called Jesus a deceiver

27:65 told by Pilate that he had a watch, and to go and make it as sure as he could

27:66 went and made the sepulcher sure, sealing the stone and setting a watch

28:11 was shown by some of the watch, all the things that were done

28:12 assembled with others, gave large money unto the soldiers, instructing them to say Jesus' disciples came by night and stole Him away while they slept (28:13)

Matt 28:14 promised to persuade the governor and secure the soldiers

Mark 8:31 would reject Jesus

10:33 Jesus would be delivered unto him

10:33 he would condemn Jesus to death, deliver Him to the Gentiles, mock Him, scourge Him, spit on Him and kill Him (10:34)

11:18 heard that Jesus cleansed the temple, and sought how he might destroy Him

11:18 feared Jesus, because all the people were astonished at His doctrine

11:27 came to Jesus in the temple and inquired as to His authority for His actions (11:28)

11:29 answered by Jesus that if he answered Jesus' question, his question would be answered

11:30 questioned by Jesus

11:31 reasoned with the others as to the effects of various possible answers to Jesus' question (11:32)

11:32 feared the people

11:33 answered that they (he) could not tell the answer to Jesus' question

11:33 was informed by Jesus that He would not answer his question

12: 1 spoken unto by Jesus in parables

12:12 sought to lay hold on Jesus because he knew He had spoken the parable against him (the chief priests)

12:12 feared the people

12:12 left Jesus and went his way

14: 1 sought how to take Jesus by craft, and put Him to death, but not on the feast day, lest there be an uproar of the people (14:2)

14:10 approached by Judas Iscariot to betray Jesus unto them

14:11 hearing Judas's proposal, was glad, and promised to give him money

14:43 had sent a great multitude with swords and staves with Judas (to take Jesus)

14:47 his servant's (Malchus) right ear was cut off (by Simon Peter)

14:53 Jesus led away unto him

14:53 was assembled with all the chief priests, elders, and scribes

14:53 the high priest

14:54 (Simon) Peter followed Jesus into his palace and sat with his servants

14:54 the high priest

14:55 sought for witness against Jesus to put Him to death, and found none

14:60 the high priest

14:60 stood and questioned Jesus concerning those who witnessed against Him

14:61 the high priest

14:61 inquired of Jesus, as to whether He were the Christ, the Son of the Blessed

43

CAIAPHAS *(continued)*

Mark	14:63	the high priest
	14:63	rent his clothes
	14:63	asked why they needed further witnesses (against Jesus)
	14:64	accused Jesus of blasphemy
	14:66	had maids
	15: 1	straightway in the morning, held a consultation with the elders, scribes, and the whole council
	15: 1	bound Jesus and carried Him away and delivered Him to Pilate
	15: 3	accused Jesus of many things (before Pilate)
	15: 4	witnessed many things against Jesus
	15:10	had delivered Jesus for envy
	15:11	moved the people that Pilate should release Barabbas unto them
	15:31	mocking, said that He saved others, but could not save Himself
Luke	3: 2	contemporary of Tiberius Caesar, Herod, Philip and Lysanias (tetrarchs) and Pontius Pilate
	3: 2	ruled along with Annas
	3: 2	one of the high priests
	9:22	Jesus prophesied he would reject Him
	19:47	sought to destroy Jesus, and could not find what he might do (19:48)
	20: 1	together with the other chief priests and the scribes and elders, came upon Jesus
	20: 2	asked Jesus by what authority He acted, and who gave Him this authority
	20: 3	questioned, in turn by Jesus, concerning the baptism of John (20:4)
	20: 5	reasoned with the others concerning the various possible answers to Jesus' question (20:6)
	20: 7	answered Jesus that he could not tell the answer to His question
	20: 8	informed by Jesus that He likewise would not answer his question
	20:19	the same hour sought to lay hands on Jesus for he perceived that He had spoken the parable against him
	20:19	feared the people
	20:20	watched Jesus
	20:20	sent forth spies that they might deliver him unto to the power and authority of the governor
	22: 2	sought how he might kill Jesus
	22: 2	feared the people
	22: 4	communed with Judas Iscariot concerning the betrayal of Jesus
	22: 5	was glad (concerning the betrayal of Jesus) and covenanted to give Judas money
	22: 6	Jesus was to be betrayed unto him in the absence of the multitude
	22:50	his servant's (Malchus) right ear was cut off by (Simon) Peter

Luke	22:51	his servant's (Malchus) right ear was healed by Jesus
	22:52	asked by Jesus if he came out as against a thief with swords and staves
	22:53	daily being with Jesus in the temple, had not stretched forth his hand against Him
	22:53	this was his hour
	22:54	Jesus brought into his house
	22:54	Simon Peter followed Jesus into his house and sat down among those present (22:55)
	22:56	had a maid
	22:66	as soon as it was day, led Jesus into the council
	22:67	asked Jesus plainly if He were the Christ
	22:67	told by Jesus that if He told him, he would not believe
	22:68	told by Jesus that he would not answer Him, nor let Him go
	22:70	asked Jesus if He were the Son of God
	22:71	declared no need for further witness, as he had heard of Jesus' own mouth
	23: 1	led Jesus unto Pilate
	23: 2	(falsely) accused Jesus of perverting the nation and forbidding to give tribute to Caesar
	23: 4	told by Pilate that he found no fault in Jesus
	23: 5	was more fierce, saying that Jesus stirred up the people, teaching throughout all Jewry
	23:10	stood and vehemently accused Jesus
	23:13	brought Jesus unto Pilate
	23:13	called together (by Pilate) along with the rulers and the people and told that he had found no fault in Jesus of those things which he had accused Him (23:14)
	23:23	his voice (among others) prevailed (before Pilate)
	24:20	delivered Jesus to be condemned to death, and crucified Him
John	7:32	sent officers to take Jesus
	7:45	the officers returned to him without Jesus
	7:48	had not believed on Jesus
	11:47	gathered with a council to decide what to do with Jesus
	11:48	feared, if left alone, Jesus would cause the Romans to come and take away his place and the nation
	11:49	the high priest that same year (as the death of Christ)
	11:50	prophesied that one should die that the whole nation perish not
	11:51	spake not of himself, but prophesied that Jesus should die for the nation and for all the chil-

44

dren of God (11:52)

John	11:51	the high priest that same year (as the death of Christ)
	11:53	from that day took council to put Him to death
	11:57	gave a commandment that if any man knew where He was, he should show it, that they might take Him
	12:10	consulted to put Lazarus also to death
	18: 3	presented a band of men and officers to Judas (Iscariot, to take Jesus)
	18:13	son-in-law of Annas
	18:13	the high priest that same year (as the death of Christ)
	18:14	had given counsel to the Jews that it was expedient that one man should die for the people
	18:15	knew John (the disciple)
	18:15	had a palace
	18:16	knew John
	18:16	Peter brought into his palace
	18:18	had servants and officers
	18:19	asked Jesus of His disciples and of His doctrine
	18:21	told to ask them that (had) heard Him
	18:24	had received Jesus bound from Annas
	18:24	the high priest
	18:26	had servants
	18:26	the high priest
	18:28	had Jesus led to the hall of judgment
	18:28	entered not into the judgment hall, lest he should be defiled
	18:30	had delivered Jesus unto Pilate
	18:35	had delivered Jesus unto Pilate
	19: 6	seeing Jesus, cried out for His crucifixion
	19: 6	told by Pilate to take Him (himself) and crucify Him
	19:11	delivered Jesus unto Pilate
	19:11	had the greater sin than Pilate
	19:15	claimed to have no king but Caesar
	19:21	endeavored to "correct" Pilate concerning the title given to Jesus (19:22)
Acts	4: 1	came upon Peter and John for teaching the people (4:2)
	4: 2	grieved that Peter and John taught the people
	4: 3	laid hands on Peter and John and put them in hold (prison) unto the next day
	4: 6	part of the committee at Jerusalem which examined Peter and John (4:7)
	4: 8	ruler of the people
	4: 8	elder of Israel
	4:13	marveled when he saw the boldness of Peter and John, perceiving that

they were unlearned and ignorant men

Acts	4:13	took knowledge of Peter and John that they had been with Jesus
	4:14	beholding the man which was healed standing with them, could say nothing against it
	4:15	conferred with the council concerning (Simon) Peter and John and could not deny the miracle (4:16)
	4:18	as part of the council, commanded (Simon) Peter and John not to speak at all nor teach in the name of Jesus
	4:21	further threatening (Simon) Peter and John, let them go, finding nothing how to punish them
	5:24	hearing these things (the escape of the apostles from prison) doubted of them whereunto this would grow
	5:25	was told that the apostles were standing in the temple teaching the people
	5:30	(had part with them who) slew Jesus, and hanged (Him) on a tree
	5:33	hearing (Simon) Peter's words, was cut to the heart and took counsel to slay the apostles
	5:40	agreed to the words of Gamaliel
	5:40	called the apostles, beat them, commanded them not to speak in the name of Jesus, and let them go
	7: 1	questioned Stephen concerning the false accusations against him
	13:27	knew not Jesus, nor the voices of the prophets
	13:27	condemned Jesus, thus fulfilling the voices of the prophets
	13:28	found no cause of death in Jesus, yet desired that He be slain
	25:15	informed Festus of Paul, desiring to have judgment against him
	26:10	had given authority to Paul to shut up in prison the saints of God
	26:12	gave authority and commission to Paul to go into Damascus

CAIN [cain = acquisition; maker; smith]
First-born son of Adam and Eve, the first child born of the human race; brother of Abel and Seth; his offering of the fruit of the ground (a faithless and bloodless sacrifice) rejected by the Lord; he became the first murderer when he slew his brother Abel. (See also Gen 4)

Heb	11: 4	his sacrifice was less excellent than was Abel's
1Joh	3:12	was of the wicked one (Satan)
	3:12	slew his brother (Abel)
	3:12	his works were evil
Jude	:11	some deceivers in Jude's day were described as going his way

CAINAN [ca'nun = acquisition]
1. Son of Arphaxad, father of Sala, and mentioned as an ancestor of Jesus.

Luke   3:35   father of Sala (3:36)
          3:36   son of Arphaxad

2. Also Old Testament Kenan, son of Enos and father of Maleleel, and an ancestor of Jesus. (See also Gen 5)

Luke   3:37   father of Maleleel
          3:38   son of Enos

CARPUS [car'-pus = fruit]
A man of Troas who held Paul's cloak (which was requested by Paul to be brought by Timothy).

2Tim   4:13   was in Troas
         4:13   had possession of Paul's cloak

CEPHAS [se'-fas = a stone] — see SIMON PETER

CHLOE♀ [clo'-e = tender verdure]
A female disciple whose household informed Paul of problems concerning contentions among the saints at Corinth.

1Cor   1:11   her house had informed Paul of the contentions among the brethren at Corinth

CHUZA [cu'-zah = a measure]
Herod Antipas's steward and husband of Joanna.

Luke   8: 3   husband of Joanna
         8: 3   Herod's steward

CIS [sis = luring one]
Old Testament Kish, father of Saul (king of Israel). (See also 1Sam 9, 10, 14; 2Sam 21)

Acts   13:21   father of (king) Saul
         13:21   of the tribe of Benjamin

CLAUDIA♀ [claw'-de-ah = whining; lame]
A female Christian at Rome who sent greetings to Timothy by Paul and possibly the wife of Pudens.

2Tim   4:21   sent greetings to Timothy by Paul

CLAUDIUS [claw'-de-us = whining; lame]
1. Caesar
The fourth emperor of Rome who succeeded Caius (Caligula), his command that all Jews depart Rome sent Aquila and Priscilla to Corinth, and during his reign a famine occurred having been prophesied by Agabus.

Acts   11:28   a great famine came to pass during his days
         18: 2   had commanded all Jews to depart from Rome

2. Lysias [li'-see-as = light, bright releaser (?)]
A chief captain of the Romans, whose actions kept Paul from possible death at the hands of the mob in Jerusalem, and obtained his Roman citizenship with a large sum of money. Full name was Claudius Lysias.

Acts   21:31   tidings came unto him that all Jerusalem was in an uproar
         21:31   chief captain of the band
         21:32   immediately took soldiers and centurions and ran down unto them
         21:32   seeing him and the soldiers, they (the crowd) left beating of Paul
         21:32   chief captain
         21:32   chief captain
         21:33   came near, took Paul, and commanded him to be bound with two chains
         21:33   demanded (of Paul) who he was, and what he had done
         21:34   not knowing the certainty for the tumult, commanded Paul to be carried into the castle
         21:37   chief captain
         21:37   asked, of Paul, for an audience
         21:37   asked Paul if he could speak Greek
         21:38   thought Paul to be Egyptian (who had earlier caused an uproar)
         21:39   besought, by Paul, to suffer him to speak unto the people
         21:40   granted Paul license (to speak)
         22:24   chief captain
         22:24   commanded Paul to be brought into the castle
         22:24   bade that Paul should be examined by scourging that he (Claudius) might know wherefore they cried so against him (Paul)
         22:26   chief captain
         22:27   asked if Paul were a Roman
         22:28   chief captain
         22:28   with a great sum had obtained his freedom
         22:29   chief captain
         22:29   was afraid after learning that Paul was a Roman, and because he had bound him
         22:30   loosed Paul from his bands
         22:30   commanded the chief priests, and all their council to appear
         22:30   brought Paul down, and set him before them
         23:10   chief captain
         23:10   fearing lest Paul should have been pulled in pieces, commanded the soldiers to take him by force and to bring him into the castle
         23:15   chief captain
         23:17   chief captain
         23:17   Paul asked a centurion to bring his nephew unto him to tell him a certain thing
         23:18   chief captain
         23:18   Paul's nephew brought before him
         23:19   chief captain
         23:19   took Paul's nephew by the hand, led him aside privately, and asked him what he had to tell him
         23:21   was asked not to yield to the desires of the Jews

CLAUDIUS *(continued)*

Acts 23:21 those Jews who desired to kill Paul, were ready, looking for a promise from him
23:22 chief captain
23:22 let the young man (Paul's nephew) depart, charging him to tell no man what they had discussed
23:23 called two centurions instructing them to prepare the necessary military forces and beast to bring Paul safely to Felix (23:24)
23:25 wrote a letter to Felix (23:30)
23:27 rescued Paul (from the Jews)
23:28 desiring to know the cause of the accusations against Paul, brought him into the council
23:30 learned that the Jews laid wait for Paul, and sent him straightway to Felix
23:30 commanded that Paul's accusers also tell, before Felix, what they had against him
24: 7 chief captian
24: 7 took Paul out of the hands of the Jews with great violence
24: 8 commanded the accusers of Paul to appear before Felix
24:22 chief captain
24:22 was to come to Caesarea

CLEMENT [clem'-ent = mild]
A fellow laborer with Paul at Philippi.

Phil 4: 3 a laborer in the gospel

CLEOPAS [cle'-o-pas = renowned father]
One of the two disciples who accompanied Jesus on the road to Emmaus after the resurrection.

Mark 16:12 Jesus appeared in another form unto him on the road to Emmaus
16:13 told other disciples of seeing Jesus on the road to Emmaus
Luke 24:13 went the same day (resurrection day) to Emmaus and on the way talked of all these things which had happened (24:14)
24:15 while he communed and reasoned, together with another, Jesus drew near and went with him
24:16 his eyes were holden that he should not know Him
24:17 walked and was sad
24:18 rehearsed to Jesus the events of the preceeding days (24:24)
24:21 had trusted that Jesus would have redeemed Israel
24:22 words of the women astonished him
24:25 was determined by Jesus to be foolish, and slow of heart to believe all that the prophets had spoken
24:27 beginning at Moses and all the prophets, Jesus expounded unto

him in all the scriptures the things concerning Himself
Luke 24:28 drew nigh unto the village (Emmaus)
24:29 constrained Jesus to abide (and stay the night)
24:30 sat at meat with Jesus and his eyes were opened and he knew Jesus and Jesus vanished out of his sight
24:32 his heart had burned within him while Jesus had talked with him on the way and while He opened to him the scriptures
24:33 the same hour rose up and returned to Jerusalem
24:34 told the eleven and others that the Lord is risen indeed
24:35 told what things were done in the way (to Emmaus) and how Jesus was known of him in breaking of bread
24:36 Jesus appeared unto him and the eleven
24:36 was terrified and affrighted and supposed he had seen a spirit (24:37)
24:38 asked by Jesus why he was troubled and why thoughts arose in his heart
24:40 was shown Jesus' hands and feet
24:41 believed not yet for joy and wondered
24:42 gave Jesus a piece of a broiled fish and of an honeycomb
24:45 his understanding was opened by Jesus that he might understand the scriptures
24:46 a witness of these things (24:48)
24:49 told to tarry in Jerusalem until endued with power from on high
Acts 13:31 was His witness unto the people

CLEOPHAS [cle'-o-fas = renowned father]
Husband of Mary (who stood at the cross of Jesus). (Possibly identical with Alphaeus)

John 19:25 husband of Mary

CORE [co'-ree = ice; hail]
Old Testament Korah, son of Hebron.

Jude :11 some deceivers in Jude's day perished in his gainsaying

CORNELIUS [cor-ne'-le-us = of a horn]
A Roman centurion (probably Italian) of Caesarea, a devout and God-fearing man who called for Peter to instruct him. He and his house were converted and they were the first Gentiles to be given the gift of the Holy Spirit.

Acts 10: 1 a man in Caesarea
10: 1 a centurion of the Italian band
10: 2 a devout man
10: 2 feared God with all his house
10: 2 gave much alms to the people and prayed to God alway

47

CORNELIUS *(continued)*

Acts 10: 3 saw an angel of God in a vision which called him by name
10: 4 looked on the angel and was afraid and questioned
10: 4 his prayers and alms came up for a memorial before God.
10: 5 told to send men to Joppa and to call for Simon Peter
10: 6 would be told by Simon Peter what to do
10: 7 sent two servants and a soldier of them that waited on him continually, declared all things unto them, and sent them to Joppa (10:8)
10:17 had sent men (who inquired for Simon's house) for Peter
10:21 sent men unto (Simon) Peter
10:22 a centurion
10:22 a just man who feared God
10:22 had good report among all the nation of the Jews
10:22 was warned from God by an holy angel to send for (Simon) Peter and to hear his words
10:24 was in Caesarea
10:24 waited for (Simon) Peter, and the others and had called together his kinsmen and near friends
10:25 meeting (Simon) Peter, fell down at his feet and worshiped him
10:26 was taken up by (Simon) Peter and told to stand, for he, himself, was also a (mere) man
10:27 talked with (Simon) Peter
10:30 had fasted
10:30 while praying, an angel stood before him
10:31 told by the angel that his prayer was heard, and his alms were in remembrance in the sight of God
10:32 had been told of the angel to send to Joppa and call for Simon Peter, who would speak unto him
10:33 immediately sent for (Simon) Peter
10:33 was ready to hear all things, commanded (of God) through (Simon) Peter
10:44 hearing the word, the Holy Ghost fell upon him
10:46 spake with tongues and magnified God
10:48 commanded to be baptized in the name of the Lord
10:48 prayed (Simon) Peter to tarry certain days
11:12 (Simon) Peter accompanied by six brethren (from Joppa), entered his house
11:13 showed (Simon) Peter how he had seen an angel which told him to send to Joppa and call for (Simon) Peter
11:14 would hear from (Simon) Peter the words whereby he and all his house would be saved
Acts 11:15 the Holy Ghost fell on him as on the disciples
11:17 God gave him the like gift (the Holy Ghost) as He had the disciples

COSAM [co'-sam = diviner]
Son of Elmodam, father of Addi, and ancestor of Jesus (through Joseph the husband of Mary of whom was born Jesus).

Luke 3:28 father of Addi
3:28 son of Elmodam

CRESCENS [cres'-sens = growing]
A disciple at Rome who went to Galatia.

2Tim 4:10 departed to Galatia

CRISPUS [cris'-pus = curled]
The chief ruler of the synagogue at Corinth who believed and was baptized by Paul

Acts 18: 8 the chief ruler of the synagogue (at Corinth)
18: 8 believed on the Lord with all his house
1Cor 1:14 baptized by Paul

CYRENIUS [si-re'-ne-us = of Cyrene]
Governor of Syria (A.Ð. 6) the first of two occasions, and full name was Publius Sulpicius Quirinius. During his first reign a census (enrollment, taxation) was made throughout the entire Roman empire. It was during this census that Jesus Christ was born.

Luke 2: 2 governor of Syria
2: 2 contemporary of Caesar Augustus

D

DAMARIS ♀ [dam-a'-ris = a heifer; a yoke-bearing wife]
A female disciple at Athens and converted under the ministry of Paul.

Acts 17:34 heard Paul at Mars Hill
17:34 clave unto Paul and believed
17:34 a woman

DANIEL [dan'-i-el = God is judge]
An Old Testament prophet of the tribe of Judah and apparently of royal lineage, taken captive to Babylon, an interpreter of dreams, the author of the Old Testament book bearing his name, cast into a den of lions and escaped without harm under king Darius for praying to his God, known by his Babylonian name Belteshazzar, appointed

DANIEL (continued)

governor over Babylon, and one of the three presidents over the Persian empire under Darius the Mede. (See also Dan 1—12)

Matt	24:15	spoke of the abomination of desolation
	24:15	a prophet
Mark	13:14	spoke of the abomination of desolation
	13:14	a prophet
Heb	11:33	through faith stopped the mouths of lions
	11:39	had obtained a good report through faith
	11:39	received not the promise

DAVID [da'-vid = beloved]

The youngest of seven brothers, the son of Jesse, grandson of Obed, great-grandson of Boaz and Ruth, second king of Israel and Judah who reigned forty years, recipient of a convenant from the Lord, a member of the tribe of Judah, a young shepherd who slew Goliath (the Philistine giant) with the sling, annointed king by the prophet Samuel, best friend of Jonathan the son of Saul who relentlessly pursued David to take his life in order to secure the kingdom for Jonathan, accomplished harpist and poet, author of many of the Old Testment Psalms, had at least five wives; the father of Solomon his successor as king, Adonijah who tried to ursurp his throne, and Absolom (among others), and a direct ancestor of Jesus. (See also 2 Sam 1, 2; 1 Kng 1, 2)

Matt	1: 1	Jesus Christ was of his lineage
	1: 6	begat by Jesse
	1: 6	the king
	1: 6	begat Solomon of her that had been the wife of Urias
	1:17	was fourteen generations from Abraham
	1:17	fourteen generations from him to Babylonian captivity
	9:27	Jesus called his Son
	12: 3	entered the house of God and ate of the shewbread when he was an hungered (12:4)
	12:23	Jesus called his Son
	15:22	Jesus was claimed by a woman of Canaan, to be his Son
	20:30	Jesus is called his Son by two blind men (20:31)
	21: 9	Jesus called his Son
	21:15	children called Jesus his Son (while in the temple)
	22:42	Pharisees called Christ his Son
	22:43	in spirit called Jesus "Lord" (22:44)
	22:45	called Christ Lord
	22:45	Christ is his Son
	27:35	a prophet
Mark	2:25	had need and hungered
	2:26	went into the house of God and ate the shewbread which was not law-

		ful for him to eat and also gave it to his men
Mark	10:47	Jesus was called his Son
	10:48	Jesus was called his Son
	11:10	considered, by the Jews, as their father
	12:35	the scribes say that Christ is his Son
	12:36	spake by the Holy Ghost
	12:37	called Christ "Lord"
Luke	1:27	Joseph was of his house
	1:32	his throne would be given to Jesus, a Son of his lineage
	1:69	God had raised up an horn of salvation for Israel in his house
	1:69	the servant of God
	2: 4	Bethlehem was called his city
	2: 4	Joseph was of his house and lineage
	2:11	Christ the Saviour was born in his city (Bethlehem)
	3:31	father of Nathan
	3:32	son of Jesse
	6: 3	was an hungered
	6: 3	had men with him (soldiers)
	6: 4	entered the house of God and ate the shewbread (which was not lawful to eat) and also gave to his men
	18:38	Jesus was considered his Son (of his lineage)
	18:39	described Jesus as his Son (of his lineage)
	20:41	Jesus asked the tempters how that Christ is his Son
	20:42	said (wrote) in the book of Psalms
	20:44	called Him (Christ) "Lord"
	20:44	Christ is his Son
John	7:42	Christ cometh of his seed
	7:42	was of the town of Bethlehem
Acts	1:16	the Holy Spirit had used his mouth to speak, concerning those things of Judas's actions in betraying Jesus
	1:20	wrote in the book of Psalms concerning Judas Iscariot
	2:25	spoke concerning Christ
	2:25	foresaw the Lord always before his face
	2:26	his heart did rejoice and his tongue was glad
	2:29	a patriarch
	2:29	dead and was buried and his sepulcher still remains
	2:30	a prophet
	2:30	God had sworn with an oath to him that of the fruit of his loins, according to the flesh, He would raise up Christ to sit on his throne
	2:31	spake of the resurrection of Christ
	2:34	was not (yet) ascended into the heavens
	4:25	his mouth had been used of the Lord to prophesy
	4:25	a servant of God
	7:45	until his days God had driven out the Gentiles

49

DAVID *(continued)*

Acts	7:46	desired to find a tabernacle for the God of Jacob
	13:22	raised up of the Lord to be king over Israel
	13:22	given testimony of the Lord that he was a man after God's own heart, who should fulfill all His will
	13:22	son of Jesse
	13:23	of his seed had God raised up unto Israel a Saviour, Jesus
	13:34	God would give the sure mercies of David
	13:36	served his own generation by the will of God
	13:36	fell asleep (died), was laid unto the fathers, and saw corruption
Rom	1: 3	Christ was made of his seed according to the flesh
	4: 6	described the blessedness of the man unto whom God imputed righteousness apart from works (4:8)
	11: 9	wrote concerning Israel (11:10)
2Tim	2: 8	Jesus Christ was of his seed
Heb	4: 7	God spake through him
	11:32	acted by faith (11:34)
	11:39	had obtained a good report through faith
	11:39	received not the promise
Rev	3: 7	Christ has his key
	5: 5	Jesus Christ was his root
	22:16	his root and offspring was Jesus

DEMAS [de'-mas = popular; a rabble]
A disciple at Rome; fellow laborer with Mark, Aristarchus, Luke, and Paul (whom he forsook, having loved this present world); and departed to Thessalonica.

Col	4:14	greeted the church at Colosse
2Tim	4:10	had forsaken Paul
	4:10	loved the present world
	4:10	departed to Thessalonica
Phle	:24	fellow laborer with Paul
	:24	Paul requested Philemon to salute him

DEMETRIUS [de-me'-tre-us = of mother earth]
1. A wealthy silversmith at Ephesus whose trade was making silver shrines of the goddess Diana, and leader of a riot over the actions and teachings of Paul.

Acts	19:24	a silversmith
	19:24	made silver shrines for Diana which brought him no small gain
	19:25	called together the workers of like occupation
	19:25	had wealth (from the making of shrines for Diana)
	19:27	his craft was in danger to be set at nought
	19:38	was implored to take to law those with whom he had a matter

2. A man of good report

| 3Joh | :12 | had good report of all men |
| | :12 | had witness of John as to the truth of reports concerning him |

DIDYMUS [did'-i-mus = twin]—see Thomas

DIONYSIUS [di-on-ish'-yus = devoted to Dionysus, i.e., Bacchus]
A Christian man of Athens, converted through the ministry of Paul, and the distinction as the "Areopagite" infers his membership in the high court.

Acts	17:34	heard Paul at Mars hill
	17:34	clave unto Paul and believed
	17:34	the areopagite

DIOTREPHES [di-ot'-re-feez = nourished by Zeus]
Loved the preeminence in the church, offered no hospitality to the apostle John, and forbade them that would by casting them out of the church.

3John	: 9	loved to have the preeminence in the church
	: 9	did not receive John
	:10	prated against John with malicious words
	:10	did not receive the brethren
	:10	forbade those members in the church to receive the brethren and even cast them out of the church

DORCAS ♀ [dor'-cas = doe; gazelle]
Also called Tabitha, a female disciple at Joppa, full of good works and almsdeeds, was brought back to life by the apostle Peter.

Acts	9:36	lived at Joppa
	9:36	a disciple
	9:36	named Tabitha, which interpreted is Dorcas
	9:36	a woman full of good works and almsdeeds
	9:37	was sick and died
	9:37	was washed and laid in an upper chamber
	9:39	(Simon) Peter was brought into the chamber where she lay
	9:39	had made coats and garments
	9:40	told by (Simon) Peter to arise
	9:40	opened her eyes, saw (Simon) Peter, and sat up
	9:41	lifted up by (Simon) Peter, and was presented to the saints and widows alive
	9:42	her resurrection was known throughout Joppa

DRUSILLA ♀ [dru-sil'-lah = watered by the dew]
A Jewess, she was a daughter of King Agrippa I, wife of governor Felix of Judea, and preached to (along with her husband) by the apostle Paul.

Acts	24:24	wife of Felix (the governor)
	24:24	a Jewess
	24:24	with her husband, heard Paul concerning the faith in Christ

E

ELEAZAR [el-e-a'-zar = God is helper]
Son of Eliud, father of Matthan, and an ancestor of Jesus (three generations before Joseph, the husband of Mary).

Matt 1:15 begotten of Eliud
     1:15 begat Matthan

ELIAKIM [e-li'-a-kim = God is setting up]
1. Son of Abiud, grandson of Zerubbabel, father of Azor, and an ancestor of Jesus. (Possibly identical with #2)

Matt 1:13 begotten by Abiud
     1:13 begat Azor
2. Son of Melea, father of Jonan, and an ancestor of Jesus. (Possibly identical with #1)

Luke 3:30 father of Jonan
     3:31 son of Melea

ELIAS [e-li'-as = my God is Jehovah]
Old Testament Elijah, an Old Testament prophet contemporary with Ahab (king of Israel), called the "Tishbite" probably in reference to his place of residence, performed many notable miracles including raising a young man from the dead, withholding rain from Heaven for the space of three and one-half years, and praying down fire from Heaven on Mount Carmel at his confrontation with the prophets of Baal. Was translated to Heaven in a chariot of fire, thus eluding death at the time, and was succeeded as prophet by Elisha, appeared with Jesus and Moses on the mount of transfiguration, and is considered by many scholars to be one of the two witnesses of the Revelation. (See also 1Kng 17—21; 2Kng 1—3)

Matt 11:14 his coming fulfilled through John the Baptist
    16:14 some claimed that Jesus was he
    17: 3 present at transfiguration of Jesus and talked with Him (17:4)
    17: 4 Peter desired to build him a tabernacle
    17: 5 overshadowed by a bright cloud
    17:10 prophecy of his coming fulfilled through John the Baptist (17:13)
    17:10 scribes said he must come first
    17:11 would truly come first and restore all things
    17:12 was come and not known, but treated as Jews desired
    27:47 people at crucifixion thought that Jesus was calling for him
    27:49 people waited to see if he would come to save Jesus
Mark 6:15 some people believed Jesus was he
    8:28 some said Jesus was he
    9: 4 along with Moses, appeared unto Peter, James, and John at the transfigurations of Jesus
    9: 4 talked with Jesus
    9: 5 Peter desired to make him a tabernacle

Mark 9:11 the scribes had said that he must come first
    9:12 Jesus said that he must come first and restore all things
    9:13 was indeed come (in the person of John the Baptist) and treated as Jews desired
   15:35 some at the crucifixion thought Jesus called for him
   15:36 some waited to see if he would come and take Jesus down from the cross
Luke 1:17 John the Baptist would go before Jesus in his spirit and power
    4:25 in his day heaven was shut up three years and six months and there was great famine throughout all the land
    4:26 sent only to a widow in Sarepta, a city of Sidon
    9: 8 some thought he had appeared in form as Jesus
    9:19 some thought him to be Jesus
    9:30 talked with Jesus and Moses at the transfiguration of Christ
    9:31 appeared in glory and spake of Jesus' death which He should accomplish at Jerusalem
    9:33 departed
    9:33 Peter desired to build him a tabernacle
    9:54 had called down fire from heaven to consume opponents
John 1:21 people questioned whether John the Baptist was he
    1:25 John stated that he was not He
Rom 11: 2 made intercession to God against Israel
    11: 3 thought he alone was left of God's servants and that his life was sought after
Jas 5:17 a man subject to like passions as we are
    5:17 prayed earnestly that it might not rain and it rained not for three years and six months
    5:18 prayed again and the heaven gave rain

ELIEZER [e-li-e'-zur = God is help]
Son of Jorim, father of Jose, and an ancestor of Jesus (through Joseph).

Luke 3:29 father of Jose
    3:29 son of Jorim

ELISABETH ♀ [e-liz'-a-beth = God is swearer]
Wife of Zacharias, mother of John the Baptist (born in her old age), a cousin of Mary the mother of Jesus, of priestly lineage (being of the daughters of Aaron), and walked blameless in all the commandments and ordinances of the Lord.

Luke 1: 5 wife of Zacharias
    1: 5 was of the daughters of Aaron

51

ELIZABETH *(continued)*

Luke 1: 6 a righteous woman
1: 6 walked blameless in all the commandments and ordinances of the Lord
1: 7 childless because she was barren
1: 7 well stricken in years
1:13 an angel announced that she would bear a son, to be named John
1:18 was well stricken in years
1:24 conceived and hid herself five months
1:25 had had reproach among men
1:36 cousin of Mary
1:36 conceived a son in her old age
1:36 was called barren
1:39 lived in the hill country in a city of Juda
1:40 saluted by Mary upon Mary's visit
1:41 her baby leaped in her womb
1:41 was filled with the Holy Ghost
1:42 blessed Mary her cousin (1:45)
1:43 Jesus was her Lord
1:44 her baby leaped in her womb
1:56 visited by Mary for about three months
1:57 brought forth a son
1:58 rejoiced
1:60 explained that her son's name would be John

ELISEUS [el-i-se'-us = my God is salvation]
Old Testament Elisha, the son of Shaphat; an Old Testament prophet and successor to and student of Elijah; his works displayed God's power and confirmation of office upon him (as the widow's cruise of oil, the healing of Naaman the leper, and the raising from the dead the son of a woman who befriended him). (See also 1Kng 19; 2Kng 2—13)

Luke 4:27 the prophet (in Israel)

ELIUD [e-li'-ud = God my praise]
Son of Achim, father of Eleazar, and an ancestor of Jesus.

Matt 1:14 begotten of Achim
1:15 begat Eleazar

ELMODAM [el-mo'-dam = measure]
Son of Er, father of Cosam, and an ancestor of Jesus.

Luke 3:28 father of Cosam
3:28 son of Er

ELYMAS [el'-i-mas = a sorcerer]
Also called Bar-jesus, a sorcerer and false prophet, a Jew on the Isle of Paphos who withstood Barnabas and Paul, and temporarily blinded as a judgment for his actions.

Acts 13: 6 was on the isle of Paphos
13: 6 a sorcerer
13: 6 a false prophet
13: 6 a Jew (son of Jesus)
13: 7 was with Sergius Paulus

Acts 13: 8 name by interpretation was Elymas
13: 8 the sorcerer
13: 8 withstood Barnabas and Saul (Paul) seeking to turn away Sergius Paulus from the faith
13: 9 a judgment was pronounced upon him by Saul (Paul) (13:11)
13:10 full of subtilty and all mischief
13:10 the child of the devil
13:10 the enemy of all righteousness
13:10 ceased not to pervert the right ways of the Lord
13:11 the hand of the Lord was upon him and a mist and a darkness (a temporary blindness) fell on him
13:11 went about seeking someone to lead him by the hand

EMMOR [em'-mor = an ass]
Old Testament Hamor, father of Sychem, and from whose sons Abraham purchased a sepulcher. (See also Gen 33—34; Josh 24; Judg 9)

Acts 7:16 had sons
7:16 Abraham bought a sepulcher from his sons
7:16 father of Sychem

ENOCH [e'-nok = tuition; teacher]
Also Old Testament Henoch, son of Jared and father of Methuselah, probably seventh in line from Adam through Seth, walked with God, and was translated that he should not see death. (See also Gen 5; 1Chron 1)

Luke 3:37 father of Mathusala
3:37 son of Jared
Heb 11: 5 by faith was translated that he should not see death
11: 5 was not found because God had translated him
11: 5 pleased God
11:13 did not receive the promises, but was persuaded of them and embraced them
11:13 confessed that he was a stranger and pilgrim on the earth
11:16 desired a better country
11:16 God is not ashamed to be called his God
11:16 God hath prepared for him a city
11:39 had obtained a good report through faith
11:39 received not the promise
Jude :14 the seventh from Adam
:14 prophesied concerning the Lord executing judgment upon the ungodly (:15)

ENOS [e'-nos = mortal man]
Son of Seth, father of Cainan, and an ancestor of Jesus. (See also Gen 4—5)

Luke 3:37 father of Cainan (3:38)
3:38 son of Seth

52

EPAENETUS [ep-en-e'-tus = praised]
A well-beloved Christian at Rome to whom Paul sends greetings, and possibly the first saved of Paul's ministry in Achaia.

Rom	16: 5	saluted by Paul
	16: 5	well-beloved of Paul
	16: 5	the firstfruits of Achaia unto Christ

EPAPHRAS [ep'-a-fras = lovely]
A fellow servant of Paul and Timothy at Colosse, and a faithful minister of Christ.

Col	1: 7	a dear fellow servant of Paul and Timothy
	1: 7	a faithful minister of Christ for the Colossian believers
	1: 8	informed Paul of the love, in the Spirit, of the Colossian Christians
	4:12	one of the Colossians
	4:12	a servant of Christ who always labored fervently for the Colossians in prayer
	4:12	saluted the Colossian church
	4:13	had a great zeal for the Colossian church, for those in Laodicea, and those in Hierapolis
Phle	:23	fellow prisoner in Christ Jesus with Paul
	:23	Paul requested Philemon to salute him

EPAPHRODITUS [e-paf-ro-di'-tus = lovely]
A (Christian) brother, companion in labor, and fellow soldier with Paul, sent to Philippi, was sick unto death but received the mercy of God, and later ministered to Paul.

Phil	2:25	Paul thought it necessary to send him to the Philippian church
	2:25	Paul's brother and companion in labor, and fellow soldier
	2:25	messenger to the Philippian church
	2:25	ministered to Paul's wants
	2:26	longed after the Philippian church and was full of heaviness because they had heard of his illness
	2:27	had been sick nigh unto death, but God had mercy on him
	2:28	was carefully sent by Paul to the Philippians to cause them to rejoice
	2:29	Philippian church was to receive him with gladness and to hold him in reputation
	2:30	was nigh unto death for the work of Christ, not regarding his life, to supply the Philippians lack of service toward Paul
	4:18	conveyed a gift of the Philippian church to Paul

ER [ur = watcher]
Son of Jose, father of Elmodam, and an ancestor of Jesus.

| Luke | 3:28 | father of Elmodam |
| | 3:29 | son of Jose |

ERASTUS [e-ras'-tus = beloved]
1. Sent, along with Timothy, into Macedonia by Paul. (May be identical with #2 and/or #3)

| Acts | 19:22 | sent into Macedonia by Paul |
| | 19:22 | ministered unto Paul |

2. Chamberlain of the city of Corinth. (May be identical with #1 and/or #3)

| Rom | 16:23 | the chamberlain of the city |
| | 16:23 | saluted the church at Rome |

3. A man of Corinth. (May be identical with #1 and/or #2)

| 2Tim | 4:20 | lived at Corinth |

ESAIAS [e-sah'-yas = save thou Jehovah]
Old Testament Isaiah; an Old Testament prophet; son of Amoz (not the prophet), married and had two sons; contemporary with Uzziah, Jotham, Ahaz, and Hezekiah (kings of Judah); and writer of the Old Testament book bearing his name. (See also 2Kng 19—20; Isa 1—40)

Matt	3: 3	the prophet
	3: 3	prophesied concerning John the Baptist
	4:14	a prophet
	8:17	the prophet
	12:17	the prophet
	13:14	prophesied
	15: 7	prophesied
Mark	7: 6	prophesied of the Pharisees and scribes
Luke	3: 4	a prophet
	3: 4	wrote concerning John the Baptist
	4:17	the prophet
	4:17	Jesus read from his words (4:19)
John	1:23	the prophet
	12:38	made a saying (a prophecy)
	12:38	a prophet
	12:39	said again (prophesied again)
	12:41	saw His glory and spake of Him
Acts	8:28	the Ethiopian eunuch was reading his words
	8:28	the prophet
	8:30	the prophet
	8:34	the prophet
	28:25	well spake the Holy Ghost by him (28:27)
	28:25	the prophet
Rom	9:27	cried (prophesied) concerning Israel
	9:29	had said (prophesied) before
	10:20	very bold in his teaching
	15:12	prophesied of the root of Jesse (Jesus) who should rise to reign over the Gentiles

ESAU [e'-saw = hairy]
Son of Isaac and Rebecca, twin brother of Jacob, a hairy man and a skilled hunter, and sold his birthright for a mess of pottage. (See also Gen 25—36)

| Rom | 9:11 | child (of Isaac and Rebecca) |

ESAU (continued)

Rom	9:11	being not yet born had done neither good nor evil
	9:12	would serve his younger brother Jacob
	9:13	hated of God
Heb	11:20	blessed by Isaac (concerning things to come)
	12:16	a fornicator
	12:16	profane person
	12:16	for one morsel of meat sold his birthright
	12:17	when he would have inherited the blessing, was rejected
	12:17	found no place of repentance, though he sought it carefully with tears

ESLI [es'-li = reserved for Jehovah]
Son of Hagge, father of Naum, and an ancestor of Jesus. (Possibly Old Testament Azaliah)

| Luke | 3:25 | father of Naum |
| | 3:25 | son of Nagge |

ESROM [es'-rom = enclosed]
Son of Phares, father of Aram, and an ancestor of Jesus. (Possibly Old Testament Hezron)

Matt	1: 3	begat by Phares
	1: 3	begat Aram
Luke	3:33	father of Aram
	3:33	son of Phares

EUBULUS [yu-bu'-lus = of good counsel]
A believer at Rome who sent greetings to Timothy by Paul.

| 2Tim | 4:21 | sent greetings to Timothy by Paul |

EUNICE ♀ [yu-ni'-see = conquering well]
Mother of Timothy, probably the daughter of Lois, wife of a Greek, and unfeigned faith was known to Paul.

Acts	16: 1	mother of Timotheus (Timothy)
	16: 1	a Jewess
	16: 1	a believer
	16: 1	the wife of a Greek
2Tim	1: 5	had unfeigned faith
	1: 5	mother of Timothy
	1: 5	daughter of Lois

EUODIAS ♀ [yu-o'-de-as = fragrant]
Euodia, a woman in the church at Philippi who evidently has a dispute or disagreement with another woman Syntyce. (Paul encouraged them to be of the same mind.)

| Phil | 4: 2 | besought (by Paul) to be of the same mind in the Lord with Syntyche |

EUTYCHUS [yu'-tik-us = fortunate]
A young man of Troas who fell asleep while sitting in a third floor window while listening to the preaching of Paul. (Eutychus was taken up dead but was restored to life by Paul.)

Acts	20: 6	was at Troas
	20: 9	sat in a window
	20: 9	a young man
	20: 9	fell into a deep sleep
	20: 9	sunk down with sleep, fell from the third loft, and was taken up dead
	20:10	was fallen upon and embraced by Paul
	20:10	his life was in him
	20:12	was alive, which fact brought comfort to many

EVE ♀ [eev = life, life-giving]
The wife of Adam; a direct creation of God from the rib of her husband; mother of Cain, Abel, Seth, and others; beguiled by the serpent, ate of the forbidden fruit and in turn gave to her husband; and the mother of all the human race. (See also Gen 3—4)

2Cor	11: 3	beguiled by the serpent
1Tim	2:13	formed after Adam
	2:14	was deceived and transgressed
	2:15	would be saved in childbearing

EZEKIAS [ez-e-ki'-as = strengthened of Jehovah]
Old Testament Hezekiah, a king of Judah, a good king unlike his father Ahaz and trusted in God, received a sign from the Lord of an additional fifteen years of life by the sundial being turned back ten degrees, and succeeded by his son Manasseh (who was born three years after the extension of his father's life). (See also 2Kng 16—21; 1Chr 3—4; 2Chr 28—33; Isa 36—39)

| Matt | 1: 9 | begotten of Achaz |
| | 1:10 | begat Manasses |

F

FELIX [fe'-lix = happy]
A Roman procurator of Judea appointed by the emperor Claudius and presided at the trial of Paul.

Acts	23:24	the governor
	23:26	most excellent governor
	23:26	recipient of a letter from Claudius Lysias concerning Paul
	23:33	was in Caesarea
	23:33	the epistle (from Claudius Lysias), and Paul were presented before him
	23:33	the governor
	23:34	the governor

FELIX *(continued)*

Acts 23:34 read the letter and asked Paul of what province he was
23:34 understood that Paul was of Cilicia
23:35 agreed to hear Paul when his accusers had come
23:35 commanded that Paul be kept in Herod's judgment hall
24: 1 governor
24: 1 informed by Tertullus, against Paul
24: 2 Paul accused by Tertullus before him
24: 2 worthy deeds were done unto the nation by his providence
24: 3 called noble
24:10 the governor
24:10 beckoned unto Paul to speak
24:10 had been many years a judge of the nation
24:21 had called Paul in question (touching the resurrection of the dead)
24:22 had more perfect knowledge of the way (of salvation)
24:22 deferred the matter until he could hear from (Claudius) Lysias
24:23 commanded a centurion to keep Paul under liberty and to forbid none of his acquaintance to minister or come unto him
24:24 his wife was Drusilla
24:24 came with his wife and heard Paul concerning the faith in Christ
24:25 trembled at Paul's words (of the scripture)
24:25 told Paul he would call for him (again) at a convenient season
24:26 hoped that Paul would give him money that he might loose him, and sent for him the oftener, communing with him
24:27 succeeded by Porcius Festus
24:27 willing to show the Jews a pleasure, left Paul bound
25:14 left Paul in bonds

FESTUS [fes'-tus = festival]—see PORCIUS FESTUS

FORTUNATUS [for-chu-na'-tus = fortunate; well-freighted]
A believer who, along with Stephanas and Achaicus, supplied Paul's need.

1Cor 16:17 had gone to Paul (along with Stephanas and Achaicus)
16:17 supplied Paul's needs (which the Corinthian church had failed to do)
16:18 had refreshed Paul's spirit and that of the Corinthian church

G

GAD [gad = the seer; an invader; fortune]
One of the patriarchs, the seventh son of Jacob, son of Zilpah the handmaid of Leah, and full brother of Asher. (See also Gen 30, 35, 42—49; Exod 1)

Matt 1: 2 begat by Jacob
John 4:12 drank of the well (Jacob's)
4:12 a child of Jacob
Acts 7: 8 begat by Jacob
7: 8 one of the patriarchs
7: 9 one of the patriarchs
7: 9 moved with envy, sold Joseph into Egypt
7:11 found no sustenance
7:12 sent by Jacob to Egypt for corn
7:13 on his second visit (to Egypt), Joseph was made known to him
7:13 was made known unto Pharaoh
7:15 went down into Egypt and died
7:16 was carried into Sychem and was laid in the sepulcher that Abraham bought
Rev 7: 5 twelve thousand sealed of his tribe
21:12 his name is inscribed upon the gates of the new Jerusalem
21:12 a child of Israel (Jacob)

GAIUS [gah'-yus = on earth]
1. A man of Macedonia, a traveling companion of Paul and seized by a mob of silversmiths at Ephesus. (May be identical with #2, #3, and #4)

Acts 19:29 was caught and was rushed into the theater (at Ephesus)
19:29 of Macedonia
19:29 Paul's companion in travel
19:37 neither a robber of churches, nor a blasphemer of Diana

2. A man of Derbe, who accompanied Paul into Asia. (May be identical with #1, #3, and #4)

Acts 20: 4 of Derbe
20: 4 accompanied Paul into Asia
20: 5 went before and tarried for Paul (and Luke) at Troas
20: 6 abode seven days with Paul (and Luke) at Troas
20:13 going before by ship, sailed unto Assos
20:14 met Paul at Assos, took him in, and came to Mitylene
20:15 sailed over against Chios, next day arrived at Samos, tarried at Trogyllium, and next day came to Miletus
20:34 Paul's hands had ministered unto his necessities

3. A host of Paul who was also baptized by him at Corinth. (May be identical with #1, #2, probably with #4)

Rom 16:23 host of Paul (and of the whole church)

GAIUS (continued)
Rom 16:23 saluted the church at Rome
1Cor 1:14 baptized by Paul

4. Addressee of Epistle of third John. (May be identical with #1, #2, probably with #3)

3Joh : 1 recipient of the third letter of John
      : 1 well-beloved of John
      : 2 soul prospered
      : 3 indwelt with the truth and walked in the truth
      : 5 did faithfully to the brethren and to strangers
      : 6 many bore witness of his charity before the church

GALLIO [gal'-le-o = a eunuch (?)]
A Roman proconsul or deputy of Achaia before whom Paul was brought by his Jewish opponents.

Acts 18:12 deputy of Achaia
      18:14 spoke to the Jews
      18:15 would not judge in such matters as the Jews had brought against Paul
      18:16 drove the Jews from the judgment seat
      18:17 cared for none of those things

GAMALIEL [gam-a'-le-el = God is recompenser]
A pharisee, a celebrated member of the Sanhedrin, instructor of Paul, and held in high esteem among his counterparts.

Acts 5:34 stood up in the council (Sanhedrin)
      5:34 a Pharisee
      5:34 a doctor of the law who had reputation among all the people
      5:34 commanded the apostles to be put forth a little space (for deliberation)
      5:35 counseled the Sanhedrin concerning their handling of the apostles (5:39)
      5:40 got the agreement of the council concerning his thoughts about the apostles
      22: 3 resided at Jerusalem
      22: 3 Paul sat at his feet

GIDEON [ghid'-e-on = feller; hewer; great warrior]
Also Old Testament Jerubbaal and Jerubbesheth; youngest son of Joash; of the tribe of Manasseh; the fifth judge, who judged Israel for forty years; and led Israel to an astounding and unique victory over the Midianites with an army of only 300 men. (See also Judg 6—8)

Heb 11:32 acted by faith (11:34)
     11:39 had obtained a good report through faith
     11:39 received not the promise

GREAT, HEROD THE [her'-od = heroic]
Son of Antipater, procurator of Judea, made king of Judea under Augustus, reigned at the time of the birth of Christ, father of Herod Antipas by Malthace, and had the temple at Jerusalem built in which Jesus taught.

Matt 2: 1 the king (tetrarch) at the time of the birth of Christ
      2: 3 the king
      2: 3 troubled (at the news of the birth of the new King of the Jews)
      2: 4 gathered all the chief priests and scribes of the people together and demanded to know the place of Christ's birth
      2: 7 demanded of the wise men the time of the star's appearance
      2: 8 sent wise men to Bethlehem to find Jesus
      2: 9 the king
      2: 9 was heard by the wise men
      2:12 mocked by the wise men who returned another way
      2:13 would seek to destroy (kill) Jesus
      2:16 was mocked of the wise men and was exceeding wroth
      2:16 had diligently inquired of the wise men
      2:16 slew all male children in Bethlehem and coasts two years and under
      2:19 died
      2:20 was dead
      2:20 had sought the young child's (Jesus' life)
      2:22 father of Archelaus
Luke 1: 5 king of Judea
Acts 23:35 had a judgment hall (in Caesarea)
      23:35 Felix commanded that Paul be kept in his judgment hall

H

HEBER [he'-bur = companion]
Son of Sala;, father of Phalec; an ancestor of Jesus; and possibly Old Testament Eber. (See also Gen 46:17; 1Chr 7:31, 32)

Luke 3:35 father of Phalec
      3:35 son of Sala

HELI [he'-li = my God]
Son of Matthat and father of Joseph, husband of Mary of whom was born Jesus; and brother of Jacob the father of the identical of Mary.

Luke 3:23 father of Joseph
      3:24 son of Matthat

HERMAS, HERMES [her'-mas, her'mees = Mercury; interpreter]
A Christian at Rome saluted by Paul.

Rom 16:14 saluted by Paul
        16:14 was with other brethren

HERMOGENES [her-moj'-e-nees = born of Hermes]
A man in Asia who turned away from Paul.

2Tim 1:15 lived in Asia
       1:15 turned away from Paul (along with Phygellus)

HEROD (A title, not a proper name: SEE A-GRIPPA I, AGRIPPA II, ANTIPAS, and the GREAT)

HERODIAS ♀ [he-ro'-de-as = heroic]
Sister of Agrippa; daughter of Aristobulus (son of Herod the Great) by Mariamne; married first to Philip, then to Herod (tetrarch of Galilee) Philip's brother; mother of Salome whose dancing pleased Herod, and responsible for the death of John the Baptist.

Matt 14: 3 John the Baptist was bound and put into prison for her sake
      14: 3 wife of Philip (brother of Herod Antipas, the tetrarch)
      14: 4 was not lawful for her to be the wife of Herod (Antipas)
      14: 6 her daughter's dancing pleased Herod on his birthday
      14: 8 had instructed her daughter to ask Herod for the head of John the Baptist in a charger
      14:11 given the head of John the Baptist by her daughter
Mark 6:17 for her sake Herod had bound John (the Baptist) in prison
      6:17 wife of Philip (King Herod's brother)
      6:17 sister-in-law of Herod the king
      6:17 married Herod
      6:18 John (the Baptist) had said it was not lawful for her to be Herod's
      6:19 had a quarrel against John (the Baptist) and would have killed him, but could not
      6:22 had a daughter
      6:22 her daughter's dancing pleased Herod and she was given her wish of him
      6:24 replied to the question of her daughter as to the nature of the wish, by requesting the head of John the Baptist in a charger (6:25)
      6:28 given the head of John the Baptist in a charger by her daughter
Luke 3:19 wife of Philip

HERODION [he-ro'-de-on = valiant]
A kinsman of Paul at Rome, probably a Jew, and saluted by Paul.

Rom 16:11 saluted by Paul
      16:11 kinsman of Paul

HYMENAEUS [hy-men-e'-us = nuptial]
A man made shipwreck by blasphemy, delivered unto Satan by Paul, and claimed no bodily resurrection from the dead.

1Tim 1:19 made shipwreck (1:20)
      1:20 delivered unto Satan, by Paul, to learn not to blaspheme
2Tim 2:16 failed to shun profane and vain babblings and increased unto more ungodliness (2:17)
      2:17 his word ate as a canker
      2:17 worked ungodliness with Philetus
      2:18 erred from the truth
      2:18 overthrew the faith of some by stating that the resurrection was already past

I

ISAAC [i'-za-ak = laughter]
Son of Abraham by Sarah, born of his parents in their very old age, the son of the promise (covenant) made to Abraham by the Lord, and father of Jacob and Esau by Rebecca. (See also Gen 17—49)

Matt 1: 2 begotten of Abraham
      1: 2 begat Jacob
      8:11 will be seated with many from the east and west and with Abraham and Jacob in the kingdom of Heaven
     22:32 God was his God
Mark 12:26 God is his God
Luke 3:34 father of Jacob
      3:34 son of Abraham
     13:28 will be present in the kingdom of God
     20:37 the Lord was his God
     20:37 recognized the same God as Moses
Acts 3:13 a father of Israel
      3:13 God was his God
      7: 8 begotten by Abraham (son of)
      7: 8 circumcised the eighth day (by his father)
      7: 8 begat Jacob
      7:32 father of Moses (his lineage)
      7:32 God was his God
Rom 9: 7 only in him (would Abraham's seed be called)

ISAAC *(continued)*

Rom	9: 9	would be born of Sarah according to the promise
	9:10	Rebecca conceived by him
	9:10	a father of the Israelites
Gal	4:28	a child of promise
	4:29	was persecuted by him that was born after the flesh
	4:29	was born after the Spirit
	4:30	son of the freewoman
	4:30	would be heir (but not with the son of the bondwoman)
Heb	11: 9	dwelt in tabernacles with Abraham and Jacob (in the land of promise)
	11: 9	heir with Abraham and Jacob of the promise
	11:13	died in faith, not having received the promises, but was persuaded of them and embraced them
	11:17	offered up by his father (Abraham)
	11:17	the only begotten son of his father (Abraham)
	11:18	in him, would Abraham's seed be called
	11:19	Abraham believed that God was able to raise him up (from the dead)
	11:19	received in a figure (by Abraham)
	11:20	by faith blessed Jacob and Esau concerning things to come
	11:39	had obtained a good report through faith
	11:39	received not the promise
Jams	2:21	son of Abraham
	2:21	offered upon the altar by his father

ISRAEL [iz'-ra-el = ruling of God]—see JACOB

ISSACHAR [is'-sa-kar = bearing hire; reward]
One of the patriarchs, the ninth son of Jacob (by Leah); the fifth son of his mother; and at least four sons were born to him. (See also Gen 30, 35; Exod 1)

Matt	1: 2	begotten by Jacob
John	4:12	drank of the well (Jacob's)
	4:12	a child of Jacob
Acts	7: 8	begotten of Jacob
	7: 8	one of the patriarchs
	7: 9	one of the patriarchs
	7: 9	moved with envy, sold Joseph into Egypt
	7:11	found no sustenance
	7:12	sent by Jacob to Egypt for corn
	7:13	on his second visit (to Egypt), Joseph was made known to him
	7:13	was made known unto Pharaoh
	7:15	went down into Egypt and died
	7:16	was carried into Sychem and was laid in the sepulcher that Abraham bought
Rev	7: 7	twelve thousand sealed of his tribe
	21:12	his name is inscribed upon the gates of the new Jerusalem
	21:12	a child of Israel (Jacob)

J

JACOB [ja'-cub = following after; supplanter]
1. Son of Isaac and Rebecca; twin brother of Esau; name changed to "Israel" by the Lord; his progeny is the true "Israel" as opposed to those of his father Isaac and his grandfather Abraham; his character seems to have well matched the meaning of his name supplanter or schemer; worked seven years for his bride Rachel, but ended up marrying her sister Leah, not by choice, but by deceit on the part of Laban their father; served another seven years for Rachel; and twelve sons and one daughter were born to him. (See also Gen 25—30)

Matt	1: 2	begotten of Isaac
	1: 2	begat Judas (Judah) and his brethren
	8:11	will be seated with many from the east and west and with Abraham and Isaac in the kingdom of Heaven
	22:32	God was his God
Mark	12:26	God is his God
Luke	1:33	Jesus would reign over his house (Israel) for ever
	1:54	servant of God
	3:33	father of Juda (3:34)
	3:34	son of Isaac
	13:28	will be present in the kingdom of God
	20:37	the Lord was his God
	20:37	recognized the same God as Moses
John	4: 5	gave a parcel of ground at Sychar to Joseph
	4: 5	father of Joseph
	4: 6	had a well at Sychar (in Samaria)
	4:12	claimed by Samaritans as their father
	4:12	gave this well to the Samaritans
	4:12	drank from the well bearing his name, along with his children and cattle
Acts	3:13	a father of Israel
	3:13	God was his God
	7: 8	begotten by Isaac
	7: 8	begat the twelve patriarchs
	7:11	found no sustenance (food)
	7:12	hearing there was corn in Egypt, sent out the patriarchs
	7:14	called to Egypt by Joseph
	7:15	went down into Egypt
	7:15	died (in Egypt)
	7:16	carried into Sychem and laid in the sepulcher that Abraham bought
	7:32	a father of Moses
	7:32	God was his God
	7:46	God was his God
Rom	9:11	child (of Isaac and Rebecca)
	9:11	being not yet born had done neither good nor evil
	9:12	would be served by his elder brother Esau
	9:13	loved of God

58

JACOB *(continued)*

Heb	11: 9	dwelt in tabernacles with Abraham and Isaac (in the land of promise)
	11: 9	heir with Abraham and Isaac of the promise
	11:13	died in faith, not having received the promises, but was persuaded of them and embraced them
	11:20	blessed by Isaac (concerning things to come)
	11:21	by faith, when dying, blessed both the sons of Joseph
	11:21	worshiped (God), leaning upon the top of his staff
	11:39	had obtained a good report through faith
	11:39	received not the promise
Rev	21:12	the names of his children (the patriarchs) are inscribed on the twelve gates of the new Jerusalem

2. Son of Matthan and father of Joseph the husband of Mary of whom was born Jesus.

| Matt | 1:15 | begotten of Matthan |
| | 1:16 | begat Joseph, the husband of Mary of whom was born Jesus Christ |

JAIRUS [ja-i'-rus = whom God enlightens]
A ruler of the synagogue, probably in or near Capernaum, whose daughter was raised from the dead by Jesus.

Matt	9:18	a ruler
	9:18	his daughter was dead
	9:18	asked Jesus to come and lay His hand upon his daughter
Mark	5:22	came to Jesus and fell at His feet
	5:22	a ruler of the synagogue
	5:23	besought Jesus on behalf of his little daughter who lay at the point of death
	5:24	was accompanied by Jesus to his house
	5:35	ruler of the synagogue
	5:35	informed from certain of his house that his daughter was dead
	5:36	ruler of the synagogue
	5:36	told by Jesus to not be afraid, but to believe
	5:37	of the multitude, only Peter, James, and John were allowed by Jesus to accompany him to the (his) house
	5:38	a ruler of synagogue
	5:39	Jesus entered his house
	5:40	entered the room of his little daughter along with the mother, Jesus, Peter, James, and John
	5:42	witnessed the raising of his daughter from the dead by Jesus
Luke	8:41	a man, a ruler of the synagogue
	8:41	fell down at Jesus' feet and besought Him that He would come into his house
	8:42	had only one daughter, twelve years of age, who lay dying

Luke	8:49	the ruler of the synagogue
	8:49	one from his house came to inform him that his daughter was dead
	8:50	told by Jesus not to fear, but only believe and his daughter would be made whole
	8:51	Jesus entered his house
	8:51	suffered to go into the house with Jesus, along with Peter, James, and John, and the mother of the maiden
	8:55	witnessed the raising of his daughter from the dead by Jesus
	8:56	was astonished at the miracle of Jesus
	8:56	charged, by Jesus, to tell no man concerning the raising of his daughter from the dead

JAMBRES [jam'-brees = foamy healer (?)]
Probably an Egyptian leader or magician who, along with Jannes, withstood Moses before Pharaoh immediately prior to the exodus.

| 2Tim | 3: 8 | withstood Moses (resisting the truth) |

JAMES [james = supplanter]
1. Son of Zebedee (BOANERGES)
An apostle of Jesus Christ, one of the twelve, son of Zebedee, brother of John the apostle, probably son of Salome, a fisherman who left his nets to follow Jesus, present at the transfiguration of Jesus, one of the inner circle with John and Peter, and first of the apostles to see death when slain with the sword by Agrippa I.

Matt	4:21	son of Zebedee
	4:21	brother of John
	4:21	was mending nets with John and Zebedee in a ship
	4:21	was called by Jesus
	4:22	left the ship and his father and followed Jesus
	8:23*	followed Jesus into a ship
	8:25*	came to and awoke Jesus and asked Him to save the disciples, for they perished
	8:26*	fearful
	8:26*	of little faith
	8:27*	marveled at Jesus
	9:10*	sat at meat with Jesus along with publicans and sinners
	9:14*	fasted not
	9:19*	followed Jesus
	9:37*	instructed to pray that the Lord would send forth laborers into His harvest (9:38)
	10: 1*	was called unto Jesus
	10: 1	one of the twelve disciples
	10: 1*	given power to cast out unclean spirits
	10: 1*	given power to heal all manner of sickness and disease
	10: 2	son of Zebedee
	10: 2	brother of John

JAMES(continued)

Matt 10: 2 one of the twelve apostles
10: 5 one of the twelve (apostles)
10: 5* commanded to go neither to the Gentiles, nor into any city of the Samaritans
10: 6* sent forth by Jesus to the lost sheep of the house of Israel
10: 7* commanded by Jesus to preach "the kingdom of heaven is at hand"
10: 8* commanded to heal the sick, cleanse the lepers, raise the dead, and cast out devils (demons)
10: 8* had freely received
10: 9* was to provide neither gold, nor silver, nor brass, nor scrip, neither two coats, neither shoes, nor staves (for himself) (10:10)
10:11* in every city or town, was to inquire who was worthy, and to abide with them
10:12* was to salute each house he entered
10:13* his peace was to come upon each worthy house, but return to him if unworthy
10:14* was to shake off the dust of his feet therein, when not received or heard by a house or city
10:16* sent forth (by Jesus) as a sheep in the midst of wolves
10:16* was to be wise as a serpent and harmless as a dove
10:17* would be delivered to the councils, scourged in synagogues, and brought before governors and kings for (Jesus') sake (10:18)
10:19* was to take no thought concerning what he would speak when delivered up, for the Spirit of his Father would speak in him (10:20)
12: 1* was an hungered and plucked corn in the field and ate
12: 2* accused by the Pharisees of acting unlawfully on the Sabbath day
12:49* called mother and brethren by Jesus
13:10* questioned Jesus about His use of parables
13:11* was given unto him to know the mysteries of the kingdom of Heaven
13:16* saw and heard (spiritually)
13:17* had seen and heard (spiritually)
13:18* had the parable of the sower explained by Jesus (13:23)
13:36* had the parable of the wheat and tares explained by Jesus (13:43)
13:51* claimed to have understood all these things (parables)
14:15* came to Jesus and requested Him to send the multitude away
14:16* instructed by Jesus to feed the multitude
14:17* requested by Jesus to bring the five loaves and two fishes to Him (14:18)

Matt 14:19* given the blessed loaves by Jesus
14:19 distributed the loaves to the multitude
14:20* took up of the fragments that remained twelve baskets full
14:22* constrained by Jesus to get into a ship and to go before Him unto the other side (of Sea of Galilee)
14:24* his ship was tossed with waves
14:25* approached by Jesus (walking on the sea)
14:26* saw Jesus walking on the water (Sea of Galilee) and was afraid
14:27* told by Jesus to be of good cheer and not be afraid
14:33* being in the ship, worshiped Jesus, claiming Him to be the Son of God
14:34* came into the land of Gennesaret
15: 2 accused by the scribes and Pharisees of transgressing the tradition of the elders by not washing his hands when he ate bread
15:12* came to Jesus, informing Him that the Pharisees were offended at His saying
15:23* came and besought Jesus to send away her that cried after him
15:32* was called (unto Jesus)
15:34* had seven loaves and a few little fishes
15:36* given the loaves and fishes (by Jesus)
15:36* gave the loaves and fishes to the multitude
15:37* took up of the broken meat that was left seven baskets full
16: 5* was come to the other side and had forgotten to take bread
16: 6* told to beware of the leaven of the Pharisees and Sadducees
16: 7 reasoned with the other disciples over Jesus' words
16: 7* had taken no bread
16: 8* of little faith
16: 8 reasoned with the other disciples (concerning the lack of bread)
16: 9* took up baskets (of fragments)
16:10* took up baskets (of fragments)
16:11* did not understand Jesus' words concerning the leaven (doctrine) of the Pharisees and Sadducees
16:12* understood how that Jesus spoke not of bread, but of the doctrine of the Pharisees and Sadducees
16:13* was in Caesarea Philippi
16:13* answered Jesus' question concerning His identity (16:14)
16:15* questioned as to his view of Jesus' identity
16:20* charged by Jesus to tell no man that He was Jesus the Christ
16:21* shown by Jesus the sufferings He

JAMES *(continued)*

must undergo

Matt 17: 1 taken up by Jesus into an high mountain apart with Peter and John

17: 1 brother of John

17: 2 witnessed the transfiguration of Jesus

17: 3 saw Moses and Elias talking with Jesus

17: 4 was present (at transfiguration of Jesus)

17: 5 hearing the voice of the Lord out of a cloud, fell on his face and was sore afraid (17:6)

17: 7 touched by Jesus and told to arise and be not afraid

17: 8 lifted up his eyes and saw no man but Jesus

17: 9 coming down from the mountain, charged by Jesus to tell the vision to no man until He was risen from the dead

17:13 understood that Jesus spoke of John the Baptist

17:22* abode in Galilee

17:23* was exceedingly sorry

17:24* came to Capernaum

18: 1* asked Jesus who is the greatest in the kingdom of Heaven

19:13* rebuked those who brought children to Jesus

19:14* was rebuked, in turn, by Jesus

19:25* exceedingly amazed at Jesus' answer to the rich young ruler and asked who could be saved

19:27* had forsaken all and followed Jesus

19:28* had followed Jesus

19:28* promised by Jesus to sit upon the twelve thrones judging the twelve tribes of Israel

20:17* going up to Jerusalem, was taken apart and foretold by Jesus of His betrayal, crucifixion, and resurrection (20:19)

20:20 son of Zebedee

20:20 came to Jesus with his mother and brother and worshiped Him

20:20 mother requested of Jesus that he and his brother John, might sit on His right and left hands in His kingdom (20:21)

20:22 was able to drink of Christ's cup and to be baptized with His baptism (20:23)

20:24 the other ten disciples were moved with indignation against him and his brother John

20:29* departed from Jericho (for Jerusalem)

21: 1* arrived in Bethphage and the Mount of Olives

21:20* saw the withered fig tree and marveled

Matt 24: 1* came to Jesus to show Him the buildings of the temple

24: 2* Jesus spoke to him of the coming destruction of the temple

24: 3* asked Jesus of the sign of His coming and of the end of the world

26: 8* was indignant at the actions of the woman

26:10* had troubled the woman

26:17* asked Jesus where he should prepare for Him the Passover

26:19* did as Jesus had appointed and made ready the Passover

26:20 celebrated the Passover with Jesus and the rest of the twelve

26:22 asked Jesus if he were the one to betray Him

26:26* while eating (the Passover) was given the bread by Jesus

26:27* given the cup (by Jesus)

26:30* having sung an hymn, went out into the Mount of Olives

26:31* Jesus predicted that he would be offended because of Him

26:35* claimed he would never deny Jesus, even though it meant death

26:36* came with Jesus to Gethsemane

26:36* instructed to sit and pray

26:37 went with Jesus

26:37 son of Zebedee

26:38* told by Jesus to tarry and watch with Him

26:40* fell asleep in the garden of Gethsemane

26:43* fell asleep again in the garden for his eyes were heavy

26:45* told to sleep on now and take his rest

26:46* told to arise and go (with Jesus)

26:56* forsook Jesus and fled

27:56 his mother beheld the crucifixion of Jesus

28:13* would be accused of stealing Jesus' body by night

28:16* went into Galilee into the place (mountain) appointed

28:17* saw Jesus and worshiped Him

28:19* was given the great commission (28:20)

28:20* Jesus would always be with him, even unto the end of the world

Mark 1:19 son of Zebedee

1:19 brother of John

1:19 seen by Jesus while in the ship mending the nets

1:20 called by Jesus and followed Him

1:20 left his father in the ship with the hired servants

1:21 went into Capernaum with Jesus

1:29 had been at the synagogue at Capernaum

1:29 along with Jesus and John, entered the house of Simon (Peter) and Andrew

JAMES *(continued)*

Mark 1:31 ministered unto by Peter's wife's mother

1:36 followed Jesus to His solitary place of prayer (1:37)

2:15 sat at meat with Jesus, Levi (Matthew), and many publicans and sinners

2:18 did not fast as the disciples of John (the Baptist) and Pharisees did

2:23 plucked ears of corn in the corn fields on the Sabbath day

3: 7 withdrew from the synagogue with Jesus to the sea

3:14* ordained by Jesus (to be with Him)

3:14* would be sent forth to preach (by Jesus)

3:15* would be given power by Jesus to heal sicknesses and to cast out devils (demons)

3:17 son of Zebedee

3:17 brother of John

3:17 along with his brother John, was surnamed by Jesus, Boanerges meaning "the sons of thunder"

3:17 a disciple of Jesus (one of the twelve)

3:20* could not eat bread with Jesus because of the multitude

4:10* asked Jesus about the parable of the sower

4:11* was given to know the mystery of the kingdom of God

4:33* had many parables taught him by Jesus

4:34* when alone, with the rest of the twelve, had all things expounded by Jesus

4:36* sent away the multitude

4:36* with the rest of the twelve, took Jesus to the other side of the sea

4:38* in fear, awakened Jesus in the midst of the storm

4:40* was fearful and had no faith

4:41* feared exceedingly

4:41* questioned among the other disciples as to what manner of man Jesus was that even the wind and the sea obey Him

5: 1* went with Jesus across the Sea of Galilee to the country of the Gadarenes

5:37 was allowed by Jesus to enter into Jairus's house with Him

5:37 brother of John

5:42 witnessed the raising of Jairus's daughter by Jesus

6: 1* followed Jesus into His own country

6: 7* sent forth two by two (by Jesus)

6: 7* given power over unclean spirits

6: 8* commanded to take nothing on his journey except a staff, and to be shod with sandals and only one coat (6:9)

Mark 6:12* went out, and preached that men should repent

6:13* cast out many devils (demons) and anointed with oil many that were sick, and healed them

6:30* an apostle

6:30* gathered together unto Jesus to report what he had done and taught

6:31* had no leisure so much as to eat

6:32* departed privately with Jesus into a desert place by ship

6:36* asked Jesus to send away the multitude into the villages to buy themselves bread

6:37* told by Jesus to give food to the multitude

6:37* asked Jesus if he should go and buy bread to feed the people

6:38* when asked by Jesus the available provisions, reported five loaves and two fishes

6:39* made the people sit down by hundreds and by fifties (6:40)

6:41* given the food blessed by Jesus to distribute to the crowd

6:43* took up twelve baskets full of fragments and of the fishes

6:45* constrained by Jesus to get into the ship and go to the other side unto Bethsaida

6:47* was alone (with the other disciples) in the ship in the midst of the sea

6:48* toiled in rowing the ship for the winds were contrary

6:48* Jesus came unto him in about the fourth watch of the night walking upon the sea

6:49* saw Jesus walking upon the sea and cried out for he supposed it had been a spirit

6:50* saw Jesus and was troubled but admonished by Him to fear not

6:51* was amazed beyond measure and wondered that the wind ceased as Jesus entered the ship

6:52* because of his hardened heart, had forgotten about the miracle of the loaves

6:53* came into the land of Gennesaret

6:54* got out of the ship

7: 5* walked not according to the traditions of the elders (ate bread with unwashed hands)

8: 5* informed Jesus of the seven loaves

8: 6* set the loaves before the people

8: 7* receiving the blessed fishes from Jesus, set them before the people

8: 8* gathered seven baskets of fragments

8:10* entered into a ship with Jesus and went into Dalmanutha

8:13* entering into the ship again with Jesus, departed to the other side

JAMES *(continued)*

Mark 8:14* had forgotten to take bread, and had only one loaf in the ship

8:16* had no bread

8:17* having seen the miracles, still did not understand as his heart was possibly yet hardened

8:19* took up twelve baskets full of fragments at the feeding of the five thousand

8:20* took up seven baskets full of fragments at the feeding of the four thousand

8:27* went into towns of Caesarea Philippi with Jesus

8:27* responded to Jesus' question concerning His identity with "John the Baptist, Elias, and one of the prophets" (8:28)

8:30* charged to tell no man that Jesus was the Christ

8:31* taught by Jesus of the things concerning Himself

9: 2 witnessed the transfiguration of Jesus (9:8)

9: 4 Elias (Elijah) and Moses appeared to him, Peter, and John at the transfiguration of Jesus

9: 6 was sore afraid

9: 7 overshadowed by a cloud and heard the voice of God

9: 9 forbidden to tell what he had seen until after the resurrection

9:10 questioned with Peter and John what the rising from the dead should mean

9:14* questioned by the scribes

9:30* passed through Galilee

9:32* did not understand the words of Jesus, but was afraid to ask

9:33* came to Capernaum

9:33* disputed with the other disciples on the way to Capernaum as to whom should be the greatest (9:34)

9:38* forbade a man from casting out devils (demons) in Jesus' name, because he did not follow him

10:13* rebuked those who brought young children to Jesus that He should touch them

10:14* rebuked, in turn, by Jesus

10:24* astonished at the words of Jesus concerning those with riches

10:26* astonished at Jesus' words

10:28* had left all and followed Jesus

10:32* went up to Jerusalem with Jesus and was amazed and afraid

10:35 son of Zebedee

10:35 brother of John

10:35 came unto Jesus and asked Him to grant his desire

10:37 asked that he and his brother John, might sit one on His right hand and the other on His left hand in His glory

Mark 10:38 told by Jesus that he did not know what he was asking

10:38 could drink of the cup that Jesus did, and could be baptized with the baptism that He was baptized with (10:39)

10:41 the other ten disciples were much displeased with him and John

10:46* went to Jericho

10:46* went out of Jericho with Jesus

11: 1* came nigh to Jerusalem, unto Bethphage and Bethany, at the Mount of Olives

11:11* went to Bethany with Jesus and stayed until the morrow (11:12)

11:14* heard Jesus curse the fig tree

11:15* returned to Jerusalem with Jesus

11:19* went out of Jerusalem (10:20)

11:20* witnessed the fig tree dried up from the roots

11:27* came again to Jerusalem

13: 3 sat upon the Mount of Olives

13: 3 asked Jesus privately concerning the sign when all things should be fulfilled (13:4)

13: 5 cautioned, by Jesus, to not be deceived

14:12 asked Jesus where he should go and prepare the Passover

14:17* in the evening of the first day of unleavened bread, went with Jesus to the upper room

14:18* sat and ate together with Jesus

14:19* began to be sorrowful over Jesus' statement of betrayal and to ask "Is it I?"

14:20* dipped with Jesus in the dish

14:22* ate the Passover with Jesus

14:23* drank of the communion cup

14:26* sung an hymn and went out to the Mount of Olives

14:31* exclaimed that even if it meant death, he would not deny Him

14:32* went to Gethsemane and was told to sit there while Jesus prayed

14:33 went apart with Jesus in the garden of Gethsemane

14:34 told, by Jesus, to tarry and watch

14:37 found sleeping by Jesus

14:40 found sleeping again by Jesus (for his eyes were heavy)

14:40 did not know what to answer Jesus

14:41 told by Jesus to sleep on and take his rest

14:42 told to rise up and go

14:50* forsook Jesus and fled

16:10* mourned and wept

16:11* believed not Mary Magdalene's account

16:14* Jesus appeared to him as he sat at meat (with the other disciples)

16:14* upbraided by Jesus for his unbelief and hardness of heart, because he

JAMES *(continued)*

believed not them which had seen Him after He was risen

Mark 16:15* commissioned to go into all the world and preach the gospel to every creature

16:20* went forth and preached everywhere, with signs following

Luke 4:39 ministered unto by Peter's wife's mother

5: 2 had a ship

5: 2 a fisherman

5: 2 was washing the nets

5: 7 went to Peter's aid to haul in his catch of fish, and filled the ship so that it began to sink

5: 9 was astonished at the draught of fishes that had been caught (5:10)

5:10 brother of John

5:10 son of Zebedee

5:10 with his brother John, was partner with Simon (Peter)

5:11 brought the ship to land

5:11 forsook all and followed Jesus

5:30* murmured against by the scribes and Pharisees

5:30* ate and drank with publicans and sinners

5:33* ate and drank instead of fasting

6: 1* plucked ears of corn and ate (rubbing them in his hands) on the Sabbath

6: 2* claimed (by the Pharisees) to be doing that which was not lawful to do on the Sabbath days

6:13 chosen as one of the twelve

6:13* also called (named) an apostle

6:14 named an apostle

6:17* came down from the mountain with Jesus and stood in the plain

8: 1* went throughout every city and village with Jesus

8: 9* questioned Jesus concerning a parable

8:10* unto him it was given to know the mysteries of the kingdom of God

8:22* went into a ship with Jesus and launched forth for the other side

8:23* the boat, filled with water, put him in jeopardy

8:24* called Jesus Master

8:24* came to Jesus and awakened Him during the storm

8:25* asked by Jesus concerning his faith

8:25* was afraid and wondered concerning Jesus' power over the elements

8:26* arrived at the country of Gadarenes (Gadara)

8:51 suffered to go into Jairus's home with Jesus, Peter, John, and the father and mother of the maiden

8:55 witnessed the raising of Jairus's daughter from the dead by Jesus

9: 1* given power and authority over all devils (demons) and to cure diseases

Luke 9: 2* sent by Jesus to preach the kingdom of God and to heal the sick

9: 3* was to take neither staves, nor scrip, neither bread, neither money, neither have two coats

9: 4* was to abide in whatever house he entered

9: 6* went through the towns, preaching the gospel, and healing everywhere

9:10* returned and told Jesus all he had done

9:10* went privately with Jesus into a desert place belonging to the city called Bethsaida

9:12* requested that Jesus send away the multitude, so that they might go into the towns and lodge and get victuals (food)

9:13* had only five loaves and two fishes but was requested by Jesus to give food to the multitude

9:14* made the multitude sit down in companies by fifties (9:15)

9:16* gave the blessed loaves and fish unto the multitude

9:17* took up twelve baskets of fragments

9:18* was alone with Jesus (and the rest of the twelve)

9:18* in response to Jesus' question as to His identity, responded "John the Baptist, Elias, and one of the prophets risen again" (9:19)

9:20* straitly charged and commanded to tell no man that He is the Christ (9:21)

9:28 went up into a mountain to pray with Jesus

9:32 was heavy with sleep and upon awaking saw Moses and Elias (Elijah) and the glory of Jesus

9:34 feared as he was overshadowed and entered into a cloud

9:36 told no man in those days any of those things which he had seen at the transfiguration of Christ

9:37 came down from the mount of transfiguration the next day

9:45* feared to ask Jesus concerning His teaching

9:46* reasoned with the other disciples as to which of them should be greatest

9:49* forbade a man from casting out devils (demons) in Jesus' name because he followed not with the disciples

9:54 questioned the Lord if he should command fire to come down from heaven and consume a village of the Samaritans

9:55 rebuked by Jesus

10:24* saw and heard what many prophets

JAMES *(continued)*

and kings had desired to experience

Luke 12: 1* warned by Jesus to beware of the leaven of the Pharisees

12: 4* friend of Jesus

17: 5* asked Jesus to increase his faith

18:15* rebuked those who brought infants to Jesus

18:16* rebuked, in turn, by Jesus

18:28* had left all and followed Jesus

18:31* taken unto Jesus and instructed of things to come (18:33)

18:34* understood none of these teachings of Jesus

19:29* with Jesus came nigh to Bethphage and Bethany at the Mount of Olives

19:37* rejoiced and praised God with a loud voice (19:38)

22:14* sat down with Jesus (in the upper room for the Passover)

22:14* was called an apostle

22:15* Jesus truly desired his presence in eating the Passover

22:19* partook of the first Lord's Supper (22:20)

22:23* inquired among the disciples as to which of them would betray Jesus

22:24* a strife existed among him and the other disciples as to which one should be accounted the greatest

22:28* had continued with Jesus in His temptations

22:29* was appointed a kingdom (that he might eat and drink at Jesus' table in His kingdom and sit on thrones judging the twelve tribes of Israel) (22:30)

22:35* had lacked nothing

22:36* told to prepare (for his new task)

22:39* followed Jesus to the Mount of Olives

22:40* told to pray that he enter not into temptation

22:45* found sleeping for sorrow (by Jesus)

22:46* told to rise and pray, lest he enter into temptation

22:49* perceiving the forthcoming events, asked Jesus if he should use his sword

24: 9* was told all things concerning the resurrection by Mary Magdalene, Joanna, Mary the mother of James, and the other women

24:10* an apostle

24:11* the words of the women seemed to him as idle tales and he believed them not

24:33* being gathered together (with the other disciples), Cleopas found him and declared that the Lord was risen indeed and had appeared to Simon (24:34)

Luke 24:36* Jesus appeared unto him (after the resurrection) but he was terrified and affrightened and supposed that he had seen a spirit (24:37)

24:38* asked by Jesus why he was troubled and why thoughts arose in his heart

24:40* was shown Jesus' hands and feet

24:41* believed not yet for joy, and wondered

24:42* gave Jesus a piece of a broiled fish and of an honeycomb

24:45* his understanding was opened by Jesus that he might understand the scriptures

24:46* was witness of these things (24:48)

24:49* told to tarry in Jerusalem until he was endued with power from on high

24:50* led by Jesus out as far as to Bethany and was blessed of Him

24:52* worshiped Jesus and returned to Jerusalem with great joy

24:53* was continually in the temple, praising and blessing God

John 2: 2* was called to the marriage in Cana of Galilee

2:11* believed on Jesus

2:12* went to Capernaum and continued there not many days

2:17* remembered that it was written of Him, "the zeal of thine house hath eaten me up"

2:22* after the resurrection, remembered Jesus' words and believed the scriptures, and the words which Jesus had said

3:22* came into the land of Judea with Jesus and tarried there with Him

4: 2* did baptize

4: 8* had gone away unto the city to buy meat

4:27* came unto Jesus and marveled that He talked with the Samaritan woman, yet did not question Him

4:31* called Jesus Master

4:31* implored Jesus to eat

4:33* questioned among the disciples if Jesus had been brought food to eat

4:35* told to look on the fields for they were white already to harvest

4:38* had been sent to reap where he had not labored, and had entered into others' labors

6: 3* went up into a mountain and sat with Jesus

6:10* instructed by Jesus to have the multitude sit down

6:11* distributed the loaves and fishes to the multitude

6:13* gathered twelve baskets of fragments

6:16* went down to the sea, entered a ship and went toward Capernaum (6:17)

JAMES (*continued*)

John 6:19* after rowing twenty-five to thirty furlongs, saw Jesus walking on the sea and was afraid
6:20* told to not be afraid
6:21* willingly received Him into the ship
6:22* was entered into the only boat there
6:22* was apart from Jesus in the boat alone (with the other disciples)
6:67* asked, by Jesus, if he would also go away
6:69* believed and was sure that Jesus was the Christ, the Son of the living God
6:70* chosen as one of the twelve
9: 2* questioned Jesus concerning the man born blind
11: 8* called Jesus "Master"
11:11* friend of Lazarus
11:54* continued with Jesus at Ephraim
12:16* understood not, at first, the events of the triumphal entry of Jesus
12:16* after Jesus' glorification, remembered that these events had been written of Jesus, and had been done unto Him
13: 5* feet washed by Jesus
13:12* had his feet washed by Jesus
13:13* called Jesus "Master" and "Lord"
13:14* had his feet washed by Jesus
13:14* told, by Jesus, that he ought to wash one another's feet
13:15* had been given an example that he should do as Jesus had done to him
13:18* was known and chosen of Jesus
13:21* when told that one of them would betray Jesus, looked on the others doubting of whom He spoke (13:22)
13:28* knew not for what intent Jesus spoke these words to Judas Iscariot
13:34* given a new commandment to love one another
13:34* loved of Jesus
13:35* love one to another was a mark that he was a true disciple of Jesus
14:25* was with Jesus
14:26* would be instructed by the Holy Spirit in all things
14:26* the words Jesus had spoken would be brought to his remembrance
14:27* Jesus' peace was given to him and left with him
14:31* was told to arise and go with Jesus
15: 3* was clean through the Word
15: 9* loved of Jesus
15:12* commanded to love one another
15:12* loved of Jesus
15:16* chosen of Jesus, and ordained of Him to go and bring forth fruit, and that his fruit should remain
15:17* commanded to love one another
15:19* not of the world
15:19* chosen out of the world by Jesus

John 15:19* hated of the world
15:27* would bear witness because he had been with Jesus from the beginning
16: 4* was with Jesus
16: 6* sorrow had filled his heart
16:12* could not bear the words of Jesus
16:22* presently had sorrow
16:24* had asked nothing of the Father in Jesus' name
16:27* loved of the Father
16:27* loved Jesus, and believed that He came from God
16:29* could now understand plainly Jesus' words
16:30* was sure that Jesus knew all things
16:30* believed that Jesus came forth from God
18: 1* went with Jesus over the brook Cedron and went into a garden (Gethsemane)
18: 2* often resorted there with Jesus
20:18* told by Mary Magdalene that she had seen the Lord and that He had spoken unto her
20:19* while assembled together (with the other disciples) with the doors shut for fear of the Jews, Jesus appeared in the midst
20:20* saw Jesus' hands and side and was glad
20:21* sent by Jesus and given His peace
20:22* breathed on by Jesus and received the Holy Ghost
20:25* told Thomas that he had seen the Lord
20:25* informed by Thomas that he would not believe without specific conditions being met
20:26* the doors being shut again, Jesus appeared the second time to him and the apostles
20:30* many other signs were done in his presence which are not written (in this book)
21: 1 saw Jesus at the Sea of Tiberias (Sea of Galilee) while with a group of disciples (21:2)
21: 2 a son of Zebedee
21: 2 had a brother
21: 3 entering a ship, went fishing, and caught nothing
21: 4 knew (recognized) not Jesus
21: 5 had no meat (had caught nothing)
21: 6 obeying Jesus' command, cast the net on the right side of the ship
21: 6 was not able to draw the net for the multitude of fishes
21: 8 being not far from land, came in a little ship dragging the net with fishes
21: 9 coming to land, saw a fire of coals there, with fish and bread thereon
21:10 told by Jesus, to bring of the fish which had been caught

66

JAMES *(continued)*

John   21:12   told to come and dine
     21:12   dared not ask who He was, knowing it was the Lord
     21:13   given bread and fish by Jesus
     21:14   the third appearance of Jesus unto the disciples after His resurrection
     21:15   had dined with Jesus

Acts   1: 2*   had been given commandments by Jesus (through the Holy Ghost)
     1: 2*   chosen by Jesus
     1: 3*   was shown Jesus alive after His passion
     1: 3*   spoken to by Jesus of the things pertaining to the kingdom of God
     1: 3*   saw Jesus forty days
     1: 4*   commanded, by Jesus, not to depart from Jerusalem, but to wait for the promise of the Father
     1: 5*   would be baptized with the Holy Ghost
     1: 6*   questioned Jesus concerning the restoration of the kingdom to Israel
     1: 7*   was not to know the times or the seasons which the Father had put in His own power
     1: 8*   after receiving the Holy Spirit, would receive power and would be witness unto Jesus Christ throughout the earth
     1: 9*   beheld as Jesus was taken up into Heaven at His ascension
     1:10*   was joined by two men in white apparel while he looked steadfastly toward Heaven
     1:11*   a man of Galilee
     1:11*   was gazing up into Heaven
     1:11*   Jesus was taken up from him into Heaven
     1:11*   was told that Jesus would come in like manner as he had seen Him go into Heaven
     1:12*   returned to Jerusalem and went into an upper room (1:13)
     1:14*   continued in prayer and supplication with the women, Mary the mother of Jesus, and with His brethen
     1:21*   was with the Lord Jesus at various times
     1:24*   prayed concerning the ordination of one to be a witness of Jesus' resurrection
     1:26*   gave forth his lot (concerning Judas Iscariot's successor)
     2: 1*   present at the day of Pentecost
     2: 2*   while sitting in the house, cloven tongues like as of fire sat upon him, he was filled with the Holy Ghost, and spoke with other tongues (2:4)
     2: 6*   his speech confounded the multitude because every man heard in his own language
     2: 7*   a Galilean

Acts   2:13*   mocked by some who claimed him as full of new wine
     2:14*   stood with (Simon) Peter
     2:15*   was not drunk
     2:32*   was a witness to the resurrection of Jesus
     2:37*   asked by the multitude on the day of Pentecost what they should do
     2:42*   many continued steadfastly in his doctrine and fellowship
     2:43*   many wonders and signs were done by him
     4:33*   with great power gave witness of the resurrection of the Lord Jesus
     4:33*   great grace was upon him
     4:35*   the price of possessions sold by Christians was laid at his feet
     4:35*   distributed to every man (of the Christian community) as he had need
     4:36*   gave Joses a surname of Barnabas
     4:37*   Joses's money was laid at his feet
     5: 2*   the gift of Ananias and Sapphira was laid at his feet
     5:12*   by his hands were many signs and wonders wrought among the people
     5:12*   was with one accord with the others in Solomon's porch
     5:13*   no man durst join himself to him (the apostles)
     5:13*   was magnified of the people
     5:16*   healed the multitude of sicknesses and unclean spirits
     5:18*   placed in the common prison by the high priest and Sadducees
     5:19*   released from prison by the angel of the Lord and told to go, stand, and speak in the temple (5:20)
     5:21*   entered into the temple early in the morning and taught
     5:22*   was not found in the prison
     5:25*   was standing in the temple and teaching the people
     5:26*   brought without violence and set before the council (5:27)
     5:27*   questioned by the high priest (5:28)
     5:28*   had been commanded not to teach in this (Jesus') name
     5:28*   had filled Jerusalem with his doctrine and had (seemingly) intended to bring Jesus' blood upon his accusers
     5:29*   believed that he ought to obey God rather than men
     5:32*   witness of God (and of His works)
     5:33*   Jewish leaders took counsel to slay him
     5:34*   put a little space from the Sanhedrin (for their deliberation)
     5:40*   called back before the council, beaten, commanded not to speak in the name of Jesus, and let go
     5:41*   departed from the council rejoicing

JAMES *(continued)*

Acts

that he was counted worthy to suffer shame for His name
5:42* daily in the temple and in every house, ceased not to teach and preach Jesus Christ
6: 2* called the multitude together and stated it was not reasonable that he should leave the Word of God and serve tables
6: 3* instructed that seven men of honest report be chosen to be appointed to serve tables
6: 4* determined to give himself continually to prayer and to the ministry of the Word
6: 6* the chosen seven were set before him, for whom he prayed and laid his hands on them
8: 1* remained in Jerusalem in the midst of great persecution
8:14* was in Jerusalem
8:14* hearing that Samaria had received the Word of God, sent Peter and John to Samaria
9:27* Saul (Paul) was brought to him by Barnabas and he was informed of Saul's (Paul's) conversion experience and his bold preaching at Damascus
9:28* was accompanied by Saul (Paul) in coming in and going out at Jerusalem
10:39* was witness of all things Jesus did both in the land of the Jews and in Jerusalem
10:41* a witness, chosen before of God
10:41* ate and drank with Jesus after His resurrection
10:42* commanded of Jesus to preach unto the people, and testified that it was Jesus which was ordained of God to be the Judge of quick and dead
11: 1* was in Judea
11: 1* heard that the Gentiles had also received the Word of God
11:15* the Holy Ghost fell on him at the beginning (Pentecost)
12: 2 killed with the sword by Herod
12: 2 brother of John
13:31* saw Jesus many days
13:31* came up with Jesus from Galilee to Jerusalem
13:31* was His (Jesus') witness unto the people
15: 2* Paul, Barnabas, and others were sent by the church at Antioch to consult with him over the matter of circumcision
15: 4* received Paul, Barnabas, and the others from Antioch
15: 6* came together (with the elders) to consider the matter (of circumcision)

Acts

15: 8* given the Holy Ghost
15: 9* God made no difference between him and a Gentile
15:10* was not able to bear the yoke
15:22* acting with the elders, sent chosen men back to Antioch with Paul and Barnabas
15:23* acting with the elders and brethren, wrote letters of instruction to the Gentiles at Antioch, Syria, and Cilicia
15:24* gave no commandment that Gentile believers must be circumcised and keep the law
15:25* considered it good, being assembled, to send chosen men unto the believers
15:25* loved Barnabas and Paul
15:27* sent Judas and Silas to the Gentile believers
15:33* Judas (Barsabas) and Silas returned unto him
16: 4* with the elders, ordained decrees
16: 4* was at Jerusalem

Rom

16: 7* Andronicus and Junia were well known to him

1Cor

4: 9* Paul thought God had set him (and the apostles) forth last, as it were appointed to death
4: 9* made a spectacle unto the world, to the angels, and to men
4:10* a fool for Christ's sake
4:10* weak, despised
4:11* hungered, thirsted, was naked, was buffeted, and had no certain dwelling place
4:12* labored, working with his own hands
4:12* being reviled, he blessed; being persecuted, he suffered it; being defamed, he entreated (4:13)
4:13* made as the filth of the world, and the offscouring of all things
9: 5* had power to lead about a sister, a wife
15: 5* had seen the risen Lord
15: 7* the risen Lord was seen of him
15:11* preached

2Pet

1:18 heard the voice of God the Father while with Jesus in the holy mount

Rev

21:14* name inscribed in the twelve foundations of the new Jerusalem
21:14* an apostle of the Lamb

2. Son of Alphaeus, "the Less," an apostle of Jesus Christ, one of the twelve, and possibly identical with James the half-brother of Jesus and/or James the son of Mary and brother of Joses.

Matt

8:23* followed Jesus into a ship
8:25* came to and awoke Jesus, and asked Him to save the disciples, for they perished
8:26* fearful
8:26* of little faith

JAMES *(continued)*

Matt 8:27* marveled at Jesus

9:10* sat at meat with Jesus along with publicans and sinners

9:14* fasted not

9:19* followed Jesus

9:37* instructed to pray that the Lord would send forth laborers into His harvest (9:38)

10: 1* was called unto Jesus

10: 1* one of the twelve disciples

10: 1* given power to cast out unclean spirits

10: 1* give power to heal all manner of sickness and disease

10: 2 one of the twelve apostles

10: 3 son of Alphaeus

10: 5 one of the twelve (apostles)

10: 5* commanded to go neither to the Gentiles, nor into any city of the Samaritans

10: 6* sent forth by Jesus to the lost sheep of the house of Israel

10: 7* commanded by Jesus to preach "the kingdom of heaven is at hand"

10: 8* commanded to heal the sick, cleanse the lepers, raise the dead, cast out devils (demons)

10: 8* had freely received

10: 9* was to provide neither gold, nor silver, nor brass, nor scrip, neither two coats, neither shoes, nor staves (for himself) (10:10)

10:11* in every city or town, was to inquire who was worthy, and to abide with them

10:12* was to salute each house he entered

10:13* his peace was to come upon each worthy house, but return to him if unworthy

10:14* was to shake off the dust of his feet therein, when not received or heard by a house or city

10:16* sent forth (by Jesus) as a sheep in the midst of wolves

10:16* was to be wise as a serpent and harmless as a dove

10:17* would be delivered to the councils, scourged in synagogues, and brought before governors and kings for (Jesus') sake (10:18)

10:19* was to take no thought concerning what he would speak when delivered up, for the Spirit of his Father would speak in him (10:20)

12: 1* was an hungered and plucked corn in the field and ate

12: 2* accused by the Pharisees of acting unlawfully on the Sabbath day

12:49* called mother and brethren by Jesus

13:10* questioned Jesus about His use of parables

Matt 13:11* was given unto him to know the mysteries of the kingdom of Heaven

13:16* saw and heard (spiritually)

13:17* had seen and heard (spiritually)

13:18* had the parable of the sower explained by Jesus (13:23)

13:36* had the parable of the wheat and tares explained by Jesus (13:43)

13:51* claimed to have understood all these things (parables)

14:15* came to Jesus and requested Him to send the multitude away

14:16* instructed by Jesus to feed the multitude

14:17* requested by Jesus to bring the five loaves and two fishes to Him (14:18)

14:19* given the blessed loaves by Jesus

14:19* distributed the loaves to the multitude

14:20* took up of the fragments that remained twelve baskets full

14:22* constrained by Jesus to get into a ship and to go before Him unto the other side (of Sea of Galilee)

14:24* his ship was tossed with waves

14:25* approached by Jesus (walking on the sea)

14:26* saw Jesus walking on the water (Sea of Galilee) and was afraid

14:27* told by Jesus to be of good cheer and not be afraid

14:33* being in the ship, worshiped Jesus, claiming Him to be the Son of God

14:34* came into the land of Gennesaret

15: 2* accused by the scribes and Pharisees, of transgressing the tradition of the elders by not washing his hands when he ate bread

15:12* came to Jesus, informing Him that the Pharisees were offended at His saying

15:23* came and besought Jesus to send away her that cried after him

15:32* was called (unto Jesus)

15:34* had seven loaves and a few little fishes

15:36* given the loaves and fishes (by Jesus)

15:36* gave the loaves and fishes to the multitude

15:37* took up of the broken meat that was left seven baskets full

16: 5* was come to the other side and had forgotten to take bread

16: 6* told to beware of the leaven of the Pharisees and Sadducees

16: 7* reasoned with the other disciples over Jesus' words

16: 7* had taken no bread

16: 8* of little faith

16: 8* reasoned with the other disciples (concerning the lack of bread)

16: 9* took up baskets (of fragments)

JAMES *(continued)*

Matt 16:10* took up baskets (of fragments)
16:11* did not understand Jesus' words concerning the leaven (doctrine) of the Pharisees and Sadducees
16:12* understood how that Jesus spoke not of bread, but of the doctrine of the Pharisees and Sadducees
16:13* was in Caesarea Philippi
16:13* answered Jesus' question concerning His identity (16:14)
16:15* questioned as to his view of Jesus' identity
16:20* charged by Jesus to tell no man that He was Jesus the Christ
16:21* shown by Jesus the sufferings He must undergo
17:15* could not cure the lunatic boy (17:16)
17:19* asked Jesus why he could not cast out the devil (demon)
17:20* could not cast out the devil (demon) because of unbelief
17:22* abode in Galilee
17:23* was exceedingly sorry
17:24* came to Capernaum
18: 1* asked Jesus who is the greatest in the kingdom of Heaven
19:13* rebuked those who brought children to Jesus
19:14* rebuked, in turn, by Jesus
19:25* exceedingly amazed at Jesus' answer to the rich young ruler and asked who could be saved
19:27* had forsaken all and followed Jesus
19:28* had followed Jesus
19:28* promised by Jesus to sit upon the twelve thrones judging the twelve tribes of Israel
20:17* going up to Jerusalem, taken apart and foretold by Jesus of His betrayal, crucifixion, and resurrection (20:19)
20:24* was moved with indignation towards James and John because of their request of Jesus
20:29* departed from Jericho (for Jerusalem)
21: 1* arrived in Bethphage and the Mount of Olives
24: 1* came to Jesus to show Him the buildings of the temple
24: 2* Jesus spoke to him of the coming destruction of the temple
24: 3* asked Jesus of the sign of His coming and of the end of the world
26: 8* was indignant at the actions of the woman
26:10* had troubled the woman
26:17* asked Jesus where he should prepare for Him the Passover
26:19* did as Jesus had appointed and made ready the Passover
26:20 celebrated Passover with Jesus and the rest of the twelve

Matt 26:22 asked Jesus if he were the one to betray Him
26:26* while eating (the Passover) was given the bread by Jesus
26:27* given the cup (by Jesus)
26:30* having sung a hymn, went out into the Mount of Olives
26:31* Jesus predicted that he would be offended because of Him
26:35* claimed he would never deny Jesus, even though it meant death
26:36* came with Jesus to Gethsemane
26:36* instructed to sit and pray
26:40* fell asleep in the garden of Gethsemane
26:43* fell asleep again in the garden (of Gethsemane)
26:45* told to sleep on now and take his rest
26:46* told to arise and go (with Jesus)
26:56* forsook Jesus and fled
28:13* would be accused of stealing Jesus' body by night
28:16* went into Galilee into the place (mountain) appointed
28:17* saw Jesus and worshiped Him
28:19* given the great commission (28:20)
28:20* Jesus would always be with him, even unto the end of the world

Mark 3:14* ordained by Jesus (to be with Him)
3:14* would be sent forth to preach (by Jesus)
3:15* would be given power, by Jesus, to heal sicknesses and to cast out devils (demons)
3:18 a disciple of Jesus (one of the twelve)
3:18 son of Alphaeus
3:20* could not eat bread with Jesus because of the multitude
4:10* asked Jesus about the parable of the sower
4:11* was given to know the mystery of the kingdom of God
4:33* had many parables taught him by Jesus
4:34* when alone, with the rest of the twelve, had all things expounded by Jesus
4:36* sent away the multitude
4:36* with the rest of the twelve, took Jesus to the other side of the sea
4:38* in fear, awakened Jesus in the midst of the storm
4:40* was fearful and had no faith
4:41* feared exceedingly
4:41* questioned among the other disciples as to what manner of man Jesus was that even the wind and the sea obey Him
5: 1* went with Jesus across the Sea of Galilee to the country of the Gadarenes

70

JAMES *(continued)*

Mark 6: 1* followed Jesus into His own country

6: 7* sent forth two by two (by Jesus)

6: 7* given power over unclean spirits

6: 8* commanded to take nothing on his journey except a staff, and to be shod with sandals and only one coat (6:9)

6:12* went out, and preached that men should repent

6:13* cast out many devils (demons) and anointed with oil many that were sick, and healed them

6:30* an apostle

6:30* gathered together unto Jesus to report what he had done and taught

6:31* had no leisure so much as to eat

6:32* departed privately with Jesus into a desert place by ship

6:36* asked Jesus to send away the multitude into the villages to buy themselves bread

6:37* told by Jesus to give food to the multitude

6:37* asked Jesus if he should go and buy bread to feed the people

6:38* when asked by Jesus the available provisions, reported five loaves and two fishes

6:39* made the people sit down by hundreds and by fifties (6:40)

6:41* given the food blessed by Jesus, to distribute to the crowd

6:43* took up twelve baskets full of fragments and of the fishes

6:45* constrained by Jesus to get into the ship and go to the other side unto Bethsaida

6:47* was alone (with the other disciples) in the ship in the midst of the sea

6:48* toiled in rowing the ship for the winds were contrary

6:48* Jesus came unto him in about the fourth watch of the night walking upon the sea

6:49* saw Jesus walking upon the sea and cried out for he supposed it had been a spirit

6:50* saw Jesus and was troubled but admonished by him to fear not

6:51* was amazed beyond measure and wondered that the wind ceased as Jesus entered the ship

6:52* because of his hardened heart, had forgotten about the miracle of the loaves

6:53* came into the land of Gennesaret

6:54* got out of the ship

7: 5* walked not according to the traditions of the elders (ate bread with unwashed hands)

8: 5* informed Jesus of the seven loaves

8: 6* set the loaves before the people

Mark 8: 7* receiving the blessed fishes from Jesus, set them before the people

8: 8* gathered seven baskets of fragments

8:10* entered into a ship with Jesus and went into Dalmanutha

8:13* entering into the ship again with Jesus, departed to the other side

8:14* had forgotten to take bread, and had only one loaf in the ship

8:16* had no bread

8:17* having seen the miracles, still did not understand as his heart was possibly yet hardened

8:19* took up twelve baskets full of fragments at the feeding of the five thousand

8:20* took up seven baskets full of fragments at the feeding of the four thousand

8:27* went into the towns of Caesarea Philippi with Jesus

8:27* responded to Jesus' question concerning His identity with "John the Baptist, Elias, and one of the prophets" (8:28)

8:30* charged to tell no man that Jesus was the Christ

8:31* taught by Jesus of the things concerning Himself

9:14* questioned by the scribes

9:18* could not cast out a dumb spirit

9:30* passed through Galilee

9:32* did not understand the words of Jesus, but was afraid to ask

9:33* came to Capernaum

9:33* disputed with the other disciples on the way to Capernaum as to whom should be the greatest (9:34)

9:38* forbade a man from casting out devils (demons) in Jesus' name because he did not follow him

10:13* rebuked those who brought young children to Jesus that He should touch them

10:14* rebuked, in turn, by Jesus

10:24* astonished at the words of Jesus concerning those with riches

10:26* astonished at Jesus' words

10:28* had left all and followed Jesus

10:32* went up to Jerusalem with Jesus and was amazed and afraid

10:41 was much displeased with James and John

10:46* went to Jericho

10:46* went out of Jericho with Jesus

11: 1* came nigh to Jerusalem unto Bethphage and Bethany, at the Mount of Olives

11:11* went to Bethany with Jesus and stayed unto the morrow (11:12)

11:14* heard Jesus curse the fig tree

11:15* returned to Jerusalem with Jesus

11:19* went out of Jerusalem (10:20)

JAMES *(continued)*

Mark 11:20* witnessed the fig tree dried up from the roots

11:27* came again to Jerusalem

13: 3 sat upon the Mount of Olives

14:12* asked Jesus where he should go and prepare the Passover

14:17* in the evening of the first day of unleavened bread, went with Jesus to the upper room

14:18* sat and ate together with Jesus

14:19* began to be sorrowful over Jesus' statement of betrayal and to ask "Is it I?"

14:20* dipped with Jesus in the dish

14:22* ate the Passover with Jesus

14:23* drank of the communion cup

14:26* sung an hymn and went out to the Mount of Olives

14:31* exclaimed that even if it meant death, he would not deny Him

14:32* went to Gethsemane and was told to sit there while Jesus prayed

14:50* forsook Jesus and fled

15:40 called "the less"

15:40 son of Mary

15:40 brother of Jesus

16:10* mourned and wept

16:11* believed not Mary Magdalene's account

16:14* Jesus appeared unto him as he sat at meat (with the other disciples)

16:14* upbraided by Jesus for his unbelief and hardness of heart, because he believed not them which had seen Him after He was risen

16:15* commissioned to go into all the world and preach the gospel to every creature

16:20* went forth and preached everywhere, with signs following

Luke 6: 1* plucked ears of corn and ate (rubbing them in his hands) on the Sabbath

6: 2* claimed (by the Pharisees) to be doing that which was not lawful to do on the Sabbath days

6:13 chosen as one of the twelve

6:13* also called (named) an apostle

6:15 an apostle

6:15 the son of Alphaeus

6:16 brother of Judas (probably Thaddeus)

6:17* came down from the mountain with Jesus and stood in the plain

8: 1* went throughout every city and village with Jesus

8: 9* questioned Jesus concerning a parable

8:10* unto him it was given to know the mysteries of the kingdom of God

8:22* went into a ship with Jesus and launched forth for the other side

8:23* the boat, filled with water, put him in jeopardy

Luke 8:24* called Jesus Master

8:24* came to Jesus and awakened Him during the storm

8:25* asked by Jesus concerning his faith

8:25* was afraid and wondered concerning Jesus' power over the elements

8:26* arrived at the country of the Gadarenes (Gadara)

9: 1* given power and authority over all devils (demons) and to cure diseases

9: 2* sent, by Jesus, to preach the kingdom of God and to heal the sick

9: 3* was to take neither staves, nor scrip, neither bread, neither money, neither have two coats

9: 4* was to abide in whatever house he entered

9: 6* went through the towns, preaching the gospel, and healing everywhere

9:10* returned and told Jesus all he had done

9:10* went privately with Jesus into a desert place belonging to the city called Bethsaida

9:12* requested that Jesus send away the multitude, so that they might go into the towns and lodge and get victuals (food)

9:13* had only five loaves and two fishes, but was requested by Jesus to give food to the multitude

9:14* made the multitude sit down in companies by fifties (9:15)

9:16* gave the blessed loaves and fish unto the multitude

9:17* took up twelve baskets of fragments

9:18* was alone with Jesus (and the rest of the twelve)

9:18* in response to Jesus' question as to His identity, responded "John the Baptist, Elias, and one of the prophets risen again" (9:19)

9:20* straitly charged and commanded to tell no man that He is the Christ (9:21)

9:40* could not cast the spirit (demon) out of a boy

9:45* feared to ask Jesus concerning His teaching

9:46* reasoned with the other disciples as to which of them should be greatest

9:49* forbade a man from casting out devils (demons) in Jesus' name because he followed not with the disciples

10:24* saw and heard what many prophets and kings had desired to experience

12: 1* warned by Jesus to beware of the leaven of the Pharisees

12: 4* friend of Jesus

17: 5* asked Jesus to increase his faith

72

JAMES *(continued)*

Luke 18:15* rebuked those who brought infants to Jesus

18:16* rebuked, in turn, by Jesus

18:28* had left all and followed Jesus

18:31* taken unto Jesus and instructed of things to come (18:33)

18:34* understood none of these teachings of Jesus

19:29* with Jesus, came nigh to Bethphage and Bethany at the Mount of Olives

19:37* rejoiced and praised God with a loud voice (19:38)

22:14* sat down with Jesus (in the upper room for the Passover)

22:14* was called an apostle

22:15* Jesus truly desired his presence in eating the Passover

22:19* partook of the first Lord's Supper (22:20)

22:23* inquired among the disciples as to which of them would betray Jesus

22:24* a strife existed among him and the other disciples as to which one should be accounted the greatest

22:28* had continued with Jesus in His temptations

22:29* was appointed a kingdom (that he might eat and drink at Jesus' table in His kingdom and sit on thrones judging the twelve tribes of Israel) (22:30)

22:35* had lacked nothing

22:36* told to prepare (for his new task)

22:39* followed Jesus to the Mount of Olives

22:40* told to pray that he enter not into temptation

22:45* found sleeping for sorrow (by Jesus)

22:46* told to rise and pray, lest he enter into temptation

22:49* perceiving the forthcoming events, asked Jesus if he should use his sword

24: 9* was told all things concerning the resurrection by Mary Magdalene, Joanna, Mary the mother of James, and the other women (24:10)

24:10* an apostle

24:11* the words of the women seemed to him as idle tales and he believed them not

24:33* being gathered together (with the other disciples) Cleopas found him and declared that the Lord was risen indeed and had appeared to Simon (24:34)

24:36* Jesus appeared unto him (after the resurrection) but he was terrified and affrighted, and supposed he had seen a spirit (24:37)

24:38* asked by Jesus why he was troubled and why thoughts arose in his heart

Luke 24:40* was shown Jesus' hands and feet

24:41* believed not yet for joy, and wondered

24:42* gave Jesus a piece of a broiled fish and of a honeycomb

24:45* his understanding was opened by Jesus that he might understand the scriptures

24:46* was witness of these things (24:48)

24:49* told to tarry in Jerusalem until he was endued with power from on high

24:50* led by Jesus out as far as to Bethany and was blessed of Him

24:52* worshiped Jesus and returned to Jerusalem with great joy

24:53* was continually in the temple, praising and blessing God

John 2: 2* was called to the marriage in Cana of Galilee

2:11* believed on Jesus

2:12* went to Capernaum and continued there not many days

2:17* remembered that it was written of Him, "the zeal of thine house hath eaten me up"

2:22* after the resurrection, remembered Jesus' words and believed the scriptures and the words which Jesus had said

3:22* came into the land of Judea with Jesus and tarried there with Him

4: 2* did baptize

4: 8* had gone away unto the city to buy meat

4:27* came unto Jesus and marveled that He talked with the Samaritan woman, yet did not question Him

4:31* called Jesus "Master"

4:31* implored Jesus to eat

4:33* questioned among the disciples if Jesus had been brought food to eat

4:35* told to look on the fields for they were white already to harvest

4:38* had been sent to reap where he had not sown, and had entered into others' labors

6: 3* went up into a mountain and sat with Jesus

6:10* instructed by Jesus to have the multitude sit down

6:11* distributed the loaves and fishes to the multitude

6:13* gathered twelve baskets of fragments

6:16* went down to the sea, entered a ship, and went toward Capernaum (6:17)

6:19* after rowing twenty-five to thirty furlongs, saw Jesus walking on the sea and was afraid

6:20* told to not be afraid

6:21* willingly received Him into the ship

JAMES *(continued)*

John 6:22* was entered into the only boat there
      6:22* was apart from Jesus in the boat alone (with the other disciples)
      6:67* asked, by Jesus, if he would also go away
      6:69* believed and was sure that Jesus was the Christ, the Son of the living God
      6:70* chosen as one of the twelve
      9: 2* questioned Jesus concerning the man born blind
      11: 8* called Jesus Master
      11:11* friend of Lazarus
      11:54* continued with Jesus at Ephraim
      12:16* understood not, at first, the events of the triumphal entry of Jesus
      12:16* after Jesus' glorification, remembered that these events had been written of Jesus, and had been done unto Him
      13: 5* feet washed by Jesus
      13:12* had his feet washed by Jesus
      13:13* call Jesus "Master" and "Lord"
      13:14* had his feet washed by Jesus
      13:14* told, by Jesus, that he ought to wash one another's feet
      13:15* had been given an example that he should do as Jesus had done to him
      13:18* was known and chosen of Jesus
      13:21* when told that one of them would betray Jesus, looked on the others doubting of whom He spoke (13:22)
      13:28* knew not for what intent Jesus spoke these words to Judas Iscariot
      13:34* given a new commandment to love one another
      13:34* loved of Jesus
      13:35* love one to another was a mark that he was a true disciple of Jesus
      14:25* was with Jesus
      14:26* would be instructed by the Holy Spirit in all things
      14:26* the words Jesus had spoken would be brought to his remembrance
      14:27* Jesus' peace was given to him and left with him
      14:31* was told to arise and go with Jesus
      15: 3* was clean through the Word
      15: 9* loved of Jesus
      15:12* commanded to love one another
      15:12* loved of Jesus
      15:16* chosen of Jesus, and ordained of Him to go and bring forth fruit, and that his fruit should remain
      15:17* commanded to love one another
      15:19* not of the world
      15:19* chosen out of the world by Jesus
      15:19* hated of the world
      15:27* would bear witness, because he had been with Jesus from the beginning
      16: 4* was with Jesus
      16: 6* sorrow had filled his heart

John 16:12* could not bear the words of Jesus
      16:22* presently had sorrow
      16:24* had asked nothing of the Father in Jesus' name
      16:27* loved of the Father
      16:27* loved Jesus, and believed that He came from God
      16:29* could now understand plainly Jesus' words
      16:30* was sure that Jesus knew all things
      16:30* believed that Jesus came forth from God
      18: 1* went with Jesus over the brook Cedron and entered into a garden (Gethsemane)
      18: 2* often resorted there with Jesus
      20:18* told by Mary Magdalene that she had seen the Lord and that He had spoken unto her
      20:19* while assembled together (with the other disciples) with the doors shut for fear of the Jews, Jesus appeared in the midst
      20:20* saw Jesus' hands and side and was glad
      20:21* sent by Jesus and given His peace
      20:22* breathed on by Jesus and received the Holy Ghost
      20:25* told Thomas that he had seen the Lord
      20:25* informed by Thomas that he would not believe without specific conditions being met
      20:26* the doors being shut again, Jesus appeared the second time to him and the apostles
      20:30* many other signs were done in his presence which are not written (in this book)

Acts   1: 2* had been given commandments by Jesus (through the Holy Ghost)
       1: 2* chosen by Jesus
       1: 3* was shown Jesus alive after His passion
       1: 3* spoken to by Jesus of the things pertaining to the kingdom of God
       1: 3* saw Jesus forty days
       1: 4* commanded, by Jesus, not to depart from Jerusalem, but to wait for the promise of the Father
       1: 5* would be baptized with the Holy Ghost
       1: 6* questioned Jesus concerning the restoration of the kingdom to Israel
       1: 7* was not to know the times or the seasons which the Father had put in His own power
       1: 8* after receiving the Holy Spirit, would receive power and would be witness unto Jesus Christ throughout the earth
       1: 9* beheld as Jesus was taken up into Heaven at His ascension
       1:10* was joined by two men in white

JAMES *(continued)*

apparel while he looked steadfastly toward Heaven

Acts 1:11* a man of Galilee
1:11* was gazing up into Heaven
1:11* Jesus was taken up from him into Heaven
1:11* was told that Jesus would come in like manner as he had seen Him go into Heaven
1:12* returned to Jerusalem and went into an upper room (1:13)
1:14* continued in prayer and supplication with the women, Mary the mother of Jesus, and with His brethren
1:21* was with the Lord Jesus at various times
1:24* prayed concerning the ordination of one to be a witness of Jesus' resurrection
1:26* gave forth his lot (concerning Judas Iscariot's successor)
2: 1* present at the day of Pentecost
2: 2* while sitting in the house, cloven tongues like as of fire sat upon him, he was filled with the Holy Ghost, and spoke with other tongues (2:4)
2: 6* his speech confounded the multitude because every man heard in his own language
2: 7* a Galilean
2:13* mocked by some who claimed him as full of new wine
2:14* stood with (Simon) Peter
2:15* was not drunk
2:32* was a witness to the resurrection of Jesus
2:37* asked by the multitude on the day of Pentecost what they should do
2:42* many continued steadfastly in his doctrine and fellowship
2:43* many wonders and signs were done by him
4:33* with great power gave witness of the resurrection of the Lord Jesus
4:33* great grace was upon him
4:35* the price of possessions sold by Christians was laid at his feet
4:35* distributed to every man (of the Christian community) as he had need
4:36* gave Joses a surname of Barnabas
4:37* Joses's money was laid at his feet
5: 2* the gift of Ananias and Sapphira was laid at his feet
5:12* by his hands were many signs and wonders wrought among the people
5:12* was with one accord with the others in Solomon's porch
5:13* no man durst join himself to him (the apostles)
5:13* was magnified of the people

Acts 5:16* healed the multitude of sicknesses and unclean spirits
5:18* placed in the common prison by the high priest and Sadducees
5:19* released from prison by the angel of the Lord and told to go, stand, and speak in the temple (5:20)
5:21* entered into the temple early in the morning and taught
5:22* was not found in the prison
5:25* was standing in the temple and teaching the people
5:26* brought without violence and set before the council (5:27)
5:27* questioned by the high priest (5:28)
5:28* had been commanded not to teach in this (Jesus') name
5:28* had filled Jerusalem with his doctrine and had (seemingly) intended to bring Jesus' blood upon his accusers
5:29* believed that he ought to obey God rather than men
5:32* witness of God (and of His works)
5:33* Jewish leaders took counsel to slay him
5:34* put a little space from the Sanhedrin (for their deliberation)
5:40* called back before the council, beaten, commanded not to speak in the name of Jesus, and let go
5:41* departed from the council rejoicing that he was counted worthy to suffer shame for His name
5:42* daily in the temple and in every house, ceased not to teach and preach Jesus Christ
6: 2* called the multitude together and stated it was not reasonable that he should leave the Word of God and serve tables
6: 3* instructed that seven men of honest report be chosen to be appointed to serve tables
6: 4* determined to give himself continually to prayer and to the ministry of the Word
6: 6* the chosen seven were set before him, for whom he prayed and laid his hands on them
8: 1* remained in Jerusalem in the midst of great persecution
8:14* was in Jerusalem
8:14* hearing that Samaria had received the Word of God, sent Peter and John to Samaria
9:27* Saul (Paul) was brought to him by Barnabas and he was informed of Saul's (Paul's) conversion experience and his bold preaching at Damascus
9:28* was accompanied by Saul (Paul) in coming in and going out at Jerusalem

75

JAMES *(continued)*

Acts 10:39* was witness of all things Jesus did both in the land of the Jews and in Jerusalem
10:41* a witness chosen before of God
10:41* ate and drank with Jesus after His resurrection
10:42* commanded of Jesus to preach unto the people, and testified that it was Jesus which was ordained of God to be the Judge of quick and dead
11: 1* was in Judea
11: 1* heard that the Gentiles had also received the Word of God
11:15* the Holy Ghost fell on him at the beginning (Pentecost)
13:31* saw Jesus many days
13:31* came up with Jesus from Galilee to Jerusalem
13:31* was His (Jesus') witness unto the people
15: 2* Paul, Barnabas, and others were sent by the church at Antioch to consult with him over the matter of circumcision
15: 4* received Paul, Barnabas, and the others from Antioch
15: 6* came together (with the elders) to consider the matter (of circumcision)
15: 8* given the Holy Ghost
15: 9* God made no difference between him and a Gentile
15:10* was not able to bear the yoke
15:22* acting with the elders, sent chosen men back to Antioch with Paul and Barnabas
15:23* acting with the elders and brethren, wrote letters of instruction to the Gentiles at Antioch, Syria, and Cilicia
15:24* gave no commandment that Gentile believers must be circumcised and keep the law
15:25* considered it good, being assembled, to send chosen men unto the believers
15:25* loved Barnabas and Paul
15:27* sent Judas and Silas to the Gentile believers
15:33* Judas (Barsabas) and Silas returned unto him
16: 4* with the elders, ordained decrees
16: 4* was at Jerusalem
Rom 16: 7* Andronicus and Junia were well known to him
1Cor 4: 9* Paul thought God had set him (and the apostles) forth last, as it were, appointed to death
4: 9* made a spectacle unto the world, to the angels, and to men
4:10* a fool for Christ's sake
4:10* weak, despised
4:11* hungered, thirsted, was naked, was buffeted, and had no certain dwelling place
1Cor 4:12* labored, working with his own hands
4:12* being reviled, he blessed; being persecuted, he suffered it; being defamed, he entreated (4:13)
4:13* made as the filth of the world, and the offscouring of all things
9: 5* had power to lead about a sister, a wife
15: 5* had seen the risen Lord
15: 7* the risen Lord was seen of him
15:11* preached
Rev 21:14* name inscribed in the twelve foundations of the new Jerusalem
21:14* an apostle of the Lamb

3. Half brother of Jesus, possibly identical with James the son of Alphaeus and/or James the son of Mary and brother of Joses, and generally identified as the writer of the epistle of James.

Matt 12:46 a (half) brother of Jesus
12:46 stood without, desiring to speak with Jesus
12:46 had brothers and a mother
12:47 had brothers and a mother
12:47 stood without, desiring to speak with Jesus
13:55 assumed to be the son of Joseph and Mary
13:55 thought to be the brother of Jesus, Joses, Simon, and Judas
13:56 had sisters
Mark 3:31 a brother of Jesus
3:31 had brothers and a mother
3:31 came with his brethren and mother, stood without, and sent and called for Jesus
3:32 had brothers and a mother
3:32 sought Jesus
6: 3 (half) brother of Jesus
6: 3 brother of Joses, Juda, and Simon
6: 3 son of Mary
6: 3 had sisters
Luke 8:19 came to Jesus (along with his mother and his brethren)
8:19 could not come at Jesus for the press (crowd)
8:20 stood without, with his mother and brethren desiring to see Jesus
John 2:12 went to Capernaum with his mother and brethren, and continued there not many days
7: 3 requested Jesus to depart and go into Judea, that His disciples also might see the works that He did
7: 5 did not believe in Jesus
7: 5 had brethren
7: 6 his time was always ready
7: 7 could not be hated of the world
7:10 was gone up (to the feast)
Acts 1:14 was present in the upper room
1:14 continued with one accord, in prayer and supplication, with the

JAMES (continued)

		apostles, the women, his mother, and his brethren
Acts	2: 1	present at the day of Pentecost
	2: 2	while sitting in the house, cloven tongues, like as of fire sat upon him, he was filled with the Holy Ghost and spoke with other tongues (2:4)
	12:17	(Simon) Peter instructed that he and his brethren were to be shown (told) these things
	15:13	asked for an audience of the council (and declared his views)
	15:19	gave sentence that the Gentiles who had turned to God, be not troubled with circumcision
	21:18	present with the elders (at Jerusalem)
	21:18	received Paul and his company
	21:19	saluted by Paul
	21:20	heard Paul's words and glorified the Lord
1Cor	9: 5	had power to lead about a sister, a wife
	15: 7	had seen the risen Lord
Gal	1:19	the Lord's brother
	1:19	seen by Paul in Jerusalem
	2: 9	perceived the grace given unto Paul and, with Cephas and John, gave to him and Barnabas the right hand of fellowship that they should go to the heathen
	2:12	sent certain Jews to Jerusalem
Jas	1: 1	a servant of God and of the Lord Jesus Christ
	1: 1	wrote the epistle of James to the twelve tribes which are scattered abroad
	1:18	declared that he would show his faith by his works
Jude	: 1	brother of Jude

4. "the LESS"—see JAMES (son of Alphaeus)

5. Son of Mary, brother of Joses, and possibly identical with James the son of Alphaeus and/or James the half-brother of Jesus.

Matt	27:56	son of Mary
	27:56	brother of Joses
Mark	16: 1	son of Mary
Luke	24:10	son of Mary (one of the followers of Jesus)

JANNA [jan'-nah = flourishing]
Son of Joseph, father of Melchi, and an ancestor of Jesus.

Luke	3:24	father of Melchi
	3:24	son of Joseph

JANNES [jan'-nees = he vexed; he oppressed]
Probably an Egyptian leader or magician, who, along with Jambres, withstood Moses before Pharaoh immediately prior to the exodus.

2Tim	3: 8	withstood Moses (resisted the truth)

JARED [ja'-red = descending]
Son of Maleleel, father of Enoch, and an ancestor of Jesus.

Luke	3:37	father of Enoch
	3:37	son of Maleleel

JASON [ja'-sun = healing]
1. A believer in Thessalonica who aided Paul and who was accused of treason. (Probably identical with #2)

Acts	17: 5	his house was assaulted by some in the city because of Paul and Silas
	17: 6	drawn unto the rulers of the city for his help to Paul and Silas
	17: 7	had received Paul and Silas (and Timothy)
	17: 7	accused of disloyalty to Caesar by saying there was another king
	17: 9	had security taken of him and was let go

2. A kinsman of Paul (meaning he was a Jew) and one of Paul's companions. (Probably identical with #1)

Rom	16:21	kinsman (countryman) of Paul (and Lucius and Sosipater)
	16:21	saluted the church at Rome

JECHONIAS [jek-o-ni'as = Jehovah will establish]
Old Testament Coniah, Jechoniah, and Jehoiachin; a king of Judah, the son of Jehoiakim; father of Salathiel; reigned at time Judah was taken into captivity by Babylon; and recipient of a curse from the Lord that none of his seed would prosper sitting on the throne of David. (See also Jer 22—24)

Matt	1:11	begotten of Josias
	1:11	had brethren
	1:12	begat Salathiel

JEPHTHAE [jef'-thah-e = an opposer]
Old Testament Jephthah and the ninth judge of Israel who led them in a military victory over the Ammonites. (See also Judg 11, 12; 1Sam 12)

Heb	11:32	acted by faith (11:34)
	11:39	had obtained a good report through faith
	11:39	received not the promise

JEREMIAS [jer-e-mi'as = Jehovah will cast forth]; (Jeremy; O.T. Jeremiah)
Also Jeremy; Old Testament Jeremiah, one of the major Old Testament prophets, the son of Hilkiah, of priestly lineage, from Anathoth, often called "the weeping prophet," his prophecies precluded God's judgment upon Judah; and writer of the Old Testament books of Jeremiah and Lamentations. (See also 2Chr 35—36; Jer 1; 18—51)

Matt	2:17	the prophet
	2:17	prophesied the loss of Rachel's children under Herod (2:18)
	16:14	some claimed that Jesus was he

JEREMIAS *(continued)*
Matt 27: 9 the prophet

JEREMY [jer'-e-mee = Jehovah will cast forth]
see—JEREMIAS

JESSE [jes'-se = Jehovah exists]
Son of Obed, grandson of Boaz and Ruth, father
of David, and from Bethlehem. (See also Ruth 4;
1Sam 16—25; 2Sam 20—23)

Matt	1: 5	begotten by Obed
	1: 6	begat David the king
Luke	3:31	father of David (3:32)
	3:32	son of Obed
Acts	13:22	father of David
Rom	15:12	his "root" is Christ

JESUS [je'-zus = savior]
1. Old Testament Jeshua and Joshua, son of Nun,
and a military leader.

Acts	7:45	brought the tabernacle with the other fathers of Israel
Heb	4: 8	if he had given them rest, he would not afterward have spoken of another day

2. JUSTUS [jus'-tus = just]
A Jewish fellow worker of Paul.

Col	4:11	also called Justus
	4:11	a Jewish fellow worker who had been a comfort to Paul

JEZEBEL ♀ [jez'-e-bel = unexalted; unhusband-
ed]
A (false) prophetess perceived to have seduced
God's servants to commit fornication; possibly the
daughter of Ethbaal; wife of Ahab (king of Judah);
and mother of Joram. (See also 1King 16—21;
2King 9)

Rev	2:20	called herself a prophetess
	2:20	allowed to teach and seduce God's servants to commit fornication and to eat things sacrificed unto idols
	2:21	given space to repent of her fornica-tion and she would not
	2:22	will be cast into a bed
	2:22	committed adultery (possibly spiritually)
	2:23	her children will be killed

JOANNA [jo-an'-nah = grace or gift of God]
1. An ancestor of Jesus.

Luke	3:26	father of Juda (3:27)
	3:27	son of Rhesa

♀ 2. Wife of Chuza (Herod's steward); healed of
evil spirits and infirmities; and ministered unto
Jesus of her substance. (Possibly identical with
#3)

Luke	8: 2	had been healed of evil spirits and infirmities (8:3)
	8: 3	wife of Chuza, Herod's steward
	8: 3	ministered unto Him (Christ) of her substance

♀ 3. Present at Jesus' crucifixion and present at
the tomb with spices early on resurrection day.
(Possibly identical with #2)

Luke	23:55	came with Jesus from Galilee, fol-lowed after and beheld the sepulcher, and how His body was laid
	23:56	returned and prepared spices and ointments
	23:56	rested the sabbath day according to the commandment
	24: 1	very early the first day of the week, came to the sepulcher bringing the spices she had prepared
	24: 2	found the stone rolled away from the sepulcher
	24: 3	entered the sepulcher, and found not the body of the Lord Jesus
	24: 4	while much perplexed, two men (angels) stood by in shining gar-ments
	24: 5	was afraid and bowed down her face to the earth
	24: 5	asked by the angels why she sought the living among the dead
	24: 8	remembered the words of Jesus (concerning these events)
	24: 9	returned from the sepulcher and told all these things unto the eleven and to all the rest (24:10)
	24:11	her words seemed as idle tales and the disciples believed her not
	24:22	her words astonished the hearers
	24:22	was early at the sepulcher
	24:23	not finding Jesus' body, went say-ing that she had seen a vision of angels which said that He was alive

JOATHAM [jo'-a-tham = Jehovah is perfect]
Son of Ozias (Uzziah), twelfth king of Judah, and
an ancestor of Jesus.

Matt	1: 9	begotten of Ozias
	1: 9	begat Achaz

JOB [jobe = hated; persecuted]
A perfect, righteous, and upright man; a servant
of the Lord; a wealthy Old Testament saint who
dwelt in Uz; suffered the loss of all earthly possessions; endured great physical anguish; received
the accusations of his so called "comforters," and
maintained his integrity before God. (See also Job
1—42; Ezek 14)

Jas	5:11	many had heard of his patience

JOEL [jo'-el = Jehovah is God]
An Old Testament prophet during the days of
Uzziah, the son of Pethuel, and author of the Old
Testament prophetical book bearing his name.
(See also Joel 1)

Acts	2:16	a prophet
	2:16	his prophecy preached and ex-pounded by Peter on the day of Pentecost (2:21)

JOHN [jon = Jehovah's gift]
1. The baptist (baptizer), a prophet, son of Zacharias and Elisabeth, of priestly lineage, the forerunner of Jesus, preached that Jesus was the Messiah, and was beheaded by Herod Antipas at the request of Herodias through her daughter.

Matt 3: 1 preached repentance in the wilderness of Judea (3:2)
3: 3 man whom Esaias (Isaiah) prophesied would be the voice of one crying in the wilderness
3: 4 had raiment of camel's hair and a leather girdle
3: 4 his meat was locusts and wild honey
3: 5 people came to him from Jerusalem, all Judea, and all the region around about Jordan and were baptized (3:6)
3: 6 baptized (many) in the Jordan (river)
3: 7 did baptize
3: 7 condemned Pharisees and Sadducees and warned of judgment (3:12)
3:11 baptized with water unto repentance
3:11 Jesus is mightier than he
3:11 not worthy to bear Jesus' shoes (unloose them)
3:13 Jesus came to be baptized of him
3:13 was at Jordan
3:14 forbade Jesus to be baptized (of him)
3:14 had need to be baptized of Jesus
3:15 suffered Jesus (to be baptized)
4:12 cast into prison
9:14 had disciples who questioned Jesus concerning fasting
11: 2 was in prison
11: 2 had heard the works of Christ
11: 2 sent two disciples to inquire of Jesus concerning His identity (11:3)
11: 7 Jesus spoke unto the multitudes concerning him (11:11)
11: 9 more than a prophet
11:10 Christ's messenger who would prepare His way
11:11 none greater among them that are born of women
11:11 he that is least in the kingdom of Heaven is greater than he (John)
11:12 the Baptist (baptizer)
11:14 called Elias (Elijah) by Jesus
11:18 came neither eating nor drinking
11:18 claimed by some to have a devil (demon)
14: 2 claimed by Herod that Jesus was he, risen from the dead
14: 2 the baptist (the baptizer)
14: 3 bound and put into prison by Herod (Antipas) for Herodias's sake

Matt 14: 4 told Herod (Antipas) it was not lawful to have Herodias as his wife
14: 5 would have been put to death by Herod (Antipas), but was not, for Herod feared the multitude
14: 5 people counted him as a prophet
14: 8 his head was requested by Herodias's daughter
14:10 beheaded by Herod in prison
14:11 head brought in a charger and given to the damsel
14:11 his head brought to Herodias by her daughter
14:12 his disciples took his body and buried it
16:14 some claimed that Jesus was he (the baptist)
17:10 claimed by Jesus to be Elias who had already come (17:13)
17:13 the baptist
21:25 did baptize
21:26 the people held him as a prophet
21:32 went to the people with the way of righteousness and was not believed (by the chief priests and elders)
21:32 believed by the publicans and harlots
Mark 1: 4 baptized in the wilderness
1: 4 preached the baptism of repentance for the remission of sins
1: 5 baptized all the land of Judea, and they of Jerusalem in the Jordan river
1: 6 clothed with camel's hair and a girdle of skin around his loins
1: 6 ate locusts and wild honey
1: 7 preached that a mightier one than he would come after him, the latchet of whose shoes he was not worthy to stoop down and unloose
1: 8 baptized with water
1: 9 baptized Jesus in the Jordan river
1:14 was put in prison
2:18 had disciples (who fasted)
6:14 Herod believed that Jesus was he (John) risen from the dead and performing mighty works
6:16 Herod declared that Jesus was he (John) whom he (Herod) had beheaded, risen from the dead
6:17 had been taken by Herod and bound in prison for Herodias's sake
6:18 told Herod it was not lawful to have Herodias his brother's wife
6:19 Herodias had a quarrel against him and would have killed him, but could not
6:20 feared by Herod, observed by him, and heard by him gladly
6:20 a just man
6:20 holy
6:24 his head (in a charger) was asked by Herodias's daughter in response to her wish after dancing for the

79

JOHN *(continued)*

king (6:25)

Mark	6:27	beheaded in the prison on the command of king Herod
	6:28	his head (in a charger) was given to Herodias's daughter, who gave it to Herodias
	6:29	had disciples
	6:29	his disciples came and took up his corpse, and laid it in a tomb
	8:28	some said Jesus was he
	9:13	Jesus said that the coming of Elijah was accomplished (in the form of John the Baptist)
	11:30	did baptize
	11:32	all men counted him as a prophet
Luke	1:13	an angel informed his father of his impending birth
	1:13	was to be named John
	1:14	many would rejoice at his birth
	1:15	he would be great in the sight of the Lord
	1:15	he would drink neither wine nor strong drink
	1:15	he would be filled with the Holy Ghost even from his mother's womb
	1:16	he would turn many of the children of Israel to the Lord their God
	1:17	would go before Jesus in the spirit and power of Elias (Elijah)
	1:41	as a babe, leaped in the womb of his mother
	1:41	Elisabeth was his mother
	1:44	leaped in his mother's womb for joy
	1:57	was born
	1:59	circumcised the eighth day
	1:59	others originally named him Zacharias after his father
	1:60	mother named him John
	1:63	his father named him John
	1:66	the people wondered what manner of child he would be
	1:66	the hand of the Lord was with him
	1:67	Zacharias was his father
	1:76	his father prophesied that he would be called the prophet of the Highest
	1:76	he would go before the face of the Lord to prepare His ways
	1:80	grew and waxed strong in spirit
	1:80	resided in the desert till the day of his showing unto Israel
	3: 2	the Word of God came upon him in the wilderness
	3: 2	son of Zacharias
	3: 3	preached the baptism of repentance for the remission of sins in all the country about Jordan
	3: 7	called the multitude that came to be baptized by him a generation of vipers
	3:12	publicans came to be baptized by him, and called him Master
	3:15	people questioned in their hearts, the possibility of his being the Christ
Luke	3:16	baptized with water
	3:16	claimed himself to be greatly inferior to Jesus
	3:16	was not worthy to unloose the latchet of Jesus' shoes
	3:18	preached many things unto the people
	3:19	reproved Herod concerning Herodias and for all the evils which Herod had done
	3:20	shut up in prison by Herod
	3:21	baptized Jesus (in the Jordan)
	5:33	had disciples who often fasted and prayed
	7:18	had disciples
	7:19	called two of his disciples and sent them to Jesus to inquire if He were the One that should come, or should he look for another
	7:20	sent (two) disciples to Jesus with a query
	7:24	Jesus spoke of him to the people
	7:26	a prophet and much more than a prophet
	7:27	Jesus' messenger who would prepare the way before Him
	7:28	no person born of women was greater than John the Baptist
	7:28	the greatest prophet
	7:28	he that is least in the kingdom of God is greater than he (John)
	7:29	baptized many with his baptism
	7:30	Pharisees and lawyers were not baptized by him
	7:33	came neither eating bread nor drinking wine
	7:33	Pharisees and lawyers (7:30) claimed that he had a devil (demon)
	9: 7	some thought him risen from the dead
	9: 9	beheaded by Herod
	9:19	some say that Jesus was he
	11: 1	taught his disciples to pray
	20: 4	did baptize
	20: 5	was not believed by the chief priests, scribes, and elders
	20: 6	people were persuaded that he was a prophet
John	1: 6	a man sent from God
	1: 7	came as a witness to bear witness of the Light
	1: 8	was not that Light, but sent to bear witness of that Light
	1:15	bore witness of Him (Christ) who was before him (John)
	1:19	his record (1:27)
	1:20	confessed that he was not the Christ
	1:21	questioned if he were Elias or "that prophet" to which he answered "no"
	1:23	claimed to be the voice of one cry-

John
	ing in the wilderness
1:25	asked why he did baptize
1:26	did baptize with water
1:27	came before Christ but was preferred after Him
1:27	not worthy to unloose the latchet of Jesus' shoes
1:28	did baptize in Bethabara beyond Jordan
1:29	saw Jesus and said, "Behold the Lamb of God which taketh away the sin of the world"
1:30	came before Jesus who was preferred and was before him
1:31	knew not Him (Jesus)
1:31	came baptizing with water
1:32	bore record of the Spirit descending from Heaven like a dove, and abiding upon Him
1:33	knew Him not
1:33	was sent of Him to baptize with water
1:33	saw and bore record that the One upon whom the Spirit descended and remained was the Son of God (1:34)
1:35	stood with two of his disciples
1:36	looking upon Jesus said, "Behold the Lamb of God"
1:37	two of his disciples heard him speak and followed Jesus
1:40	one of his disciples was Andrew
3:23	was baptizing in Enon near to Salim
3:24	not yet cast into prison
3:25	had disciples
3:26	was with Jesus beyond the Jordan and bore witness of Him
3:26	was called "Rabbi"
3:28	had witnesses to his testimony that he was not the Christ, but was sent before Him
3:29	a friend of the Bridegroom whose joy was fulfilled (at the Bridegroom's voice)
3:30	he must decrease (as Christ increased)
4: 1	made and baptized disciples
5:33	bore witness unto the truth
5:35	a burning and shining light
5:36	Jesus had a greater witness than he
10:40	first baptized beyond Jordan
10:41	did no miracle
10:41	all things he spoke of the man (Jesus) were true

Acts
1: 5	baptized with water
1:22	baptized Jesus
10:37	had preached a baptism
11:16	indeed baptized with water
13:24	had preached the baptism of repentance to all the people of Israel
13:25	fulfilled his course
13:25	declared that he was not the Christ

Acts
18:25	had a baptism
19: 3	disciples in Ephesus had been baptized unto his baptism
19: 4	baptized with the baptism of repentance

2. Son of Zebedee (BOANERGES: the ELDER)
An apostle of Jesus Christ, one of the twelve; son of Zebedee; brother of James the apostle; probably his mother was Salome; a fisherman who left his nets to follow Jesus, present at the transfiguration of Jesus; known as "the disciple whom Jesus loved"; one of the inner three with James and Peter; and writer of the gospel of John, the epistles of John, and the prophetical book of the Revelation. (Identical with #5)

Matt
4:21	son of Zebedee
4:21	brother of James
4:21	was mending nets with Zebedee and James in a ship
4:21	was called by Jesus
4:22	left the ship and his father and followed Jesus
8:23*	followed Jesus into a ship
8:25*	came to and awoke Jesus and asked Him to save the disciples, for they perished
8:26*	fearful
8:26*	of little faith
8:27*	marveled at Jesus
9:10*	sat at meat with Jesus along with publicans and sinners
9:14*	fasted not
9:19*	followed Jesus
9:37*	instructed to pray that the Lord would send forth laborers into His harvest (9:38)
10: 1*	was called unto Jesus
10: 1	one of the twelve disciples
10: 1*	given power to cast out unclean spirits
10: 1*	given power to heal all manner of sickness and disease
10: 2	son of Zebedee
10: 2	one of the twelve disciples
10: 2	brother of James (the apostle)
10: 5	one of the twelve (apostles)
10: 5*	commanded to go neither to the Gentiles, nor into any city of the Samaritans
10: 6*	sent forth by Jesus to the lost sheep of the house of Israel
10: 7*	commanded by Jesus to preach "the kingdom of heaven is at hand"
10: 8*	commanded to heal the sick, cleanse the lepers, raise the dead, cast out devils (demons)
10: 8*	had freely received
10: 9*	was to provide neither gold, nor silver, nor brass, nor scrip, neither two coats, neither shoes, nor staves (for himself) (10:10)
10:11*	in every city or town, was to inquire

JOHN *(continued)*

who was worthy, and to abide with them

Matt 10:12* was to salute each house he entered

10:13* his peace was to come upon each worthy house, but return to him if unworthy

10:14* was to shake off the dust of his feet therein, when not received or heard by a house or city

10:16* sent forth (by Jesus) as a sheep in the midst of wolves

10:16* was to be wise as a serpent and harmless as a dove

10:17* would be delivered to the councils, scourged in synagogues, and brought before governors and kings for Jesus' sake (10:18)

10:19* was to take no thought concerning what he would speak when delivered up, for the Spirit of his Father would speak in him (10:20)

12: 1* was an hungered and plucked corn in the field and ate

12: 2* accused by the Pharisees of acting unlawfully on the Sabbath day

12:49* called mother and brethren by Jesus

13:10* questioned Jesus about His use of parables

13:11* was given unto him to know the mysteries of the kingdom of Heaven

13:16* saw and heard (spiritually)

13:17* had seen and heard (spiritually)

13:18* had the parable of the sower explained by Jesus (13:23)

13:36* had the parable of the wheat and tares explained by Jesus (13:43)

13:51* claimed to have understood all these things (parables)

14:15* came to Jesus and requested Him to send the multitude away

14:16* instructed by Jesus to feed the multitude

14:17* requested by Jesus to bring the five loaves and two fishes to Him (14:18)

14:19* given the blessed loaves by Jesus

14:19* distributed the loaves to the multitude

14:20* took up of the fragments that remained twelve baskets full

14:22* constrained by Jesus to get into a ship and to go before Him unto the other side (of Sea of Galilee)

14:24* his ship was tossed with waves

14:25* approached by Jesus (walking on the sea)

14:26* saw Jesus walking on the water (Sea of Galilee) and was afraid

14:27* told by Jesus to be of good cheer and not be afraid

14:33* being in the ship, worshiped Jesus, claiming Him to be the Son of God

Matt 14:34* came into the land of Gennesaret

15: 2* accused by the scribes and Pharisees of transgressing the tradition of the elders by not washing his hands when he ate bread

15:12* came to Jesus, informing Him that the Pharisees were offended at His saying

15:23* came and besought Jesus to send away her that cried after him

15:32* was called (unto Jesus)

15:34* had seven loaves and a few little fishes

15:36* given the loaves and fishes (by Jesus)

15:36* gave the loaves and fishes to the multitude

15:37* took up of the broken meat that was left seven baskets full

16: 5* was come to the other side and had forgotten to take bread

16: 6* told to beware of the leaven of the Pharisees and Sadducees

16: 7* reasoned with the other disciples over Jesus' words

16: 7* had taken no bread

16: 8* of little faith

16: 8 reasoned with the other disciples (concerning the lack of bread)

16: 9* took up baskets (of fragments)

16:10* took up baskets (of fragments)

16:11* did not understand Jesus' words concerning the leaven (doctrine) of the Pharisees and Sadducees

16:12* understood how that Jesus spoke not of bread, but of the doctrine of the Pharisees and Sadducees

16:13* was in Caesarea Philippi

16:13* answered Jesus' question concerning His identity (16:14)

16:15* questioned as to his view of Jesus' identity

16:20* charged by Jesus to tell no man that He was Jesus the Christ

16:21* shown by Jesus the sufferings He must undergo

17: 1 taken up by Jesus into a high mountain

17: 2 witnessed the transfiguration of Jesus

17: 3 saw Moses and Elias talking with Jesus

17: 4 was present (at transfiguration of Jesus)

17: 5 hearing the voice of the Lord out of a cloud, fell on his face and was sore afraid (17:6)

17: 7 touched by Jesus and told to arise and be not afraid

17: 8 lifted up his eyes and saw no man but Jesus

17: 9 coming down from the mountain, charged by Jesus to tell the vision to no man until He be risen from

JOHN (continued)

		the dead
Matt	17:13	understood that Jesus spoke of John the Baptist
	17:22*	abode in Galilee
	17:23*	was exceedingly sorry
	17:24*	came to Capernaum
	18: 1*	asked Jesus who is the greatest in the kingdom of Heaven
	19:13*	rebuked those who brought children to Jesus
	19:14*	rebuked, in turn, by Jesus
	19:25*	exceedingly amazed at Jesus' answer to the rich young ruler and asked who could be saved
	19:27*	had forsaken all and followed Jesus
	19:28*	had followed Jesus
	19:28*	promised by Jesus to sit upon the twelve thrones judging the twelve tribes of Israel
	20:17*	going up to Jerusalem, taken apart and foretold by Jesus of His betrayal, crucifixion, and resurrection (20:19)
	20:20	son of Zebedee
	20:21	his mother requested that he and his brother James might sit on Jesus' right and left hands in His kingdom
	20:22	was able to drink of Christ's cup and to be baptized with His baptism
	20:24	the other ten disciples were moved with indignation against him and his brother James
	20:29*	departed from Jericho (for Jerusalem)
	21: 1*	arrived in Bethphage and the Mount of Olives
	21:20*	saw the withered fig tree and marveled
	24: 1*	came to Jesus to show Him the buildings of the temple
	24: 2*	Jesus spoke to him of coming destruction of the temple
	24: 3*	asked Jesus of the sign of His coming and of the end of the world
	26: 8*	was indignant at the actions of the woman
	26:10*	had troubled the woman
	26:17*	asked Jesus where he should prepare for Him the Passover
	26:19*	did as Jesus had appointed and made ready the Passover
	26:20	celebrated the Passover with Jesus and the rest of the twelve
	26:22*	asked Jesus if he were the one to betray Him
	26:26*	while eating (the Passover) given the bread by Jesus
	26:27*	given the cup (by Jesus)
	26:30*	having sung a hymn, went out into the Mount of Olives
	26:31*	Jesus predicted that he would be

		offended because of Him
Matt	26:35*	claimed he would never deny Jesus, even though it meant death
	26:36*	came with Jesus to Gethsemane
	26:36*	instructed to sit and pray
	26:37	went with Jesus
	26:37	son of Zebedee
	26:38*	told by Jesus to tarry and watch with Him
	26:40*	fell asleep in the garden of Gethsemane
	26:43*	fell asleep again in the garden for his eyes were heavy
	26:45*	told to sleep on now and take his rest
	26:46*	told to arise and go (with Jesus)
	26:56*	forsook Jesus and fled
	27:56	his mother beheld the crucifixion of Jesus
	28:13*	would be accused of stealing Jesus' body by night
	28:16*	went into Galilee into the place (mountain) appointed
	28:17*	saw Jesus and worshiped Him
	28:19*	given the great commission(28:20)
	28:20*	Jesus would always be with him, even unto the end of the world
Mark	1:19	son of Zebedee
	1:19	brother of James
	1:19	seen by Jesus while in the ship mending the nets
	1:20	called by Jesus and followed Him
	1:20	left his father in the ship with the hired servants
	1:21	went into Capernaum with Jesus
	1:29	had been at the synagogue at Capernaum
	1:29	along with James and Jesus, entered the home of Simon (Peter) and Andrew
	1:31	ministered unto by Peter's wife's mother
	1:36	followed Jesus to His solitary place of prayer (1:37)
	2:15	sat at meat with Jesus, Levi (Matthew), and many publicans and sinners
	2:18	did not fast as the disciples of John (the Baptist) and Pharisees did
	2:23	plucked ears of corn in the corn fields on the Sabbath day
	3: 7	withdrew from the synagogue with Jesus to the sea
	3:14*	ordained by Jesus (to be with Him)
	3:14*	would be sent forth to preach (by Jesus)
	3:15*	would be given power, by Jesus, to heal sicknesses and to cast out devils (demons)
	3:17	son of Zebedee
	3:17	brother of James
	3:17	along with his brother, was surnamed Boanerges meaning the "sons of thunder" by Jesus

JOHN *(continued)*

Mark 3:17 a disciple of Jesus (one of the twelve)

3:20* could not eat bread with Jesus because of the multitude

4:10* asked Jesus about the parable of the sower

4:11* was given to know the mystery of the kingdom of God

4:33* had many parables taught him by Jesus

4:34* when alone, with the rest of the twelve, had all things expounded by Jesus

4:36* sent away the multitude

4:36* with the rest of the twelve, took Jesus to the other side of the sea

4:38* in fear, awakened Jesus in the midst of the storm

4:40* was fearful and had no faith

4:41* feared exceedingly

4:41* questioned among the other disciples as to what manner of man Jesus was that even the wind and the sea obey Him

5: 1* went with Jesus across the Sea of Galilee to the country of the Gadarenes

5:37 brother of James

5:37 was allowed by Jesus to enter into Jarius's house with Him

5:42 witnessed the raising of Jarius's daughter by Jesus

6: 1* followed Jesus into His own country

6: 7* sent forth two by two (by Jesus)

6: 7* given power over unclean spirits

6: 8* commanded to take nothing on his journey, except a staff, and to be shod with sandals and only one coat (6:9)

6:12* went out, and preached that men should repent

6:13* cast out many devils (demons) and anointed with oil many that were sick, and healed them

6:30* an apostle

6:30* gathered together unto Jesus to report what he had done and taught

6:31* had no leisure so much as to eat

6:32* departed privately with Jesus into a desert place by ship

6:36* asked Jesus to send away the multitude into the villages to buy themselves bread

6:37* told by Jesus to give food to the multitude

6:37* asked Jesus if he should go and buy bread to feed the people

6:38* when asked by Jesus the available provisions, reported five loaves and two fishes

6:39* made the people sit down by hundreds and by fifties (6:40)

Mark 6:41* given the food blessed by Jesus to distribute to the crowd

6:43* took up twelve baskets full of fragments and of the fishes

6:45* constrained by Jesus to get into the ship and go to the other side unto Bethsaida

6:47* was alone (with the other disciples) in the ship in the midst of the sea

6:48* toiled in rowing the ship for the winds were contrary

6:48* Jesus came unto him in about the fourth watch of the night walking upon the sea

6:49* saw Jesus walking upon the sea and cried out for he supposed it had been a spirit

6:50* saw Jesus and was troubled but admonished by Him to fear not

6:51* was amazed beyond measure and wondered that the wind ceased as Jesus entered the ship

6:52* because of his hardened heart, had forgotten about the miracle of the loaves

6:53* came into the land of Gennesaret

6:54* got out of the ship

7: 5* walked not according to the traditions of the elders (ate bread with unwashed hands)

8: 5* informed Jesus of the seven loaves

8: 6* set the loaves before the people

8: 7* receiving the blessed fishes from Jesus, set them before the people

8: 8* gathered seven baskets of fragments

8:10* entered into a ship with Jesus and went into Dalmanutha

8:13* entering into the ship again with Jesus, departed to the other side

8:14* had forgotten to take bread, and had only one loaf in the ship

8:16* had no bread

8:17* having seen the miracles, still did not understand as his heart was possibly yet hardened

8:19* took up twelve baskets full of fragments at the feeding of the five thousand

8:20* took up seven baskets full of fragments at the feeding of the four thousand

8:27* went into the towns of Caesarea Philippi with Jesus

8:27* responded to Jesus' question concerning His identity, with "John the Baptist, Elias, and one of the prophets" (8:28)

8:30* charged to tell no man that Jesus was the Christ

8:31* taught by Jesus of the things concerning Himself

9: 2 witnessed the transfiguration of Jesus (9:8)

84

Mark 9: 4   Elias (Elijah) and Moses appeared to him, Peter, and James at the transfiguration of Jesus

9: 6   was sore afraid

9: 7   overshadowed by a cloud and heard the voice of God

9: 9   forbidden to tell what he had seen until after the resurrection

9:10   questioned with Peter and James as to what the rising from the dead should mean

9:14*   questioned by the scribes

9:30*   passed through Galilee

9:32*   did not understand the words of Jesus, but was afraid to ask

9:33*   came to Capernaum

9:33*   disputed with the other disciples on the way to Capernaum as to whom should be the greatest (9:34)

9:38*   forbade a man from casting out devils (demons) in Jesus' name, because he did not follow him

10:13*   rebuked those who brought young children to Jesus that He should touch them

10:14*   rebuked, in turn, by Jesus

10:24*   astonished at the words of Jesus concerning those with riches

10:26*   astonished at Jesus' words

10:28*   had left all and followed Jesus

10:32*   went up to Jerusalem with Jesus and was amazed and afraid

10:35   son of Zebedee

10:35   brother of James

10:35   came unto Jesus and asked Him to grant his desire

10:37   asked that he and his brother James might sit one on His right and the other on His left hand in His glory

10:38   told by Jesus that he did not know what he was asking

10:38   would drink of the cup that Jesus did, and would be baptized with the baptism that He was baptized with (10:39)

10:41   the other ten disciples were much displeased with him and James

10:46*   went to Jericho

10:46*   went out of Jericho with Jesus

11: 1*   came nigh to Jerusalem, unto Bethphage and Bethany, at the Mount of Olives

11:11*   went to Bethany with Jesus and stayed until the morrow (11:12)

11:14*   heard Jesus curse the fig tree

11:15*   returned to Jerusalem with Jesus

11:19*   went out of Jerusalem (10:20)

11:20*   witnessed the fig tree dried up from the roots

11:27*   came again to Jerusalem

13: 3   sat upon the Mount of Olives

13: 3   asked Jesus privately concerning the sign when all things should be fulfilled (13:4)

Mark 13: 5   cautioned, by Jesus, to not be deceived

14:12   asked Jesus where he should go and prepare the Passover

14:13   sent by Jesus to prepare the Passover (14:15)

14:17*   in the evening of the first day of unleavened bread, went with Jesus to the upper room

14:18*   sat and ate together with Jesus

14:19*   began to be sorrowful over Jesus' statement of betrayal and to ask "Is it I?"

14:20*   dipped with Jesus in the dish

14:22*   ate the Passover with Jesus

14:23*   drank of the communion cup

14:26*   sung a hymn and went out to the Mount of Olives

14:31*   exclaimed that even if it meant death, he would not deny Him

14:32*   went to Gethsemane and was told to sit there while Jesus prayed

14:33   went apart with Jesus in the garden of Gethsemane

14:34   asked by Jesus to tarry and watch

14:37   found sleeping by Jesus

14:40   found sleeping again by Jesus (for his eyes were heavy)

14:40   did not know what to answer Jesus

14:41   told by Jesus to sleep on and take his rest

14:42   told to rise up and go

14:50*   forsook Jesus and fled

16:10*   mourned and wept

16:14*   Jesus appeared unto him as he sat at meat (with the other disciples)

16:14*   upbraided by Jesus for his unbelief and hardness of heart, because he believed not them which had seen Him after He was risen

16:15*   commissioned to go into all the world and preach the gospel to every creature

16:20*   went forth and preached everywhere, with signs following

Luke 4:39   ministered unto by Peter's wife's mother

5: 2   had a ship

5: 2   a fisherman

5: 2   was washing the nets

5: 7   went to Peter's aid to haul in his catch of fish, and filled the ship so that it began to sink

5: 9   was astonished at the draught of fishes that had been caught (5:10)

5:10   brother of James

5:10   son of Zebedee

5:10   with his brother James, was partner with Simon (Peter)

5:11   brought the ship to land

5:11   forsook all and followed Jesus

5:30*   murmured against by scribes and Pharisees

JOHN *(continued)*

Luke 5:30* ate and drank with publicans and sinners

5:33* ate and drank instead of fasting

6: 1* plucked ears of corn and ate (rubbing them in his hands) on the Sabbath

6: 2* claimed (by the Pharisees) to be doing that which was not lawful to do on the Sabbath days

6:13 chosen as one of the twelve

6:13* also called (named) an apostle

6:14 an apostle

6:17* came down from the mountain with Jesus and stood in the plain

8: 1* went throughout every city and village with Jesus

8: 9* questioned Jesus concerning a parable

8:10* unto him it was given to know the mysteries of the kingdom of God

8:22* went into a ship with Jesus and launched forth for the other side

8:23* the boat, filled with water, put him in jeopardy

8:24* called Jesus Master

8:24* came to Jesus and awakened Him during the storm

8:25* asked by Jesus concerning his faith

8:25* was afraid and wondered concerning Jesus' power over the elements

8:26* arrived at the country of the Gadarenes (Gadara)

8:51 suffered to go into Jairus's house with Jesus, along with Peter and James and the father and mother of the maiden

8:55 witnessed the raising of Jairus's daughter from the dead, by Jesus

9: 1* given power and authority over all devils (demons) and to cure diseases

9: 2* sent by Jesus to preach the kingdom of God and to heal the sick

9: 3* was to take neither staves, nor scrip, neither bread, neither money, neither have two coats

9: 4* was to abide in whatever house he entered

9: 6* went through the towns, preaching the gospel, and healing everywhere

9:10* returned and told Jesus all he had done

9:10* went privately with Jesus into a desert place belonging to the city called Bethsaida

9:12* requested that Jesus send away the multitude so that they might go into the towns and lodge and get victuals (food)

9:13* had only five loaves and two fishes, but was requested by Jesus to give food to the multitude

9:14* made the multitude sit down in companies by fifties (9:15)

Luke 9:16* gave the blessed loaves and fish unto the multitude

9:17* took up twelve baskets of fragments

9:18* was alone with Jesus (and the rest of the twelve)

9:18* in response with Jesus' question as to His identity, responded "John the Baptist, Elias and one of the prophets risen again" (9:19)

9:20* straitly charged and commanded to tell no man that He is the Christ (9:21)

9:28 went up into a mountain to pray with Jesus

9:32 was heavy with sleep and upon awaking saw Moses and Elias (Elijah) and the glory of Jesus

9:34 feared as he was overshadowed and entered into a cloud

9:36 told no man in those days, any of those things which he had seen at the transfiguration of Christ

9:37 came down from the mount of transfiguration the next day

9:45* feared to ask Jesus concerning His teaching

9:46* reasoned with the other disciples as to which of them should be greatest

9:49* forbade a man from casting out devils (demons) in Jesus' name because he followed not with the disciples

9:49 called Jesus Master

9:52 sent as (Jesus') messenger to Samaria, along with James

9:54 questioned the Lord if he should command fire to come down from heaven and consume a village of Samaritans

9:55 rebuked by Jesus

10:24* saw and heard what many prophets and kings had desired to experience

12: 1* warned by Jesus to beware of the leaven of the Pharisees

12: 4* friend of Jesus

17: 5* asked Jesus to increase his faith

18:15* rebuked those who brought infants to Jesus

18:16* rebuked, in turn, by Jesus

18:28* had left all and followed Jesus

18:31* taken unto Jesus and instructed of things to come (18:33)

18:34* understood none of these teachings of Jesus

19:29* with Jesus, came nigh to Bethphage and Bethany at the Mount of Olives

19:37* rejoiced and praised God with a loud voice (19:38)

22: 8 sent by Jesus along with Simon Peter to prepare the Passover

22:13 went into the city, found it as Jesus

Luke 22:14* said, and made ready the Passover
sat down with Jesus (in the upper room for the Passover)

22:14* was called an apostle

22:15* Jesus truly desired his presence in eating the Passover

22:19* partook of the first Lord's Supper (22:20)

22:23* inquired among the disciples as to which of them would betray Jesus

22:24* a strife existed among him and the other disciples as to which one should be accounted the greatest

22:28* had continued with Jesus in His temptations

22:29* was appointed a kingdom (that he might eat and drink at Jesus' table in His kingdom and sit on thrones judging the twelve tribes of Israel) (22:30)

22:35* had lacked nothing

22:36* told to prepare (for his new task)

22:39* followed Jesus to the Mount of Olives

22:40* told to pray that he enter not into temptation

22:45* found sleeping for sorrow (by Jesus)

22:46* told to rise and pray, lest he enter into temptation

22:49* perceiving the forthcoming events, asked Jesus if he should use his sword

24: 9* was told all things concerning the resurrection by Mary Magdalene, Joanna, Mary the mother of James, and the other women

24:10* an apostle

24:11* the words of the women seemed to him as idle tales and he believed them not

24:24 went to the sepulcher and found it even as the women had said, but saw not Jesus

24:33* being gathered together (with the other disciples), Cleopas found him and declared that the Lord was risen indeed and had appeared to Simon (24:34)

24:36* Jesus appeared unto him (after the resurrection) but he was terrified and affrighted, and supposed that he had seen a spirit (24:37)

24:38* asked by Jesus why he was troubled and why thoughts arose in his heart

24:40* was shown Jesus' hands and feet

24:41* believed not yet for joy, and wondered

24:42* gave Jesus a piece of a broiled fish and of a honeycomb

24:45* his understanding was opened by Jesus that he might understand the scriptures

Luke 24:46* was witness of these things (24:48)

24:49* told to tarry in Jerusalem until he was endued with power from on high

24:50* led by Jesus out as far as to Bethany and was blessed of Him

24:52* worshiped Jesus and returned to Jerusalem with great joy

24:53* was continually in the temple, praising and blessing God

John 2: 2* was called to the marriage in Cana of Galilee

2:11* believed on Jesus

2:12* went to Capernaum and continued there not many days

2:17* remembered that it was written of Him, "the zeal of thine house hath eaten me up"

2:22* after the resurrection, remembered Jesus' words and believed the scriptures, and the words which Jesus had said

3:22* came into the land of Judea with Jesus and tarried there with Him

4: 2* did baptize

4: 8* had gone away unto the city to buy meat

4:27* came unto Jesus and marveled that He talked with the Samaritan woman, yet did not question Him

4:31* called Jesus Master

4:31* implored Jesus to eat

4:33* questioned among the disciples if Jesus had been brought food to eat

4:35* told to look on the fields for they were white already to harvest

4:38* had been sent to reap where he had not sown, and had entered into others' labors

6: 3* went up into a mountain and sat with Jesus

6:10* instructed, by Jesus to have the multitude sit down

6:11* distributed the loaves and fishes to the multitude

6:13* gathered twelve baskets of fragments

6:16* went down to the sea, entered a ship, and went toward Capernaum (6:17)

6:19* after rowing twenty-five to thirty furlongs, saw Jesus walking on the sea and was afraid

6:20* told to not be afraid

6:21* willingly received Him into the ship

6:22* was entered into the only boat there

6:22* was apart from Jesus in the boat alone (with the other disciples)

6:67* asked by Jesus if he would also go away

6:69* believed and was sure that Jesus was the Christ, the Son of the living God

6:70* chosen as one of the twelve

John 9: 2* questioned Jesus concerning the man born blind

11: 8* called Jesus Master

11:11* friend of Lazarus

11:54* continued with Jesus at Ephraim

12:16* understood not, at first, the events of the triumphal entry of Jesus

12:16* after Jesus' glorification, remembered that these events had been written of Jesus and had been done unto Him

13: 5* feet washed by Jesus

13:12* had his feet washed by Jesus

13:13* called Jesus Master and Lord

13:14* had his feet washed by Jesus

13:14* told by Jesus that he ought to wash one another's feet

13:15* had been given an example that he should do as Jesus had done to him

13:18* was known and chosen of Jesus

13:21* when told that one of them would betray Jesus, looked on the others doubting of whom He spoke (13:22)

13:23 leaned upon Jesus' bosom

13:23 one of the disciples

13:23 loved of Jesus

13:24 beckoned by Simon Peter to ask Jesus who it was that should betray Him

13:25 was lying on Jesus' breast

13:25 asked Jesus who it was (that would betray Him)

13:28* knew not for what intent Jesus spoke these words to Judas Iscariot

13:34* was given a new commandment to love one another

13:34* loved of Jesus

13:35* love one to another was a mark that he was a true disciple of Jesus

14:25* was with Jesus

14:26* would be instructed by the Holy Spirit in all things

14:26* the words Jesus had spoken would be brought to his remembrance

14:27* Jesus' peace was given to him and left with him

14:31* was told to arise and go with Jesus

15: 3* was clean through the Word

15: 9* loved of Jesus

15:12* commanded to love one another

15:12* loved of Jesus

15:16* chosen of Jesus, and ordained of Him to go and bring forth fruit, and that his fruit should remain

15:17* commanded to love one another

15:19* not of the world

15:19* chosen out of the world by Jesus

15:19* hated of the world

15:27* would bear witness, because he had been with Jesus from the beginning

16: 4* was with Jesus

16: 6* sorrow had filled his heart

John 16:12* could not bear the words of Jesus

16:22* presently had sorrow

16:24* had asked nothing of the Father in Jesus' name

16:27* loved of the Father

16:27* loved Jesus, and believed that He came from God

16:29* could now understand plainly Jesus' words

16:30* was sure that Jesus knew all things

16:30* believed that Jesus came forth from God

18: 1* went with Jesus over the brook Cedron and entered into a garden (Gethsemane)

18: 2* often resorted there with Jesus

18:15 followed Jesus (to the trial)

18:15 a disciple

18:15 was known unto the high priest

18:15 went in with Jesus into the palace of the high priest

18:16 a disciple

18:16 was known of the high priest

18:16 went out and spoke unto her that kept the door and brought in Simon (Peter)

19:26 was seen by Jesus at the cross

19:26 the disciple whom Jesus loved

19:26 would now be the son of Jesus' mother

19:27 the disciple

19:27 told by Jesus to behold his mother (Mary)

19:27 from that hour took Jesus' mother unto his own house

20: 2 informed by Mary Magdalene that Jesus was taken out of the sepulcher

20: 3 went with (Simon) Peter to the sepulcher

20: 4 outran (Simon) Peter and came first to the sepulcher

20: 5 stooping down and looking in, saw the linen clothes lying, yet went not in

20: 8 after Peter, went also into the sepulcher, saw, and believed

20: 9 as yet knew not the scripture, that He must rise again from the dead

20:10 went away unto his own home

20:18* told by Mary Magdalene that she had seen the Lord and that He had spoken unto her

20:19* while assembled together (with the other disciples) with the doors shut for fear of the Jews, Jesus appeared in the midst

20:20* saw Jesus' hands and side and was glad

20:21* sent by Jesus and given His peace

20:22* breathed on by Jesus and received the Holy Ghost

20:25* told Thomas that he had seen the Lord

20:25* informed by Thomas that he would

JOHN (continued)

not believe without specific conditions being met

John 20:26* the doors being shut again, Jesus appeared the second time to him and the apostles

20:30* many other signs were done in his presence which are not written (in this book)

29:31 wrote the gospel of John that men might believe that Jesus is the Christ, the Son of God, and that believing they might have life through His name

21: 1 saw Jesus at the Sea of Tiberias (Sea of Galilee) while with a group of disciples

21: 2 a son of Zebedee

21: 3 entering a ship, went fishing and caught nothing

21: 4 knew (recognized) not Jesus

21: 5 had no meat (had caught nothing)

21: 6 obeying Jesus' command, cast the net on the right side of the ship

21: 6 was not able to draw the net for the multitude of fishes

21: 7 loved of Jesus

21: 7 recognized Jesus and informed (Simon) Peter

21: 8 being not far from land, came in a little ship, dragging the net with fishes

21: 9 coming to land, saw a fire of coals there, with fish and bread thereon

21:10 told by Jesus to bring of the fish which he had caught

21:12 told to come and dine

21:12 dared not ask who He was, knowing it was the Lord

21:13 given bread and fish by Jesus

21:14 third appearance of Jesus unto him (the disciples) after His resurrection

21:15 had dined with Jesus

21:20 loved of Jesus

21:20 followed Jesus and (Simon) Peter

21:20 had leaned on His breast at supper and asked Jesus who it was that should betray Him

21:23 because of Jesus' statement to Simon Peter (21:22), began the saying of him that he should not die

21:24 writer of the gospel of John

Acts 1: 2* had been given commandments by Jesus (through the Holy Ghost)

1: 2* chosen by Jesus

1: 3* was shown Jesus alive after His passion

1: 3* spoken to by Jesus of the things pertaining to the kingdom of God

1: 3* saw Jesus forty days

1: 4* commanded, by Jesus, not to depart from Jerusalem, but to wait for the promise of the Father

Acts 1: 5* would be baptized with the Holy Ghost

1: 6* questioned Jesus concerning the restoration of the kingdom to Israel

1: 7* was not to know the times or the seasons which the Father had put in His own power

1: 8* after receiving the Holy Spirit, would receive power and would be witness unto Jesus Christ throughout the earth

1: 9* beheld as Jesus was taken up into Heaven at His ascension

1:10* was joined by two men in white apparel while he looked steadfastly toward Heaven

1:11* a man of Galilee

1:11* was gazing up into Heaven

1:11* Jesus was taken up from him into Heaven

1:11* was told that Jesus would come in like manner as he had seen Him go into Heaven

1:12* returned to Jerusalem and went into an upper room (1:13)

1:14* continued in prayer and supplication with the women, Mary the mother of Jesus, and with His brethren

1:21* was with the Lord Jesus at various times

1:24* prayed concerning the ordination of one to be a witness of Jesus' resurrection

1:26* gave forth his lot (concerning Judas Iscariot's successor)

2: 1* present at the day of Pentecost

2: 2* while sitting in the house, cloven tongues like as of fire sat upon him, he was filled with the Holy Ghost, and spoke with other tongues (2:4)

2: 6* his speech confounded the multitude because every man heard in his own language

2: 7* a Galilean

2:13* mocked by some who claimed him as full of new wine

2:14* stood with (Simon) Peter

2:15* was not drunk

2:32* was a witness to the resurrection of Jesus

2:37* asked by the multitude on the day of Pentecost what they should do

2:42* many continued steadfastly in his doctrine and fellowship

2:43* many wonders and signs were done by him

3: 1 went into the temple with (Simon) Peter at the hour of prayer

3: 3 was asked an alms by the lame man at the gate of the temple

3: 4 fastened his eyes upon the lame man

3: 8 entered into the temple with

JOHN *(continued)*

(Simon) Peter and the formerly lame man

Acts 3:11 held by the formerly lame man in Solomon's porch

3:15 a witness of the resurrected (Jesus)

4: 1 priests, captain of the temple, and the Sadducees laid hands on him (and Peter) and put them in hold (prison) overnight for preaching through Jesus, the resurrection (4:3)

4: 7 set in the midst of the examining council and questioned concerning the healing of the lame man

4:13 had boldness

4:13 an unlearned and ignorant man who had been with Jesus

4:15 commanded to go aside out of the council

4:16 had performed a notable miracle

4:18 commanded not to speak at all or to teach in the name of Jesus (by the examining council)

4:20 could not but speak the things which he had seen and heard

4:21 being guiltless, was released

4:23 reported the words of the chief priests and elders to the believers

4:33* with great power gave witness of the resurrection of the Lord Jesus

4:33* great grace was upon him

4:35* the price of possessions sold by Christians was laid at his feet

4:35* distributed to every man (of the Christian community) as he had need

4:36* gave Joses a surname of Barnabas

4:37* Joses's money was laid at his feet

5: 2* the gift of Ananias and Sapphira was laid at his feet

5:12* by his hands were many signs and wonders wrought among the people

5:12* was with one accord with the others in Solomon's porch

5:13* no man durst join himself to him (the apostles)

5:13* was magnified of the people

5:16* healed the multitude of sicknesses and unclean spirits

5:18* placed in the common prison by the high priest and Sadducees

5:19* released from prison by the angel of the Lord and told to go, stand, and speak in the temple (5:20)

5:21* entered into the temple early in the morning and taught

5:22* was not found in the prison

5:25* was standing in the temple and teaching the people

5:26* brought without violence and set before the council (5:27)

5:27* questioned by the high priest (5:28)

Acts 5:28* had been commanded not to teach in this (Jesus') name

5:28* had filled Jerusalem with his doctrine and had (seemingly) intended to bring Jesus' blood upon his accusers

5:29* believed that he ought to obey God rather than men

5:32* witness of God (and of His works)

5:33* Jewish leaders took counsel to slay him

5:34* put a little space from the Sanhedrin (for their deliberation)

5:40* called back before the council, beaten, commanded not to speak in the name of Jesus, and let go

5:41* departed from the council rejoicing that he was counted worthy to suffer shame for His name

5:42* daily in the temple and in every house, ceased not to teach and preach Jesus Christ

6: 2* called the multitude together and stated it was not reasonable that he should leave the Word of God and serve tables

6: 3* instructed that seven men of honest report be chosen to be appointed to serve tables

6: 4* determined to give himself continually to prayer and to the ministry of the Word

6: 6* the chosen seven were set before him, for whom he prayed and laid his hands on them

8: 1* remained in Jerusalem in the midst of great persecution

8:14* was in Jerusalem

8:14 sent (along with Simon Peter) to Samaria by the other apostles

8:15 prayed for the Samaritans that they might receive the Holy Ghost

8:17 laid his hands on the Samaritans and they received the Holy Ghost

8:18 by the laying on of his hands the Holy Ghost was given

8:18 was offered money by Simon (the sorcerer) for the ability to impart the Holy Ghost (8:19)

8:25 testified and preached the word of the Lord and returned to Jerusalem

8:25 preached the gospel in many villages of Samaritans

9:27* Saul (Paul) was brought to him by Barnabas and he was informed of Saul's (Paul's) conversion experience and his bold preaching at Damascus

9:28* was accompanied by Saul (Paul) in coming in and going out at Jerusalem

10:39* was witness of all things Jesus did both in the land of the Jews and in Jerusalem

Acts 10:41* a witness, chosen before of God

10:41* ate and drank with Jesus after His resurrection

10:42* commanded of Jesus to preach unto the people, and testified that it was Jesus which was ordained of God to be the Judge of quick and dead

11: 1* was in Judea

11: 1* heard that the Gentiles had also received the Word of God

11:15* the Holy Ghost fell on him at the beginning (Pentecost)

12: 2 brother of James

12: 2 his brother James was killed with the sword by Herod

13:31* saw Jesus many days

13:31* came up with Jesus from Galilee to Jerusalem

13:31* was His (Jesus') witness unto the people

15: 2* Paul, Barnabas, and others were sent by the church at Antioch to consult with him over the matter of circumcision

15: 4* received Paul, Barnabas, and the others from Antioch

15: 6* came together (with the elders) to consider the matter (of circumcision)

15: 8* given the Holy Ghost

15: 9* God made no difference between him and a Gentile

15:10* was not able to bear the yoke

15:22* acting with the elders, sent chosen men back to Antioch with Paul and Barnabas

15:23* acting with the elders and brethren, wrote letters of instruction to the Gentiles at Antioch, Syria, and Cilicia

15:24* gave no commandment that Gentile believers must be circumcised and keep the law

15:25* considered it good, being assembled, to send chosen men unto the believers

15:25* loved Barnabas and Paul

15:27* sent Judas and Silas to the Gentile believers

15:33* Judas (Barsabas) and Silas returned unto him

16: 4* with the elders, ordained decrees

16: 4* was at Jerusalem

Rom 16: 7* Andronicus and Junia were well known to him

1Cor 4: 9* Paul thought God had set him (and the apostles) forth last, as it were appointed to death

4: 9* made a spectacle unto the world, to the angels, and to men

4:10* a fool for Christ's sake

4:10* weak, despised

4:11* hungered, thirsted, was naked, was buffeted, and had no certain dwelling place

1Cor 4:12* labored, working with his own hands

4:12* being reviled, he blessed; being persecuted, he suffered it; being defamed, he entreated (4:13)

4:13* made as the filth of the world, and the offscouring of all things

9: 5* had power to lead about a sister, a wife

15: 5* had seen the risen Lord

15: 7* the risen Lord was seen of him

15:11* preached

Gal 2: 9 perceived the grace given unto Paul, and with Cephas and James, gave to Paul and Barnabas the right hand of fellowship

2: 9 sent to the circumcision

2Pet 1:18 heard the voice of God the Father while with Jesus in the holy mount

1Joh 1: 1 had heard, seen, looked upon, and his hands had handled the Word of life (Jesus Christ)

1: 2 had seen, borne witness to, and shown others the eternal life which was with the Father

1: 2 the eternal life was manifested unto him

1: 3 had declared that which he had seen and heard unto others that they might have fellowship with himself and other believers

1: 3 his fellowship was with the Father and with His Son Jesus Christ

1: 4 wrote in order that others' joy might be full

1: 5 had both heard and then declared the message that God is light and in Him is no darkness at all

2: 8 wrote a new commandment to his readers

3:23 given commandment of the Lord to love one another

4:14 had seen and given testimony that the Father sent the Son to be the Saviour of the world

5:13 wrote this epistle to those that believe on the name of the Son of God that they might know that they have eternal life

2Joh : 1 author of the book of 2 John

: 1 the elder

: 1 loved the "elect lady"

: 2 the truth dwelled in him and would be with him forever

: 4 rejoiced greatly to find others walking in truth according to a commandment from the Father

: 5 besought the "elect lady" to walk after the commandment that we love one another

: 6 defined "love"

: 6 statement of the commandment

JOHN *(continued)*

2Joh : 7 gave definition of antichrist and deceiver

:12 desired to be present with and to speak face-to-face with the "elect lady" rather than writing with paper and ink

3Joh : 1 the elder

: 1 author of the epistle of 3 John

: 1 loved Gaius in the truth

: 3 rejoiced over Gaius who walked in the truth

: 4 rejoiced that his children (spiritual) walked in the truth

: 9 wrote to the church

: 9 rejected by Diotrephes

:10 Diotrephes prated against him with malicious words

:13 trusted to shortly see Gaius face to face rather than write with ink and pen (:14)

Rev 1: 1 received the revelation of Jesus Christ by angelic message

1: 1 a servant of God

1: 2 bore record of the Word of God, of the testimony of Jesus Christ, and of all things that he saw

1: 4 writer of the book of the Revelation

1: 4 addressed the seven churches of Asia

1: 9 a (Christian) brother and companion in tribulation

1: 9 was in the isle of Patmos

1:10 was in the Spirit on the Lord's day

1:10 heard a great voice as of a trumpet

1:11 told to write what he saw in a book and to send it to the seven churches in Asia

1:12 turned to see the voice that spoke with him

1:12 saw seven golden candlesticks (and one like unto the Son of man) (1:13)

1:17 seeing Jesus, fell dead at His feet

1:17 touched by Jesus' right hand

1:17 spoken to by Jesus

1:19 commanded to write the things he had seen, the things which are, and things which shall be hereafter

1:20 beheld the seven stars in the right hand of Jesus

1:20 saw the seven golden candlesticks

2: 1 commanded to write unto the angel of the church at Ephesus

2: 8 commanded to write unto the angel of the church at Smyrna

2:12 commanded to write unto the angel of the church in Pergamos

2:18 commanded to write unto the angel of the church in Thyatira

3: 1 commanded to write unto the angel of the church in Sardis

3: 7 commanded to write unto the angel of the church in Philadelphia

3:14 commanded to write unto the angel of the church of the Laodiceans

Rev 4: 1 beheld a door opened in Heaven

4: 1 heard a voice as of a trumpet talking with him

4: 2 was immediately in the spirit

4: 4 saw twenty-four elders seated around a throne in Heaven

5: 1 saw a seven-sealed book (in the right hand of God)

5: 2 saw a strong angel asking who was worthy to open the book and loose the seals thereof

5: 4 wept much because no one was worthy to open the book or look thereon

5: 5 told by one of the elders to weep not because Jesus was worthy to open the book and to loose the seven seals thereof

5: 6 beheld the Lamb of God

5:11 beheld and heard the voice of many angels round about the throne and the beasts and the elders

5:13 heard every creature blessing Him that sitteth upon the throne, and blessing the Lamb

6: 1 saw the Lamb open the first seal

6: 1 heard one of the four beasts saying "Come and see"

6: 2 saw and beheld a white horse and him that sat upon it

6: 3 heard the second beast say "Come and see"

6: 4 saw a red horse and his rider

6: 5 heard the third beast say "Come and see"

6: 5 saw a black horse and he that sat upon him

6: 6 heard a voice in the midst of the four beasts

6: 7 heard the voice of the fourth beast say "Come and see"

6: 8 saw a pale horse and his rider Death, followed by Hell

6: 9 saw under the altar the souls of martyred saints

6:12 saw the sixth seal opened and the accompanying phenomena (6:17)

7: 1 saw four angels standing on the four corners of the earth, holding the four winds

7: 2 saw another angel with the seal of God

7: 4 heard the number of them which were sealed (144,000)

7: 9 saw an innumerable multitude standing before the Lamb

7:13 questioned by an elder concerning those in white robes

7:14 answers the elder

7:14 informed that those in white robes were come out of great tribulation

8: 2 saw the seven angels which stood before God

JOHN (continued)

Rev 8:13 beheld and heard an angel flying through the midst of Heaven

9: 1 saw a star fall from Heaven unto the earth

9:13 heard a voice from the four horns of the golden altar commanding to loose the four angels which are bound in the great river Euphrates (9:14)

9:16 heard the number of the army of the horsemen

9:17 saw the horses in the vision, and them that sat on them

10: 1 saw another mighty angel come down from Heaven

10: 4 was about to write when he heard a voice from Heaven telling him to seal up those things which the seven thunders uttered

10: 5 saw the angel stand upon the sea and upon the earth

10: 8 heard again the voice from Heaven which spoke unto him, instructing him to go and take the little book

10: 9 went unto the angel requesting the little book

10: 9 was told by the angel to take and eat the (little) book

10:10 took the little book out of the angel's hand, and ate it up

10:10 in his mouth, the little book was sweet as honey

10:10 after eating the little book, his belly was bitter

10:11 told by the angel that he must prophesy again before many peoples, and nations, and tongues, and kings

11: 1 given a reed like unto a rod

11: 1 told to rise and measure the temple of God, the altar, and them that worshiped therein

11: 2 instructed to leave out and measure not the court which was without the temple

13: 1 stood upon the sand of the sea and saw a beast rise up out of the sea

13: 2 described the beast which he saw (rise up out of the sea)

13: 3 saw one of the beasts' heads as it were, wounded to death

13:11 beheld another beast coming up out of the earth

14: 1 looked and beheld a Lamb standing on Mount Zion and with Him an hundred forty and four thousand (persons)

14: 2 heard a voice from Heaven, as the voice of many waters and as the voice of a great thunder

14: 2 heard the voice of harpers harping with their harps

14: 6 saw another angel fly in the midst of Heaven, having the everlasting gospel

Rev 14:13 heard a voice from Heaven saying unto him "write"

14:14 looked and beheld a white cloud and upon it one like unto the Son of Man

15: 1 saw another great and marvelous sign in Heaven

15: 2 saw as it were a sea of glass mingled with fire, and the victors standing on it

15: 5 looked and beheld the temple of the tabernacle of the testimony in Heaven was opened

16: 1 heard a great voice out of the temple speaking to the seven angels

16: 5 heard the angel of the waters speak concerning God (16:6)

16: 7 heard another out of the altar speak concerning God

16:13 saw three unclean spirits like frogs come out of the mouths of the dragon, the beast, and the false prophet

17: 1 talked with one of the seven angels which had the seven vials

17: 1 was told to "come hither" and see the judgment of the great whore

17: 3 was carried away in the spirit into the wilderness

17: 3 saw a woman sit upon a scarlet colored beast

17: 6 saw the woman drunken with the blood of the saints and of the martyrs of Jesus and wondered with great admiration

17: 7 questioned by the angel as to why he marveled

17:15 had seen the waters where the whore sat, and had their meaning interpreted

17:16 had seen the ten horns upon the beast

18: 1 saw another angel come down from Heaven and lighten the earth with his glory

18: 4 heard another voice from Heaven speaking

19: 1 heard a great voice of much people in Heaven praising God

19: 6 heard as it were the voices of a great multitude, many waters, and mighty thunderings praising God

19: 9 told to write these true sayings of God

19:10 fell at his feet to worship him, but was rebuked and told to worship God

19:10 fellow servant (with the angel)

19:11 saw Heaven opened and beheld a white horse and Him that sat upon him

19:17 saw an angel standing in the sun

19:19 saw the beast, the kings of the

JOHN (continued)

earth, and their armies gathered together to make war against Him that sat on the horse and against His army

Rev 20: 1 saw an angel come down from Heaven having the key of the bottomless pit and a great chain in his hand

20: 4 saw thrones, and the souls of them that were beheaded

20:11 saw a great white throne and Him that sat on it

20:12 saw the dead, small and great, stand before God

21: 1 saw a new Heaven and a new earth

21: 2 identified himself as John (writer of the book of the Revelation)

21: 2 saw the holy city, new Jerusalem, coming down from God out of Heaven

21: 3 heard a great voice out of Heaven speaking

21: 5 told to write these true and faithful words (he had heard)

21: 6 spoken to by God

21: 9 spoken to by one of the seven angels and told to come and see the bride, the Lamb's wife

21:10 was carried away (by the angel) in the spirit to a great and high mountain and shown the great city, the holy Jerusalem

21:14* name inscribed in the twelve foundations of the new Jerusalem

21:14* an apostle of the Lamb

21:15 talked with one who had a golden reed to measure the city, the gates, and the walls

21:22 saw no temple (in the new Jerusalem)

22: 1 shown a pure river of water of life proceeding out of the throne of God and of the Lamb

22: 6 was told that these sayings are faithful and true

22: 8 identified himself as John (the writer of the book of Revelation)

22: 8 saw and heard these things (the sayings of the prophecy of this book)

22: 8 fell down to worship before the feet of the angel and was instructed not to do so, but to worship God (22:9)

22: 9 fellow servant (with the angel)

22:10 told to seal not the sayings of the prophecy of this book

3. A kinsman of the high priest and one of the council members who examined Peter and John.

Acts 4: 6 kindred of the high priest

4: 6 part of the committee at Jerusalem which examined (Simon) Peter and John (4:7)

Acts 4: 8 ruler of the people

4: 8 elder of Israel

4:15 conferred with the council concerning (Simon) Peter and John and could not deny the miracle (4:16)

4:18 as part of the council, commanded (Simon) Peter and John not to speak at all or teach in the name of Jesus

4:21 further threatening (Simon) Peter and John, let them go, finding nothing how to punish them

4. John MARK—see MARK

5. the elder—see JOHN (son of Zebedee - #2)

JONA [jo'-nah = dove]—see JONAS (father of Simon Peter)

JONAH [jo'-nan = dove]—see JONAS (the prophet)

JONAN [jo'-nah = gift or grace of God]
Son of Eliakim, father of Joseph, and ancestor of Jesus.

Luke 3:30 father of Joseph

3:30 son of Eliakim

JONAS [jo'-nas = dove]
1. An Old Testament prophet and identical with Old Testament Jonah, son of Amittai, sent to Nineveh, disobedient to God, fled to Tarshish, obeyed the Lord after three days and nights in the belly of the great fish, and preached in Ninevah where the Lord brought about national repentance. (See also Jona 1—4)

Matt 12:39 prophet

12:40 was three days and three nights in the whale's belly

12:41 men of Ninevah repented at his preaching

12:41 Jesus is greater than he

16: 4 the prophet

16: 4 his sign would be the only one the Pharisees and Sadducees would receive

Luke 11:29 his sign would be the only one given to the evil generation

11:29 the prophet

11:30 was himself a sign unto the Ninevites

11:32 the men of Ninevah repented at his preaching

11:32 one greater than he had come

2. Also Jona, and father of Simon Peter.

Matt 16:17 father of Simon Peter

John 1:42 father of Simon (Peter) and Andrew

21:15 father of Simon (Peter)

21:16 father of Simon (Peter)

21:17 father of Simon (Peter)

JORAM [jo'-ram = Jehovah is high or exalted]
Also Old Testament Jehoram, a wicked king of Judah, son of Josaphat, father of Ozias (Uzziah),

JORAM (*continued*)
husband of Athaliah (daughter of Ahab and Jezebel), and succeeded by Ahaziah (Jehoahaz) his son. (See also 1Kng 22; 2Kng 1,8,12; 2Chr 21—22)

Matt   1: 8   begotten of Josaphat
          1: 8   begat Ozias

JORIM [jo'-rim = whom Jehovah has exalted]
Son of Matthat; father of Eliezer; and an ancestor of Jesus.

Luke   3:29   father of Eliezer
        3:29   son of Matthat

JOSAPHAT [jos'-a-fat = Jehovah is judge]
Old Testament Jehoshaphat; son of Asa; a good king of Judah; and an ancestor of Jesus. (See also 1Kng 15,22; 2Kng 1,3,8,12; 2Chr 17—22)

Matt   1: 8   begotten of Asa
          1: 8   begat Joram

JOSE [jo'-ze = Jesus]
Son of Eliezer, father of Er, and an ancestor of Jesus.

Luke   3:28   father of Er (3:29)
        3:29   son of Eliezer

JOSEPH [jo'-zef = increaser; son of Saba]
1. The eleventh patriarch; son of Jacob; mother was Rachel; an interpreter of dreams; sold into slavery in Egypt by his elder brothers; became second only to the Pharaoh in Egypt; was instrumental in saving his family from famine in Israel. (See also Gen 30—50; Exod 1,13; Num 1,13,26,36; Deut 27,33; Josh 14—17,24)

Matt   1: 2   begotten of Jacob
John   4: 5   recipient of a parcel of ground in Sychar from Jacob
        4: 5   son of Jacob
        4:12   drank of the well (Jacob's)
        4:12   a child of Jacob
Acts   7: 8   one of the patriarchs
        7: 8   begotten by Jacob
        7: 9   one of the patriarchs
        7: 9   sold into Egypt (by his brothers)
        7: 9   God was with him and delivered him out of all his afflictions (7:10)
        7:10   given favor and wisdom in the sight of Pharaoh (by God)
        7:10   made governor over Egypt and all his house
        7:13   on their second visit, made himself known to his brethren
        7:13   his kindred was made known unto Pharaoh
        7:14   called his father Jacob and all his kindred to him
        7:14   his kindred equaled threescore and fifteen souls
        7:16   carried into Sychem and laid in the sepulcher that Abraham bought
        7:18   a new king (Pharaoh) arose who knew him not

Heb   11:21   sons blessed by Jacob
       11:22   by faith when he died, made mention of the departing of the children of Israel
       11:22   gave commandment concerning his bones

2. Of Arimathaea, a rich man, disciple of Jesus, begged the body of Jesus from Pontius Pilate, and buried Jesus' body in his own tomb.

Matt   27:57   of Arimathaea
       27:57   a rich man
       27:57   a disciple of Jesus
       27:58   went to Pilate and begged the body of Jesus
       27:59   wrapped Jesus' body in a clean linen cloth
       27:60   laid Jesus' body in his own new tomb hewn out of the rock
       27:60   rolled a great stone to the door of the sepulcher and departed
Mark 15:43   of Arimathaea
       15:43   an honorable counselor who waited for the kingdom of God
       15:43   went boldly unto Pilate and craved the body of Jesus
       15:45   given the body of Jesus by Pilate
       15:46   bought fine linen and wrapped Jesus, after taking Him down from the cross
       15:46   laid Him in a sepulcher (hewn out of a rock)
       15:46   rolled a stone unto the door of the sepulcher
Luke   23:50   a counselor
       23:50   a good man, and just
       23:51   had not consented to the counsel or their deed
       23:51   of Arimathaea
       23:51   waited for the kingdom of God
       23:52   went to Pilate and begged the body of Jesus
       23:53   took down the body of Jesus, wrapped it in linen, and laid it in a sepulcher
John   19:38   of Arimathaea
       19:38   a secret disciple of Jesus, for fear of the Jews
       19:38   besought Pilate that he might take away the body of Jesus, and was given leave
       19:38   came and took the body of Jesus
       19:40   along with Nicodemus, wound the body of Jesus in linen clothes with the spices
       19:41   laid Jesus in a new sepulcher, in a garden, wherein was never man yet laid (19:42)

3. Husband of Mary of whom was born Jesus; a carpenter by trade; a just man; and of the lineage of David.

Matt   1:16   begat by Jacob
        1:16   husband of Mary of whom was born Jesus

JOSEPH (continued)

Matt 1:18 espoused to Mary
1:19 husband of Mary
1:19 a just man
1:19 not wililng to make her (Mary) a public example, wanted to put her away privily
1:20 while thinking on these things, told by an angel of the Lord in a dream to fear not to take Mary to wife
1:20 son of David
1:24 being raised from sleep, obeyed the angel of the Lord and took Mary as his wife
1:25 knew not his wife until after the birth of Jesus
1:25 called His name JESUS
2:13 warned in a dream by an angel of the Lord to take Jesus and Mary and flee to Egypt, and to remain there until further word was given
2:14 arose and departed by night into Egypt with Jesus and Mary
2:15 remained in Egypt until the death of Herod
2:19 recalled (through a dream) to Israel from Egypt (2:20)
2:21 arose, took the young child and His mother, and came into Israel
2:22 heard that Archelaus did reign in Judea in the room of his father Herod (the Great)
2:22 feared to go to Judea
2:22 being warned of God in a dream, turned aside into parts of Galilee
2:23 came and dwelt in the city of Nazareth
13:55 known as a carpenter and thought, by some, to be the father of Jesus
13:55 possibly the father of James, Joses, Simon, and Judas

Luke 1:27 a man
1:27 espoused to Mary
1:27 was of the house of David
2: 4 lived in Nazareth of Galilee
2: 4 journeyed to Bethlehem of Judea to be taxed with Mary (2:5)
2: 4 was of the house and lineage of David
2: 5 Mary was his espoused wife
2: 7 could find no room in the inn
2:16 found by the shepherds
2:22 took Jesus to Jerusalem, to present Him to the Lord and to offer a sacrifice (2:24)
2:27 brought the child Jesus to the temple to do for Him after the custom of the law
2:33 marveled at those things spoken of Jesus
2:34 blessed by Simeon
2:39 returned to Nazareth of Galilee
2:41 went to the feast of the Passover every year in Jerusalem

Luke 2:42 went to Jerusalem for the feast of the Passover with Jesus when Jesus was twelve years old
2:43 as he returned from Jerusalem, knew not that Jesus had tarried behind
2:44 having gone a day's journey, sought Jesus among the kinsfolk and acquaintance
2:45 not finding Jesus, returned to Jerusalem seeking Him
2:46 after three days, found Jesus in the temple
2:48 was amazed at Jesus
2:48 had sought Jesus sorrowing
2:49 did not understand Jesus' explanation (2:50)
2:51 went back to Nazareth with Jesus
2:51 Jesus was subject unto him
3:23 supposedly the father of Jesus
3:23 son of Heli
4:22 the people questioned that Jesus was his Son

John 1:45 Jesus of Nazareth was his (supposed) son
6:42 the Jews believed him to be the father of Jesus
6:42 was known of the Jews

4. Son of Mattathias; father of Janna; and an ancestor of Jesus.

Luke 3:24 father of Janna
3:24 son of Mattathias (3:25)

5. Son of Juda; father of Semei; and an ancestor of Jesus.

Luke 3:26 father of Semei
3:26 son of Juda

6. Son of Jonan; father of Juda; and an ancestor of Jesus.

Luke 3:30 father of Juda
3:30 son of Jonan

7. Surnamed Justus; also named Barsabas; accompanied the apostles in their travels; appointed as possible successor to the apostleship in place of Judas Iscariot; and lost the lot of election to Matthias.

Acts 1:22 appointed as a possible successor to the position vacated by Judas Iscariot, as a witness to the resurrection of Christ (1:23)
1:23 called Barsabas
1:23 surnamed Justus

JOSES [jo'-zez = "exalted"]
1. Half-brother of Jesus. (Possibly identical with #2)

Matt 12:46 a (half) brother of Jesus
12:46 stood without, desiring to speak with Jesus
12:46 had brothers
12:47 had brothers
12:47 stood without, desiring to speak with Jesus
13:55 thought to be the brother of Jesus,

96

JOSES *(continued)*

James, Simon, and Judas

Matt 13:55 assumed to be the son of Mary and (Joseph) the carpenter
13:56 had sisters
Mark 3:31 a brother of Jesus
3:31 came with his brethren and his mother, stood without, and sent and called for Jesus
3:32 sought Jesus
6: 3 (half) brother of Jesus
6: 3 brother of James, Juda, and Simon
6: 3 son of Mary
6: 3 had sisters
Luke 8:19 came to Jesus (along with his mother and brethren)
8:19 could not come at Jesus for the press (crowd)
8:20 stood without, desiring to see Jesus
John 2:12 went to Capernaum with his mother and brethren and continued there not many days
7: 3 he and his brothers requested Jesus to depart and go into Judea, that His disciples also might see the works that He did
7: 5 did not believe in Jesus, nor did his brothers
7: 6 his time was always ready
7: 7 cannot be hated of the world
7:10 was gone up (to the feast)
Acts 1:14 was present in the upper room
1:14 continued with one accord, in prayer and supplication, with the apostles, the women, his mother, and his brethren
2: 1 present at the day of Pentecost
2: 2 while sitting in the house, cloven tongues like as of fire sat upon him; he was filled with the Holy Ghost and spoke with other tongues (2:4)
1Cor 9: 5 had power to lead about a sister, a wife

2. Son of Mary and brother of James. (Possibly identical with #1)
Matt 27:56 brother of James
27:56 son of Mary
Mark 15:40 son of Mary
15:40 brother of James ("the less")
15:47 son of Mary

3. Surnamed Barnabas (son of exhortation), a Levite from Cyprus, took part in the first missionary journey with Paul, and along with John Mark did missionary work in Cyprus.
Acts 4:36 surnamed Barnabas by the apostles
4:36 his name means son of consolation
4:36 a Levite from Cyprus
4:37 sold his land and brought the money and laid it at the apostles' feet

JOSIAS [jo-si'-as = he will be sustained of Jehovah]
Old Testament Josiah, son of Amon, a king of Judah, began to reign at eight years of age, a good king who discovered a copy of the Law in the temple. (See also 2Kng 21—23; 1Chr 3; 2Chr 33—36; Jer 1,3,22—26)
Matt 1:10 begotten of Amon
1:11 begat Jechonias and his brethren
1:11 was carried away to Babylon

JUDA [ju'-dah = praise]
1. The patriarch—see JUDAS
2. Half-brother of Jesus—see JUDAS
3. Son of Joanna, father of Joseph, and an ancestor of Jesus.
Luke 3:26 father of Joseph
3:26 son of Joanna (3:27)
4. Son of Joseph, father of Simeon, and an ancestor of Jesus.
Luke 3:30 father of Simeon
3:30 son of Joseph

JUDAS [ju'-das = praise]
1. ISCARIOT [is-car'-e-ot = man of kerioth (?)]
Surnamed Iscariot, son of Simon, an apostle of Jesus Christ, one of the twelve, betrayed Jesus for thirty pieces of silver, hanged himself, called the son of perdition.
Matt 8:23* followed Jesus into a ship
8:25* came to and awoke Jesus and asked Him to save the disciples, for they perished
8:26* fearful
8:26* of little faith
8:27* marveled at Jesus
9:10* sat at meat with Jesus, along with publicans and sinners
9:14* fasted not
9:19* followed Jesus
9:37* instructed to pray that the Lord would send forth laborers into His harvest (9:38)
10: 1* was called unto Jesus
10: 1 one of the twelve disciples (of Jesus)
10: 1* given power to cast out unclean spirits
10: 1* given power to heal all manner of sickness and disease
10: 2 one of the twelve apostles (10:4)
10: 4 one of the twelve apostles
10: 4 betrayed Jesus
10: 5 one of the twelve (apostles)
10: 5* commanded to go neither to the Gentiles, nor into any city of the Samaritans
10: 6* sent forth by Jesus to the lost sheep of the house of Israel
10: 7* commanded by Jesus to preach "the kingdom of heaven is at hand"
10: 8* commanded to heal the sick, cleanse the lepers, raise the dead, cast out devils (demons)
10: 8* had freely received
10: 9* was to provide neither gold, nor silver, nor brass, nor scrip, neither

two coats, neither shoes, nor staves (for himself) (10:10)

Matt 10:11* in every city or town, was to inquire who was worthy, and to abide with them

10:12* was to salute each house he entered

10:13* his peace was to come upon each worthy house, but return to him if unworthy

10:14* was to shake off the dust of his feet therein, when not received or heard by a house or city

10:16* sent forth (by Jesus) as a sheep in the midst of wolves

10:16* was to be wise as a serpent and harmless as a dove

12: 1* was an hungered and plucked corn in the field and ate

12: 2* accused by the Pharisees of acting unlawfully on the Sabbath day

12:49* called mother and brethren by Jesus

13:10* questioned Jesus about His use of parables

13:11* was given unto him to know the mysteries of the kingdom of Heaven

13:16* saw and heard (spiritually)

13:17* had seen and heard (spiritually)

13:18* had the parable of the sower explained by Jesus (13:23)

13:36* had the parable of the wheat and tares explained by Jesus (13:43)

13:51* claimed to have understood all these things (parables)

14:15* came to Jesus and requested Him to send the multitude away

14:16* instructed by Jesus to feed the multitude

14:17* requested by Jesus to bring the five loaves and two fishes to Him (14:18)

14:19* given the loaves blessed by Jesus

14:19* distributed the loaves to the multitude

14:20* took up of the fragments that remained twelve baskets full

14:22* constrained by Jesus to get into a ship and to go before Him unto the other side (of the Sea of Galilee)

14:24* his ship was tossed with waves

14:25* approached by Jesus (walking on the sea)

14:26* saw Jesus walking on the water (Sea of Galilee) and was afraid

14:27* told by Jesus to be of good cheer and not be afraid

14:33* being in the ship, worshiped Jesus, claiming Him to be the Son of God

14:34* came into the land of Gennesaret

15: 2* accused, by the scribes and Pharisees, of transgressing the tradition of the elders by not washing his hands when he ate bread

Matt 15:12* came to Jesus, informing Him that the Pharisees were offended at His saying

15:23* came and besought Jesus to send away her that cried after him

15:32* was called unto Jesus

15:34* had seven loaves and a few little fishes

15:36* given the loaves and fishes (by Jesus)

15:36* gave the loaves and fishes to the multitude

15:37* took up of the broken meat that was left seven baskets full

16: 5* was come to the other side and had forgotten to take bread

16: 6* told to beware of the leaven of the Pharisees and Sadducees

16: 7* reasoned with the other disciples over Jesus' words

16: 7* had taken no bread

16: 8* of little faith

16: 8* reasoned with the other disciples (concerning the lack of bread)

16: 9* took up baskets (of fragments)

16:10* took up baskets (of fragments)

16:11* did not understand Jesus' words concerning the leaven (doctrine) of the Pharisees and Sadducees

16:12* understood how that Jesus spoke not of bread, but of the doctrine of the Pharisees and Sadducees

16:13* was in Caesarea Philippi

16:13* answered Jesus' question concerning His identity (16:14)

16:15* questioned as to his view of Jesus' identity

16:20* charged by Jesus to tell no man that He was Jesus the Christ

16:21* shown by Jesus the sufferings He must undergo

17:15* could not cure the lunatic boy (17:16)

17:19* asked Jesus why he could not cast out the devil (demon)

17:20* could not cast out the devil (demon) because of unbelief

17:22* abode in Galilee

17:23* was exceedingly sorry

17:24* came to Capernaum

18: 1* asked Jesus who is the greatest in the kingdom of Heaven

19:13* rebuked those who brought children to Jesus

19:14* rebuked, in turn, by Jesus

19:25* exceedingly amazed at Jesus' answer to the rich young ruler and asked who could be saved

19:28* had followed Jesus

20:17* going up to Jerusalem, taken apart and foretold by Jesus of His betrayal, crucifixion, and resurrection (20:19)

20:24* was moved with indignation

JUDAS *(continued)*

toward James and John because of their request of Jesus

Matt 20:29* departed from Jericho (for Jerusalem)
21: 1* arrived in Bethphage and the Mount of Olives
21:20* saw the withered fig tree and marveled
24: 1* came to Jesus to show Him the buildings of the temple
24: 2* Jesus spoke to him of coming destruction of the temples
24: 3* asked Jesus of the sign of His coming and of the end of the world
26: 8* was indignant at the actions of the woman
26:10* had troubled the woman
26:14 one of the twelve (disciples)
26:14 covenanted with the chief priests for thirty pieces of silver for betrayal of Jesus (26:15)
26:16 sought opportunity to betray Jesus
26:17* asked Jesus where he should prepare for Him the Passover
26:19* did as Jesus had appointed and made ready the Passover
26:20 celebrated the Passover with Jesus and the rest of the twelve
26:24 a woe pronounced upon him as the betrayer
26:24 Jesus stated it would have been good if he had never been born
26:25 betrayed Jesus
26:25 Jesus confirmed that he was the one who would betray Him
26:46 was at hand to betray Jesus
26:47 one of the twelve (disciples)
26:47 came with a great multitude
26:48 betrayed Jesus
26:48 his betrayal sign would be a kiss
26:49 gave the kiss of betrayal to Jesus
26:50 called "friend" by Jesus
27: 3 had betrayed Jesus
27: 3 was condemned
27: 3 repented and returned the money to the chief priests and elders
27: 4 stated that he had sinned in betraying the innocent blood
27: 5 cast down the silver in the temple and went and hanged himself
Mark 3:14* ordained by Jesus (to be with Him)
3:14* would be sent forth to preach (by Jesus)
3:15* would be given power by Jesus to heal sicknesses and to cast out devils (demons)
3:19* a disciple of Jesus (one of the twelve)
3:19 betrayed Him (Jesus)
3:20* could not eat bread with Jesus because of the multitude
4:10* asked Jesus about the parable of the sower

Mark 4:11* was given to know the mystery of the kingdom of God
4:33* had many parables taught him by Jesus
4:34* when alone, with the rest of the twelve, had all things expounded by Jesus
4:36* sent away the multitude
4:36* with the twelve, took Jesus to the other side of the sea
4:38* in fear, awakened Jesus in the midst of the storm
4:40* was fearful and had no faith
4:41* feared exceedingly
4:41* questioned among the other disciples as to what manner of man Jesus was that even the wind and the sea obey Him
5: 1* went with Jesus across the Sea of Galilee to the country of the Gadarenes
6: 1* followed Jesus into His own country
6: 7* sent forth two by two (by Jesus)
6: 7* given power over unclean spirits
6: 8* commanded to take nothing on his journey except a staff, and to be shod with sandals and only one coat (6:9)
6:12* went out and preached that men should repent
6:13* cast out many devils (demons) and anointed with oil many that were sick, and healed them
6:30* apostle
6:30* gathered together unto Jesus to report what he had done and taught
6:31* had no leisure so much as to eat
6:32* departed privately with Jesus into a desert place by ship
6:36* asked Jesus to send away the multitude into the villages to buy themselves bread
6:37* told by Jesus to give food to the multitude
6:37* asked Jesus if he should go and buy bread to feed the people
6:38* when asked by Jesus the available provisions, reported five loaves and two fishes
6:39* made the people sit down by hundreds and by fifties (6:40)
6:41* given the food blessed by Jesus to distribute to the crowd
6:43* took up twelve baskets full of fragments and of the fishes
6:45* constrained by Jesus to get into the ship and go to the other side unto Bethsaida
6:47* was alone (with the other disciples) in the midst of the sea
6:48* toiled in rowing the ship for the winds were contrary
6:48* Jesus came unto him in about the

JUDAS *(continued)*

Matt

fourth watch of the night walking upon the sea
6:49* saw Jesus walking upon the sea and cried out for he supposed it had been a spirit
6:50* saw Jesus and was troubled but admonished by Him to fear not
6:51* was amazed beyond measure and wondered that the wind ceased as Jesus entered the ship
6:52* because of his hardened heart, had forgotten about the miracle of the loaves
6:53* came into the land of Gennesaret
6:54* got out of the ship
7: 5* walked not according to the traditions of the elders (ate bread with unwashed hands)
8: 5* informed Jesus of the seven loaves
8: 6* set the loaves before the people
8: 7* receiving the blessed fishes from Jesus, set them before the people
8: 8* gathered seven baskets of fragments
8:10* entered into a ship with Jesus and went into Dalmanutha
8:13* entering into the ship again with Jesus, departed to the other side
8:14* had forgotten to take bread, and had only one loaf in the ship
8:16* had no bread
8:17* having seen the miracles, still did not understand as his heart was possibly yet hardened
8:19* took up twelve baskets full of fragments at the feeding of the five thousand
8:20* took up seven baskets full of fragments at the feeding of the four thousand
8:27* went into the towns of Caesarea Philippi with Jesus
8:27* responded to Jesus' question concerning His identity with "John the Baptist, Elias, and one of the prophets" (8:28)
8:30* charged to tell no man that Jesus was the Christ
8:31* taught by Jesus of the things concerning Himself
9:14* questioned by the scribes
9:18* could not cast out a dumb spirit
9:30* passed through Galilee
9:32* did not understand the words of Jesus, but was afraid to ask
9:33* came to Capernaum
9:33* disputed with the other disciples on the way to Capernaum as to whom should be the greatest (9:34)
9:38* forbade a man from casting out devils (demons) in Jesus' name, because he did not follow him
10:13* rebuked those who brought young children to Jesus that He should touch them

Mark

10:14* rebuked, in turn, by Jesus
10:24* astonished at the words of Jesus concerning those with riches
10:26* astonished at Jesus' words
10:28* had left all and followed Jesus
10:32* went up to Jerusalem with Jesus and was amazed and afraid
10:41 was much displeased with James and John
10:46* went to Jericho
10:46* went out of Jericho with Jesus
11: 1* came nigh to Jerusalem, unto Bethphage and Bethany, at the Mount of Olives
11:11* went to Bethany with Jesus and stayed until the morrow (11:12)
11:14* heard Jesus curse the fig tree
11:15* returned to Jerusalem with Jesus
11:19* went out of Jerusalem (10:20)
11:20* witnessed the fig tree dried up from the roots
11:27* came again to Jerusalem
14: 4* indignant at the woman for the waste of the ointment
14:10 one of the twelve
14:10 went unto the chief priests to betray Jesus unto them
14:11 was promised money by the chief priests (for his betrayal of Jesus)
14:11 sought how he might conveniently betray Jesus
14:17* in the evening of the first day of unleavened bread, went with Jesus to the upper room
14:18* sat and ate together with Jesus
14:19* began to be sorrowful over Jesus' statement and to ask, "Is it I?"
14:20* dipped with Jesus in the dish
14:21 a woe pronounced upon him by Jesus that it were good if he had never been born
14:42 was at hand (to betray Jesus)
14:43 one of the twelve
14:43 came to betray Jesus (with a great multitude)
14:44 had given a token of a kiss, as the betrayal sign
14:45 went straightway to Jesus, called Him "Master, Master" and kissed Him

Luke

6: 1* plucked ears of corn and ate (rubbing them in his hands) on the Sabbath
6: 2* claimed (by the Pharisees) to be doing that which was not lawful to do on the Sabbath days
6:13 chosen as one of the twelve
6:13* also called (named) an apostle
6:16 an apostle
6:16 the traitor
6:17* came down from the mountain with Jesus and stood in the plain

JUDAS *(continued)*

Luke 8: 1* went throughout every city and village with Jesus

8: 9* questioned Jesus concerning a parable

8:10* unto him it was given to know the mysteries of the kingdom of God

8:22* went into a ship with Jesus and launched forth for the other side

8:23* the boat, filled with water, put him in jeopardy

8:24* called Jesus Master

8:24* came to Jesus and awakened Him during the storm

8:25* asked by Jesus, concerning his faith

8:25* was afraid and wondered concerning Jesus' power over the elements

8:26* arrived at the country of the Gadarenes (Gadara)

9: 1* given power and authority over all devils (demons) and to cure diseases

9: 2* sent by Jesus to preach the kingdom of God and to heal the sick

9: 3* was to take neither staves, nor scrip, neither bread, neither money, neither have two coats

9: 4* was to abide in whatever house he entered

9: 6* went through the towns, preaching the gospel and healing everywhere

9:10* returned and told Jesus all he had done

9:10* went privately with Jesus into a desert place belonging to the city called Bethsaida

9:12* requested that Jesus send away the multitude, so that they might go into the towns and lodge and get victuals (food)

9:13* had only five loaves and two fishes, but was requested by Jesus to give food to the multitude

9:14* made the multitude sit down in companies by fifties (9:15)

9:16* gave the blessed loaves and fish unto the multitude

9:17* took up twelve baskets of fragments

9:18* was alone with Jesus (and the rest of the twelve)

9:18* in response to Jesus' question as to His identity, responded, "John the Baptist, Elias, and one of the prophets risen again" (9:19)

9:20* straitly charged and commanded to tell no man that He is the Christ (9:21)

9:40* could not cast the spirit (demon) out of a boy

9:45* feared to ask Jesus concerning His teaching

9:46* reasoned with the other disciples as to which of them should be greatest

Luke 9:49* forbade a man from casting out devils (demons) in Jesus' name because he followed not with the disciples

10:24* saw and heard what many prophets and kings had desired to experience

12: 1* warned by Jesus to beware of the leaven of the Pharisees

12: 4* friend of Jesus

17: 5* asked Jesus to increase his faith

18:15* rebuked those who brought infants to Jesus

18:16* rebuked, in turn, by Jesus

18:28* had left all and followed Jesus

18:31* taken unto Jesus and instructed of things to come (18:33)

18:34* understood none of these teachings of Jesus

19:29* with Jesus, came nigh to Bethphage and Bethany at the Mount of Olives

19:37* rejoiced and praised God with a loud voice (19:38)

22: 3 Satan entered into him

22: 3 surnamed Iscariot

22: 3 of the number of the twelve

22: 4 went his way, communed with the chief priests and captains, how he might betray Jesus unto them

22: 5 covenanted (with the chief priests and captains) for money

22: 6 promised and sought opportunity to betray Jesus in the absence of the multitude

22:14 * sat down with Jesus (in the upper room for the Passover)

22:14* was called an apostle

22:15* Jesus truly desired his presence in eating the Passover

22:21 his hand was on the table with Jesus at the feast of Passover

22:22 a woe pronounced upon him by Jesus for the betrayal

22:23* inquired among the disciples as to which of them would betray Jesus

22:24* a strife existed among him and the other disciples as to which one should be accounted the greatest

22:28* had continued with Jesus in His temptations

22:35* had lacked nothing

22:47 was called Judas

22:47 led a multitude to Jesus (for the betrayal)

22:47 one of the twelve

22:47 drew near unto Jesus to kiss Him

22:48 betrayed the Son of man with a kiss

John 2: 2* was called to the marriage in Cana of Galilee

2:11* believed on Jesus

2:12* went to Capernaum and continued there not many days

2:17* remembered that it was written of Him, "the zeal of thine house hath

JUDAS *(continued)*

eaten me up"

John	3:22*	came into the land of Judea with Jesus and tarried there with Him
	4: 2*	did baptize
	4: 8*	had gone away unto the city to buy meat
	4:27*	came unto Jesus and marveled that He talked with the Samaritan woman yet did not question Him
	4:31*	called Jesus Master
	4:31*	implored Jesus to eat
	4:33*	questioned among the other disciples if Jesus had been brought food to eat
	4:35*	told to look on the fields for they were white already to harvest
	4:38*	had been sent to reap where he had not labored, and had entered into others' labors
	6: 3*	went up into a mountain and sat with Jesus
	6:10*	instructed by Jesus, to have the multitude sit down
	6:11*	distributed the loaves and fishes to the multitude
	6:13*	gathered twelve baskets of fragments
	6:16*	went down to the sea, entered a ship and went toward Capernaum (6:17)
	6:19*	after rowing twenty-five to thirty furlongs, saw Jesus walking on the sea and was afraid
	6:20*	told to not be afraid
	6:21*	willingly received Him into the ship
	6:22*	was entered into the only boat there
	6:22*	was apart from Jesus in the boat alone (with the other disciples)
	6:64	was known of Jesus from the beginning that he would betray Him
	6:67*	asked, by Jesus, if he would also go away
	6:69*	believed and was sure that Jesus was the Christ, the Son of the living God
	6:70*	chosen as one of the twelve
	6:70	called a "devil" by Jesus (6:71)
	6:71	son of Simon
	6:71	would betray Jesus
	6:71	one of the twelve
	9: 2*	questioned Jesus concerning the man born blind
	11: 8*	called Jesus Master
	11:11*	friend of Lazarus
	11:54*	continued with Jesus at Ephraim
	12: 4	one of the disciples
	12: 4	son of Simon
	12: 4	would betray Jesus
	12: 5	questioned why the ointment was not sold for three hundred pence and given to the poor
	12: 6	cared not for the poor
	12: 6	was a thief

John	12: 6	had the bag, and bare what was put therein
	12:16*	understood not, at first, the events of the triumphal entry of Jesus
	13: 2	the devil put into his heart to betray Jesus
	13: 2	Simon's son
	13: 5*	feet washed by Jesus
	13:10	claimed by Jesus to not be clean (spiritually)
	13:11	was known by Jesus as the one who should betray Him
	13:11	Jesus claimed he was not clean (spiritually)
	13:12*	had his feet washed by Jesus
	13:13*	called Jesus Master and Lord
	13:14*	told, by Jesus, that he ought to wash one another's feet
	13:14*	had his feet washed by Jesus
	13:15*	had been given an example that he should do as Jesus had done to him
	13:18*	was known and chosen of Jesus
	13:18	ate bread with Jesus, yet lifted up his heel against Him
	13:21*	when told that one of them would betray Jesus, looked on the others doubting of whom He spoke (13:22)
	13:21	would betray Jesus
	13:26	given the sop by Jesus after He had dipped it
	13:26	son of Simon
	13:27	after taking the sop, Satan entered into him
	13:27	Jesus told him that what he should do, do quickly
	13:29	had the bag
	13:29	some thought Jesus had told him to buy things needed for the feast, or to give something to the poor
	13:30	having received the sop, went immediately out
	13:31	was gone out (from the upper room)
	17:12	the son of perdition
	17:12	was lost (that the scripture might be fulfilled)
	18: 2	betrayed Jesus
	18: 2	knew the place (the garden of Gethsemane)
	18: 2*	often resorted there with Jesus
	18: 3	having received a band of men and officers from the chief priests and Pharisees, came with lanterns and torches and weapons
	18: 5	betrayed Jesus
	18: 5	stood with the crowd (at the betrayal)
Acts	1:16	was guide to them that took Jesus
	1:17	had been numbered with the disciples and had obtained part of the ministry
	1:18	purchased a field with the reward of iniquity

JUDAS *(continued)*

Acts	1:18	fell headlong to his death, burst asunder, and all his bowels gushed out
	1:19	his death was known to all the dwellers at Jerusalem
	1:20	had been written about in the book of Psalms
	1:20	his bishopric another would take
	1:25	fell, by transgression, that he might go to his own place
2The	2: 3	the son of perdition

2. Half-brother of Jesus, called Juda, and possibly identical with Thaddaeus (Lebbaeus) and Jude.

Matt	12:46	a (half) brother of Jesus
	12:46	stood without, desiring to speak with Jesus
	12:46	had brothers
	12:47	had brothers
	12:47	stood without, desiring to speak with Jesus
	13:55	(thought to be) the brother of Jesus, James, Joses, and Simon
	13:55	assumed to be the son of Joseph and Mary
	13:56	had sisters
Mark	3:31	a (half) brother of Jesus
	3:31	came with his brethren and his mother, stood without, and sent and called for Jesus
	3:32	sought Jesus with his mother and brethren
	6: 3	(half) brother of Jesus
	6: 3	brother of James, Joses, and Simon
	6: 3	son of Mary
	6: 3	had sisters
Luke	8:19	came to Jesus (along with his mother and his brethren)
	8:19	could not come at Jesus for the press (crowd)
	8:20	stood without with his mother and brethren, desiring to see Jesus
John	2:12	went to Capernaum with his mother and brethren and continued there not many days
	7: 3	he and his brethren requested Jesus to depart and go into Judea, that His disciples also might see the works that He did
	7: 5	did not believe in Jesus
	7: 6	his time was always ready
	7: 7	cannot be hated of the world
	7:10	was gone up (to the feast) with his brothers
Acts	1:14	was present in the upper room
	1:14	continued with one accord, in prayer and supplication, with the apostles, the women, his mother, and his brethren
	2: 1	present at the day of Pentecost
	2: 2	while sitting in the house, cloven tongues like as of fire, sat upon him, he was filled with the Holy Ghost and spoke with other tongues (2:4)
1Cor	9: 5	had power to lead about a sister, a wife

3. A Galilean who stirred up rebellion and revolt at the time of the Roman taxation, and immediately prior to the birth of Christ.

Acts	5:37	of Galilee
	5:37	drew away much people after him
	5:37	perished

4. A man of Damascus, who lodged Paul in his house.

Acts	9:11	lived in a house on the street called Straight (in Damascus)
	9:11	Saul (Paul) was in his house
	9:17	Ananias entered his house to minister to Saul (Paul)

5. Also Barsabas, a prophet sent, along with Paul and Barnabas, to Antioch with letters from the apostles to the Gentile brethren in Antioch, Syria, and Cilicia concerning the rite of circumcision.

Acts	15:22	sent (along with Silas) to Antioch with Paul and Barnabas
	15:22	a chosen man of the company (of the Jerusalem church)
	15:22	surnamed Barsabas
	15:22	a chief man among the brethren
	15:23	bearer of letters from the apostles to the Gentile brethren in Antioch, Syria, and Cilicia
	15:25	a chosen man, sent with Barnabas and Paul
	15:27	sent by the Jerusalem council to confirm by mouth the message of the letter
	15:30	dismissed, came to Antioch, gathered the multitude together; and delivered the epistle
	15:32	a prophet
	15:32	exhorted the brethren with many words and confirmed them
	15:33	tarried a space, and then returned in peace unto the apostles

6. an apostle—see THADDAEUS

7. Also Juda (Old Testament Judah), one of the patriarchs, and fourth son of Jacob by Leah. (See also Gen 29, 35—38, 43—49)

Matt	1: 2	begotten of Jacob
	1: 2	had brothers
	1: 3	begat Phares and Zara of Thamar
Luke	3:33	father of Phares
	3:33	son of Jacob (3:34)
John	4:12	drank of the well (Jacob's)
	4:12	a child of Jacob
Acts	7: 8	begotten of Jacob
	7: 8	one of the patriarchs
	7: 9	one of the patriarchs
	7: 9	moved with envy, sold Joseph into Egypt
	7:11	father of Israel
	7:11	found no sustenance
	7:12	sent by Jacob to Egypt for corn
	7:13	on his second visit (to Egypt), Joseph was made known to him
	7:13	was made known unto Pharaoh

JUDAS *(continued)*

Acts 7:15 went down into Egypt and died
      7:16 was carried into Sychem and was laid in the sepulcher that Abraham bought
Heb 7:14 the Lord (Christ) sprang from him (through his tribe)
      7:14 Moses spoke nothing concerning a priesthood of his tribe
Rev 5: 5 the Lion of his tribe was Jesus
      7: 5 twelve thousand sealed of his tribe
    21:12 his name is inscribed upon the gates of the new Jerusalem
    21:12 a child of Israel (Jacob)

JUDE [jood = he shall be praised]
Half-brother of Jesus, brother of James, and author of the New Testament book of Jude. (Possibly identical with Thaddaeus, Lebbaeus, Judas)

Jude : 1 the servant of Jesus Christ
     : 1 brother of James
     : 3 wrote the book of Jude to Christians exhorting them to earnestly contend for the faith

JULIA ♀ [ju'-le-ah = soft-haired]
A female believer of Rome, saluted or greeted by Paul, and possibly a relative of Philologus.

Rom 16:15 saluted by Paul
    16:15 was with the saints

JULIUS [ju'-le-us = soft-haired]
A Roman centurion in whose responsibility Paul and other prisoners were placed while on the journey to Rome.

Acts 27: 1 Paul (and the other prisoners) were delivered unto him (to sail to Italy)
    27: 1 a centurion of Augustus's band
    27: 2 entered into a ship of Adramyttium and launched, meaning to sail by the coasts of Asia
    27: 3 the next day touched at Sidon
    27: 3 courteously entreated Paul and gave him liberty to go unto his friends to refresh himself
    27: 4 launched from Sidon and sailed under Cyprus, because the winds were contrary
    27: 5 sailed over the sea of Cilicia and Pamphylia, and came to Myra
    27: 6 the centurion
    27: 6 found a ship of Alexandria sailing into Italy, and put Paul and Aristarchus (and Luke) therein
    27: 7 sailed under Crete, over against Salmone, and came to the Fair Havens near the city of Lasea (27:8)
    27:11 the centurion
    27:11 believed the master and the owner of the ship more than Paul
    27:13 sailed close by Crete
    27:16 ran under the island of Clauda
    27:16 had much work to come by the boat

Acts 27:18 was exceedingly tossed with a tempest
    27:19 cast out the tackling of the ship
    27:20 saw neither sun nor stars in many days and all hope that he should be saved was taken away
    27:21 had loosed from Crete
    27:22 exhorted by Paul to be of good cheer
    27:23 his safety assured to Paul by the Lord in a dream (27:24)
    27:27 had been driven up and down in Adria fourteen nights
    27:31 instructed by Paul to abide in the ship
    27:33 besought by Paul to take meat
    27:33 had tarried and continued fasting fourteen days
    27:34 prayed by Paul to take some meat (for his health)
    27:34 not one hair would fall from his head
    27:36 was of good cheer, and took some meat
    27:37 one of 276 passengers in the ship
    27:43 willing to save Paul alive, kept the soldiers from their purpose (killing the prisoners)
    27:43 commanded that they which could swim should cast themselves first into the sea and get to land and the rest to find boards or broken pieces of the ship (27:44)
    28: 1 had escaped to the island of Melita
    28: 2 was shown no little kindness (by the people of Melita)
    28: 2 was received because of the present rain and the cold
    28:11 after three months departed in a ship of Alexandria
    28:12 landed at Syracuse and tarried three days
    28:13 sailed on to Rhegium and then to Puteoli
    28:14 went toward Rome
    28:15 went to Appii forum and The three taverns
    28:16 came to Rome and delivered the prisoners to the captain of the guard
    28:16 the centurion

JUNIA [ju'-ne-ah = continue thou Jehovah]
Probably should be "Junias," a kinsman of Paul (meaning he was a Jew), fellow prisoner of Paul and Andronicus, well-known among the apostles, and a believer prior to Paul's conversion.

Rom 16: 7 saluted by Paul
    16: 7 kinsman of Paul
    16: 7 fellow prisoner of Paul and Andronicus
    16: 7 of note (well known) among the apostles
    16: 7 was in Christ (saved) before Paul

JUSTUS [jus'-tus = just]
1. A man of Corinth with whom Paul lodged.

Acts   18: 7   Paul entered his house (which was
                 joined hard to the synagogue at
                 Corinth)
        18: 7   one who worshiped God
2. Jesus—see JESUS (Justus)
3. Joseph Barsabas—see JOSEPH (surnamed
JUSTUS BARSABAS)

L

LAMECH [la'-mek = overthrower; wild man]
Son of Methuselah, father of Noah, and an ancestor of Jesus. (See also Gen 5; 1Chr 1)

Luke   3:36   father of Noe (Noah)
        3:37   son of Mathusala

LAZARUS [laz'-a-rus = God has helped]
1. A beggar who laid at the gate of a rich man.
His death and subsequent events portray the difference between the eternal state of the saved and
the wicked.

Luke   16:20   a beggar
        16:20   laid at the gate of the rich man full
                 of sores
        16:21   desired to be fed with the crumbs
                 which fell from the rich man's table
        16:21   the dogs licked his sores
        16:22   died
        16:22   was carried by the angels into
                 Abraham's bosom
        16:23   seen by the rich man (in hell) in
                 Abraham's bosom
        16:24   help desired of him by the rich man
        16:25   during his lifetime received evil
                 things, but in death was now com-
                 forted
        16:27   asked by the rich man to be sent
                 to his father's house to testify unto
                 them (16:28)
2. A man of Bethany, brother of Mary and Martha,
friend of Jesus and greatly beloved of Him, raised
to life again by Jesus after having lain in the tomb
four days, and an instrument of the Lord by reason
of his resurrection through which many Jews believed on Jesus.

John   11: 1   a sick man
        11: 1   of Bethany
        11: 1   brother of Mary and Martha (11:2)
        11: 2   was sick
        11: 3   had sisters
        11: 3   loved by Jesus
        11: 3   was sick
        11: 4   his sickness was not unto death but
                 for the glory of God
        11: 5   loved by Jesus
        11: 6   was sick

John   11:11   slept (was dead) (11:13)
        11:11   friend of Jesus and the twelve
        11:14   was dead
        11:17   had lain four days in the grave
                 when Jesus arrived
        11:19   his sisters were comforted by many
                 Jews concerning him
        11:23   would rise again
        11:24   would rise again in the resurrection
                 at the last day
        11:34   Jesus inquired where he was laid
        11:36   greatly loved by Jesus
        11:38   his grave was a cave with a stone
                 upon it
        11:39   was dead
        11:39   his sister said that he would stink
                 being dead four days
        11:41   was dead (the stone was taken
                 away from the grave)
        11:43   commanded to come forth (from
                 the grave by Jesus)
        11:44   was dead
        11:44   came forth (from the dead) bound
                 hand and foot with grave clothes
                 and his face bound about with a
                 napkin
        11:44   was to be loosed and let go
        12: 1   was in Bethany
        12: 1   had been dead
        12: 1   had been raised from the dead (by
                 Jesus)
        12: 2   made Jesus a supper
        12: 2   sat at the table with Jesus
        12: 9   many of the Jews came to see him
                 who had been raised from the dead
        12:10   chief priests consulted to also put
                 him to death
        12:11   by reason of him, many of the Jews
                 went away and believed on Jesus
        12:17   called out of his grave and raised
                 from the dead (by Jesus)

LEBBAEUS [leb-be'-us = a man of heart]—see
THADDAEUS

LEVI [le'-vi = joined]
1. One of the patriarchs, the third son of Jacob
by Leah, descendants (called Levites) of whom
served in the ministry of the tabernacle and the
priesthood. (See also Gen 29,34,49; Exod 1,6;
Num 3,26)

Matt   1: 2   begotten by Jacob
John   4:12   drank of the well (Jacob's)
        4:12   a child of Jacob
Acts   7: 8   begat by Jacob
        7: 8   one of the patriarchs
        7: 9   one of the patriarchs
        7: 9   moved with envy, sold Joseph into
                 Egypt
        7:11   found no sustenance
        7:12   sent by Jacob to Egypt for corn
        7:13   on his second visit (to Egypt),
                 Joseph was made known to him
        7:13   was made known unto Pharaoh

LEVI *(continued)*

Acts   7:15   went down into Egypt and died
        7:16   was carried into Sychem and was laid in the sepulcher that Abraham bought
Heb   7: 5   had sons (who received the office of the priesthood)
        7: 9   received tithes
        7: 9   payed tithes in Abraham
        7:10   met by Melchisedec while still in the loins of his father (Abraham)
Rev   7: 7   twelve thousand sealed of his tribe
      21:12   his name is inscribed upon the gates of the new Jerusalem
      21:12   a child of Israel (Jacob)
2. Son of Melchi, father of Matthat, and an ancestor of Jesus.

Luke   3:24   father of Matthat
      3:24   son of Melchi
3. Son of Simeon, father of Matthat, and an ancestor of Jesus.

Luke   3:29   father of Matthat
      3:30   son of Simeon
4. an apostle—see MATTHEW

LINUS [li'-nus = linen]
A Christian friend of Paul at Rome who sent greetings to Timothy.

2Tim   4:21   sent greetings to Timothy by Paul

LOIS ♀ [lo'-is = agreeable; no standard-bearer]
Grandmother of Timothy, probably mother of Eunice, from Lystra, and known for her unfeigned faith.

2Tim   1: 5   had unfeigned faith
      1: 5   grandmother of Timothy (Timotheaus)
      1: 5   mother of Eunice

LOT [lot = concealed; dark colored]
Son of Haran, nephew of Abraham, a "righteous" man, resided at Sodom, wife turned to a pillar of salt, became the father of Moab and Benammi (progenitors of the Moabites and the Ammonites) by incest with his two daughters (through their conspiracy and not of his own volition). (See also Gen 11—14)

Luke 17:28   as it was in his days, so shall it be in the day when the Son of Man is revealed (17:30)
     17:29   went out of Sodom
     17:32   had a wife
2Pet   2: 7   a just man, delivered by God from judgment
      2: 7   vexed with the filthy conversation of the wicked
      2: 8   a righteous man
      2: 8   vexed his righteous soul from day to day with the unlawful deeds of the people of Sodom and Gomorrah

LUCAS [lu'-cas = light-giving]—see LUKE

LUCIUS [lu'-she-us = of light]
1. A prophet and/or teacher in the church at Antioch, from Cyprus, and participated in the commissioning and sending out of Paul and Barnabas for missionary service. (Possibly identical with #2)

Acts   13: 1   was in the church at Antioch
      13: 1   a prophet and/or teacher
      13: 1   of Cyrene
      13: 2   ministered to the Lord and fasted
      13: 3   fasted, prayed, and laid hands on Barnabas and Saul (Paul) and sent them away
2. A kinsman of Paul who saluted the church at Rome. (Possibly identical with #1)

Rom   16:21   kinsman of Paul (and Jason and Sosipater)
     16:21   saluted the church at Rome

LUKE [luke = light-giving]; (Lucas)
Also Lucas, a Gentile physician, traveling companion of Paul, writer of the New Testament books of the gospel of Luke and the Acts of the Apostles, and a participant with Paul in his travels.

Luke   1: 3   had perfect understanding of all things from the very first
      1: 3   wrote the gospel of Luke to Theophilus
Acts   1: 1   made the former treatise of all that Jesus began both to do and to teach
      1: 1   addressed Theophilus
     16:10   endeavored to go into Macedonia, assured that the Lord had called him to preach the gospel unto them
     16:11   loosing from Troas, took a straight course to Samothracia
     16:11   the next day went on to Neapolis
     16:12   went on to Philippi and abode there certain days
     16:13   on the Sabbath went out of the city to a place of prayer and spoke unto the women
     16:14   heard by Lydia
     16:15   constrained by Lydia to abide at her house
     16:16   met by a damsel possessed with a spirit of divination as he went to prayer
     16:17   followed by a damsel possessed with a spirit of divination
     16:17   said to be one of the servants of the most high God, which show unto us the way of salvation
     20: 5   a group of traveling companions waited for him and Paul at Troas
     20: 6   sailed from Philippi and came to Troas in five days
     20: 6   abode seven days in Troas
     20:13   going before by ship, sailed unto Assos
     20:14   met Paul at Assos, took him in, and came to Mitylene

Acts 20:15 sailed over against Chios, the next day arrived at Samos, tarried at Trogyllium, and the next day came to Miletus

21: 1 having launched, came with a straight course unto Coos and the day following to Rhodes, and from there to Patara

21: 2 found a ship sailing to Phenicia, went aboard and set forth

21: 3 after discovering Cyprus, sailed unto Syria, landing at Tyre

21: 4 found disciples (at Tyre)

21: 4 tarried seven days (at Tyre)

21: 5 departed from Tyre and was brought on his way out of the city by the people

21: 5 kneeled down on the shore and prayed

21: 6 took leave one of another and took ship

21: 7 finishing his course from Tyre, came to Ptolemais

21: 7 saluted the brethren and abode with them one day

21: 8 was of Paul's company

21: 8 departed and came unto Caesarea

21: 8 entered into the house of Philip the evangelist

21: 8 abode with Philip the evangelist

21:10 tarried many days (with Philip the evangelist)

21:12 hearing these things, besought Paul not to go to Jerusalem

21:13 wept and broke Paul's heart

21:14 ceased persuading Paul

21:15 took up the carriages and went up to Jerusalem

21:16 accompanied by disciples of Caesarea among whom was Mnason

21:17 gladly received by the brethren at Jerusalem

21:18 went in unto James and all the elders (at Jerusalem)

27: 1 was to sail into Italy

27: 2 entered into a ship (with Paul and Aristarchus) of Adramyttium and launched, meaning to sail by the coasts of Asia

27: 3 the next day touched at Sidon

27: 4 launched from Sidon and sailed under Cyprus, because the winds were contrary

27: 5 sailed over the sea of Cilicia and Pamphylia, and came to Myra

27: 6 put on a ship of Alexandria sailing into Italy

27: 7 sailed slowly many days, scarcely coming over against Cnidus, not being suffered of the wind

27: 7 sailed under Crete, over against Salmone, and came to the Fair Ha-

vens, near the city of Lasea (27:8)

Acts 27:13 sailed close by Crete

27:16 ran under the island of Clauda

27:16 had much work to come by the boat

27:18 exceedingly tossed with a tempest

27:19 cast out, with his own hands, the tackling of the ship

27:20 saw neither sun nor stars in many days, and all hope that he should be saved was taken away

27:27 had been driven up and down in Adria fourteen nights

27:33 besought by Paul to take meat

27:33 had tarried and continued fasting fourteen days

27:34 was prayed to take some meat for his health

27:34 not one hair would fall from his head

27:36 was of good cheer and took meat

27:37 was one of 276 passengers in the ship

27:44 escaped safely to land

28: 1 had escaped to the island of Melita

28: 2 was shown no little kindness (by the people of Melita)

28: 2 received because of the present rain and the cold

28: 7 received by Publius and lodged three days courteously

28:10 honored with many honors

28:10 when he departed, was laded with such things as were necessary

28:11 after three months departed in a ship of Alexandria

28:12 landed at Syracuse and tarried three days

28:13 sailed on to Rhegium and then to Puteoli

28:14 found brethren (at Puteoli) and desired to tarry with them seven days

28:14 went toward Rome

28:15 met by the brethren at Appii forum and the three taverns

28:16 came to Rome

2Cor 8:18 sent, by Paul, to accompany Titus

8:18 a (Christian) brother of Paul

8:18 his praise is in the gospel throughout all the churches

8:19 chosen of the churches, to travel with Paul

8:19 administered grace (to the churches) to the glory of the Lord

8:20 avoided that any man should blame him in the abundance (of grace) which he ministered

8:21 provided for honest things, not only in the sight of the Lord, but also in the sight of men

8:23 a messenger of the churches and the glory of Christ

9: 3 sent by Paul to the Corinthian church

LUKE *(continued)*

2Cor	9: 5	exhorted to go before (to Corinth) and make up the bounty (for the saints)
	12:17	sent by Paul unto the Corinthians
	12:18	sent with Titus, by Paul (to the Corinthians)
	12:18	a (Christian) brother (of Paul)
Col	4:14	the beloved physician
	4:14	greeted the church at Colosse
2Tim	4:11	was alone with Paul
Phle	:24	fellow laborer with Paul
	:24	Paul requested Philemon to salute him

LYDIA ♀ [lid'-e-ah = to firebrand; travailing]
A seller of purple from Thyatira, baptized along with her household after hearing the preaching of Paul at Philippi, and opened her home hospitably to the missionaries.

Acts	16:13	was by the river side on the Sabbath day (16:14)
	16:14	a seller of purple
	16:14	of the city of Thyatira
	16:14	worshiped God
	16:14	her heart being opened by the Lord, heard the message and attended unto the things spoken of Paul
	16:15	was baptized (and her household)
	16:15	constrained Paul and his company to abide at her house
	16:40	Paul and Silas entered her house after being brought out of the prison

LYSANIAS [li-sa'-ne-as = relaxing sadness]
Tetrarch of Abilene during the reign of Tiberius Caesar.

Luke	3: 1	contemporary of Tiberius Casesar, and Pontius Pilate, Herod and Philip (tetrarchs) and Annas and Caiaphas (high priests) (3:2)
	3: 1	tetrarch of Abilene

LYSIAS [li'-see-as = light, bright releaser (?)]— see CLAUDIUS LYSIAS

M

MAATH [ma'-ath = from this time; small]
Son of Mattathias, father of Nagge, and an ancestor of Jesus.

Luke	3:25	father of Nagge (3:26)
	3:26	son of Mattathias

MAGDALENE ♀ [mag'-da-leen = of Magdala] —see MARY (#2)

MALCHUS [mal'-kus = counselor; king]
The servant of Caiaphas (the high priest) whose right ear was cut off by Simon Peter with a sword in the garden of Gethsemane and healed by Jesus.

Matt	26:51	servant of the high priest
	26:51	ear smote off with a sword
Mark	14:47	servant of the high priest
	14:47	ear cut off with a sword
Luke	22:50	right ear cut off when smitten by Simon Peter with a sword
	22:50	the servant of the high priest
	22:51	Jesus touched his ear and healed him
John	18:10	the servant of the high priest
	18:10	right ear cut off with a sword by Simon Peter
	18:26	had a kinsman who also was a servant of the high priest
	18:26	ear cut off by (Simon) Peter

MALELEEL [mal'e-le-el = praise of God]
Old Testament Mahalaleel, son of Cainan, father of Jared, and an ancestor of Jesus. (See also Gen 5; 1Chr 1)

Luke	3:37	father of Jared
	3:37	son of Cainan

MANAEN [man'-a-en = comforter]
A prophet and teacher in the church at Antioch, brought up with Herod Antipas (evidently a foster brother), and participated in the commissioning and sending out of Paul and Barnabas for missionary service.

Acts	13: 1	was in the church at Antioch
	13: 1	a prophet and teacher
	13: 1	had been brought up with Herod (Antipas)
	13: 2	ministered to the Lord and fasted
	13: 3	fasted, prayed, and laid his hands on Barnabas and Saul (Paul) and sent them away

MANASSES [ma-nas'-sez, ma-nas'-seh = causing forgetfulness]
1. Old Testament Manasseh, son of Ezekias (Hezekiah), father of Amon, a wicked king of Judah, and reintroduced idolatry.

Matt	1:10	begotten by Ezekias
	1:10	begat Amon

2. Old Testament Manasseh, elder brother of Ephraim, the son of Joseph but not of his grandfather Jacob, son of Asenath, and progenitor of the tribe bearing his name. (See also Gen 41,46,48,50)

Rev	7: 6	twelve thousand sealed of his tribe
	21:12	his name is inscribed upon the gates of the new Jerusalem
	21:12	a child of Israel (Jacob)

MARCUS [mar'-cus = a defense]—see MARK

MARK [mark = a defense]

Also Marcus, John Mark (John, surnamed Mark), the son of Mary, from Jerusalem, a relative (probably cousin) of Barnabas, friend of Simon Peter, traveling companion of Paul, and author of the gospel of Mark.

Mark	14:51	followed Jesus (after the betrayal)
	14:51	a young man
	14:51	had a linen cloth cast about his naked body
	14:51	the young men laid hands on him
	14:52	left the linen cloth and fled naked
Acts	12:12	son of Mary
	12:12	surnamed Mark
	12:15	thought Rhoda to be mad
	12:15	thought Peter to be his (Peter's) angel
	12:16	saw Peter and was astonished
	12:17	beckoned unto by Peter to hold his peace and told to go show these things unto James and to the brethren
	12:25	taken by Barnabas and Saul (Paul) to Jerusalem
	12:25	surnamed Mark
	13: 4	departed with Barnabas and Saul (Paul) unto Seleucia and then sailed to Cyprus
	13: 5	assisted Barnabas and Saul (Paul)
	13: 6	on the isle of Paphos found Bar-Jesus, with Sergius Paulus
	13:13	left Paphos with Barnabas and Saul (Paul) and came to Perga in Pamphylia
	13:13	departed from Barnabas and Saul (Paul) and returned to Jerusalem
	15:37	Barnabas determined to take him along with him and Paul (on a return missionary journey)
	15:37	surname was Mark
	15:38	Paul thought it not good to take him with him and Barnabas
	15:38	had departed from them (Paul and Barnabas) from Pamphylia and went not with them to the work
	15:39	a contention over him caused Paul and Barnabas to part company
	15:39	sailed unto Cyprus with Barnabas
Col	4:10	saluted the church at Colosse
	4:10	nephew of Barnabas
	4:11	a Jewish fellow worker who had been a comfort to Paul
2Tim	4:11	Paul asked Timothy to bring him
	4:11	was profitable to Paul for the ministry
Phle	:24	fellow laborer with Paul
	:24	saluted Philemon
1Pet	5:13	saluted the believers who were recipients of the epistle of 1 Peter
	5:13	a son (spiritual) of Paul

MARTHA ♀ [mar'-thah = mistress]

Sister of Mary and Lazarus of Bethany, concerned more with hospitality than fellowship with Jesus, and witnessed the resurrection of her brother Lazarus from the dead.

Luke	10:38	a woman
	10:38	received Jesus into her home
	10:39	had a sister called Mary
	10:40	was cumbered about much serving
	10:40	concerned that Jesus seemed not to care that her sister had left her to serve alone
	10:40	asked Jesus to have her sister Mary to help her serve
	10:41	careful and troubled about many things
John	11: 1	of the town of Bethany
	11: 1	sister of Lazarus and Mary (11:2)
	11: 3	sister of Lazarus and Mary
	11: 3	sent a message to Jesus that Lazarus was sick
	11: 5	loved of Jesus
	11: 5	sister of Mary
	11:19	many Jews came to her and Mary to comfort them concerning their brother
	11:20	hearing that Jesus was coming, went and met Him
	11:21	told Jesus that if He had been present her brother would not have died
	11:23	told by Jesus that her brother would rise again
	11:24	knew that her brother would rise again in the resurrection at the last day
	11:27	believed that Jesus was the Christ, the Son of God
	11:28	secretly called her sister Mary
	11:28	called Jesus Master
	11:30	met Jesus outside of Bethany
	11:39	sister of Lazarus
	12: 2	made Jesus a supper
	12: 2	served at the supper

MARY ♀ [ma'-ry = bitter; their rebellion]

1. The virgin mother of Jesus, wife of Joseph, and cousin of Elisabeth the mother of John the Baptist.

Matt	1:16	wife of Joseph
	1:16	mother of Jesus
	1:18	mother of Jesus
	1:18	found with child of the Holy Ghost while espoused to Joseph
	1:19	wife of Joseph
	1:19	Joseph, not willing to make her a public example, was minded to put her away privily
	1:20	subject of Joseph's dream
	1:20	had conceived by the Holy Ghost
	1:21	would bring forth a Son and call him Jesus
	1:23	virgin who conceived
	1:24	taken unto Joseph as his wife
	1:25	was not known (of Joseph) till she had brought forth her firstborn Son
	2:11	mother of Jesus

MARY *(continued)*

Matt	2:14	departed into Egypt with Joseph and Jesus
	2:14	mother of Jesus
	2:15	remained in Egypt until the death of Herod
	2:20	mother of Jesus
	2:21	mother of Jesus
	2:21	returned to Israel with Joseph and Jesus
	12:46	had other sons besides Jesus
	12:46	stood without, desiring to speak with Jesus
	12:47	stood without, desiring to speak with Jesus
	13:55	thought to be the mother of Jesus
	13:55	possibly mother of James, Joses, Simon, and Judas
Mark	3:31	called Jesus and sought for Him (3:32)
	6: 3	mother of Jesus
	6: 3	mother of James, Joses, Juda, and Simon
	6: 3	mother of daughters
Luke	1:26	lived in Nazareth of Galilee (1:27)
	1:26	visited by the angel (Gabriel) (1:28)
	1:27	a virgin
	1:27	espoused to Joseph
	1:28	was highly favored and the Lord was with her
	1:28	was blessed among women
	1:29	was troubled at the sayings of the angel
	1:30	had found favor with God
	1:31	would conceive and bring forth a Son and call his name Jesus
	1:34	had not known a man
	1:35	was told that the Holy Ghost would come upon her, and the power of the Highest would overshadow her
	1:35	would bear the Son of God
	1:36	cousin of Elisabeth
	1:38	the handmaid of the Lord
	1:38	consented to the angel's words
	1:39	arose with haste and went into a city of Juda
	1:40	entered into the house of Zacharias
	1:40	saluted Elisabeth
	1:42	blessed among women
	1:43	the mother of the Lord
	1:45	blessed for her belief
	1:46	her soul magnified the Lord
	1:47	God was her Saviour
	1:48	was of low estate
	1:48	the handmaiden of the Lord
	1:48	all generations would call her blessed
	1:49	great things were done to her by the Lord
	1:56	vistied with Elisabeth about three months and then returned home
	2: 4	journeyed to Bethlehem with Joseph to be taxed (2:5)

Luke	2: 5	the espoused wife of Joseph
	2: 5	was great with child
	2: 7	brought forth her firstborn Son, wrapped Him in swaddling clothes, and laid Him in a manger
	2: 7	could find no room in the inn
	2:16	found by the shepherds
	2:19	kept all these things (concerning Jesus) and pondered them in her heart
	2:21	Jesus was conceived in her womb
	2:21	called His name Jesus (as instructed by the angel)
	2:22	was purified (according to the law of Moses)
	2:22	took Jesus to Jerusalem to present Him to the Lord and to offer a sacrifice (2:24)
	2:27	brought the child Jesus to the temple to do for Him after the custom of the law
	2:33	marveled at those things spoken of her Son Jesus
	2:34	blessed by Simeon (the priest)
	2:35	a sword would pierce her soul
	2:39	performed all things according to the law of the Lord and returned to Nazareth into Galilee
	2:41	went to the feast of the Passover every year in Jerusalem
	2:42	went to Jerusalem for the feast of the Passover with Jesus when He was twelve years old
	2:43	as she returned from Jerusalem, knew not that Jesus had tarried behind
	2:44	having gone a day's journey, sought Jesus among the kinsfolk and acquaintance
	2:45	not finding Jesus, returned to Jerusalem seeking Him
	2:46	after three days, found Jesus in the temple
	2:48	was amazed at Jesus
	2:48	had sought Jesus sorrowing
	2:49	did not understand Jesus' explanation (2:50)
	2:51	went back to Nazareth with Jesus
	2:51	Jesus was subject unto her
	2:51	kept all Jesus' sayings in her heart
	8:19	came to Jesus but held back by the press (crowd)
	8:20	desired to see Jesus
John	2: 1	attended a marriage in Cana of Galilee
	2: 1	mother of Jesus
	2: 3	the mother of Jesus
	2: 3	informed Jesus of the absence of wine
	2: 5	the mother of Jesus
	2: 5	told the servants to follow Jesus' instructions
	2:12	went to Capernaum and continued there not many days.

MARY (continued)

John	6:42	mother of Jesus
	6:42	was known of the Jews
	19:25	stood by the cross of Jesus
	19:25	sister of Mary (wife of Cleophas)
	19:25	mother of Jesus
	19:26	mother of Jesus
	19:26	seen by Jesus
	19:26	told by Jesus to behold her son (John, the apostle)
	19:27	she would now be the mother of John
	19:27	from that hour was taken by John unto his own house
Acts	1:14	was with the apostles in the upper room
	1:14	mother of Jesus
	2: 1	present at the day of Pentecost
	2: 2	while sitting in the house, cloven tongues like as of fire, sat upon her, she was filled with the Holy Ghost and spoke with other tongues (2:4)

2. MARY Magdalene ♀ [mag'-da-leen = of Magdala]
A female disciple from Magdala, a follower of Jesus from whom He had cast seven demons, and the first person to whom Jesus appeared after His resurrection.

Matt	27:55	beheld the crucifixion from afar off (27:56)
	27:55	followed Jesus from Galilee, ministering unto Him (27:56)
	27:61	sat at the sepulcher of Jesus
	28: 1	came to the sepulcher of Jesus at dawn on the first day of the week
	28: 5	told by an angel to fear not
	28: 5	sought Jesus
	28: 6	told by an angel to come see the place where the Lord lay and to go quickly and tell His disciples that He was risen from the dead (28:7)
	28: 8	departed quickly from the sepulcher with fear and great joy and ran to bring His disciples word
	28: 9	met Jesus on the way, held Him by the feet, and worshiped Him
	28:10	told by Jesus to be not afraid
	28:10	told by Jesus to tell His brethren to go to Galilee to see Him
Mark	15:40	looked on afar off (at the crucifixion of Jesus)
	15:41	followed Jesus when He was in Galilee, ministering unto Him
	15:47	beheld where Jesus was laid
	16: 1	had bought sweet spices to anoint Jesus (body)
	16: 2	very early the first day of the week, came to the sepulcher
	16: 3	questioned who should roll away the stone from the door of the sepulcher
	16: 4	looked and saw that the stone was rolled away

Mark	16: 5	entered the sepulcher and saw a young man sitting clothed in a long white garment
	16: 5	was afraid
	16: 6	told to not be afraid
	16: 7	instructed to go tell His disciples and Peter, that He goeth into Galilee and there they would see Him
	16: 8	quickly fled from the sepulcher for she trembled and was amazed
	16: 8	said nothing to anyone because of fear
	16: 9	first person to whom Jesus appeared (after His resurrection)
	16: 9	Jesus had previously cast seven devils (demons) out of her
	16:10	went and told them that had been with Him (that He had risen from the dead)
	16:11	had seen the risen Lord
Luke	8: 2	had been healed of evil spirits and infirmities
	8: 2	seven devils (demons) cast out of her
	8: 2	ministered unto Him of her substance (8:3)
	23:49	observed the cross from afar
	23:55	came with Jesus from Galilee, followed after and beheld the sepulcher, and how His body was laid
	23:56	returned and prepared spices and ointments
	23:56	rested the Sabbath day according to the commandment
	24: 1	very early the first day of the week came to the sepulcher bringing the spices she had prepared
	24: 2	found the stone rolled away from the sepulcher
	24: 3	entered the sepulcher and found not the body of the Lord Jesus
	24: 4	while much perplexed, two men (angels) stood by in shining garments
	24: 5	was afraid and bowed down her face to the earth
	24: 5	asked by the angels why she sought the living among the dead
	24: 8	remembered the words of Jesus (concerning these events)
	24: 9	returned from the sepulcher and told all these things unto the eleven and to all the rest (24:10)
	24:11	her words seemed as idle tales and the disciples believed her not
	24:22	her words astonished the hearers
	24:22	was early at the sepulcher
	24:23	not finding Jesus' body, went saying she had seen a vision of angels which said that He was alive
John	19:25	stood by the cross of Jesus
	20: 1	very early the first day of the week,

MARY *(continued)*

came to the sepulcher and saw the stone taken away

John 20: 2   ran to Simon Peter and John and informed them that the Lord had been taken away out of the sepulcher and she knew not where they laid Him

20:11   stood without the sepulcher weeping

20:11   as she wept, stooped down and looked into the sepulcher and saw two angels in white sitting (20:12)

20:13   wept because they had taken away her Lord and she knew not where they had laid Him

20:14   saw Jesus standing but knew not that it was He

20:15   asked by Jesus why she wept and whom she sought

20:15   supposing Jesus to be the gardener, told Him to tell her if He had moved His body and she would take Him away

20:16   recognized Jesus when He spoke her name

20:16   called Jesus Rabboni, meaning Master

20:17   told not to touch Jesus, but to go to His brethren and tell them He would ascend to His Father

20:18   told the disciples that she had seen the Lord and that He had spoken unto her

3. Mother of James and Joses, one of a group of women who ministered to Jesus during His ministry, and observed His crucifixion. (May be identical with #5)

Matt 27:55   beheld, afar off, the crucifixion of Jesus (27:56)

27:55   followed Jesus from Galilee, ministering unto Him

27:56   mother of James and Joses

27:61   sat at the sepulcher of Jesus

28: 1   came to the sepulcher of Jesus at dawn on the first day of the week

28: 5   told by an angel to fear not

28: 5   sought Jesus

28: 7   told by an angel that Jesus had risen and that she should go and tell His disciples that they could see Him in Galilee

28: 8   departed quickly from the sepulcher with fear and great joy and ran to bring His disciples word

28: 9   met Jesus on the way, held Him by the feet and worshiped Him

28:10   told by Jesus to be not afraid

28:10   told to tell His brethren to go to Galilee to see Him

Mark 15:40   mother of James the less and Joses

15:40   looked on afar off (at the crucifixion of Jesus)

15:41   followed Jesus when He was in Galilee, ministering unto Him

Mark 15:47   beheld where Jesus was laid

15:47   mother of Joses

16: 1   mother of James

16: 1   brought sweet spices to anoint Jesus' (body)

16: 2   very early the first day of the week, came to the sepulcher

16: 3   questioned who should roll away the stone from the door of the sepulcher

16: 4   looked and saw that the stone was rolled away

16: 5   entered the sepulcher and saw a young man sitting clothed in a long white garment

16: 5   was afraid

16: 6   told to not be afraid

16: 7   instructed to go tell His disciples and Peter that He goeth into Galilee and there they would see Him

16: 8   quickly fled from the sepulcher, for she trembled and was amazed

16: 8   said nothing to anyone because of fear

Luke 23:49   observed the cross from afar

23:55   came with Jesus from Galilee, followed after and beheld the sepulcher, and how His body was laid

23:56   returned and prepared spices and ointments

23:56   rested the Sabbath day according to the commandment

24: 1   very early the first day of the week came to the sepulcher bringing the spices she had prepared

24: 2   found the stone rolled away from the sepulcher

24: 3   entered the sepulcher, and found not the body of the Lord Jesus

24: 4   while much perplexed, two men (angels) stood by in shining garments

24: 5   was afraid and bowed down her face to the earth

24: 5   asked by the angels why she sought the living among the dead

24: 8   remembered the words of Jesus (concerning these events)

24: 9   returned from the sepulcher and told all these things unto the eleven and to all the rest (24:10)

24:10   mother of James

24:11   her words seemed as idle tales and the disciples believed her not

24:22   her words astonished the hearers

24:22   was very early at the sepulcher

24:23   came, not finding Jesus' body, saying she had seen a vision of angels which said that He was alive

4. Sister of Martha and Lazarus of Bethany, one of the group of women who ministered to Jesus

MARY *(continued)*

during His ministry, observed His crucifixion, witnessed the resurrection of her brother Lazarus from the dead, and anointed Jesus' feet with ointment and wiped them with her hair.

Matt 26: 6 was in Bethany in the house of Simon the leper (26:7)
26: 7 came to Jesus and poured on His head a box of very precious ointment
26:10 freed from the troubling statement of others (by Jesus)
26:10 had wrought a good work upon Jesus
26:12 poured the ointment on Jesus' body (in anticipation of His burial)
26:13 her actions would be told wherever the gospel was preached, for a memorial of her
Mark 14: 3 a woman
14: 3 in Bethany, at house of Simon the leper
14: 3 broke an alabaster box of ointment of spikenard and poured it on Jesus' head
14: 5 was murmured against for her kind act
14: 6 wrought a good work on Jesus
14: 8 anointed Jesus' body aforehand for the burying
14: 9 a memorial of her would be given wherever this gospel was preached
Luke 10:39 sister of Martha
10:39 sat at Jesus' feet and heard His words
10:40 had left her sister to serve alone
10:42 had chosen that good part which would not be taken away from her
John 11: 1 sister of Lazarus and Martha (11:2)
11: 1 of the town of Bethany
11: 2 had anointed the Lord with ointment and wiped His feet with her hair
11: 2 Lazarus's sister
11: 3 sister of Lazarus and Martha
11: 3 sent a message to Jesus that Lazarus was sick
11: 5 loved of Jesus
11: 5 sister of Martha
11:19 many Jews came to her and Martha to comfort them concerning their brother
11:20 hearing that Jesus was coming, sat still in the house
11:23 Jesus stated that her brother would rise again
11:28 called by her sister, Martha
11:29 arose quickly and came to Jesus
11:31 comforted in the house by many Jews
11:31 rose up hastily and went out (of the house)
11:31 many thought she went to Lazarus's grave to weep

John 11:32 came to Jesus, saw Him, fell down at His feet, saying that if He had been there, her brother would not have died
11:33 wept
11:33 accompanied by weeping Jews
11:45 many of the Jews had come to her (at the death of her brother)
12: 2 made Jesus a supper
12: 3 anointed Jesus' feet with ointment of spikenard, and wiped His feet with her hair
12: 7 had kept the ointment against the day of Jesus' burying

5. Wife of Cleophas, sister of Mary (mother of Jesus), and present at the crucifixion of Jesus. (May be identical with #3)

John 19:25 stood by the cross of Jesus
19:25 sister of Mary (mother of Jesus)
19:25 wife of Cleophas

6. A resident of Jerusalem, possibly provided the meeting place for the church, and mother of John Mark.

Acts 12:12 (Simon) Peter had come to her house
12:12 mother of John Mark
12:12 many were gathered together praying at her house
12:13 (Simon) Peter knocked at the door of the gate of her house
12:15 thought Rhoda to be mad
12:15 thought Peter to be his (Peter's) angel
12:16 saw Peter and was astonished
12:17 beckoned unto by Peter to hold her peace

7. A female believer at Rome who was sent greetings by Paul.

Rom 16: 6 greeted by Paul
16: 6 bestowed much labor on Paul

MATHUSALA [ma-thu'-sa-lah = man of the javelin]
Old Testament Methuselah, son of Enoch, father of Lamech, grandfather of Noah, and oldest man recorded in the Bible (lived 969 years). (See also Gen 5)

Luke 3:36 father of Lamech (3:37)
3:37 son of Enoch

MATTATHA [mat'-ta-thah = gift]
Son of Nathan, father of Menan, and an ancestor of Jesus.

Luke 3:31 father of Menan
3:31 son of Nathan

MATTATHIAS [mat-ta-thi'-as = gift of Jehovah]
1. Son of Amos, father of Joseph, and an ancestor of Jesus.

Luke 3:24 father of Joseph (3:25)
3:25 son of Amos

MATTATHIAS *(continued)*
2. Son of Semei, father of Maath, and an ancestor of Jesus.

Luke   3:26   father of Maath
          3:26   son of Semei

MATTHAN [mat'-than = gift]
Son of Eleazar, father of Jacob, and an ancestor of Jesus.

Matt   1:15   begotten of Eleazar
        1:15   begat Jacob

MATTHAT [mat'-that = gift of God]
1. Son of Levi, father of Heli, grandfather of Joseph, the husband of Mary of whom was born Jesus, and an ancestor of Jesus.

Luke   3:23   father of Heli (3:24)
        3:24   son of Levi
2. Son of Levi, father of Jorim, and an ancestor of Jesus.

Luke   3:29   father of Jorim
        3:29   son of Levi

MATTHEW [math'-ew = gift of Jehovah]
Also Levi, an apostle of Jesus Christ, one of the twelve, called "Levi," son of Alphaeus (although not identical with Alphaeus the father of the apostle James), a collector of customs (taxes) at Capernaum who left his lucrative position to follow Jesus, and writer of the New Testament book bearing his name.

Matt   8:23*   followed Jesus into a ship
        8:25*   came to and awoke Jesus, and asked Him to save the disciples, for they perished
        8:26*   fearful
        8:26*   of little faith
        8:27*   marveled at Jesus
        9: 9   collector of customs (at Capernaum)
        9: 9   called by, and followed, Jesus
        9:10*   sat at meat with Jesus, along with publicans and sinners
        9:14*   fasted not
        9:19*   followed Jesus
        9:37*   instructed to pray that the Lord would send forth laborers into His harvest (9:38)
      10: 1*   was called unto Jesus
      10: 1*   one of the twelve disciples (of Jesus)
      10: 1*   given power to cast out unclean spirits
      10: 1*   given power to heal all manner of sickness and disease
      10: 2   one of the twelve apostles (10:3)
      10: 3   a publican
      10: 5   one of the twelve (apostles)
      10: 5*   commanded to go neither to the Gentiles, nor into any city of the Samaritans
      10: 6*   sent forth by Jesus to the lost sheep of the house of Israel

Matt 10: 7*   commanded by Jesus to preach "the kingdom of heaven is at hand"
      10: 8*   commanded to heal the sick, cleanse the lepers, raise the dead, cast out devils (demons)
      10: 8*   had freely received
      10: 9*   was to provide neither gold, nor silver, nor brass, nor scrip, neither two coats, neither shoes, nor staves (for himself) (10:10)
     10:11*   in every city or town, was to inquire who was worthy, and abide with them
     10:12*   was to salute each house he entered
     10:13*   his peace was to come upon each worthy house, but return to him if unworthy
     10:14*   was to shake off the dust of his feet therein, when not received or heard by a house or city
     10:16*   sent forth (by Jesus) as a sheep in the midst of wolves
     10:16*   was to be wise as a serpent and harmless as a dove
     10:17*   would be delivered to the councils, scourged in synagogues, and brought before governors and kings for (Jesus') sake (10:18)
     10:19*   was to take no thought concerning what he would speak when delivered up, for the Spirit of his Father would speak in him (10:20)
     12: 1*   was an hungered and plucked corn in the field and ate
     12: 2*   accused by the Pharisees of acting unlawfully on the Sabbath day
     12:49*   called mother and brethren by Jesus
     13:10*   questioned Jesus about His use of parables
     13:11   was given unto him to know the mysteries of the kingdom of heaven
     13:16*   saw and heard (spiritually)
     13:17*   had seen and heard (spiritually)
     13:18*   had the parable of the sower explained by Jesus (13:23)
     13:36*   had the parable of the wheat and tares explained by Jesus (13:43)
     13:51*   claimed to have understood all these things (parables)
     14:15*   came to Jesus and requested Him to send the multitude away
     14:16*   instructed by Jesus to feed the multitude
     14:17*   requested by Jesus to bring the five loaves and two fishes to Him (14:18)
     14:19*   given the loaves blessed by Jesus
     14:19*   distributed the loaves to the multitude
     14:20*   took up of the fragments that remained twelve baskets full
     14:22*   constrained by Jesus to get into a ship and to go before Him unto the

the other side (of the Sea of Galilee)
Matt 14:24* his ship was tossed with waves
14:25* approached by Jesus (walking on the sea)
14:26* saw Jesus walking on the water (Sea of Galilee) and was afraid
14:27* told by Jesus to be of good cheer and not be afraid
14:33* being in the ship, worshiped Jesus, claiming Him to be the Son of God
14:34* came into the land of Gennesaret
15: 2* accused by the scribes and Pharisees of transgressing the tradition of the elders by not washing his hands when he ate bread
15:12* came to Jesus, informing Him that the Pharisees were offended at His saying
15:23* came and besought Jesus to send away her that cried after him
15:32* was called (unto Jesus)
15:34* had seven loaves and a few little fishes
15:36* given the loaves and fishes (by Jesus)
15:36* gave the loaves and fishes to the multitude
15:37* took up of the broken meat that was left seven baskets full
16: 5* was come to the other side and had forgotten to take bread
16: 6* told to beware of the leaven of the Pharisees and Sadducees
16: 7* reasoned with the other disciples over Jesus' words
16: 7* had taken no bread
16: 8* of little faith
16: 8* reasoned with the other disciples (concerning the lack of bread)
16: 9* took up baskets (of fragments)
16:10* took up baskets (of fragments)
16:11* did not understand Jesus' words concerning the leaven (doctrine) of the Pharisees and Sadducees
16:12* understood not that Jesus spoke not of bread, but of the doctrine of the Pharisees and Sadducees
16:13* was in Caesarea Philippi
16:13* answered Jesus' question concerning His identity (16:14)
16:15* questioned as to his view of Jesus' identity
16:20* charged by Jesus to tell no man that He was Jesus the Christ
16:21* shown by Jesus the sufferings He must undergo
17:15* could not cure the lunatic boy (17:16)
17:19* asked Jesus why he could not cast out the devil (demon)
17:20* could not cast out the devil (demon) because of unbelief
17:22* abode in Galilee
17:23* was exceedingly sorry

Matt 17:24* came to Capernaum
18: 1* asked Jesus who is the greatest in the kingdom of Heaven
19:13* rebuked those who brought children to Jesus
19:14* rebuked, in turn, by Jesus
19:25* exceedingly amazed at Jesus' answer to the rich young ruler and asked who could be saved
19:27* had forsaken all and followed Jesus
19:28* had followed Jesus
19:28* promised by Jesus to sit upon the twelve thrones judging the twelve tribes of Israel
20:17* going up to Jerusalem, was taken apart and foretold by Jesus of His betrayal, crucifixion, and resurrection (20:19)
20:24* was moved with indignation towards James and John because of their request of Jesus
20:29* departed from Jericho (for Jerusalem)
21: 1* arrived in Bethphage and the Mount of Olives
21:20* saw the withered fig tree and marveled
24: 1* came to Jesus to show Him the buildings of the temple
24: 2* Jesus spoke to him of the coming destruction of the temple
24: 3* asked Jesus of the sign of His coming and of the end of the world
26: 8* was indignant at the actions of the woman
26:10* had troubled the woman
26:17* asked Jesus where he should prepare for Him the Passover
26:19* did as Jesus had appointed and made ready the Passover
26:20 celebrated Passover with Jesus and the rest of the twelve
26:22 asked Jesus if he were the one to betray Him
26:26* while eating (the Passover) was given the bread by Jesus
26:27* given the cup (by Jesus)
26:30* having sung an hymn, went out into the Mount of Olives
26:31* Jesus predicted that he would be offended because of Him
26:35* claimed he would never deny Jesus, even though it meant death
26:36* came with Jesus to Gethsemane
26:36* instructed to sit and pray
26:38* told by Jesus to tarry and watch with Him
26:40* fell asleep in the garden of Gethsemane
26:43* fell asleep again in the garden (of Gethsemane)
26:45* told to sleep on now and take his rest
26:46* told to arise and go (with Jesus)

MATTHEW *(continued)*

Matt 26:56* forsook Jesus and fled

28:13* would be accused of stealing Jesus' body by night

28:16* went into Galilee into the place (mountain) appointed

28:17* saw Jesus and worshiped Him

28:19* given the great commission (28:20)

28:20* Jesus would always be with him, even unto the end of the world

Mark 2:14 seen by Jesus sitting at the receipt of custom

2:14 son of Alphaeus

2:14 arose and followed Jesus, at His command

2:15 Jesus sat at meat in his house (with some disciples and many publicans and sinners)

2:18 did not fast as the disciples of John (the Baptist) and the Pharisees did

2:23 plucked ears of corn in the corn fields, on the Sabbath day

3: 7 withdrew from the synagogue with Jesus to the sea

3:14* ordained by Jesus (to be with Him)

3:14* would be sent forth to preach (by Jesus)

3:15* would be given power, by Jesus, to heal sicknesses and to cast out devils (demons)

3:18 a disciple of Jesus (one of the twelve)

3:20* could not eat bread with Jesus because of the multitude

4:10* asked Jesus about the parable of the sower

4:11* was given to know the mystery of the kingdom of God

4:33* had many parables taught him by Jesus

4:34* when alone, with the rest of the twelve, had all things expounded by Jesus

4:36* sent away the multitude

4:36* with the twelve, took Jesus to the other side of the sea

4:38* in fear, awakened Jesus in the midst of the storm

4:40* was fearful and had no faith

4:41* feared exceedingly

4:41* questioned among the other disciples as to what manner of man Jesus was that even the wind and the sea obey Him

5: 1* went with Jesus across the Sea of Galilee to the country of the Gadarenes

6: 1* followed Jesus into His own country

6: 7* sent forth two by two (by Jesus)

6: 7* given power over unclean spirits

6: 8* commanded to take nothing on his journey, except a staff, and to be shod with sandals and only one

coat (6:9)

Mark 6:12* went out and preached that men should repent

6:13* cast out many devils (demons) and anointed with oil many that were sick and healed them

6:30* an apostle

6:30* gathered together unto Jesus to report what he had done and taught

6:31* had no leisure so much as to eat

6:32* departed privately with Jesus into a desert place by ship

6:36* asked Jesus to send away the multitude into the villages to buy themselves bread

6:37* told by Jesus to give food to the multitude

6:37* asked Jesus if he should go and buy bread to feed the people

6:38* when asked by Jesus the available provisions, reported five loaves and two fishes

6:39* made the people sit down by hundreds and by fifties (6:40)

6:41* given the food blessed by Jesus to distribute to the crowd

6:43* took up twelve baskets full of fragments and of the fishes

6:45* constrained by Jesus to get into the ship and go to the other side unto Bethsaida

6:47* was alone with the other disciples in the ship in the midst of the sea

6:48* toiled in rowing the ship for the winds were contrary

6:48* Jesus came unto him in about the fourth watch of the night walking upon the sea

6:49* saw Jesus walking upon the sea and cried out for he supposed it had been a spirit

6:50* saw Jesus and was troubled but admonished by Him to fear not

6:51* was amazed beyond measure and wondered that the wind ceased as Jesus entered the ship

6:52* because of his hardened heart, had forgotten about the miracle of the loaves

6:53* came into the land of Gennesaret

6:54* got out of the ship

7: 5* walked not according to the traditions of the elders (ate bread with unwashed hands)

8: 5* informed Jesus of the seven loaves

8: 6* set the loaves before the people

8: 7* receiving the blessed fishes from Jesus, set them before the people

8: 8* gathered seven baskets of fragments

8:10* entered into a ship with Jesus and went into Dalmanutha

8:13* entering into the ship again with Jesus, departed to the other side

8:14* had forgotten to take bread, and

MATTHEW *(continued)*

Mark

had only one loaf in the ship

8:16* had no bread

8:17* having seen the miracles, still did not understand as his heart was possibly yet hardened

8:19* took up twelve baskets full of fragments at the feeding of the five thousand

8:20* took up seven baskets full of fragments at the feeding of the four thousand

8:27* went into the towns of Caesarea Philippi with Jesus

8:27* responded to Jesus' question concerning His identity with "John the Baptist, Elias, and one of the prophets" (8:28)

8:30* charged to tell no man that Jesus was the Christ

8:31* taught by Jesus of the things concerning Himself

9:14* questioned by the scribes

9:18* could not cast out a dumb spirit

9:30* passed through Galilee

9:32* did not understand the words of Jesus, but was afraid to ask

9:33* came to Capernaum

9:33* disputed with the other disciples on the way to Capernaum as to whom should be the greatest (9:34)

9:38* forbade a man from casting out devils (demons) in Jesus' name, because he did not follow him

10:13* rebuked those who brought young children to Jesus that He should touch them

10:14* rebuked, in turn, by Jesus

10:24* astonished at the words of Jesus concerning those with riches

10:26* astonished at Jesus' words

10:28* had left all and followed Jesus

10:32* went up to Jerusalem with Jesus and was amazed and afraid

10:41 was much displeased with James and John

10:46* went to Jericho

10:46* went out of Jericho with Jesus

11: 1* came nigh to Jerusalem, unto Bethphage and Bethany, at the Mount of Olives

11:11* went to Bethany with Jesus and stayed until the morrow (11:12)

11:14* heard Jesus curse the fig tree

11:15* returned to Jerusalem with Jesus

11:19* went out of Jerusalem

11:20* witnessed the fig tree dried up from the roots

11:27* came again to Jerusalem

14:17* in the evening of the first day of unleavened bread, went with Jesus to the upper room

14:18* sat and ate together with Jesus

14:19* began to be sorrowful over Jesus' statement of betrayal and to ask

"Is it I?"

Mark

14:20* dipped with Jesus in the dish

14:22* ate the Passover with Jesus

14:23* drank of the communion cup

14:26* sung an hymn and went out to the Mount of Olives

14:31* exclaimed that even if it meant death, he would not deny Him

14:32* went to Gethsemane and was told to sit there while Jesus prayed

14:50* forsook Jesus and fled

16:10* mourned and wept

16:11* believed not Mary Magdalene's account

16:14* Jesus appeared unto him as he sat at meat (with the other disciples)

16:14* upbraided by Jesus for his unbelief and hardness of heart, because he believed not them which had seen Him after He was risen

16:15* commissioned to go into all the world and preach the gospel to every creature

16:20* went forth and preached everywhere, with signs following

Luke

5:27 a publican (tax collector)

5:27 sat at the receipt of custom

5:27 commanded by Jesus to follow Jesus

5:28 left all, rose up, and followed Jesus

5:29 made a great feast in his own house, to which a great company of publicans and others were invited

6: 1* plucked ears of corn and ate (rubbing them in his hands) on the Sabbath

6: 2* claimed by the Pharisees to be doing that which was not lawful to do on the Sabbath day

6:13 chosen as one of the twelve

6:13* also called (named) an apostle

6:15 an apostle

6:17* came down from the mountain with Jesus and stood in the plain

8: 1* went throughout every city and village with Jesus

8: 9* questioned Jesus concerning a parable

8:10* unto him it was given to know the mysteries of the kingdom of God

8:22* went into a ship with Jesus and launched forth for the other side

8:23* the boat, filled with water, put him in jeopardy

8:24* called Jesus Master

8:24* came to Jesus and awakened Him during the storm

8:25* asked by Jesus concerning his faith

8:25* was afraid and wondered concerning Jesus' power over the elements

8:26* arrived at the country of the Gadarenes (Gadara)

9: 1* given power and authority over all devils (demons) and to cure diseases

Luke 9: 2* sent by Jesus, to preach the kingdom of God and to heal the sick

9: 3* was to take neither staves, nor scrip, neither bread, neither money, neither have two coats

9: 4* was to abide in whatever house he entered

9: 6* went through the towns, preaching the gospel, and healing everywhere

9:10* returned and told Jesus all he had done

9:10* went privately with Jesus into a desert place belonging to the city called Bethsaida

9:12* requested that Jesus send away the multitude, so that they might go into the towns and lodge and get victuals (food)

9:13* had only five loaves and two fishes, but was requested by Jesus to give food to the multitude

9:14* made the multitude sit down in companies by fifties (9:15)

9:16* gave the blessed loaves and fish unto the multitude

9:17* took up twelve baskets of fragments

9:18* was alone with Jesus (and the rest of the twelve)

9:18* in response to Jesus' question as to His identity, responded, "John the Baptist, Elias, and one of the prophets risen again" (9:19)

9:20* straitly charged and commanded to tell no man that He is the Christ (9:21)

9:40* could not cast the spirit (demon) out of a boy

9:45* feared to ask Jesus concerning His teaching

9:46* reasoned with the other disciples as to which of them should be greatest

9:49* forbade a man from casting out devils (demons) in Jesus' name because he followed not with the disciples

10:24* saw and heard what many prophets and kings had desired to experience

12: 1* warned by Jesus to beware of the leaven of the Pharisees

12: 4* friend of Jesus

17: 5* asked Jesus to increase his faith

18:15* rebuked those who brought infants to Jesus

18:16* rebuked, in turn, by Jesus

18:28* had left all, and followed Jesus

18:31* taken unto Jesus and instructed of things to come (18:33)

18:34* understood none of these teachings of Jesus

19:29* with Jesus, came nigh to Bethphage and Bethany at the Mount of Olives

Luke 19:37* rejoiced and praised God with a loud voice (19:38)

22:14* sat down with Jesus (in the upper room for the Passover)

22:14* was called an apostle

22:15* Jesus truly desired his presence in eating the Passover

22:19* partook of the first Lord's Supper (22:20)

22:23* inquired among the disciples as to which of them would betray Jesus

22:24* a strife existed between him and the other disciples as to which one should be accounted the greatest

22:28* had continued with Jesus in His temptations

22:29* was appointed a kingdom (that he might eat and drink at Jesus' table in His kingdom and sit on thrones judging the twelve tribes of Israel) (22:30)

22:35* had lacked nothing

22:36* told to prepare (for his new task)

22:39* followed Jesus to the Mount of Olives

22:40* told to pray that he enter not into temptation

22:45* found sleeping for sorrow (by Jesus)

22:46* told to rise and pray, lest he enter into temptation

22:49* perceiving the forthcoming events, asked Jesus if he should use his sword

24: 9* was told all things concerning the resurrection by Mary Magdalene, Joanna, Mary the mother of James, and the other women

24:10* an apostle

24:11* the words of the women seemed to him as idle tales and he believed them not

24:33* being gathered together (with the other disciples), Cleopas found him and declared that the Lord was risen indeed and had appeared to Simon (24:34)

24:36* Jesus appeared unto him (after the resurrection) but he was terrified and affrighted, and supposed that he had seen a spirit (24:37)

24:38* asked by Jesus why he was troubled and why thoughts arose in his heart

24:40* was shown Jesus' hands and feet

24:41* believed not yet for joy and wondered

24:42* gave Jesus a piece of a broiled fish and of an honeycomb

24:45* his understanding was opened by Jesus that he might understand the scriptures

24:46* was a witness of these things (24:48)

24:49* told to tarry in Jerusalem until he

MATTHEW *(continued)*

was endued with power from on high

Luke 24:50* led by Jesus out as far as to Bethany and was blessed of Him

24:52* worshiped Jesus and returned to Jerusalem with great joy

24:53* was continually in the temple praising and blessing God

John 2: 2* was called to the marriage in Cana of Galilee

2:11* believed on Jesus

2:12* went to Capernaum and continued there not many days

2:17* remembered that it was written of Him, "the zeal of thine house hath eaten me up"

2:22* after the resurrection, remembered Jesus' words and believed the scriptures and the words which Jesus had said

3:22* came into the land of Judea with Jesus and tarried there with Him

4: 2* did baptize

4: 8* had gone away unto the city to buy meat

4:27* came unto Jesus and marveled that He talked with the Samaritan woman, yet did not question Him

4:31* called Jesus Master

4:31* implored Jesus to eat

4:33* questioned among the disciples if Jesus had been brought food to eat

4:35* told to look on the fields for they were white already to harvest

4:38* had been sent to reap where he had not sown, and had entered into others' labors

6: 3* went up into a mountain and sat with Jesus

6:10* instructed by Jesus to have the multitude sit down

6:11* distributed the loaves and fishes to the multitude

6:13* gathered twelve baskets of fragments

6:16* went down to the sea, entered a ship and went toward Capernaum (6:17)

6:19* after rowing twenty-five to thirty furlongs, saw Jesus walking on the sea and was afraid

6:20* told to not be afraid

6:21* willingly received Him into the ship

6:22* was entered into the only boat there

6:22* was apart from Jesus in the boat alone (with the other disciples)

6:67* asked by Jesus if he would also go away

6:69* believed and was sure that Jesus was the Christ, the Son of the living God

6:70* chosen as one of the twelve

9: 2* questioned Jesus concerning the man born blind

John 11: 8* called Jesus Master

11:11* friend of Lazarus

11:54* continued with Jesus at Ephraim

12:16* understood not at first, the events of the triumphal entry of Jesus

12:16* after Jesus' glorification, remembered that these events had been written of Jesus, and had been done unto Him

13: 5* feet washed by Jesus

13:12* had his feet washed by Jesus

13:13* called Jesus Master and Lord

13:14* had his feet washed by Jesus

13:14* told, by Jesus, that he ought to wash one another's feet

13:15* had been given an example that he should do as Jesus had done to him

13:18* was known and chosen of Jesus

13:21* when told that one of them would betray Jesus, looked on the others, doubting of whom He spoke (13:22)

13:28* knew not for what intent Jesus spoke these words to Judas Iscariot

13:34* given a new commandment to love one another

13:34* loved of Jesus

13:35* love one to another was a mark that he was a true disciple of Jesus

14:25* was with Jesus

14:26* would be instructed by the Holy Spirit in all things

14:26* the words Jesus had spoken would be brought to his remembrance

14:27* Jesus' peace was given to him and left with him

14:31* was told to arise and go with Jesus

15: 3* was clean through the Word

15: 9* loved of Jesus

15:12* commanded to love one another

15:12* loved of Jesus

15:16* chosen of Jesus and ordained of Him to go and bring forth fruit, and that his fruit should remain

15:17* commanded to love one another

15:19* not of the world

15:19* chosen out of the world by Jesus

15:19* hated of the world

15:27* would bear witness, because he had been with Jesus from the beginning

16: 4* was with Jesus

16: 6* sorrow had filled his heart

16:12* could not bear the words of Jesus

16:22* presently had sorrow

16:24* had asked nothing of the Father in Jesus' name

16:27* loved of the Father

16:27* loved Jesus, and believed that He came from God

16:29* could now understand plainly Jesus' words

16:30* was sure that Jesus knew all things

16:30* believed that Jesus came forth from God

MATTHEW *(continued)*

John 18: 1* went with Jesus over the brook Cedron and entered into a garden (Gethsemane)

18: 2* often resorted there with Jesus

20:18* told by Mary Magdalene that she had seen the Lord and that He had spoken unto her after the resurrection

20:19* while assembled together (with the other disciples) with the doors shut for fear of the Jews, Jesus appeared in the midst

20:20* saw Jesus' hands and side and was glad

20:21* sent by Jesus and given His peace

20:22* breathed on by Jesus and received the Holy Ghost

20:25* told Thomas that he had seen the Lord

20:25* informed by Thomas, that he would not believe without specific conditions being met

20:26* the doors being shut again, Jesus appeared the second time to him and the apostles

20:30* many other signs were done in his presence which are not written (in this book)

Acts 1: 2* had been given commandments by Jesus (through the Holy Ghost)

1: 2* chosen by Jesus

1: 3* was shown Jesus alive after His passion

1: 3* spoken to by Jesus of the things pertaining to the kingdom of God

1: 3* saw Jesus forty days

1: 4* commanded, by Jesus, not to depart from Jerusalem, but to wait for the promise of the Father

1: 5* would be baptized with the Holy Ghost

1: 6* questioned Jesus concerning the restoration of the kingdom to Israel

1: 7* was not to know the times or the seasons which the Father had put in His own power

1: 8* after receiving the Holy Spirit, would receive power and would be witness unto Jesus Christ throughout the earth

1: 9* beheld as Jesus was taken up into Heaven at His ascension

1:10* was joined by two men in white apparel while he looked steadfastly toward Heaven

1:11* a man of Galilee

1:11* was gazing up to Heaven

1:11* Jesus was taken up from him into Heaven

1:11* was told that Jesus would come in like manner as he had seen Him go into Heaven

1:12* returned to Jerusalem and went

into an upper room (1:13)

Acts 1:14* continued in prayer and supplication with the women, Mary the mother of Jesus, and with His brethren

1:21* was with the Lord Jesus at various times

1:24* prayed concerning the ordination of one to be a witness of Jesus' resurrection

1:26* gave forth his lot (concerning Judas Iscariot's successor)

2: 1* present at the day of Pentecost

2: 2* while sitting in the house, cloven tongues like as of fire sat upon him, he was filled with the Holy Ghost, and spoke with other tongues (2:4)

2: 6* his speech confounded the multitude because every man heard in his own language

2: 7* a Galilean

2:13* mocked by some who claimed him as full of new wine

2:14* stood with (Simon) Peter

2:15* was not drunk

2:32* was a witness to the resurrection of Jesus

2:37* asked by the multitude on day of Pentecost what they should do

2:42* many continued steadfastly in his doctrine and fellowship

2:43* many wonders and signs were done by him

4:33* with great power gave witness of the resurrection of the Lord Jesus

4:33* great grace was upon him

4:35* the price of possessions sold by Christians was laid at his feet

4:35* distributed to every man (of the Christian community) as he had need

4:36* gave Joses a surname of Barnabas

4:37* Joses's money was laid at his feet

5: 2* the gift of Ananias and Sapphira was laid at his feet

5:12* by his hands were many signs and wonders wrought among the people

5:12* was with one accord with the others in Solomon's porch

5:13* no man durst join himself to him (the apostles)

5:13* was magnified of the people

5:16* healed the multitude of sicknesses and unclean spirits

5:18* placed in the common prison by the high priest and Sadducees

5:19* released from prison by the angel of the Lord and told to go, stand, and speak in the temple (5:20)

5:21* entered into the temple early in the morning and taught

5:22* was not found in the prison

5:25* was standing in the temple, and teaching the people

Acts 5:26* brought without violence and set before the council (5:27)

5:27* questioned by the high priest (5:28)

5:28* had been commanded not to teach in this (Jesus') name

5:28* had filled Jerusalem with his doctrine and had (seemingly) intended to bring Jesus' blood upon his accusers

5:29* believed that he ought to obey God rather than men

5:32* witness of God (and of His works)

5:33* Jewish leaders took counsel to slay him

5:34* put a little space from the Sanhedrin (for their deliberation)

5:40* called back before the council, beaten, commanded not to speak in the name of Jesus, and let go

5:41* departed from the council rejoicing that he was counted worthy to suffer shame for His name

5:42* daily in the temple and in every house, ceased not to teach and preach Jesus Christ

6: 2* called the multitude together and stated it was not reasonable that he should leave the Word of God and serve tables

6: 3* instructed that seven men of honest report be chosen to be appointed to serve tables

6: 4* determined to give himself continually to prayer and to the ministry of the Word

6: 6* the chosen seven were set before him, for whom he prayed and laid his hands on them

8: 1* remained in Jerusalem in the midst of great persecution

8:14* was in Jerusalem

8:14* hearing that Samaria had received the Word of God, sent Peter and John to Samaria

9:27* Saul (Paul) was brought to him by Barnabas and he was informed of Saul's (Paul's) conversion experience and his bold preaching at Damascus

9:28* was accompanied by Saul (Paul) in coming in and going out at Jerusalem

10:39* was witness of all things Jesus did both in the land of the Jews and in Jerusalem

10:41* a witness, chosen before of God

10:41* ate and drank with Jesus after His resurrection

10:42* commanded of Jesus to preach unto the people, and testified that it was Jesus which was ordained of God to be the Judge of quick and dead

11: 1* was in Judea

Acts 11: 1* heard that the Gentiles had also received the Word of God

11:15* the Holy Ghost fell on him at the beginning (Pentecost)

13:31* saw Jesus many days

13:31* came up with Jesus from Galilee to Jerusalem

13:31* was His (Jesus') witness unto the people

15: 2* Paul, Barnabas, and others were sent by the church at Antioch to consult with him over the matter of circumcision

15: 4* received Paul, Barnabas, and the others from Antioch

15: 6* came together (with the elders) to consider the matter (of circumcision)

15: 8* given the Holy Ghost

15: 9* God made no difference between him and a Gentile

15:10* was not able to bear the yoke

15:22* acting with the elders, sent chosen men back to Antioch with Paul and Barnabas

15:23* acting with the elders and brethren, wrote letters of instruction to the Gentiles at Antioch, Syria, and Cilicia

15:24* gave no commandment that Gentile believers must be circumcised and keep the law

15:25* considered it good, being assembled, to send chosen men unto the believers

15:25* loved Barnabas and Paul

15:27* sent Judas and Silas to the Gentile believers

15:33* Judas (Barsabas) and Silas returned unto him

16: 4* with the elders, ordained decrees

16: 4* was at Jerusalem

Rom 16: 7* Andronicus and Junia were well known to him

1Cor 4: 9* Paul thought God had set him (and the apostles) forth last, as it were appointed to death

4: 9* made a spectacle unto the world, to the angels, and to men

4:10* a fool for Christ's sake

4:10* weak, despised

4:11* hungered, thirsted, was naked, was buffeted, and had no certain dwelling place

4:12* labored, working with his own hands

4:12* being reviled, he blessed; being persecuted, he suffered it; being defamed, he entreated (4:13)

4:13* made as the filth of the world, and the offscouring of all things

9: 5* had power to lead about a sister, a wife

15: 5* had seen the risen Lord

MATTHEW *(continued)*

1Cor 15: 7* the risen Lord was seen of him
      15:11* preached
Rev   21:14* name inscribed in the twelve foun-
              dations of the new Jerusalem
      21:14* an apostle of the Lamb

MATTHIAS [mat'-thias = given of Jehovah]
Nominated and chosen by lot by the eleven as the
successor to Judas Iscariot's vacated position as
"witness" and apostle.

Acts 1:22 appointed as possible successor to
            position vacated by Judas Iscariot,
            as a witness to the resurrection of
            Christ (an apostle) (1:23)
      1:26 the lot fell upon him (to take the
            apostleship) and he was numbered
            with the eleven apostles

Possible references to Matthias

      2: 1 present at the day of Pentecost
      2: 2 while sitting in the house, cloven
            tongues like as of fire sat upon him,
            he was filled with the Holy Ghost,
            and spoke with other tongues (2:4)
      2: 6* his speech confounded the mul-
             titude because every man heard in
             his own language
      2: 7* a Galilean
      2:13* mocked by some who claimed him
             as full of new wine
      2:14* stood with (Simon) Peter
      2:15* was not drunk
      2:32* was a witness to the resurrection of
             Jesus
      2:37* asked by the multitude on day of
             Pentecost what they should do
      2:42* many continued steadfastly in his
             doctrine and fellowship
      2:43* many wonders and signs were done
             by him
      4:33* with great power gave witness of
             the resurrection of the Lord Jesus
      4:33* great grace was upon him
      4:35* the price of possessions sold by
             Christians was laid at his feet
      4:35* distributed to every man (of the
             Christian community) as he had
             need
      4:36* gave Joses a surname of Barnabas
      4:37* Joses's money was laid at his feet
      5: 2* the gift of Ananias and Sapphira
             was laid at his feet
      5:12* by his hands were many signs and
             wonders wrought among the
             people
      5:12* was with one accord with the disci-
             ples in Solomon's porch
      5:13* no man durst join himself to him
             (as the apostles)
      5:13* was magnified of the people
      5:16* healed the multitude of sicknesses
             and unclean spirits
      5:18* placed in the common prison by
             the high priest and Sadducees

Acts 5:19* released from prison by the angel
             of the Lord and told to go, stand,
             and speak in the temple (5:20)
      5:21* entered into the temple early in the
             morning and taught
      5:22* was not found in the prison
      5:25* was standing in the temple and
             teaching the people
      5:26* brought without violence and set
             before the council (5:27)
      5:27* questioned by the high priest (5:28)
      5:28* had been commanded not to teach
             in this (Jesus') name
      5:28* had filled Jerusalem with his doc-
             trine and had (seemingly) intended
             to bring Jesus' blood upon his ac-
             cusers
      5:29* believed he ought to obey God
             rather than men
      5:32* witness of God (and of His works)
      5:33* Jewish leaders took counsel to slay
             him
      5:34* put a little space from the council
             (for their deliberation)
      5:40* called back before the council,
             beaten, commanded not to speak
             in the name of Jesus, and let go
      5:41* departed from the council rejoicing
             that he was counted worthy to suf-
             fer shame for His name
      5:42* daily in the temple and in every
             house, ceased not to teach and
             preach Jesus Christ
      6: 2* called the multitude together and
             stated it was not reasonable that
             he should leave the Word of God
             and serve tables
      6: 3* instructed that seven men of honest
             report be chosen to be appointed
             to serve tables
      6: 4* determined to give himself continu-
             ally to prayer and to the ministry
             of the Word
      6: 6* the chosen seven were set before
             him, for whom he prayed and laid
             his hands on them
      8: 1* remained in Jerusalem in the midst
             of great persecution
      8:14* was in Jerusalem
      8:14* hearing that Samaria had received
             the Word of God, sent Peter and
             John to Samaria
      9:27* Saul (Paul) was brought to him by
             Barnabas and he was informed of
             Saul's (Paul's) conversion experi-
             ence and his bold preaching at
             Damascus
      9:28* was accompanied by Saul (Paul)
             in coming in and going out at
             Jerusalem
     10:39* was witness of all things Jesus did
             both in the land of the Jews and in
             Jerusalem

122

MATTHIAS *(continued)*

Acts 10:41* a witness, chosen before God
      10:41* ate and drank with Jesus after His resurrection
      10:42* commanded of Jesus to preach unto the people, and testified that it was Jesus which was ordained of God to be the Judge of quick and dead
      11: 1* was in Judea
      11: 1* heard that the Gentiles had also received the Word of God
      11:15* the Holy Ghost fell on him at the beginning (Pentecost)
      13:31* saw Jesus many days
      13:31* came up with Jesus from Galilee to Jerusalem
      13:31* was His (Jesus') witness unto the people
      15: 2* Paul, Barnabas, and others were sent by the church at Antioch to consult with him over the matter of circumcision
      15: 4* received Paul, Barnabas, and the others from Antioch
      15: 6* came together (with the elders) to consider the matter (of circumcision)
      15: 8* given the Holy Ghost
      15: 9* God made no difference between him and a Gentile
      15:10* was not able to bear the yoke
      15:22* acting with the elders, sent chosen men back to Antioch with Paul and Barnabas
      15:23* acting with the elders and brethren, wrote letters of instruction to the Gentiles at Antioch, Syria, and Cilicia
      15:24* gave no commandment that Gentile believers must be circumcised and keep the law
      15:25* considered it good, being assembled, to send chosen men unto the believers
      15:25* loved Barnabas and Paul
      15:27* sent Judas and Silas to the Gentile believers
      15:33* Judas (Barsabas) and Silas returned unto him
      16: 4* with the elders, ordained decrees
      16: 4* was at Jerusalem
Rom   16: 7* Andronicus and Junia were well known to him
1Cor   4: 9* Paul thought God had set him (and the apostles) forth last, as it were appointed to death
       4: 9* made a spectacle unto the world, to the angels, and to men
       4:10* a fool for Christ's sake
       4:10* weak, despised
       4:11* hungered, thirsted, was naked, was buffeted, and had no certain dwelling place
       4:12* labored, working with his own hands
       4:12* being reviled, he blessed; being persecuted, he suffered it; being defamed, he entreated (4:13)
       4:13* made as the filth of the world, and the offscouring of all things
       9: 5* had power to lead about a sister a wife
      15: 5* had seen the risen Lord
      15: 7* the risen Lord was seen of him
      15:11* preached

MELCHI [mel'-ki = my king; my counsel]
1. Son of Janna, father of Levi, and an ancestor of Jesus.

Luke   3:24 father of Levi
       3:24 son of Janna

2. Son of Addi, father of Neri, and an ancestor of Jesus.

Luke   3:27 father of Neri (3:28)
       3:28 son of Addi

MELCHISEDEC [mel-kis'-e-dek = my king is righteous (?)]
Old Testament Melchizedek (king of righteousness), king of Salem, priest of the most high God, received tithes of Abraham who blessed him, without father and mother, without beginning of days nor end of life, a type of Christ's priesthood. (See also Gen 14)

Heb   5: 6 Christ was after his order (priesthood)
       5:10 Christ was after his order (priesthood)
       6:20 Jesus was after his order (priesthood)
       7: 1 king of Salem
       7: 1 priest of the most high God
       7: 1 met Abraham returning from the slaughter of the kings, and blessed him
       7: 2 received a tenth part (tithe) from Abraham
       7: 2 king of righteousness
       7: 2 king of Salem (king of peace)
       7: 3 without father or mother
       7: 3 without descent
       7: 3 had neither beginning of days nor end of life
       7: 3 made like unto the Son of God
       7: 3 abideth a priest continually
       7: 4 a great man, unto whom even Abraham gave the tenth (tithe) of the spoils
       7: 6 his descent is not counted from them (the descendants of Abraham)
       7: 6 received tithes of Abraham
       7: 6 blessed Abraham
       7: 7 better than Abraham, whom he blessed
       7:10 met Levi while Levi was yet in the loins of his father (Abraham)

MELCHISEDEC *(continued)*
Heb 7:11 had an order (a priesthood)
7:15 after his similitude there arose another priest
7:17 Christ was after his order (priesthood)
7:21 Christ was a priest after his order (priesthood)

MELEA [mel'-e-ah = my dear friend]
Son of Menan, father of Eliakim, and an ancestor of Jesus through Mary.
Luke 3:30 father of Eliakim (3:31)
3:31 son of Menan

MENAN [me'-nan = soothsayer; enchanted]
Son of Mattatha, father of Melea, great-grandson of David, and an ancestor of Jesus through the line of Mary.
Luke 3:31 father of Melea
3:31 son of Mattatha

MNASON [na'-son = remembering; solicitor]
An old disciple of Cyprus who accompanied Paul to Jerusalem and with whom he lodged.
Acts 21:15 accompanied Paul to Jerusalem (21:16)
21:16 an old disciple
21:16 of Cyprus
21:16 would lodge Paul (and Luke)
21:17 gladly received by the brethren at Jerusalem
21:18 went in unto James and all the elders (at Jerusalem)

MOSES [mo'-zez = drawn out]
Born in Egypt while Israel lived in bondage, the younger brother of Aaron and Miriam, the son of Amram and Jochebed, raised as the "son of Pharaoh's daughter," educated in all the learning of the Egyptians, an Old Testament prophet, led the Israelites out of Egypt to the promised land, forbidden to enter the land because of sin, and author of the Pentateuch. (See also Exod 2—40; Lev 8—16; Num 1—36; Deut 1—5; 27—34)
Matt 8: 4 commanded a specific gift be given to the priest for a testimony
17: 3 present at transfiguration of Jesus and talked with Him (17:4)
17: 4 Peter desired to build him a tabernacle
17: 5 overshadowed by a bright cloud
19: 7 his commandment to write a bill of divorcement was explained by Jesus to the Pharisees (19:8)
19: 8 suffered (the Israelites) to put away their wives
22:24 gave commandment concerning a man who dies childless
23: 2 his authority assumed by the scribes and Pharisees
Mark 1:44 had commanded an offering for cleansing

Mark 7:10 commanded to honor father and mother, and whoso curseth father or mother was to die the death
9: 4 along with Elias (Elijah), appeared unto Peter, James, and John at the transfiguration of Jesus
9: 4 was talking with Jesus
9: 5 Peter desired to make him a tabernacle
10: 3 commanded the people
10: 4 suffered to write a bill of divorcement (to put away a wife) due to the hardness of the people's hearts (10:5)
12:19 wrote concerning raising up seed to one's brother
12:26 author of the book(s) of the law
12:26 God spoke unto him in the bush
Luke 2:22 commanded a law of purification
5:14 had commanded an offering for cleansing
9:30 talked with Jesus and Elias (Elijah) at the transfiguration of Jesus
9:31 appeared in glory and spoke of Jesus' death which He should accomplish at Jerusalem
9:33 departed
16:29 he and the prophets had testified of God
16:31 those who would not hear him (his words) would not be persuaded though one rose from the dead
20:28 wrote concerning raising up seed to one's brother
20:37 showed at the burning bush that the dead were raised when he called the Lord the God of Abraham, Isaac, and Jacob
24:27 Jesus began with his words (writings) to expound in all the scriptures the things concerning Himself
24:44 wrote the law
John 1:17 giver of the law
1:45 wrote concerning Jesus in the law
3:14 lifted up the serpent in the wilderness
5:45 the accuser of the Israelites
5:45 the Jews trust in him
5:46 had not been believed by the Jews
5:46 wrote of Jesus
5:47 his writings not believed by the Jews
6:32 gave not that (true) bread from Heaven
7:19 gave the law
7:22 gave circumcision not of himself, but of the fathers
7:23 gave the law (which should not be broken)
8: 5 commanded in the law that those guilty of adultery should be stoned
9:28 the Pharisees claimed to be his disciples
9:29 God had spoken unto him

124

MOSES *(continued)*

Acts	3:22	prophesied concerning Christ
	3:22	a prophet
	6:11	certain men falsely accused Stephen of speaking blasphemy against him
	6:14	had delivered customs to the Jews
	7:20	was born
	7:20	exceeding fair
	7:20	was nourished up in his father's house three months
	7:21	when cast out, Pharaoh's daughter took him up and nourished him for her own son
	7:22	was learned in all the wisdom of the Egyptians
	7:22	was mighty in words and in deeds
	7:23	at forty years of age, decided to visit his brethren
	7:24	seeing one of his brethren suffer wrong, defended, and avenged him
	7:24	smote (killed) the Egyptian
	7:25	was misunderstood by his brethren
	7:26	seeing his brethren strive, tried to set them at one
	7:27	was considered to think himself a ruler and a judge over them (the Israelites)
	7:28	killed an Egyptian
	7:29	fled from Egypt to Madian, where he was a stranger
	7:29	begat two sons
	7:30	after forty years, an angel of the Lord appeared to him in a burning bush in the wilderness of Mount Sina (Sinai)
	7:31	seeing the burning bush, wondered, drew near to behold it, and heard the voice of the Lord
	7:32	trembled and durst not behold
	7:33	told to put off his shoes for he stood on holy ground
	7:34	would be sent by God into Egypt
	7:35	having been refused by the Israelites before, was now sent of God to be a ruler and a deliverer
	7:35	an angel had appeared unto him in a (burning) bush
	7:36	brought the Israelites out after he had shown wonders and signs in the land of Egypt, in the Red Sea, and in the wilderness for forty years
	7:37	spoke of a prophet whom the Lord would raise up among the brethren, like unto him
	7:38	had been spoken to by the angel in Mount Sina (Sinai)
	7:38	received the lively oracles to give unto the Israelites
	7:39	was not obeyed, but thrust away
	7:40	brought the Israelites out of the land of Egypt
	7:40	the Israelites did not know what had become of him

Acts	7:44	was instructed by the Lord to make the tabernacle according to the fashion (pattern) he had seen
	13:39	giver of the law
	15: 1	had taught circumcision
	15: 5	gave the law
	15:21	in old time, had in every city them that preached him, being read in the synagogues every Sabbath day
	26:22	told of what should come concerning Christ (26:23)
	28:23	giver of the law
Rom	5:14	death reigned from Adam to him
	9:15	spoken to by the Lord
	10: 5	described the righteousness which is of the law
1Cor	9: 9	giver of the law
	10: 2	all Israel (the fathers of the Jews) were baptized unto him in the cloud and in the sea
2Cor	3: 7	the children of Israel could not steadfastly behold his face
	3: 7	his countenance was glorious
	3:13	put a veil over his face, that the children of Israel could not steadfastly look
	3:15	his writings (the law) were read
2Tim	3: 8	withstood by Jannes and Jambres
Heb	3: 2	was faithful in all his house
	3: 3	counted worthy of less glory than Christ
	3: 5	verily was faithful in all his house, as a servant, for a testimony
	3:16	led (Israel) out of Egypt
	7:14	spoke nothing concerning a priesthood of the tribe of Juda
	8: 5	was admonished of God to make all things (of the tabernacle) according to the pattern shown him in the mount
	9:19	spoke every precept to all people according to the law
	9:19	took the blood of calves and of goats, with water and scarlet wool, and hyssop and sprinkled both the book and all the people
	9:21	sprinkled with blood both the tabernacle and all the vessels of the ministry
	10:28	giver of the law
	11:23	after birth was hid three months by his parents
	11:23	a proper child
	11:24	by faith, when come to years, refused to be called the son of Pharaoh's daughter
	11:25	chose to suffer affliction with the people of God than to enjoy the pleasures of sin for a season
	11:26	esteemed the reproach of Christ greater riches than the treasures of Egypt
	11:26	had respect unto the recompense of the reward

MOSES *(continued)*

Heb 11:27 by faith, forsook Egypt, not fearing the wrath of the king
    11:27 endured as seeing him who is invisible
    11:28 through faith kept the Passover and the sprinkling of blood
    11:39 had obtained a good report through faith
    11:39 received not the promise
    12:21 exceedingly feared and quaked
Jude   : 9 Michael the archangel and the devil contended over his body
Rev   15: 3 his song was sung by those victorious over the beast
    15: 3 servant of God

N

NAAMAN [na'-a-man = pleasant]
A Syrian military leader, inflicted with leprosy, traveled to Israel where he followed the instructions of the prophet Elisha to obtain a cure. (See also 2Kng 5)

Luke 4:27 a leper (who was cleansed)
    4:27 a Syrian
    4:27 contemporary with Elisha the prophet

NAASSON [na'-as-son = enchanter]
Son of Aminadab, father of Salmon, and an ancestor of Jesus.

Matt 1: 4 begotten of Aminadab
    1: 4 begat Salmon
Luke 3:32 father of Salmon
    3:32 son of Aminadab (3:33)

NACHOR [na'-kor = snorting]
Old Testament Nahor, son of Saruch, father of Thara, grandfather of Abraham, and an ancestor of Jesus.

Luke 3:34 father of Thara
    3:34 son of Saruch (3:35)

NAGGE [nag'-e = illuminating]
Son of Maath, father of Esli, and an ancestor of Jesus.

Luke 3:25 father of Esli
    3:25 son of Maath (3:26)

NARCISSUS [nar-sis'-sus = flower]
A believer at Rome whose household was greeted by Paul.

Rom 16:11 those of his household which were in the Lord were greeted by Paul

NATHAN [na'-than = given; gift]
Son of David, father of Mattatha, and an ancestor of Jesus.

Luke 3:31 father of Mattatha
    3:31 son of David

NATHANAEL [na-than'-a-el = gift of God]
A man of Cana in Galilee, an Israelite in whom was no guile, and some authorities think he is identical with Bartholomew the apostle.

John 1:45 found by Philip
    1:46 questioned as to whether any good thing could come out of Nazareth
    1:46 told by Philip to come and see
    1:47 seen by Jesus
    1:47 an Israelite in whom there was no guile
    1:48 was called by Philip
    1:48 seen by Jesus while under the fig tree
    1:49 called Jesus Rabbi
    1:49 confessed Jesus to be the Son of God and King of Israel
    1:50 because of Jesus' statement to him, believed
    1:50 had been seen by Jesus while under the fig tree
    1:50 would see greater things than these
    1:51 would hereafter see Heaven open and the angels of God ascending and descending upon the Son of man
    21: 1 saw Jesus at the Sea of Tiberias (Sea of Galilee) while with a group of disciples (21:2)
    21: 2 of Cana in Galilee
    21: 3 entering a ship, went fishing, and caught nothing
    21: 4 knew (recognized) not Jesus
    21: 5 had no meat (had caught nothing)
    21: 6 obeying Jesus' command, cast the net on the right side of the ship
    21: 6 was not able to draw the net for the multitude of fishes
    21: 8 being not far from land, came in a little ship, dragging the net with fishes
    21: 9 coming to land, saw a fire of coals there, with fish and bread thereon
    21:10 told, by Jesus, to bring of the fish which he had caught
    21:12 told to come and dine
    21:12 dared not ask who He was, knowing that it was the Lord
    21:13 given bread and fish by Jesus
    21:14 saw the resurrected Jesus
    21:15 had dined with Jesus

NAUM [na'-um = comfort]
Son of Esli, father of Amos, and an ancestor of Jesus through Mary.

Luke 3:25 father of Amos
    3:25 son of Esli

NEPHTHALIM [nef'-tha-lim = my wrestling]
Old Testament Naphtali, one of the patriarchs, the son of Jacob and Rachel's handmaid Bilhah, and a full brother of Dan. (See also Gen 30,35,46,49; Exod 1)

Matt	1: 2	begotten of Jacob
John	4:12	drank of the well (Jacob's)
	4:12	a child of Jacob
Acts	7: 8	begat by Jacob
	7: 8	one of the patriarchs
	7: 9	one of the patriarchs
	7: 9	moved with envy, sold Joseph into Egypt
	7:11	a father of the Jews
	7:11	found no sustenance
	7:12	sent by Jacob to Egypt for corn
	7:12	a father of the Jews
	7:13	on his second visit (to Egypt), Joseph was made known to him
	7:13	a brother of Joseph
	7:13	was made known unto Pharaoh
	7:15	went down into Egypt and died
	7:15	a father of the Jews
	7:16	was carried into Sychem and was laid in the sepulcher that Abraham bought

NEREUS [ne'-re-us = lamp]
A believer at Rome, who along with his sister, was greeted by Paul.

Rom	16:15	saluted by Paul
	16:15	was with the saints
	16:15	had a sister

NERI [ne'-ri = Jehovah my lamp]
Son of Melchi, father of Salathiel, and an ancestor of Jesus.

Luke	3:27	father of Salathiel
	3:27	son of Melchi (3:28)

NICANOR [ni-ca'-nor = conqueror]
One of seven men of honest report, full of the Holy Ghost, chosen to serve tables as a deacon in the Jerusalem church, and received the laying on of hands by the apostles.

Acts	6: 3	of honest report
	6: 3	full of the Holy Ghost and wisdom
	6: 5	chosen to serve tables
	6: 6	was set before the apostles
	6: 6	apostles prayed and laid their hands on him

NICODEMUS nic-o-de'-mus = innocent blood]
A Pharisee who came to Jesus by night and along with Joseph of Arimathaea prepared the body of Jesus for burial.

John	3: 1	a man of the Pharisees
	3: 1	a ruler of the Jews
	3: 2	came to Jesus by night
	3: 2	called Jesus Rabbi
	3: 2	knew Jesus was a teacher come from God because of His miracles
	3: 4	questioned as to how a man could be born again
	3: 9	questioned the process of spiritual birth
	3:10	a master of Israel
	7:50	came to Jesus by night
	7:50	a Pharisee
	7:53	went unto his own house
	19:39	at first had come to Jesus by night
	19:39	came bringing an hundred pound mixture of myrrh and aloes
	19:40	along with Joseph (of Arimathaea), wound the body of Jesus in linen clothes with the spices
	19:41	laid Jesus in a new sepulcher in a garden wherein was never man yet laid (19:42)

NICOLAS [nic'-o-las = conqueror of the people]
A proselyte of Antioch, one of seven men of honest report, full of the Holy Ghost, chosen to serve tables as a deacon in the Jerusalem church, and received the laying on of hands by the apostles.

Acts	6: 3	of honest report
	6: 3	full of the Holy Ghost and wisdom
	6: 5	chosen to serve tables
	6: 5	a proselyte of Antioch
	6: 6	was set before the apostles
	6: 6	apostles prayed and laid their hands on him

NOAH [no'-ah = rest]
Also Noe, of the line of Seth, the son of Lamech, father of Shem, Ham, and Japheth, built an ark to the saving of his family, and thereby became the father of all mankind after the flood. (See also Gen 5—10)

Matt	24:37	Jesus prophesied that the last days shall be as the days of Noe (Noah) (24:39)
	24:38	entered into the ark
Luke	3:36	father of Sem (Shem)
	3:36	son of Lamech
	17:26	as it was in his days, so shall it be also in the days of the Son of man
	17:27	entered into the ark
Heb	11: 7	being warned of God of things not seen, was moved with fear
	11: 7	by faith prepared an ark to the saving of his house and thus condemned the world
	11: 7	became heir of the righteousness which is by faith
	11:13	died in faith, not having received the promises, but was persuaded of them and embraced them
	11:13	confessed that he was a stranger and pilgrim on the earth
	11:16	desired a better country
	11:16	God is not ashamed to be called His God
	11:16	God hath prepared for him a city
	11:39	had obtained a good report through faith

NOAH *(continued)*

Heb	11:39	received not the promise
1Pet	3:20	the longsuffering of God waited in his days while the ark was being prepared
2Pet	2: 5	saved from judgment by God
	2: 5	the eighth person (saved through the flood)
	2: 5	a preacher of righteousness

NOE [no'-e = rest]—see NOAH

NYMPHAS [nim'-fas = bridegroom]
A believer to whom Paul sent a salutation and a host of the church which met in his house.

| Col | 4:15 | saluted by Paul |
| | 4:15 | hosted a church which met in his house |

O

OBED [o'-bed = serving]
Son of Boaz by Ruth, father of Jesse, and grand-father of David. (See also Ruth 4; 1Chr 2)

Matt	1: 5	begotten by Booz (Boaz) of Ruth
	1: 5	begat Jesse
Luke	3:32	father of Jesse
	3:32	son of Booz (Boaz)

OLYMPAS [o-lim'-pas = heavenly]
A believer of Rome to whom Paul sent greetings.

| Rom | 16:15 | saluted by Paul |
| | 16:15 | was with the saints |

ONESIMUS [o-nes'-i-mus = profitable]
A man of Colosse, a slave of Philemon (who had escaped to Rome), converted under the ministry of Paul, sent back to Philemon to be received as a Christian brother, and his debts to Philemon would be cared for by Paul.

Col	4: 7	sent (by Paul) with Tychicus to report the state (affairs) of Paul to the Colossian church (4:9)
	4: 9	a faithful and beloved brother (one of the Colossians) of Paul
Phle	:10	spiritual son of Paul (begotten in Paul's bonds)
	:10	Paul besought his master, Philemon, on his behalf (:18)
	:11	before an unprofitable servant, but now profitable to Philemon and to Paul
	:12	sent again to Philemon
	:12	Paul desired that Philemon receive him
	:13	was desired to be retained by Paul to minister to him in the Gospel
Phle	:15	departed for a season
	:16	beloved of Paul
	:16	was to be received not as a servant, but as a brother beloved by Philemon
	:17	Paul desired Philemon to receive him as he would receive Paul
	:18	any debts he owed to Philemon were to be paid by Paul

ONESIPHORUS [o-ne-sif'-o-rus = bringing profit]
A believer of Ephesus who often ministered unto the needs of Paul, and often under dangerous circumstances.

2Tim	1:16	Paul asked God's mercy upon his house
	1:16	often refreshed Paul
	1:16	was not ashamed of Paul's chain
	1:17	when in Rome, sought diligently for Paul and found him
	1:18	ministered much to Paul at Ephesus
	4:19	Paul requested Timothy to salute his household

OSEE [o'-see = to save]
Old Testament Hosea, son of Berri, an Old Testament prophet who ministered to the kingdom of Israel, contemporary with Uzziah, Jotham, Ahaz, and Hezekiah (kings of Judah), and Jeroboam (king of Israel), and author of the prophetical book of Hosea. (See also Hos 1)

| Rom | 9:25 | prophesied concerning relationships to Christ |

OZIAS [o-zi'-as = strength from the Lord]
Old Testament Uzziah, son of Joram, reigned as king of Judah, judged of God and became leprous for his usurpation into the activities of the priesthood, and succeeded by his son Jotham as king. (Also possibly identical with Azariah). (See also 2Kng 15; 2Chr 26,27; Isa 1,6,7; Hos 1)

| Matt | 1: 8 | begotten of Joram |
| | 1: 9 | begat Joatham |

P

PARMENAS [par'-me-nas = abiding]
One of seven men of honest report, full of the Holy Ghost, chosen to serve tables as a deacon in the Jerusalem church, and received the laying on of hands by the apostles.

| Acts | 6: 3 | of honest report |
| | 6: 3 | full of the Holy Ghost and wisdom |

PARMENAS *(continued)*

Acts   6: 5 chosen to serve tables
        6: 6 was set before the apostles
        6: 6 apostles prayed and laid their hands on him

PATROBAS [pat'-ro-bas = paternal]
A Christian at Rome saluted by Paul.

Rom 16:14 saluted by Paul
      16:14 was with other brethren

PAUL [pawl = little]
Also Saul, an apostle of Jesus Christ to the Gentiles, a Pharisee, a Hebrew of the tribe of Benjamin, born in Tarsus, a Roman citizen, zealously persecuted the Christians until converted on the road to Damascus, fervently pursued the preaching of the Lord Jesus Christ, performed three major missionary endeavors, endured great persecution, imprisoned for his preaching, executed in Rome, and writer of at least thirteen (possibly fourteen) New Testament books.

Acts   7:58 a young man
       7:58 witnesses to Stephen's stoning laid down their clothes at his feet
       8: 1 consented unto the death of Stephen
       8: 3 made havoc of the church
       8: 3 entered every house and hailing men and women, committed them to prison
       9: 1 breathed out threatenings and slaughter against the disciples of the Lord
       9: 1 went unto the high priest, and desired letters that he might bring any disciples of the Lord, bound unto Jerusalem (9:2)
       9: 3 journeyed near Damascus
       9: 3 fell to earth when he saw a light from Heaven and heard the voice of the Lord (9:4)
       9: 4 had persecuted the Lord
       9: 5 spoke to the Lord, whom he had persecuted
       9: 6 trembling and astonished, asked what the Lord would have him to do
       9: 6 told to go into the city (Damascus) and receive instruction
       9: 7 journeyed with other men
       9: 8 arose from the earth and opened his eyes, but saw no man (was blinded)
       9: 8 was led by the hand and brought into Damascus
       9: 9 was in Damascus three days without sight
       9: 9 neither ate nor drank for three days
       9:11 was in the house of Judas
       9:11 of Tarsus
       9:11 prayed

       9:12 had seen a vision (of his healing)
       9:13 had done much evil to the saints at Jerusalem
       9:14 had authority from the chief priests to bind all that call on the name of the Lord
       9:15 a chosen vessel unto God
       9:15 would bear the name of the Lord before the Gentiles, and kings, and the children of Israel
       9:16 would suffer great things for the Lord's name's sake
       9:17 Ananias placed his hands on him that he might receive his sight and be filled with the Holy Ghost
       9:18 scales fell from his eyes and he received his sight
       9:18 arose and was baptized
       9:19 received meat and was strengthened
       9:19 stayed certain days with the disciples at Damascus
       9:20 preached in the synagogues that Christ is the Son of God
       9:21 amazed his hearers
       9:21 had destroyed them which called on His name in Jerusalem and had come to Damascus for that intent
       9:22 increased more in strength
       9:22 confounded the Jews which dwelt in Damascus, proving that this is very Christ
       9:23 the Jews took counsel to kill him
       9:24 knew of the Jews intention to kill him
       9:25 was let down at night by the wall in a basket by the disciples
       9:26 came to Jerusalem
       9:26 desired to join himself with the disciples (of Jerusalem), but they were afraid of him and believed not that he was a disciple
       9:27 taken by Barnabas to the apostles and his conversion and bold preaching at Damascus were declared unto them
       9:28 went with the apostles in and out at Jerusalem
       9:29 spoke boldly in the name of the Lord Jesus
       9:29 disputed against the Grecians
       9:29 the Grecians went about to slay him
       9:30 was sent to Caesarea and on to Tarsus by the brethren
     11:25 was in Tarsus
     11:25 sought by Barnabas
     11:26 found by Barnabas and brought to Antioch
     11:26 a whole year assembled with the church and taught much people
     11:29 along with Barnabas, carried the relief to the elders from the brethren in Judea (11:30)

PAUL *(continued)*

Acts 12:25 along with Barnabas, returned to Jerusalem when he had fulfilled his ministry

12:25 took John Mark with him (and Barnabas) to Jerusalem

13: 1 was in the church at Antioch

13: 1 a prophet and teacher

13: 2 ministered to the Lord and fasted

13: 2 the Holy Spirit required he be separated unto the work to which He had called him

13: 3 the prophets and teachers laid their hands on him, and sent him away

13: 4 sent forth by the Holy Ghost

13: 4 departed with Barnabas unto Seleucia and then sailed to Cyprus

13: 5 at Salamis, preached the Word of God in the synagogues

13: 5 had John (Mark) to his minister (as an assistant)

13: 6 on the isle of Paphos found Bar-jesus (Elymas) with Sergius Paulus, who desired to hear the Word of God (13:7)

13: 8 withstood by Bar-jesus (Elymas)

13: 9 also called Paul

13: 9 filled with the Holy Ghost

13: 9 set his eyes on Bar-jesus (Elymas) and pronounced judgment against him (13:11)

13:13 left Paphos (with Barnabas and John Mark) and came to Perga in Pamphylia

13:13 John (Mark) left him (and Barnabas) and returned to Jerusalem

13:14 departed from Perga and came to Antioch in Pisidia

13:14 entered the synagogue on the Sabbath day and sat down

13:15 invited to speak by the rulers of the synagogue

13:16 stood up and beckoned with his hand and asked audience

13:32 declared the good tidings that God had fulfilled His promise in raising up Jesus (13:33)

13:42 besought of the Gentiles to preach the Word unto them

13:43 many followed him and Barnabas being persuaded to continue in the grace of God

13:45 the Jews contradicted and blasphemed his words

13:46 waxed bold, rebuked the Jews, and turned the ministry to the Gentiles

13:47 the Lord commanded that He had set him (and Barnabas) to be a light of the Gentiles

13:50 the Jews raised persecution against him (and Barnabas) and expelled them out of their coasts

13:51 shook off the dust of his feet against them of Antioch of Pisidia, and

went to Iconiom

Acts 14: 1 entered the synagogue at Iconium

14: 1 so spoke that a great multitude believed

14: 3 abode a long time in Iconium speaking boldly in the Lord

14: 3 granted, of the Lord, that signs and wonders might be done by his hands

14: 4 part of the city followed him (and Barnabas)

14: 4 called an apostle

14: 5 object of a planned assault by both Jews and Gentiles to despitefully use him and stone him

14: 6 fled to Lystra, and Derbe, and the surrounding region

14: 7 preached the gospel

14: 8 healed the crippled man at Lystra (14:10)

14:11 seeing his works, the people at Lystra thought he and Barnabas to be gods

14:12 was called Mercurius (a god)

14:12 was the chief speaker

14:13 hearing the people would have sacrificed unto him, rent his clothes and ran in among the people (14:14)

14:14 called an apostle

14:15 man of like passions as the people of Lystra, who preached unto them the living God

14:18 scarcely restrained the people from doing sacrifice unto him

14:19 was stoned, drawn out of the city, being left for dead

14:20 rose up, came into the city (of Lystra)

14:20 next day departed with Barnabas to Derbe

14:21 preached the gospel and taught many in Derbe

14:21 returned to Lystra, Iconium, and Antioch confirming the souls of the disciples and exhorting them to continue in the faith (14:22)

14:23 ordained elders in every church and commended them to the Lord

14:23 prayed with fasting

14:24 passed throughout Pisidia and came to Pamphylia

14:25 having preached the Word in Perga, went down into Attalia

14:26 sailed to Antioch, from whence he had been recommended to the grace of God

14:26 had fulfilled his work (his mission)

14:27 gathered the church together and rehearsed all that God had done with him (and Barnabas)

14:28 abode a long time with the disciples (at Antioch)

15: 2 along with Barnabas, had no small

PAUL *(continued)*

PAUL *(continued)*

PAUL *(continued)*

		all the disciples
Acts	19: 1	passed through the upper coasts and came to Ephesus
	19: 1	found disciples who had neither received, nor heard about the Holy Ghost (19:2)
	19: 6	laid his hands upon the Ephesian believers (to receive the Holy Ghost)
	19: 8	spoke boldly in the synagogue for three months disputing and persuading the things concerning the kingdom of God
	19: 9	departed from the unbelievers, and separated the disciples, disputing daily in the school of Tyrannus for two years (19:10)
	19:11	God wrought special miracles by his hands
	19:12	handkerchiefs and aprons, from his body, healed from disease and cast out evil spirits
	19:13	preached Jesus
	19:15	was known by an evil spirit
	19:21	purposed in the spirit to go to Jerusalem
	19:21	determined also to see Rome
	19:22	sent Timotheus (Timothy) and Erastus into Macedonia
	19:22	ministered unto by Timotheus (Timothy) and Erastus
	19:22	stayed in Asia (for a season)
	19:26	at Ephesus and throughout all Asia had persuaded much people that there be no gods which are made with hands
	19:29	was a traveling companion of Gaius and Aristarchus
	19:30	would have entered the theater (at Ephesus), but the disciples suffered him not
	19:31	desired by certain of the chief of Asia, which were his friends, not to adventure into the theater (at Ephesus)
	20: 1	called together the disciples (of Ephesus), embraced them, and departed for Macedonia
	20: 2	going over those parts, gave much exhortation as he went
	20: 2	came into Greece and abode three months (20:3)
	20: 3	the Jews laid wait for him as he was about to sail into Syria, but he purposed to return through Macedonia
	20: 4	accompanied into Asia by Sopater, Aristarchus, Secundus, Gaius, Timotheus (Timothy), Tychicus, and Trophimus
	20: 5	his companions waited for him (and Luke) at Troas
	20: 6	sailed from Philippi and came to Troas in five days
Acts	20: 6	abode seven days in Troas
	20: 7	ready to depart on the morrow, preached unto the disciples until midnight
	20: 9	was long preaching
	20:10	went down, fell on Eutychus, and embraced him
	20:11	came up again, broke bread, ate, talked a long while, and departed
	20:13	appointed the others to go before as he minded to go afoot
	20:14	met his companions at Assos, was taken in by them, and came to Mitylene
	20:15	sailed over against Chios, next day arrived at Samos, tarried at Trogyllium, and the next day came to Miletus
	20:16	had determined to sail by Ephesus, not spending time in Asia, hasting to be in Jerusalem on the day of Pentecost if possible
	20:17	from Miletus, sent to Ephesus and called the elders of the church
	20:17	the elders of the church (at Ephesus) came to him (20:18)
	20:18	had been with them (at Ephesus) at all seasons
	20:19	served the Lord with all humility of mind, and with many tears and temptations, which befell him by the laying in wait of the Jews
	20:20	had kept back nothing that was profitable from the Ephesians
	20:20	had taught (the Ephesians) publicly, and from house to house
	20:21	testified both to Jews and Greeks repentance toward God and faith toward our Lord Jesus Christ
	20:22	went to Jerusalem bound in the spirit, not knowing the things that should befall him there
	20:23	the Holy Ghost witnessed in every city that bonds and afflictions would come to him
	20:24	was not moved by these things, neither counted his life dear unto himself, so that he might finish his course with joy
	20:24	had received a ministry of the Lord Jesus
	20:25	those to whom he had preached (in Ephesus) the kingdom of God, would see his face no more
	20:26	exclaimed that he was pure from the blood of all men
	20:27	had not shunned to declare all the counsel of God
	20:31	for three years had not ceased to warn every one night and day with tears
	20:32	commended the Ephesians to God and to the Word of His grace

PAUL *(continued)*

Acts 20:33 coveted no man's silver, gold, or apparel

20:34 his own hands had ministered to the necessities of himself and those that were with him

20:35 had showed them (at Ephesus) all things

20:36 kneeled down and prayed with them all (the Ephesians) after speaking

20:37 the elders (of Ephesus) fell on his neck, and kissed him

20:38 many sorrowed over his words that they would see his face no more

20:38 accompanied to the ship

21: 1 having launched, came with a straight course unto Coos, and the day following to Rhodes, and from thence to Patara

21: 2 found a ship sailing to Phenicia, and went aboard and set forth

21: 3 after discovering Cyprus, sailed into Syria, landing at Tyre

21: 4 found disciples (at Tyre) who through the Spirit, said he should not go up to Jerusalem

21: 4 tarried seven days (at Tyre)

21: 5 having accomplished those days, departed from Tyre and was brought on his way out of the city by the people

21: 5 kneeled down on the shore and prayed

21: 6 took leave one of another and took ship

21: 7 finishing his course from Tyre, came to Ptolemais

21: 7 saluted the brethren and abode with them one day

21: 8 departed and came to Caesarea

21: 8 entered into the house of Philip the evangelist and abode with him

21:10 tarried many days (with Philip the evangelist)

21:11 Agabus took his girdle, bound his own hands and feet, and prophesied by the Holy Ghost that this would happen to him should he go to Jerusalem

21:12 besought by others not to go up to Jerusalem

21:13 those who besought him not to go to Jerusalem broke his heart

21:13 was not only ready to be bound, but also to die at Jerusalem for the name of the Lord Jesus

21:14 would not be persuaded

21:15 took up the carriages and went up to Jerusalem

21:16 accompanied by disciples of Caesarea among whom was Mnason

21:17 gladly received by the brethren at Jerusalem

Acts 21:18 went unto James and all the elders (at Jerusalem)

21:19 saluted James and the elders and declared what things God had wrought among the Gentiles by his ministry

21:21 was claimed to have taught the Jews to forsake Moses, not to circumcise their children, neither to walk after the customs

21:22 was come (to Jerusalem)

21:24 walked orderly and kept the law

21:26 purified himself along with others, and entered into the temple

21:27 was seen in the temple by the Jews of Asia who laid hands on him

21:28 accused of teaching against the law and the temple, and of bringing Greeks into the temple, and polluting the holy place

21:29 had been seen in the city with Trophimus, an Ephesian, whom they supposed he had brought into the temple

21:30 drawn out of the temple

21:31 people went about to kill him

21:32 was left off beating by the people

21:33 taken by the chief captain, bound with two chains, and commanded to be carried into the castle (21:34)

21:35 borne of the soldiers

21:36 the multitude cried "away with him"

21:36 asked the chief captain for an audience

21:37 was asked if he could speak Greek

21:38 was thought to be an Egyptian (by the chief captain)

21:39 a Jew of Tarsus

21:39 a citizen of no mean city

21:39 sought permission to speak to the people

21:40 given license to address the people

21:40 stood on the stairs, beckoned the people with his hands, and spoke to them in the Hebrew tongue

22: 1 presented his defense

22: 2 spoke in the Hebrew tongue

22: 3 a Jew

22: 3 born in Tarsus

22: 3 brought up (in Jerusalem) at the feet of Gamaliel

22: 3 was taught according to the perfect manner of the law of the fathers

22: 3 was zealous toward God

22: 4 persecuted this way unto death, binding and delivering into prison both men and women

22: 5 receiving letters from the high priest, went to Damascus to bring bound to Jerusalem those to be punished

22: 6 on his journey to Damascus saw a

134

PAUL *(continued)*

135

PAUL *(continued)*

before the governor (Felix)

Acts 23:34 was of the province of Cilicia
23:35 Felix agreed to hear him when his accusers had come
23:35 was commanded to be kept in Herod's judgment hall
24: 1 Felix informed by Tertullus against him
24: 2 was called forth (to hear the accusations)
24: 5 accused by Tertullus as being pestilent, a mover of sedition among all the Jews, a ringleader of the sect of the Nazarenes, and a profaner of the temple (24:6)
24: 6 had been taken and would have been judged according to the law of the Jews
24: 7 taken away from the Jews by (Claudius) Lysias
24: 8 his accusers had been commanded to appear before Felix concerning him
24: 8 was accused
24:10 beckoned of the governor (Felix) to speak
24:10 knew that Felix had been many years a judge unto this nation
24:10 cheerfully answered for himself
24:11 only twelve days had elapsed since he went up to Jerusalem to worship
24:12 was not found in the temple disputing with any man, neither raising up the people in the synagogues nor in the city
24:13 the accusations against him could not be proven by the Jews
24:14 confessed that he did worship in the way that the Jews called heresy, believing all things written in the law and in the prophets
24:15 had hope toward God in a resurrection
24:16 exercised himself always to have a conscience void of offense
24:17 after many years had come to bring alms and offerings to his nation
24:18 found, by certain Jews, purified in the temple neither with multitude nor with tumult
24:20 stood before the council
24:21 had cried before the council that he was called in question concerning the resurrection
24:21 had been called in question before Felix
24:23 commanded to be kept by a centurion with liberty and not forbidden to be seen or to be ministered to by any of his acquaintance
24:24 sent for by Felix, and heard by him and his wife, concerning the faith in Christ

Acts 24:25 reasoned of righteousness, temperance, and judgment to come
24:25 would be called for again when Felix had a more convenient season
24:26 Felix hoped that he would give him money, to be loosed
24:26 called before Felix the oftener to commune with him
24:27 left bound (after two years) by Felix
25: 1 the high priest and chief of the Jews informed Festus against him, desired favor against him, and plotted to kill him (25:3)
25: 4 Festus determined that he should be kept at Caesarea
25: 6 was commanded to be brought before Festus
25: 7 many and grievous complaints were laid against him by the Jews which could not be proved
25: 8 answered for himself (before Festus)
25: 8 neither against the law of the Jews and the temple, nor against Caesar had he offended any thing at all
25: 9 asked by Festus if he were willing to go to Jerusalem to be judged
25:10 stood at Caesar's judgment seat where he ought to be judged
25:10 to the Jews had done no wrong
25:11 refused not to die if he were an offender or had committed anything worthy of death
25:11 would not be delivered unto them on false accusations
25:11 appealed unto Caesar
25:12 his appeal unto Caesar was granted by Festus
25:14 Festus declared his cause unto the king (Agrippa) (25:21)
25:14 left in bonds by Felix
25:15 the Jews desired Festus to have judgment against him
25:17 was commanded to be brought forth before Festus
25:19 was accused according to his accusers' own superstition
25:19 affirmed Jesus to be alive
25:20 had been asked by Festus to go to Jerusalem to be judged
25:21 had appealed to be reserved unto the hearing of Augustus
25:21 commanded to be kept till Festus might send him to Caesar
25:23 at Festus's command, was brought forth into the place of hearing (before Agrippa)
25:24 seen by Agrippa and others
25:24 Festus informed Agrippa of the Jews' desire that he live no longer
25:25 found by Festus to have committed nothing worthy of death
25:25 had appealed to Augustus
25:26 brought before King Agrippa that,

PAUL *(continued)*

upon examination, Festus might have somewhat to write to Augustus

Acts 25:27 a prisoner

25:27 Festus thought it unreasonable to send him without signifying the crimes laid against him

26: 1 permitted to answer for himself before Agrippa for that whereof he was accused of the Jews (26:2)

26: 2 was happy to answer for himself touching all things whereof he was accused of the Jews

26: 3 besought Agrippa to patiently hear him

26: 4 his manner of life from his youth was known by all the Jews

26: 4 lived at Jerusalem

26: 5 known of the Jews from the beginning

26: 5 lived after the most straitest sect of his religion as a Pharisee

26: 6 stood and was judged for the hope of the promise made of God unto the fathers

26: 7 told Agrippa he was accused of the Jews for his belief in the hope to come

26: 9 had thought to do many things contrary to the name of Jesus of Nazareth in Jerusalem (26:10)

26:10 shut up in prison, many of the saints in Jerusalem having received authority from the chief priest

26:10 gave his voice against them who were put to death (for their belief)

26:11 often punished (believers) in every synagogue, compelling them to blaspheme

26:11 being exceedingly mad against the believers, persecuted them even unto strange cities

26:12 went to Damascus with authority and commission from the chief priests

26:13 at midday saw a light from Heaven, above the brightness of the sun, shining around about him and his companions

26:14 fell to the earth and heard a voice in the Hebrew tongue asking why he persecuted (the Lord)

26:14 called Saul (his former name) by Jesus

26:15 called Jesus Lord

26:15 had persecuted Jesus

26:16 told by Jesus to rise and stand upon his feet

26:16 Jesus had appeared unto him for the purpose of making him a minister and a witness of what he had seen and of those things in the which God would appear unto him

Acts 26:17 delivered from the people and from the Gentiles

26:17 was now being sent to the Gentiles

26:19 was not disobedient unto the heavenly vision

26:20 showed unto them of Damascus, at Jerusalem, and throughout all the coasts of Judea and then to the Gentiles that they should repent and turn to God and do works meet for repentance

26:21 for his witness, the Jews caught him in the temple and went about to kill him

26:22 obtaining the help of God, continued to witness, saying nothing other than those things which the prophets and Moses did say should come

26:24 spoke for himself

26:24 Festus claimed that he was beside himself, and that much learning had made him mad

26:25 was not mad, but spoke forth the words of truth and soberness

26:26 spoke freely before Agrippa

26:26 was persuaded that none of these things were hidden from Agrippa

26:27 knew that King Aprippa believed the prophets

26:28 almost persuaded Agrippa to become a Christian

26:29 desired that all who heard him were as he was, except for the bonds

26:29 was in bonds

26:30 Agrippa, Festus, Bernice, and others agreed that he had done nothing worthy of death or of bonds (26:31)

26:32 might have been set at liberty if he had not appealed unto Caesar

27: 1 delivered (along with other prisoners) unto Julius (to sail to Italy)

27: 2 entered a ship of Adramyttium, and launched, meaning to sail by the coasts of Asia

27: 2 Aristarchus (and Luke) sailed with him

27: 3 the next day touched at Sidon

27: 3 courteously entreated by Julius and given liberty to go unto his friends to refresh himself

27: 4 launched from Sidon and sailed under Cyprus because the winds were contrary

27: 5 sailed over the sea of Cilicia and Pamphylia, and came to Myra

27: 6 put on a ship of Alexandria sailing into Italy

27: 7 sailed slowly many days, scarcely coming over against Cnidus, not being suffered of the wind

27: 7 sailed under Crete, over against Salmone, and came to the fair ha-

PAUL *(continued)*

ens, near the city of Lasea (27:8)

Acts 27: 9 admonished those in authority of the danger which lay ahead on the voyage (27:10)

27:10 perceived that the voyage would be with hurt and much damage, not only of the lading and ship, but also of lives

27:11 not fully believed by the centurion

27:13 sailed close by Crete

27:16 ran under the island of Clauda

27:16 had much work to come by the boat

27:18 was exceedingly tossed with a tempest

27:19 cast out, with his own hands, the tackling of the ship

27:20 saw neither sun nor stars in many days, and all hope that he should be saved was taken away

27:21 after long abstinence, stood in the midst saying that they should have hearkened unto him and not loosed from Crete

27:22 exhorted them to be of good cheer, for no man would lose his life

27:23 an angel of God stood by him (that night)

27:23 belonged to the Lord and served Him

27:24 told by the angel of God to fear not, for he must be brought before Caesar

27:24 God hath given him all that sailed with him

27:25 believed God

27:27 had been driven up and down in Adria fourteen nights

27:31 instructed the centurion and the soldiers

27:33 besought all to take meat

27:33 had tarried and continued fasting fourteen days

27:34 prayed the passengers to take some meat

27:35 took bread and gave thanks to God in the presence of all, broke it, and began to eat

27:37 one of 276 passengers in the ship

27:42 the soldiers counsel was to kill him, lest he swim out and escape

27:43 the centurion was willing to save him (alive)

27:44 escaped safely to land

28: 1 had escaped to the island of Melita

28: 2 was shown no little kindness (by the people of Melita)

28: 2 was received because of the present rain and the cold

28: 3 gathered a bundle of sticks and laid them on the fire

28: 3 a viper came out of the heat and fastened on his hand

28: 4 seeing the venomous beast hang on

his hand, the barbarians considered him a murderer, whom, though having escaped vengeance suffered not to live

Acts 28: 5 shook off the beast into the fire and felt no harm

28: 6 when he should have swollen and fallen dead, no harm came to him

28: 6 the people, having seen no harm come to him, changed their minds and said that he was a god

28: 7 received by Publius and lodged three days courteously

28: 8 prayed and laid his hands on Publius's father and healed him

28: 9 healed others on the island

28:10 honored with many honors

28:10 when he departed, was laded with such things as were necessary

28:11 after three months departed in a ship of Alexandria

28:12 landed at Syracuse and tarried three days

28:13 sailed on to Rhegium and then to Puteoli

28:14 found brethren (at Puteoli) and desired to tarry with them seven days

28:14 went toward Rome

28:15 being met by the brethren at Appii forum and the three taverns, thanked God and took courage

28:16 came to Rome

28:16 delivered by the centurion to the captain of the guard

28:16 suffered to dwell by himself with a soldier that kept him

28:17 called together the chief of the Jews

28:17 had committed nothing against the people or customs of the fathers, yet was delivered prisoner from Jerusalem into the hands of the Romans

28:18 after examination by the Romans, would have been let go, as there was no cause of death in him

28:19 was constrained to appeal unto Caesar

28:19 had nought to accuse his nation

28:20 had called to see, and speak with the Jews

28:20 bound with a chain

28:21 the Jews of Rome had neither received letters out of Jerusalem concerning him, nor heard from any brethren any harm of him

28:22 Jews desired to hear his thoughts

28:23 was appointed a day in which he expounded and testified the kingdom of God, persuading them concerning Jesus from morning till evening

28:23 many came to his lodging to hear him

138

PAUL (continued)

Acts 28:25 people departed from him upon hearing the words of Esaias (Isaiah)

28:30 dwelt two whole years in his own hired house

28:30 received all that came in unto him, preaching the kingdom of God and teaching those things which concern the Lord Jesus Christ with all confidence (28:31)

28:31 no man forbade him (to preach and teach)

Rom 1: 1 a servant of Jesus Christ

1: 1 called to be an apostle

1: 1 separated unto the gospel of God

1: 5 had received grace and apostleship (by Christ)

1: 8 thanked his God through Jesus Christ for the Roman believers

1: 9 God was his witness

1: 9 served God with his spirit in the gospel of His Son

1: 9 without ceasing, made mention of Roman believers always in his prayers that he might have a prosperous journey to come to them (1:10)

1:11 longed to see Roman believers in order to impart to them some spiritual gift

1:12 desired to be comforted together with the Roman believers by the mutual faith

1:13 had often purposed to go to the brethren in Rome

1:13 desired fruit among Roman brethren, as among other Gentiles

1:14 debtor to Greeks, barbarians, wise and unwise

1:15 was ready to preach the gospel to those at Rome

1:16 was not ashamed of the gospel of Christ

3: 5 spoke as a man

3: 8 was slanderously reported that he taught that Christians should do evil that good may come

3: 9 a Jew

6:19 spoke after the manner of men (to the Romans)

7: 7 had not known sin but by the law

7: 7 had not known lust except the law had said, "Thou shalt not covet"

7: 8 sin wrought all manner of concupiscence in him

7: 9 was alive without the law once

7: 9 when the commandment came, sin revived, and he died (spiritually)

7:10 found the commandment ordained to life, to be unto death

7:11 sin, taking occasion by the commandment, deceived him and by it, slew him

Rom 7:13 sin worked death in him by that which is good

7:14 was carnal, sold under sin

7:15 that which he would, he did not, but that which he hated, that he did

7:17 indwelt by sin

7:18 in his flesh, dwelt no good thing

7:18 to will was present with him, but how to perform that which is good, he found not

7:19 the good he would, he did not, but the evil which he would not, that he did

7:21 found a law that when he would do good, evil was present with him

7:22 delighted in the law of God after the inward man

7:23 saw another law in his members, warring against the law of his mind, and bringing him into captivity to the law of sin

7:23 the law of sin was in his members

7:24 a wretched man (in the flesh)

7:25 with the mind served the law of God, but with the flesh the law of sin

8:38 persuaded that nothing should be able to separate (the believer) from the love of God which is in Christ Jesus our Lord (8:39)

9: 1 spoke the truth in Christ

9: 1 lied not

9: 1 his conscience also bore him witness in the Holy Ghost

9: 2 had great heaviness and continual sorrow in his heart

9: 3 could wish that he himself were accursed from Christ for his brethren, his kinsmen, according to the flesh

9: 4 an Israelite

10: 1 his heart's desire and prayer for Israel was that they might be saved

10: 2 bore record that Israelites had a zeal of God, but not according to knowledge

10: 8 preached the word of faith

11: 1 an Israelite

11: 1 of the seed of Abraham

11: 1 of the tribe of Benjamin

11:13 spoke to the Gentiles (of Rome)

11:13 the apostle of the Gentiles

11:13 magnified his office

11:14 by any means endeavored to provoke to emulation them which were his flesh (Israel) that he might save some

11:25 desired that the Gentiles not be ignorant of the mystery

14:14 knew and was persuaded that there was nothing unclean of itself

15:14 persuaded of the Romans (his brethren) that they were full of goodness, filled with all knowledge,

PAUL *(continued)*

to admonish one another

Rom 15:15 had written the more boldly (unto the Romans)

15:15 grace was given him of God

15:16 the minister of Jesus Christ to the Gentiles ministering the gospel of God

15:17 had whereof he could glory through Jesus Christ (in those things which pertain to God)

15:18 would not dare to speak of those things which Christ had not wrought by him

15:19 from Jerusalem unto Illyricum fully preached the gospel of Christ

15:20 strove to preach the gospel, not where Christ was named, lest he build upon another man's foundation

15:22 had been much hindered from coming to the Romans

15:23 had a great desire many years to come unto the Roman believers

15:24 when taking his journey to Spain, would come (also) to Rome

15:24 trusted to see the Romans in his journey and to be brought on his way by them

15:25 went unto Jerusalem to minister unto the saints

15:28 after performing his work in Rome and sealing to them the fruit, would come by Rome into Spain

15:29 was sure that when he came to Rome, he would come in the fullness of the blessing of the gospel of Christ

15:30 besought the Roman brethren to strive together in prayers to God for him

15:31 desired prayer to be delivered from them in Judea who did not believe

15:31 desired prayer that his service in Jerusalem might be accepted of the saints

15:32 desired prayer that he might come unto the Romans with joy and be refreshed

16: 1 commended Phebe unto the church at Rome

16: 1 his sister (in Christ) was Phebe

16: 2 had been succoured of Phebe

16: 3 sent his greeting to Priscilla and Aquila by the church at Rome

16: 3 Priscilla and Aquila were his helpers in Christ Jesus

16: 4 Priscilla and Aquila had laid down their own necks for his life

16: 4 gave thanks to Priscilla and Aquila

16: 5 greeted the church that met in the house of Priscilla and Aquila

16: 5 saluted his well-beloved Epaenetus

16: 6 greeted Mary who bestowed much

labor on him

Rom 16: 7 saluted Andronicus and Junia

16: 7 kinsman of Andronicus and Junia

16: 7 fellow prisoner of Andronicus and Junia

16: 7 in Christ (saved) after Andronicus and Junia

16: 8 greeted Amplias his beloved in the Lord

16: 9 saluted Urbane

16: 9 his helper in Christ was Urbane

16: 9 saluted Stachys his beloved

16:10 saluted Apelles

16:10 saluted them of Aristobulus's household

16:11 saluted Herodion

16:11 kinsman of Herodion

16:11 greeted them of the household of Narcissus which are in the Lord

16:12 saluted Tryphena and Tryphosa

16:12 saluted the beloved Persis

16:13 saluted Rufus

16:13 saluted Rufus and his mother

16:14 saluted Asyncritus, Phlegon, Hermas, Patrobas, Hermes, and the brethren with them

16:15 saluted Philologus, Julia, Nereus, and his sister, Olympas, and all the saints with them

16:17 besought the brethren to mark them who caused divisions and offenses and to avoid them

16:19 was glad on behalf of the Romans that their obedience was come abroad unto all men

16:19 desired that the Romans be wise unto that which is good and simple concerning evil

16:21 a workfellow of Timotheus (Timothy)

16:21 kinsman of Lucius, Jason, and Sosipater

16:23 hosted by Gaius

1Cor 1: 1 called an apostle of Jesus Christ through the will of God

1: 1 (Christian) brother of Sosthenes

1: 1 author of 1 Corinthians (1:2)

1: 4 thanked God always on behalf of the Corinthian brothers for the grace of God given unto them

1:10 besought the Corinthian believers to speak alike and have no divisions, but to be perfectly joined together

1:11 had heard that there were contentions among the Corinthian believers

1:12 some of the Corinthian believers claimed to be (followers) of him

1:14 baptized none of the Corinthians but Crispus and Gaius

1:15 wanted none to be able to say that he had baptized in his own name

1:16 baptized also the household of

Stephanas

1Cor 1:16 knew not whether he baptized any other

1:17 sent by Christ not to baptize, but to preach the gospel

1:23 preached Christ crucified

2: 1 came to the Corinthians, not with excellency of speech or wisdom

2: 1 declared unto the Corinthians the testimony of God

2: 2 determined not to know anything among the Corinthians save Jesus Christ and Him crucified

2: 3 was with the Corinthians in weakness, in fear, and in much trembling

2: 4 his speech and preaching were not with enticing words of man's wisdom, but in demonstration of the Spirit and of power

2: 6 spoke wisdom among the believers

2: 7 spoke the wisdom of God in a mystery

3: 1 could not speak to the Corinthians as unto spiritual, but as unto carnal, as babes in Christ

3: 2 had fed the Corinthians with milk (not with meat)

3: 4 some Corinthian believers said they were (followers) of him

3: 5 a minister (by whom the Corinthians believed)

3: 6 had planted (the gospel in the hearts of the Corinthians)

3:10 a wise master builder who laid the foundation

3:22 was the believers' (possession)

4: 1 the minister of Christ

4: 1 the steward of the mysteries of God

4: 3 considered it a very small thing to be judged of the Corinthians

4: 3 did not judge his own self

4: 4 knew nothing by himself

4: 4 was justified and judged by the Lord

4: 6 had in a figure transferred to himself and Apollos, those faults of others (for instructional purposes)

4: 9* thought God had set him (and the apostles) forth last, as it were appointed to death

4: 9* made a spectacle unto the world, to the angels, and to men

4:10* a fool for Christ's sake

4:10* weak and despised

4:11* hungered, thirsted, was naked, was buffeted, and had no certain dwelling place

4:12* labored, working with his own hands

4:12* being reviled, he blessed; being persecuted, he suffered it; being defamed, he entreated (4:13)

1Cor 4:13* was made as the filth of the world, and was the offscouring of all things

4:14 wrote not to shame them, but as his beloved sons, to warn them

4:15 had begotten them (the Corinthian believers) through the gospel

4:16 besought the Corinthians to be followers of him

4:17 had sent Timotheus (Timothy) to bring them into remembrance of his ways

4:17 Timotheus (Timothy) was his beloved (spiritual) son

4:17 taught the ways of Christ everywhere in every church

4:18 some thought he would not come

4:19 would come shortly, if the Lord willed, to the Corinthians and know their power, not their speech

4:21 questioned the Corinthians as to whether he should come to them with a rod or in love and the spirit of meekness

5: 3 although absent in body, but present in spirit, had judged (specific sins) as though he were present

5: 4 his spirit would be present in their gathering together

5: 9 had previously written an epistle to the Corinthians not to company with fornicators

5:11 wrote concerning the Christians' relationship with other believers who continually practice sin

5:12 was not a judge of the actions of those outside the church

6: 5 spoke to the shame of the Corinthian church

6:12 all things were lawful unto him, but all things were not expedient

6:12 although all things were lawful, he would not be brought under the power of any

7: 6 spoke by permission and not of commandment

7: 7 desired that all men were even as he

7: 8 suggested that the unmarried and widows remain (unmarried) as he was

7:10 was commanded of the Lord to speak concerning separation and divorce (7:11)

7:12 gave his opinion concerning marital situations (7:17)

7:25 had no commandment of the Lord concerning virgins, but gave his judgment

7:25 had obtained mercy of the Lord to be faithful

7:26 thought it good for a man to stay a virgin

7:35 spoke for the profit of the Corinthians, not to cast a snare upon them

141

PAUL *(continued)*

1Cor	7:40	believed that he had the Spirit of God (in his judgment)
	8:13	if eating meat made his brother to offend, he would eat no flesh while the world standeth, lest he offend his brother
	9: 1	an apostle
	9: 1	free
	9: 1	had seen Jesus Christ the Lord
	9: 1	the Corinthians were his work in the Lord
	9: 2	if he were not an apostle to others, he certainly was to the Corinthians
	9: 2	the seal of his apostleship was the Corinthian believers
	9: 3	was examined by some
	9: 4	had power (right) to eat and to drink
	9: 5	had power (right) to lead about a sister, a wife (the right to marry)
	9: 6	had the power (right) to forbear working
	9: 8	said the same things the law said
	9:11	had not used the right to material support from his Corinthians (9:12)
	9:15	had used none of his rights (as a minister) and did not write now for this to be done
	9:15	felt it better to die than that any man should make his glorying void
	9:16	preached the gospel of necessity, not for glory
	9:16	a woe would be on him if he preached not the gospel
	9:17	if he preached willingly, he would have a reward
	9:17	if he preached against his will, a dispensation of the gospel (responsibility still) was committed unto him
	9:18	his reward was that the gospel would be without charge, that he abused not his power in the gospel
	9:19	was free from all men
	9:19	made himself a servant unto all, that he might gain the more
	9:20	unto the Jews he became as a Jew that he might gain the Jews
	9:20	unto those under the law, became as under the law, that he might gain them
	9:21	to them without law, became as without law that he might gain them
	9:21	not without law to God, but under the law to Christ
	9:22	to the weak, became as weak to gain them
	9:22	made all things to all men, that he might by all means save some
	9:23	did what he did for the gospel's sake, that he might be a partaker with the Corinthians
1Cor	9:26	ran with certainty
	9:26	fought not as one that beateth the air
	9:27	kept his body under subjection lest when he had preached to others, he himself should be a castaway
	10: 1	would not that the Corinthians should be ignorant concerning their Jewish fathers
	10:15	spoke as to wise men
	10:20	would not that the Corinthian believers should have fellowship with devils
	10:23	all things were lawful for him, but all things were not expedient
	10:23	all things were lawful for him, but not all things edify
	10:33	pleased all men in all things, not seeking his own profit, but the profit of many, that they might be saved
	11: 1	a follower of Christ
	11: 2	praised the brethren at Corinth for their remembrance of him
	11: 2	delivered the ordinances to the brethren at Corinth
	11:17	praised not the Corinthian church
	11:18	heard of divisions among the Corinthian church and partly believed it
	11:22	praised not the Corinthian church (for their conduct at the Lord's supper)
	11:23	received of the Lord, that which also he delivered unto them
	11:34	would set the rest (of the doctrine) in order when he came (to Corinth)
	12: 1	desired that the Corinthians not be ignorant concerning spiritual gifts
	13:11	when a child, he spoke as a child, understood as a child, thought as a child
	13:11	when he became a man, he put away childish things
	13:12	knew (only) in part, but would know even as he was known
	14: 5	would that they spoke in tongues, but rather that they prophesied
	14:15	would pray with the spirit and with understanding
	14:15	would sing with the spirit and with understanding
	14:18	thanked God that he spoke with tongues more than all others (of the Corinthian church)
	14:19	in the church would rather speak five words with understanding than ten thousand words in a tongue
	14:37	the things that he wrote (to the church) were the commandments of the Lord
	15: 1	declared the gospel unto the Corinthians

PAUL *(continued)*

1Cor 15: 1 preached (the gospel) unto the Corinthians

15: 2 preached unto the Corinthians

15: 3 delivered unto the Corinthians that which he also received (from the Lord)

15: 8 had seen the risen Lord

15: 8 born out of due time

15: 9 the least of the apostles

15: 9 not meet to be called an apostle because he persecuted the church of God

15:10 by the grace of God he was what he was

15:10 the grace of God was bestowed unto him

15:10 labored more abundantly than they all by the grace of God which was with him

15:11 preached

15:15 testified of God that He raised up Christ

15:31 died daily (figurative)

15:34 spoke to the shame of the Corinthians (that some had not the knowledge of God)

16: 1 had given order to the churches of Galatia concerning the collection for the saints, and repeated it for the Corinthian church

16: 2 anticipated a visit to Corinth (16:3)

16: 3 would send the church's appointees to Jerusalem with their gift

16: 4 if he went to Jerusalem himself, the church's appointees would go with him

16: 5 would visit Corinth when he passed through Macedonia

16: 6 possibly would abide and winter at Corinth that they might bring him on his journey wherever he went

16: 7 would not see them now by the way, but trusted to tarry a while with them if the Lord permitted

16: 8 would tarry at Ephesus until Pentecost

16: 9 a great door and effectual was opened unto him and there were many adversaries

16:10 worked the work of the Lord

16:11 looked for Timotheus (Timothy) to come with the brethren

16:12 Apollos was his (Christian) brother

16:12 greatly desired Apollos to come to Corinth (with the brethren)

16:15 besought the Corinthians to submit themselves to them who ministered to the saints (16:16)

16:17 was glad of the coming of Stephanas, Fortunatus, and Achaicus

16:17 what the Corinthians had not supplied for him, Stephanas, Fortunatus, and Achaicus had

1Cor 16:21 gave the salutation (of the letter) in his own hand (writing)

16:24 gave his love to the Corinthian church

2Cor 1: 1 an apostle of Jesus Christ by the will of God

1: 1 author of the second epistle to the Corinthians

1: 1 (Christian) brother of Timothy

1: 7 his hope of the Corinthians was steadfast

1: 8 would not have the Corinthian brethren ignorant of his trouble in Asia

1: 8 (in Asia) was pressed out of measure, above strength, insomuch that he despaired even of life

1: 9 had the sentence of death in himself, that he should not trust in himself, but in God who raised the dead

1:10 delivered of the Lord from so great a death, and trusted that He would yet deliver

1:11 was helped in prayer by the Corinthians

1:11 had a gift bestowed upon him

1:12 his rejoicing was the testimony of his conscience

1:12 in simplicity and godly sincerity, not with fleshly wisdom, but by the grace of God, had had his conversation in the world

1:13 wrote no other thing to the Corinthians except what they read or acknowledged

1:14 had been acknowledged in part (by the Corinthians) as he was their rejoicing

1:14 his rejoicing was the Corinthians in the day of the Lord Jesus

1:15 was minded to come unto them before that they might have a second benefit

1:16 was minded to pass by (Corinth) into Macedonia, and come again out of Macedonia unto them

1:16 thought to be brought on his way toward Judea by the Corinthians

1:17 did not use lightness, nor did he purpose according to the flesh

1:18 his word toward the Corinthians was not yea and nay, but in Christ was yea (1:19)

1:19 preached the Son of God, Jesus Christ, among the Corinthians

1:23 with God as his witness, had not come to Corinth as yet, in an effort to spare the Corinthians

1:24 had not dominion over their faith, but was a helper of their joy

2: 1 determined that he would not come again to the Corinthians in heavi-

PAUL (*continued*)
ness

PAUL *(continued)*

2Cor 7:13 joyed for the joy of Titus

7:14 boasted to Titus of the Corinthians, but was not ashamed because it was truth

7:14 spoke all things in truth

7:16 rejoiced that he had confidence in the Corinthians in all things

8: 1 wanted the Corinthians to know of the grace of God bestowed on the churches of Macedonia

8: 3 bore record to the power of the Macedonian churches

8: 4 entreated by the Macedonians to receive the gift, and take the fellowship of the ministering to the saints

8: 6 desired Titus to finish in the Corinthians this same grace

8: 7 loved of the Corinthians

8: 8 spoke not (to the Corinthians) by commandment, but by occasion of the forwardness of others, and to prove the sincerity of their love

8:10 advised the Corinthians

8:18 sent Luke with Titus

8:18 (Christian) brother of Luke

8:19 traveled with Luke

8:19 the churches had chosen Luke (and possibly Titus) to travel with him

8:19 administered grace (to the churches) to the glory of the Lord

8:20 avoided that any man should blame him in the abundance (of grace) which he administered

8:21 provided for honest things, not only in the sight of the Lord, but also in the sight of men

8:22 sent a third brother whom he had oftentimes proved diligent in many things

8:22 had great confidence in the Corinthians

8:23 Titus was his partner, and fellow helper concerning the Corinthians

8:24 boasted on behalf of the Corinthians

9: 2 knew the forwardness of the mind of the Corinthian church

9: 2 boasted of the Corinthian church to them of Macedonia

9: 3 sent the brethren (to the Corinthians) lest his boasting should be vain

9: 4 confidently boasted (of the Corintian church)

9: 5 thought it necessary to exhort the brethren to go before (to Corinth) and make up the bounty

10: 1 besought the Corinthians that he might not (need) be bold when he was present (when he came) (10:2)

10: 1 in presence was base among the Corinthians, but being absent was bold toward them

2Cor 10: 3 walked in the flesh, but did not war after the flesh

10: 8 should boast somewhat more of his authority which the Lord had given him for edification

10:10 his letters were weighty and powerful, but his bodily presence was weak and his speech contemptible

10:11 would be the same in (bodily) presence, as in his letters (when absent)

10:12 did not compare himself to those that commend themselves

10:13 would not boast of things without (his) measure, but according to the measure of the rule which God had distributed to him

10:14 the Corinthian church was included in that area in which he had preached the gospel of Christ

10:15 boasted not of other men's labors, but that he would be enlarged by the Corinthians' ministry to preach the gospel to the regions beyond them (10:16)

11: 1 desired that the Corinthians would bear with him in his boasting

11: 2 was jealous over the Corinthians with godly jealousy

11: 2 had espoused them (the Corinthians) to one Husband that He might present them as a chaste virgin to Christ

11: 3 feared that the Corinthians' minds should be corrupted from the simplicity that is in Christ

11: 5 supposed that he was not a whit behind the very chiefest apostles

11: 6 rude in speech, but not in knowledge

11: 6 had been thoroughly made manifest among the Corinthians in all things

11: 7 questioned if he had committed an offense in abasing himself that they (the Corinthians) might be exalted

11: 7 had preached the gospel of God freely to the Corinthians

11: 8 had robbed other churches (taking wages of them), in order to serve or preach to the Corinthians

11: 9 when in Corinth and in need, was chargeable to no man (of the Corinthians), but was supplied by the brethren of Macedonia

11: 9 had kept himself from being a burden to the Corinthians and would continue to do so

11:10 the truth of God was in him

11:10 no man would stop him of his boasting in the regions of Achaia

11:12 accepted no support from the Corinthian church in order to cut off occasion for some to glory

11:16 desired the Corinthians to receive

145

PAUL *(continued)*

him that he might boast himself a little

2Cor 11:17 that which he spoke (in boasting), he spoke not after the Lord, but as it were foolishly

11:18 as others had gloried after the flesh, he would likewise glory (to show his position and authority)

11:21 (speaking foolishly) claimed boldness

11:22 a Hebrew

11:22 an Israelite

11:22 of the seed of Abraham

11:23 a minister of Christ

11:23 more abundant in labors, in stripes above measure, in prisons more frequent, in deaths oft (more than those false teachers)

11:24 five times received thirty-nine stripes (of the Jews)

11:25 thrice beaten with rods

11:25 once stoned

11:25 thrice suffered shipwreck (a night and a day in the deep)

11:26 in journeyings often, in perils of waters, robbers, by his own countrymen, by the heathen, in the city, in the wilderness, in the sea, among false brethren

11:27 in weariness and painfulness, in watchings often, in hunger and thirst, in fastings often, in cold and nakedness

11:28 had the care of all the churches

11:30 if he needed to glory, would glory of the things which concerned his infirmities

11:31 God the father was his witness that he lied not

11:32 the governor of Damascus kept the city with a garrison, desiring to apprehend him

11:33 was let down by the wall (through a window) and escaped the hand of the governor of Damascus

12: 1 was not expedient for him to glory

12: 1 would come to visions and revelations of the Lord

12: 2 knew a man in Christ (whether in the body or out of the body he could not tell) caught up to the third heaven

12: 3 knew a man, whether in the body or out of the body he could not tell

12: 4 was caught up into paradise and heard unspeakable words, not lawful for a man to utter

12: 5 would not glory of himself, but only in his infirmities

12: 6 would desire to glory but would only say the truth

12: 6 forbear (from glory) lest any man should think of him too highly

2Cor 12: 7 lest he be exalted above measure through the abundance of the revelations, was given a thorn in the flesh

12: 8 thrice besought the Lord that his thorn in the flesh might depart from him

12: 9 told of the Lord that His (God's) grace was sufficient for him

12: 9 would gladly glory in his infirmities that the power of Christ might rest upon him

12:10 took pleasure in infirmities, reproaches, necessities, persecutions, and distresses for Christ's sake

12:10 when weak, was strong (in Christ)

12:11 had been compelled to foolishly glory (boast) when he ought to have been commended

12:11 though he was nothing, was in nothing behind the very chiefest apostles

12:12 exhibited the signs of his apostleship in all patience, in signs, and wonders, and mighty deeds

12:13 was not burdensome to the church at Corinth, and asked their forgiveness for this

12:14 was ready to make his third trip to Corinth (to visit the churches)

12:14 would not be burdensome to them, for he sought them, not their possessions

12:15 would very gladly spend and be spent for the Corinthians

12:15 the more abundantly he loved the Corinthians, the less they loved him

12:16 did not burden the Corinthians

12:16 being crafty, caught the Corinthians with guile

12:17 had sent men (Titus and Luke) to the Corinthians

12:18 desired Titus (to go to the Corinthians)

12:18 sent Luke with Titus (to the Corinthians)

12:18 walked in the same spirit and steps (as Titus)

12:19 spoke before God in Christ, but did all things (to the Corinthians) for their edifying

12:20 feared that when he came (to Corinth) he would not find them as he would and that he should be found of them as they would not

12:21 feared that he would be humbled and should bewail many which had not repented, when he returned

13: 1 was making his third trip to Corinth

13: 2 had told them before, and now being absent wrote that if he came again (to Corinth), he would not

146

PAUL *(continued)*

		spare (those who had sinned)
2Cor	13: 6	not a reprobate
	13: 7	prayed that the Corinthians do no evil
	13: 8	could do nothing against the truth
	13: 9	was glad when he was weak and the Corinthians were strong
	13: 9	wished for the perfection of the Corinthians
	13:10	wrote being absent, lest being present he should use sharpness
	13:10	given power of the Lord to edification, not to destruction
	13:11	bid farewell (to the Corinthians in his letter)
Gal	1: 1	author of letter to the Galatians
	1: 1	apostle, not of men, but by Jesus Christ and God the Father
	1: 6	marveled that the Galatian Christians were so soon removed from Christ unto another gospel
	1: 8	pronounced a curse on anyone preaching another gospel (1:9)
	1:10	not a manpleaser but the servant of Christ
	1:11	gospel he preached was by the revelation of Jesus Christ (1:12)
	1:13	beforetime persecuted the church beyond measure and wasted it
	1:14	profited greatly in the Jews' religion, because of exceeding zeal for traditions of his fathers
	1:15	separated, by God, from his mother's womb and called by His grace to reveal His Son in him that he might preach Christ among the heathen (1:16)
	1:17	went into Arabia and returned again to Damascus
	1:18	went to Jerusalem to see Peter and stayed with him fifteen days
	1:19	saw no apostle other than James the Lord's brother in Jerusalem
	1:20	vindicated the truth of his words by stating that he lied not
	1:21	traveled in Syria and Cilicia and was unknown by face to the churches of Judea (1:22)
	1:23	had persecuted believers
	1:23	churches of Syria and Cilicia glorified God in him as he preached the faith which once he destroyed (1:24)
	2: 1	went to Jerusalem with Barnabas and Titus
	2: 2	went to Jerusalem by revelation to preach the gospel
	2: 2	preached among the Gentiles, but privately to those of reputation, in order to be effective
	2: 3	Titus was with him in Jerusalem
	2: 4	gave no place to false brethren who desired to bring them into bondage (2:5)

Gal	2: 7	gospel of the uncircumcision committed unto him in the apostleship of the Gentiles (2:8)
	2: 9	given right hand of fellowship by James, Cephas, and John that he might be sent to the heathen
	2:10	was forward to remember the poor
	2:11	withstood Peter face to face at Antioch for being inconsistent before the Gentiles, and spoke concerning justification by faith (2:21)
	2:15	a Jew by nature
	2:16	had believed in Jesus Christ
	2:16	justified by the faith of Christ
	2:19	dead to the law
	2:20	was crucified with Christ, yet lived
	2:20	indwelt by Christ
	2:20	lived his life in the flesh by the faith of the Son of God, Who loved him and gave Himself for him
	2:21	did not frustrate the grace of God
	4:11	feared for the Galatians, lest he had bestowed upon them labor in vain
	4:12	besought Galatians to be as he was
	4:12	was as the Galatian believers
	4:12	had not been injured by the Galatians at all
	4:13	preached the gospel through infirmity of the flesh, at first
	4:14	had a trial (thorn or temptation) in his flesh
	4:14	received by the Galatians as an angel of God, even as Christ Jesus
	4:15	his trial (thorn or temptation) was possibly related to eyes or eyesight
	4:16	was truthful with the Galatians
	4:19	Galatians were his little children (spiritual) for whom he had birth pains till Christ be formed in them
	4:20	desired to be with the Galatians and change his tone (of voice or attitude) concerning them, as previously he had doubted their sincerity
	5: 2	gave discourse on circumcision and the law (5:6)
	5: 5	waited for the hope of righteousness by faith
	5:10	had confidence in the Galatians, through the Lord, that they would be like-minded as he
	5:11	his persecution was not due to preaching "circumcision"
	5:12	desired that those who troubled the Galatians would be cut off
	5:21	informed (again) the Galatians concerning the kingdom of God
	6:11	wrote the epistle with his own hand in large letters
	6:14	wanted no glory for himself
	6:14	was crucified unto the world, and the world was crucified unto him
	6:17	bore in his body the marks of the Lord Jesus

PAUL *(continued)*

Eph 1: 1 an apostle of Jesus Christ
1: 1 writer of the epistle to the Ephesians
1:15 ceased not to give thanks for the Ephesians in his prayers after hearing of their faith in the Lord Jesus and love unto all the saints (1:16)
3: 1 prisoner of Jesus Christ for the Gentiles
3: 2 given a dispensation of the grace of God toward the Gentiles
3: 3 received the knowledge of the mystery of God by revelation (about which he had written previously)
3: 7 made a minister of the gospel by the gift of the grace of God
3: 8 less than the least of all saints
3: 8 given grace
3: 8 preached the unsearchable riches of Christ among the Gentiles
3:13 desired that Ephesians faint not at his tribulations for them
3:14 bowed his knees to God the Father
4: 1 prisoner of the Lord
4:17 commanded the Ephesian Christians not to walk as other Gentiles
5:32 spoke concerning Christ and the church
6:19 asked for prayer that utterance would be given him to open his mouth boldly to make known the mystery of the gospel
6:20 an ambassador in bonds
6:21 affairs would be reported to the Ephesians by Tychicus
6:22 sent Tychicus to the Ephesian church

Phil 1: 1 the servant of Jesus Christ
1: 1 writer of the epistle of Philippians
1: 3 thanked God upon every remembrance of the Philippians
1: 4 in his every prayer made request with joy for the Philippians (for their fellowship in the gospel)
1: 6 was confident of God's continued working in the lives of individual believers
1: 7 had the Philippians at heart, inasmuch as both in bonds and in his defense and confirmation of the gospel, they were partakers of his grace
1: 8 God bore record of his longing for the spiritual state of the Philippians
1: 9 prayed that the Philippians' love would abound yet more and more in knowledge and in all judgment
1:12 desired that the Philippians understand that the things which happened to him had fallen out rather unto the furtherance of the gospel
1:13 his bonds for Christ were known everywhere

Phil 1:14 because of his bonds, many others gained confidence to speak the word without fear
1:16 some preached Christ of contention, not sincerely, hoping to add to his bonds
1:17 was set for the defense of the gospel
1:18 rejoiced because Christ was preached (either of pretense or in truth)
1:19 this all would turn to his salvation through the prayers of the Philippians and Christ's Spirit
1:20 desired that in nothing he would be ashamed but with all boldness Christ would be magnified in his body, whether by life or by death
1:21 for him, to live was Christ and to die was gain
1:22 knew not whether to choose life or death
1:23 was in a straight between two differing desires; whether to be with Christ or to abide in the flesh
1:25 was confident that he would abide and continue with the Philippians
1:26 his return to the Philippians would bring abundant rejoicing in Jesus Christ
1:30 had suffered and was suffering for the faith
2:16 would rejoice in the day of Christ and that he had neither run nor labored in vain
2:19 trusted that the Lord Jesus would send Timotheus (Timothy) to the Philippians to report on their state (and thus bring comfort to him)
2:20 had no man like-minded as Timotheus (Timothy) who would naturally care for the state of the Philippian church
2:23 hoped to send Timotheus (Timothy) to the Philippian church
2:24 desired to personally visit the church at Philippi
2:25 thought it necessary to send Epaphroditus to Philippi
2:25 had Epaphroditus to minister to his wants
2:27 God had mercy on him in caring for Epaphroditus so that he would not have sorrow upon sorrow
2:28 carefully sent Epaphroditus to the Philippians to cause them to rejoice and to ease his own sorrow
2:29 commanded the Philippian church to receive Epaphroditus with gladness and to hold Epaphroditus in reputation
3: 4 had more human reason than the Philippians to have confidence in the flesh
3: 5 circumcised the eighth day, of the

PAUL *(continued)*

tribe of Benjamin, a Hebrew of the Hebrews

Phil 3: 5 a Pharisee

3: 6 before salvation, showed his human zeal by persecuting the church

3: 6 concerning the righteousness which was in the law, he was blameless

3: 7 counted those things of earthly gain as loss for Christ

3: 8 counted all things but loss for the excellency of the knowledge of Jesus Christ his Lord (for whom he had suffered the loss of all things and counted them but dung that he might win Christ)

3: 9 desired to be found not with his own righteousness (of the law), but with the righteousness which is of God by faith

3:10 desired to know Him (Christ) and the power of His resurrection, and the fellowship of His sufferings, being made conformable unto His death

3:14 pressed toward the mark for the prize of the high calling of God in Christ Jesus

3:17 entreated the Philippians to follow him

3:18 reminded the Philippian church (with weeping) that some are the enemies of the cross of Christ

3:20 his citizenship was in Heaven from whence he looked for the Saviour, the Lord Jesus Christ

4: 1 the Philippian church was called his dearly beloved and longed for, his joy and crown

4: 2 besought Euodias and Syntyche to be of the same mind in the Lord

4: 3 Clement, women, and others labored with him in the gospel

4:10 rejoiced in the Lord that the Philippian church had renewed its care for him

4:11 had learned to be content in whatever state he found himself

4:12 knew how to be abased and how to abound

4:12 was instructed both to be full and to be hungry, both to abound and to suffer need

4:13 could do all things through Christ (who strengthened him)

4:15 Philippians had been the only church to communicate with him concerning support when he departed from Macedonia

4:16 Philippians had given numerous times to his support while he was in Thessalonica

Phil 4:17 did not desire a gift (of support) for the gift's sake, but that they (the givers) might receive a blessing

4:18 his needs were supplied by the gifts (sent by the hand of Epaphroditus) from the Philippian church

4:21 sent greetings to every saint in Christ Jesus

Col 1: 1 an apostle of Jesus Christ by the will of God

1: 2 writer of the letter to the Colossians

1: 3 thanked God along with Timothy, for the Colossian Christians and continually prayed for them

1: 4 heard of the faith of the Colossian church and their love for the saints

1: 9 ceaseless in prayer for the Colossians

1:23 was made a minister of the gospel

1:24 rejoiced in his sufferings for the Colossian Christians and filled up that which was behind of the afflictions of Christ in his body for the sake of the Church

1:25 made a minister according to the dispensation of God which was given to him for the Colossian church to fulfill the Word of God

1:28 preached Christ and warned and taught every man in all wisdom in order that he might present every man perfect in Christ Jesus

1:29 labored in preaching and teaching Christ (in order to present every man perfect in Christ Jesus) striving according to God's working (who worked in him mightily)

2: 1 had great conflict for the Colossian church (and for others whom he had not seen face to face)

2: 5 though he was absent in the flesh (from the Colossians) he was with them in spirit, joying and beholding their order and the steadfastness of their faith in Christ

4: 3 instructed the Colossians to also pray for him that God would open unto him a door of utterance, to speak the mystery of Christ (for which he was also in bonds)

4: 4 wished to make the mystery of Christ manifest (as he ought to speak)

4: 7 his state (affairs) would be reported to the Colossians by Tychicus

4: 8 sent Tychicus to the Colossians also to be kept informed of their state and that he (Tychicus) would comfort their hearts

4: 9 sent Onesimus (with Tychicus) to help report on his affairs to the Colossian church

4:10 fellow prisoner with Aristarchus

4:10 fellow worker with Aristarchus,

PAUL *(continued)*

Marcus (Mark), and Jesus which is called Justus, and comforted by the same (4:11)

Col 4:13 bore record of Epaphras's zeal for the Colossians, the Laodiceans, and them in Hierapolis

4:15 saluted the brethren in Laodicea, and Nymphas, and the church which was in his house

4:17 instructed a message by the Colossians to Archippus

4:18 wrote the salutation of the letter to the Colossians with his own hand

4:18 asked the Colossians to remember his bonds

1The 1: 1 writer of 1 Thessalonians

1: 2 thanked God always for the Thessalonian church, mentioning them in his prayers

1: 5 gave the gospel not only in word, but in power, and in the Holy Spirit, and in much assurance

1: 5 his testimony was well known among the Thessalonian brethren for good

1: 6 the Thessalonian Christians became his followers (and the Lord's)

1: 9 people in Macedonia and Achaia knew of his good work with the Thessalonians

1:10 delivered from the wrath to come (by Christ Jesus)

2: 1 his work with the Thessalonians was not in vain

2: 2 suffered and was shamefully treated at Philippi

2: 2 was bold in God to speak the gospel of God unto the Thessalonians with much contention

2: 3 his exhortation was not of deceit, uncleanness, or in guile

2: 4 spoke the gospel of which he was allowed of God to be put in trust

2: 4 sought not to please men, but God

2: 5 God was his witness that he never used flattering words nor a cloak of covetousness

2: 6 sought not glory (support) of men, when he had the right as an apostle

2: 7 was gentle among the Thessalonians

2: 8 being affectionately desirous of the Thessalonians, he was willing to give not only the gospel of God, but even his own soul

2: 9 labored and travailed for the Thessalonian church

2: 9 labored night and day so as not to be a burden to the Thessalonians and preached the gospel of God

2:10 behaved in a holy, just, and unblameable manner among the Thessalonian believers

1The 2:11 as a father, he exhorted, comforted, and charged the Thessalonian believers to walk worthy of God (2:12)

2:13 thanked God for the reception of the Word of God among the Thessalonians

2:15 persecuted by the Jews

2:16 forbidden, by the Jews, to speak to the Gentiles concerning salvation

2:17 although absent from the Thessalonians in body, he endeavored more abundantly to see them again

2:18 endeavored to journey to Thessalonica, but was hindered by Satan on more than one occasion

2:19 his hope, joy, and crown of rejoicing was to see the Thessalonians with the Lord at His coming

2:20 the Thessalonians were his glory and joy

3: 1 stayed at Athens

3: 2 sent Timotheus (Timothy) to establish the Thessalonians, and to comfort them concerning their faith

3: 3 appointed to afflictions

3: 4 had told the Thessalonians in a previous visit, that he should suffer tribulations and he did

3: 5 sent to learn of the spiritual state of the Thessalonians, to assure that his labor among them had not been in vain

3: 6 Timotheus (Timothy) brought good tidings to him concerning the faith and charity of the Thessalonians, their good remembrance of him always, and their great desire to see him

3: 6 desired to see the Thessalonians

3: 7 comforted during his affliction and distress by the faith of the Thessalonian church

3: 9 rendered thanks to God for the joy brought him by the Thessalonian believers

3:10 prayed exceedingly night and day to see the Thessalonians, and to perfect that which was lacking in their faith

3:11 invoked the aid of God and the Lord Jesus Christ to direct him to the Thessalonians

3:12 increased and abounded in love toward the Thessalonians

4: 1 besought and exhorted the Thessalonians to walk in a manner pleasing to God, as they had received of him

4: 2 reminded the Thessalonians of other commandments of the Lord that he had given them

4:13 desired that the Thessalonians not be ignorant concerning those asleep in the Lord

PAUL *(continued)*

1The 4:15 taught by the Word of the Lord

5:14 exhorted the Thessalonians to warn the unruly, comfort the feeble-minded, support the weak, and to be patient toward all men

5:23 prayed that the Thessalonians would be preserved blameless unto the coming of Christ

5:25 requested the prayers of the Thessalonian brethren on his behalf

5:27 charged the Thessalonian church that this epistle be read unto all the holy brethren

2The 1: 1 author of epistle of 2 Thessalonians

1: 1 mentions Silvanus (Silas) and Timotheus (Timothy) in greetings to the Thessalonians

1: 3 gave thanks always to God for the Thessalonian church

1: 4 gloried in the other churches concerning the patience and faith of the Thessalonian church

1:10 his testimony was believed by the Thessalonian church

1:11 prayed always for the Thessalonian church

2: 5 reminded the Thessalonian church of his previous teaching concerning the day of Christ on his last visit

2:13 was bound to give thanks always for the Thessalonian church

2:14 Thessalonian church was called by his gospel

2:15 instructed the Thessalonian church to stand fast and hold the traditions

2:15 his epistle had been used to instruct the Thessalonian church

3: 1 asked prayer of the Thessalonian brethren

3: 1 desired the Word of the Lord to have free course and be glorified in him

3: 2 asked for prayer of Thessalonian brethren for deliverance from unreasonable and wicked men

3: 4 had confidence in the Lord as touching the Thessalonians that they would now do and continue to do his commands

3: 6 commanded the Thessalonians to withdraw themselves from every brother that walked disorderly and not after the tradition received from him

3: 7 reaffirmed the Thessalonian church's need to follow him

3: 7 did not behave disorderly among the Thessalonians

3: 8 worked for what he received of the Thessalonians so as not to be chargeable to them

3: 9 had power to live of the Thessalonians, but refused in order to make himself an example for them to follow

2The 3:10 while with the Thessalonian church commanded that those who would not work should not eat

3:12 commanded and exhorted those guilty of disorderliness to work and eat with quietness

3:14 commanded that those who obeyed not his epistle were to be noted and were to have no company with the church, that they might be ashamed

3:15 commanded that disciplined brethren not be counted as enemies, but admonished as brethren

3:17 gave the salutation of the book of 2 Thessalonians in his own hand, his custom in all of his epistles

1Tim 1: 1 an apostle of Jesus Christ by commandment of God our Saviour and Lord Jesus Christ

1: 2 wrote epistle of 1 Timothy

1: 2 Timothy was his own son in the faith

1: 3 went to Macedonia

1: 3 desired that Timothy stay at Ephesus to charge the Ephesians to teach the faith (1:4)

1:11 the gospel of God was committed to his trust

1:12 counted faithful by Christ Jesus and placed into the ministry

1:13 prior to conversion, was a blasphemer, a persecutor, and injurious, but obtained mercy because he acted ignorantly in unbelief

1:15 chief of sinners

1:16 obtained mercy, that in him Jesus Christ might show forth all longsuffering as a pattern to later Christians

1:18 charged Timothy to war a good warfare (1:19)

1:20 delivered Hymenaeus and Alexander unto Satan that they might learn not to blaspheme

2: 7 ordained a preacher

2: 7 ordained an apostle

2: 7 spoke the truth in Christ and lied not

2: 7 teacher of the Gentiles in faith and verity

2:14 hoped to visit Timothy shortly

2:15 wrote 1 Timothy so that Timothy would know how to behave himself in the house of God

6:20 charged Timothy to keep that which was committed to his trust

2Tim 1: 1 writer of epistle of 2 Timothy

1: 1 an apostle of Jesus Christ

1: 2 wrote epistle of 2 Timothy to Timothy his dear beloved (spiritual) son

151

PAUL *(continued)*

2 Tim 1: 3 thanked God that he had (without ceasing) remembered Timothy in his prayers night and day
1: 3 served God from his forefathers with pure conscience
1: 4 greatly desired to see Timothy that he (Paul) might be filled with joy
1: 5 called to remembrance the unfeigned faith that he was persuaded dwelt in Timothy
1: 6 by the laying on of his hands, Timothy had received a gift of God
1: 8 the prisoner of the Lord
1:11 was appointed a preacher
1:11 was appointed an apostle
1:11 was appointed a teacher of the Gentiles
1:12 suffered for his position with the Lord
1:12 was not ashamed of the Lord and was persuaded of His power
1:13 expounded sound words
1:15 all in Asia were turned away from him, examples of whom are Phygellus and Hermogenes
1:16 often refreshed by Onesiphorus
1:16 was shackled by a chain
1:17 when imprisoned in Rome, was sought out and found by Onesiphorus
1:18 was ministered unto by Onesiphorus at Ephesus
2: 1 called Timothy his (spiritual) son
2: 2 instructed Timothy in many things (among witnesses)
2: 8 the gospel was his gospel
2: 9 suffered trouble (as an evil doer would)
2: 9 put in bonds
2:10 endured all things for the elect's sake
3:10 fully known were his doctrine, manner of life, purpose, faith, longsufferings, charity, patience, persecutions, and afflictions
3:11 endured persecutions at Antioch, Iconium, and Lystra, but was delivered out of them all by the Lord
4: 1 charged Timothy before God, to preach the Word, to be instant in season, out of season, to reprove, rebuke, and exhort with all longsuffering and doctrine (4:2)
4: 6 was ready to be offered (to die)
4: 6 the time of his departure (his death) was at hand
4: 7 had fought a good fight
4: 7 had finished his course
4: 7 had kept the faith
4: 8 a crown of righteousness (laid up for him) would be given him by the Lord
4: 9 asked that Timothy diligently endeavor to come shortly to him

2 Tim 4:10 Demas had forsaken him and departed unto Thessalonica
4:10 Crescens and Titus had also left him
4:11 Luke was alone with him
4:11 asked that Mark be brought to him for he (Mark) was profitable to Paul for the ministry
4:12 sent Tychicus to Ephesus
4:13 asked Timothy to bring his cloak, left at Troas with Carpus, his books, and especially the parchments
4:14 was done much evil by Alexander the coppersmith
4:16 prayed God that his forsaking by all men would not be laid to their charge
4:17 the Lord had stood with him and strengthened him that the preaching might be fully known and that all Gentiles might hear
4:17 was delivered out of the mouth of the lion (figurative)
4:19 asked Timothy to salute Prisca, Aquila, and the household of Onesiphorus
4:20 left Trophimus at Miletum sick
4:21 forwarded greetings to Timothy from Eubulus, Pudens, Linus, Claudia, and all the brethren

Tit 1: 1 writer of epistle to Titus
1: 1 a servant of God
1: 1 an apostle of Jesus Christ
1: 3 the Word of God, through preaching, was committed unto him according to the commandment of God
1: 4 wrote epistle to Titus, his own son after the common faith
1: 5 left Titus in Crete to set things in order and to ordain elders in every city
1: 6 presented requirements and qualifications of elders and bishops (1:9)
1:10 instructed Titus to sharply rebuke unruly and vain talkers and deceivers (1:13)
2: 1 admonished Titus to speak the things which become sound doctrine (2:10)
3:12 determined to winter at Nicopolis

Phle : 1 author of the epistle to Philemon
: 1 a prisoner of Jesus Christ
: 1 brother (in Christ) of Timothy
: 1 fellow laborer of Philemon
: 2 friend of Apphia
: 2 fellow soldier of Archippus
: 4 always mentioned Philemon in his prayers
: 9 a prisoner of Jesus Christ
: 9 the aged

PAUL *(continued)*

Phle	:10	spiritual father of Onesimus (begotten in Paul's bonds)
	:10	besought Philemon on behalf of Onesimus
	:12	enjoined Philemon to receive Onesimus as Paul's own spiritual son
	:13	desired to have retained Onesimus as his servant in the gospel but would not without Philemon's consent (:14)
	:17	told Philemon to receive Onesimus just as he would Paul, if he counted Paul a partner
	:18	offered to pay all debts of Onesimus owed to Philemon
	:19	wrote to Philemon with his own hand concerning his offer to pay any of Onesimus's debts to Philemon
	:21	possessed confidence in Philemon to do all he had requested of him and more
	:22	requested lodging for a proposed journey
	:23	fellow prisoner of Epaphras
	:24	fellow laborer of Marcus, Aristarchus, Demas, and Lucas
2Pet	3:15	beloved (Christian) brother of Simon Peter
	3:15	given wisdom
	3:15	also wrote to the beloved
	3:16	in all his epistles, spoke of salvation and longsuffering of God
	3:16	some of his writings were hard to understand

PERSIS ♀ [pur' - sis = a persian woman]
A female disciple of Rome who was greeted by Paul and had labored much in the Lord.

Rom	16:12	saluted by Paul
	16:12	beloved
	16:12	labored much in the Lord

PETER [pe'-tur = a stone];—see SIMON PETER

PHALEC [fa'-lek = division]
Old Testament Peleg, son of Heber, father of Ragau, and an ancestor of Jesus.

| Luke | 3:35 | father of Ragau |
| | 3:35 | son of Heber |

PHANUEL ♀ [fan-u'el = vision of God]
Mother of Anna the prophetess, and a member of the tribe of Asher.

| Luke | 2:36 | a parent of Anna (the prophetess) |
| | 2:36 | of the tribe of Aser (Asher) |

PHARES [fa'-rez = breach]
Old Testament Pharez and Perez, son of Judas by Thamar, twin brother of Zara, father of Esrom,

and ancestor of Jesus.

Matt	1: 3	begat by Judas of Thamar
	1: 3	begat Esrom
Luke	3:33	father of Esrom
	3:33	son of Juda (Judas)

PHEBE ♀ [fe'-be = radiant]
A female servant of the church at Cenchrea and recommended to the Roman church by Paul to be received in the Lord and to be assisted by them in her work.

Rom	16: 1	commended of Paul to the church at Rome
	16: 1	sister (in Christ to Paul)
	16: 1	a servant of the church at Cenchrea
	16: 2	was to be received by the church at Rome as becometh saints
	16: 2	was to be assisted by the church at Rome in whatsoever business she had need of them
	16: 2	had been a succourer of many and of Paul

PHILEMON [fi-le'-mon = one who kisses]
Dearly beloved and a fellow laborer of Paul at Colosse, probably the husband of Apphia and father of Archippus, recipient of the book of Philemon, and owner of Onesimus (a slave).

Phle	: 1	corecipient, with Apphia, Archippus, and the church in his house, of the letter of Philemon
	: 1	dearly beloved and fellow laborer of Paul
	: 2	the church met in his house
	: 4	always mentioned in Paul's prayers
	: 5	had love and faith toward the Lord Jesus and toward all saints
	:10	besought by Paul on behalf of Onesimus
	:16	was requested by Paul to receive Onesimus, not as a servant, but as a brother beloved
	:17	told by Paul to receive Onesimus just as he would Paul if he counted Paul a partner
	:18	offered payment, by Paul, for all debts owed to him by Onesimus
	:19	owed even his own self to Paul
	:21	Paul had confidence in him to perform all that had been requested of him and more
	:22	received request of Paul for lodging for a future journey
	:23	was saluted, through Paul, by Epaphras, Marcus, Aristarchus, Demas, and Lucas (:24)

PHILETUS [fi-le'-tus = beloved]
A man made shipwreck by blasphemy, delivered unto Satan by Paul, and claimed there was no bodily resurrection from the dead.

| 2 Tim | 2:16 | failed to shun profane and vain babblings and increased unto more |

PHILETUS *(continued)*

ungodliness (2:17)

2Tim	2:17	his word ate as a canker
	2:17	worked ungodliness with Hymenaeus
	2:18	erred from the truth
	2:18	overthrew the faith of some by stating that the resurrection was already past

PHILIP [fil'-ip = a lover of horses]
1. an apostle of Jesus Christ, one of the twelve, and of Bethsaida.

Matt	8:23*	followed Jesus into a ship
	8:25*	came to and awoke Jesus and asked Him to save the disciples, for they perished
	8:26*	fearful
	8:26*	of little faith
	8:27*	marveled at Jesus
	9:10*	sat at meat with Jesus along with publicans and sinners
	9:14*	fasted not
	9:19*	followed Jesus
	9:37*	instructed to pray that the Lord would send forth laborers into His harvest (9:38)
	10: 1*	was called unto Jesus
	10: 1	one of the twelve disciples (of Jesus)
	10: 1*	given power to cast out unclean spirits
	10: 1*	given power to heal all manner of sickness and disease
	10: 2	one of the twelve apostles (10:3)
	10: 5	one of the twelve (apostles)
	10: 5*	commanded to go neither to the Gentiles, nor into any city of the Samaritans
	10: 6*	sent forth by Jesus to the lost sheep of the house of Israel
	10: 7*	commanded by Jesus to preach "the kingdom of heaven is at hand"
	10: 8*	commanded to heal the sick, cleanse the lepers, raise the dead, cast out devils (demons)
	10: 8*	had freely received
	10: 9*	was to provide neither gold, nor silver, nor brass, nor scrip, neither two coats, neither shoes, nor stave (for himself) (10:10)
	10:11*	in every city or town, was to inquire who was worthy, and to abide with them
	10:12*	was to salute each house he entered
	10:13*	his peace was to come upon each worthy house, but return to him if unworthy
	10:14*	was to shake off the dust of his feet therein, when not received or heard by a house or city
	10:16*	sent forth (by Jesus) as a sheep in the midst of wolves
	10:16*	was to be wise as a serpent and harmless as a dove
Matt	10:17*	would be delivered to the councils, scourged in synagogues, and brought before governors, and kings for (Jesus') sake (10:18)
	10:19*	was to take no thought concerning what he would speak when delivered up, for the Spirit of his Father would speak in him (10:20)
	12: 1*	was hungered and plucked corn in the field and ate
	12: 2*	accused by the Pharisees of acting unlawfully on the Sabbath day
	12:49*	called mother and brethren by Jesus
	13:10*	questioned Jesus about His use of parables
	13:11*	was given unto him to know the mysteries of the kingdom of Heaven
	13:16*	saw and heard (spiritually)
	13:17*	had seen and heard (spiritually)
	13:18*	had the parable of the sower explained by Jesus (13:23)
	13:36*	had the parable of the wheat and tares explained by Jesus (13:43)
	13:51*	claimed to have understood all these things (parables)
	14:15*	came to Jesus and requested Him to send the multitude away
	14:16*	instructed by Jesus to feed the multitude
	14:17*	requested by Jesus to bring the five loaves and two fishes to Him (14:18)
	14:19*	given the loaves blessed by Jesus
	14:19*	distributed the loaves to the multitude
	14:20*	took up of the fragments that remained twelve baskets full
	14:22*	constrained by Jesus to get into a ship and to go before Him unto the other side (of Sea of Galilee)
	14:24*	his ship was tossed with waves
	14:25*	approached by Jesus (walking on the sea)
	14:26*	saw Jesus walking on the water (Sea of Galilee) and was afraid
	14:27*	told by Jesus to be of good cheer and not be afraid
	14:33*	being in the ship worshiped Jesus, claiming Him to be the Son of God
	14:34*	came into the land of Gennesaret
	15: 2*	accused by the scribes and Pharisees of transgressing the tradition of the elders by not washing his hands when he ate bread
	15:12*	came to Jesus, informing Him that the Pharisees were offended at His saying
	15:23*	came and besought Jesus to send away her that cried after him
	15:32*	was called (unto Jesus)
	15:34*	had seven loaves and a few little fishes

PHILIP *(continued)*

Matt 15:36* given the loaves and fishes (by Jesus)

15:36* gave the loaves and fishes to the multitude

15:37* took up of the broken meat that was left seven baskets full

16: 5* was come to the other side and had forgotten to take bread

16: 6* told to beware of the leaven of the Pharisees and Sadducees

16: 7* reasoned with the other disciples over Jesus' words

16: 7* had taken no bread

16: 8* of little faith

16: 8 reasoned with the other disciples (concerning the lack of bread)

16: 9* took up baskets (of fragments)

16:10* took up baskets (of fragments)

16:11* did not understand Jesus' words concerning the leaven (doctrine) of the Pharisees and Sadducees

16:12* understood how that Jesus spoke not of bread, but of the doctrine of the Pharisees and Sadducees

16:13* was in Caesarea Philippi

16:13* answered Jesus' question concerning His identity (16:14)

16:15* questioned as to his view of Jesus' identity

16:20* charged by Jesus to tell no man that he was Jesus the Christ

16:21* shown by Jesus the sufferings He must undergo

17:15* could not cure the lunatic boy (17:16)

17:19* asked Jesus why he could not cast out the devil (demon)

17:20* could not cast out the devil (demon) because of unbelief

17:22* abode in Galilee

17:23* was exceedingly sorry

17:24* came to Capernaum

18: 1* asked Jesus who is the greatest in the kingdom of Heaven

19:13* rebuked those who brought children to Jesus

19:14* rebuked, in turn, by Jesus

19:25* exceedingly amazed at Jesus' answer to the rich young ruler and asked who could be saved

19:27* had forsaken all and followed Jesus

19:28* had followed Jesus

19:28* promised by Jesus to sit upon the twelve thrones judging the twelve tribes of Israel

20:17* going up to Jerusalem was taken apart and foretold by Jesus of His betrayal, crucifixion, and resurrection (20:19)

20:24* was moved with indignation towards James and John because of their request of Jesus

20:29* departed from Jericho (for Jerusalem)

Matt 21: 1* arrived in Bethphage and Mount of Olives

21:20* saw the withered fig tree and marveled

24: 1* came to Jesus to show Him the buildings of the temple

24: 2* Jesus spoke to him of the coming destruction of the temple

24: 3* asked Jesus of the sign of His coming and of the end of the world

26: 8* was indignant at the actions of the woman

26:10* had troubled the woman

26:17* asked Jesus where he should prepare for Him the Passover

26:19* did as Jesus had appointed and made ready the Passover

26:20 celebrated Passover with Jesus and the rest of the twelve

26:22 asked Jesus if he were the one to betray Him

26:26* while eating (the Passover) given the bread by Jesus

26:27* given the cup (by Jesus)

26:30* having sung an hymn, went out into the Mount of Olives.

26:31 Jesus predicted that he would be offended because of Him

26:35* claimed he would never deny Jesus, even though it meant death

26:36* came with Jesus to Gethsemane

26:36* instructed to sit and pray

26:40* fell asleep in the garden of Gethsemane

26:43* fell asleep again in the garden (of Gethsemane)

26:45* told to sleep on now and take his rest

26:46* told to arise and go (with Jesus)

26:56* forsook Jesus and fled

28:13* would be accused of stealing Jesus' body by night

28:16* went into Galilee into the place (mountain) appointed

28:17* saw Jesus and worshiped Him

28:19* given the great commission (28:20)

28:20* Jesus would always be with him, even unto the end of the world

Mark 3:14* ordained by Jesus (to be with Him)

3:14* would be sent forth to preach (by Jesus)

3:15* would be given power by Jesus to heal sicknesses and to cast out devils (demons)

3:18 a disciple of Jesus (one of the twelve)

3:20* could not eat bread with Jesus because of the multitude

4:10* asked Jesus about the parable of the sower

4:11* was given to know the mystery of the kingdom of God

4:33* had many parables taught him by

155

PHILIP *(continued)*
Jesus

Mark 4:34* when alone, with the rest of the twelve, had all things expounded by Jesus
4:36* sent away the multitude
4:36* with the twelve, took Jesus to the other side of the sea
4:38* in fear, awakened Jesus in the midst of the storm
4:40* was fearful and had no faith
4:41* feared exceedingly
4:41* questioned among the other disciples as to what manner of man Jesus was that even the wind and the sea obey Him
5: 1* went with Jesus across the Sea of Galilee to the country of the Gadarenes
6: 1* followed Jesus into His own country
6: 7* sent forth two by two (by Jesus)
6: 7* given power over unclean spirits
6: 8* commanded to take nothing on his journey except a staff, and to be shod with sandals and only one coat (6:9)
6:12* went out and preached that men should repent
6:13* cast out many devils (demons) and anointed with oil many that were sick and healed them
6:30* an apostle
6:30* gathered together unto Jesus to report what he had done and taught
6:31* had no leisure so much as to eat
6:32* departed privately with Jesus into a desert place by ship
6:36* asked Jesus to send away the multitude into the villages to buy themselves bread
6:37* told by Jesus to give food to the multitude
6:37* asked Jesus if he should go and buy bread to feed the people
6:38* when asked by Jesus the available provisions, reported five loaves and two fishes
6:39* made the people sit down by hundreds and by fifties (6:40)
6:41* given the blessed food by Jesus to distribute to the crowd
6:43* took up twelve baskets full of fragments and of the fishes
6:45 constrained by Jesus to get into the ship and go to the other side unto Bethsaida
6:47* was alone (with the other disciples) in the ship in the midst of the sea
6:48* toiled in rowing the ship for the winds were contrary
6:48* Jesus came unto him in about the fourth watch of the night walking upon the sea

Mark 6:49* saw Jesus walking upon the sea and cried out for he supposed it had been a spirit
6:50* saw Jesus and was troubled, but admonished by Him to fear not
6:51* was amazed beyond measure and wondered that the wind ceased as Jesus entered the ship
6:52* because of his hardened heart, had forgotten about the miracle of the loaves
6:53* came into the land of Gennesaret
6:54* got out of the ship
7: 5* walked not according to the traditions of the elders (ate bread with unwashed hands)
8: 5* informed Jesus of the seven loaves
8: 6* set the loaves before the people
8: 7* receiving the blessed fishes from Jesus, set them before the people
8: 8* gathered seven baskets of fragments
8:10* entered into a ship with Jesus and went into Dalmanutha
8:13* entering into the ship again with Jesus, departed to the other side
8:14* had forgotten to take bread, and had only one loaf in the ship
8:16* had no bread
8:17* having seen the miracles, still did not understand as his heart was possibly yet hardened
8:19* took up twelve baskets full of fragments at the feeding of the five thousand
8:20* took up seven baskets full of fragments at the feeding of the four thousand
8:27* went into the towns of Caesarea Philippi with Jesus
8:27* responded to Jesus' question concerning His identity with "John the Baptist, Elias, and one of the prophets" (8:28)
8:30* charged to tell no man that Jesus was the Christ
8:31* taught by Jesus of the things concerning Himself
9:14* questioned by the scribes
9:18* could not cast out a dumb spirit
9:30* passed through Galilee
9:32* did not understand the words of Jesus, but was afraid to ask
9:33* came to Capernaum
9:33* disputed with the other disciples on the way to Capernaum as to whom should be the greatest (9:34)
9:38* forbade a man from casting out devils (demons) in Jesus' name, because he did not follow him
10:13* rebuked those who brought young children to Jesus that he should touch them
10:14* rebuked, in turn, by Jesus

PHILIP (*continued*)

Mark 10:24* astonished at the words of Jesus concerning those with riches

10:26* astonished at Jesus' words

10:28* had left all and followed Jesus

10:32* went to Jerusalem with Jesus and was amazed and afraid

10:41 was much displeased with James and John

10:46* went to Jericho

10:46* went out of Jericho with Jesus

11: 1* came nigh to Jerusalem, unto Bethphage and Bethany, at the Mount of Olives

11:11* went to Bethany with Jesus and stayed until the morrow (11:12)

11:14* heard Jesus curse the fig tree

11:15* returned to Jerusalem with Jesus

11:19* went out of Jerusalem

11:20* witnessed the fig tree dried up from the roots

11:27* came again to Jerusalem

14:17* in the evening of the first day of unleavened bread, went with Jesus to the upper room

14:18* sat and ate together with Jesus

14:19* began to be sorrowful over Jesus' statement of betrayal and to ask "Is it I?"

14:20* dipped with Jesus in the dish

14:22* ate the Passover with Jesus

14:23* drank of the communion cup

14:26* sung an hymn and went out of the Mount of Olives

14:31* exclaimed that even if it meant death, he would not deny Him

14:32* went to Gethsemane and was told to sit there while Jesus prayed

14:50* forsook Jesus and fled

16:10* mourned and wept

16:11* believed not Mary Magdalene's account

16:14* Jesus appeared unto him as he sat at meat (with the other disciples)

16:14* upbraided by Jesus for his unbelief and hardness of heart, because he believed not them which had seen Him after He was risen

16:15* commissioned to go into all the world and preach the gospel to every creature

16:20* went forth and preached everywhere, with signs following

Luke 6: 1* plucked ears of corn and ate (rubbing them in his hands) on the Sabbath

6: 2* claimed (by the Pharisees) to be doing that which was not lawful to do on the Sabbath days

6:13 chosen as one of the twelve

6:13* also called (named) an apostle

6:14 an apostle

6:17* came down from the mountain with Jesus and stood in the plain

Luke 8: 1* went throughout every city and village with Jesus

8: 9* questioned Jesus concerning a parable

8:10* unto him it was given to know the mysteries of the kingdom of God

8:22* went into a ship with Jesus and launched forth for the other side

8:23* the boat, filled with water, put him in jeopardy

8:24* called Jesus Master

8:24* came to Jesus and awakened Him during the storm

8:25* asked by Jesus concerning his faith

8:25* was afraid and wondered concerning Jesus' power over the elements

8:26* arrived at the country of the Gadarenes (Gadara)

9: 1* given power and authority over all devils (demons) and to cure diseases

9: 2* sent by Jesus to preach the kingdom of God and to heal the sick

9: 3* was to take neither staves, nor scrip, neither bread, neither money, neither have two coats

9: 4* was to abide in whatever house he entered

9: 6* went through the towns, preaching the gospel, and healing everywhere

9:10* returned and told Jesus all he had done

9:10* went privately with Jesus into a desert place belonging to the city called Bethsaida

9:12* requested that Jesus send away the multitude so that they might go into the towns and lodge and get victuals (food)

9:13* had only five loaves and two fishes, but was requested by Jesus to give food to the multitude

9:14* made the multitude sit down in companies by fifties (9:15)

9:16* gave the blessed loaves and fish unto the multitude

9:17* took up twelve baskets of fragments

9:18* was alone with Jesus (and the rest of the twelve)

9:18* in response to Jesus' question as to His identity, responded "John the Baptist, Elias, and one of the prophets risen again" (9:19)

9:20* straitly charged and commanded to tell no man that He was the Christ (9:21)

9:40* could not cast the spirit (demon) out of a boy

9:45* feared to ask Jesus concerning His teaching

9:46* reasoned with the other disciples as to which of them should be greatest

9:49* forbade a man from casting out

devils (demons) in Jesus' name because he followed not with the disciples

Luke 10:24* saw and heard what many prophets
and kings had desired to experience

12: 1* warned by Jesus to beware of the
leaven of the Pharisees

12: 4* friend of Jesus

17: 5* asked Jesus to increase his faith

18:15* rebuked those who brought infants
to Jesus

18:16* rebuked, in turn, by Jesus

18:28* had left all, and followed Jesus

18:31* taken unto Jesus and instructed of
things to come (18:33)

18:34* understood none of these teachings
of Jesus

19:29* with Jesus came nigh to Bethphage
and Bethany at the Mount of
Olives

19:37* rejoiced and praised God with a
loud voice (19:38)

22:14* sat down with Jesus (in the upper
room for the Passover)

22:14* was called an apostle

22:15* Jesus truly desired his presence in
eating the Passover

22:19* partook of the first Lord's supper
(22:20)

22:23* inquired among the disciples as to
which of them would betray Jesus

22:24* a strife existed between him and
the other disciples as to which one
should be accounted the greatest

22:28* had continued with Jesus in His
temptations

22:29* was appointed a kingdom (that he
might eat and drink at Jesus' table
in His kingdom and sit on thrones
judging the twelve tribes of Israel)
(22:30)

22:35* had lacked nothing

22:36* told to prepare (for his new task)

22:39* followed Jesus to the Mount of
Olives

22:40* told to pray that he enter not into
temptation

22:45* found sleeping for sorrow (by
Jesus)

22:46* told to rise and pray, lest he enter
into temptation

22:49* perceiving the forthcoming events,
asked Jesus if he should use his
sword

24: 9* was told all things concerning the
resurrection by Mary Magdalene,
Joanna, Mary the mother of James,
and the other women

24:10* an apostle

24:11* the words of the women seemed to
him as idle tales and he believed
them not

24:33* being gathered together, (with the

other disciples) Cleopas found him
and declared that the Lord was
risen indeed and hath appeared to
Simon (24:34)

Luke 24:36* Jesus appeared unto him (after the
resurrection) but he was terrified
and affrighted, and supposed that
he had seen a spirit (24:37)

24:38* asked by Jesus why he was troubled
and why thoughts arose in his heart

24:40* was shown Jesus' hands and feet

24:41* believed not yet for joy, and wondered

24:42* gave Jesus a piece of a broiled fish
and of an honeycomb

24:45* his understanding was opened by
Jesus that he might understand the
scriptures

24:46* was a witness of these things
(24:48)

24:49* told to tarry in Jerusalem until he
was endued with power from on
high

24:50* led by Jesus out as far as to Bethany
and was blessed of Him

24:52* worshiped Jesus and returned to
Jerusalem with great joy

24:53* was continually in the temple,
praising and blessing God

John 1:43 found by Jesus, in Galilee and told
to follow him

1:44 was of Bethsaida

1:45 found Nathanael (for Jesus)

1:45 had found Him of whom Moses
and the prophets wrote

1:46 told Nathanael to come and see
(Jesus)

1:48 had called Nathanael (to Jesus)

2: 2* was called to the marriage in Cana
of Galilee

2:11* believed on Jesus

2:12* went to Capernaum and continued
there not many days

2:17* remembered that it was written of
Him, "the zeal of Thine house hath
eaten me up"

2:22* after the resurrection, remembered
Jesus' words and believed the scriptures and the words which Jesus
had said

3:22* came into the land of Judea with
Jesus and tarried there with Him

4: 2* did baptize

4: 8* had gone away unto the city to buy
meat

4:27* came unto Jesus and marveled that
He talked with the Samaritan
woman, yet did not question Him

4:31* called Jesus Master

4:31* implored Jesus to eat

4:33* questioned among the disciples if
Jesus had been brought food to eat

4:35* told to look on the fields for they
are white already to harvest

PHILIP *(continued)*

John 4:38* had been sent to reap where he had not sown, and had entered into others' labors

6: 3* went up into a mountain and sat with Jesus

6: 5 asked by Jesus where he could buy bread (in order to prove him) (6:6)

6: 7 told Jesus that two hundred pennyworth of bread was not sufficient

6:10* instructed by Jesus to have the multitude sit down

6:11* distributed the loaves and fishes to the multitude

6:13* gathered twelve baskets of fragments

6:16* went down to the sea, entered a ship, and went toward Capernaum (6:17)

6:19* after rowing twenty-five to thirty furlongs, saw Jesus walking on the sea and was afraid

6:20* told to not be afraid

6:21* willingly received Him into the ship

6:22* was entered into the only boat there

6:22* was apart from Jesus in the boat alone (with the other disciples)

6:67* asked by Jesus if he would also go away

6:69* believed and was sure that Jesus was the Christ, the Son of the living God

6:70* chosen as one of the twelve

9: 2* questioned Jesus concerning the man born blind

11: 8* called Jesus Master

11:11* friend of Lazarus

11:54* continued with Jesus at Ephraim

12:16* understood not, at first, the events of the triumphal entry of Jesus

12:16* after Jesus' glorification, remembered that these events had been written of Jesus, and had been done unto Him

12:21 certain Greeks came to him desiring to see Jesus

12:21 of Bethsaida of Galilee

12:22 came and told Andrew

12:22 along with Andrew, told Jesus that certain Greeks sought to see Him

13: 5* feet washed by Jesus

13:12* had his feet washed by Jesus

13:13* called Jesus Master and Lord

13:14* had his feet washed by Jesus

13:14* told by Jesus that he ought to wash one another's feet

13:15* had been given an example that he should do as Jesus had done to him

13:18* was known and chosen of Jesus

13:21* when told that one of them would betray Jesus, looked on the others doubting of whom He spoke (13:22)

13:28* knew not for what intent Jesus

spoke these words to Judas Iscariot

John 13:34* given a new commandment to love one another

13:34* loved of Jesus

13:35* love one to another was a mark that he was a true disciple of Jesus

14: 8 asked Jesus to show him the Father and he would be satisfied

14: 9 had been a long time with Jesus, yet had not really known Him

14:25* was with Jesus

14:26* would be instructed by the Holy Spirit in all things

14:26* the words Jesus had spoken would be brought to his remembrance

14:27* Jesus' peace was given to him and left with him

14:31* was told to arise and go with Jesus

15: 3* is clean through the Word

15: 9* loved of Jesus

15:12* commanded to love one another

15:12* loved of Jesus

15:16* chosen of Jesus, and ordained of Him to go and bring forth fruit, and that his fruit should remain

15:17* commanded to love one another

15:19* not of the world

15:19* chosen out of the world, by Jesus

15:19* hated of the world

15:27* would bear witness, because he had been with Jesus from the beginning

16: 4* was with Jesus

16: 6* sorrow had filled his heart

16:12* could not bear the words of Jesus

16:22* presently had sorrow

16:24* had asked nothing of the Father in Jesus' name

16:27* loved of the Father

16:27* loved Jesus, and believed that He came from God

16:29* could now understand plainly Jesus' words

16:30* was sure that Jesus knew all things

16:30* believed that Jesus came forth from God

18: 1* went with Jesus over the brook Cedron and entered into a garden (Gethsemane)

18: 2* often resorted there with Jesus

20:18* told by Mary Magdalene that she had seen the Lord and that He had spoken unto her

20:19* while assembled together (with the other disciples) with the doors shut for fear of the Jews, Jesus appeared in the midst

20:20* saw Jesus' hands and side and was glad

20:21* sent by Jesus and given His peace

20:22* breathed on by Jesus and received the Holy Ghost

20:25* told Thomas that he had seen the Lord

20:25* informed by Thomas that he would

PHILIP (continued)

not believe without specific conditions being met

John 20:26* the doors being shut again, Jesus appeared the second time to him and the apostles

20:30* many other signs were done in his presence which are not written (in this book)

Acts 1: 2* had been given commandments by Jesus (through the Holy Ghost)

1: 2* chosen by Jesus

1: 3* was shown Jesus alive after His passion

1: 3* spoken to by Jesus of the things pertaining to the kingdom of God

1: 3* saw Jesus forty days

1: 4* commanded, by Jesus, not to depart from Jerusalem, but to wait for the promise of the Father

1: 5* would be baptized with the Holy Spirit

1: 6* questioned Jesus concerning the restoration of the kingdom to Israel

1: 7* was not to know the times or the seasons which the Father had put in His own power

1: 8* after receiving the Holy Spirit, would receive power and would be witness unto Jesus Christ throughout the earth

1: 9* beheld as Jesus was taken up into Heaven at His ascension

1:10* was joined by two men in white apparel while he looked steadfastly toward Heaven

1:11* a man of Galilee

1:11* was gazing up into Heaven

1:11* Jesus was taken up from him into Heaven

1:11* was told that Jesus would come in like manner as he had seen Him go into Heaven

1:12* returned to Jerusalem and went into an upper room (1:13)

1:14* continued in prayer and supplication with the women, Mary the mother of Jesus, and with His brethren

1:21* was with the Lord Jesus at various times

1:24* prayed concerning the ordination of one to be a witness of Jesus' resurrection

1:26* gave forth his lot (concerning Judas Iscariot's successor)

2: 1* present at the day of Pentecost

2: 2* while sitting in the house, cloven tongues like as of fire sat upon him, he was filled with the Holy Ghost, and spoke with other tongues (2:4)

2: 6* his speech confounded the multitude because every man heard in his own language

Acts 2: 7* a Galilean

2:13* mocked by some who claimed him as full of new wine

2:14* stood with (Simon) Peter

2:15* was not drunk

2:32* was a witness to the resurrection of Jesus

2:37* asked by the multitude on day of Pentecost what they should do

2:42* many continued steadfastly in his doctrine and fellowship

2:43* many wonders and signs were done by him

4:33* with great power gave witness of the resurrection of the Lord Jesus

4:33* great grace was upon him

4:35* the price of possessions sold by Christians was laid at his feet

4:35* distributed to every man (of the Christian community) as he had need

4:36* gave Joses a surname of Barnabas

4:37* Joses's money was laid at his feet

5: 2* the gift of Ananias and Sapphira was laid at his feet

5:12* by his hands were many signs and wonders wrought among the people

5:12* was with one accord with the others in Solomon's porch

5:13* no man durst join himself to him (the apostles)

5:13* was magnified of the people

5:16* healed the multitude of sicknesses and unclean spirits

5:18* placed in the common prison by the high priest and Sadducees

5:19* released from prison by the angel of the Lord and told to go, stand, and speak in the temple (5:20)

5:21* entered into the temple early in the morning and taught

5:22* was not found in the prison

5:25* was standing in the temple and teaching the people

5:26* brought without violence and set before the council (5:27)

5:27* questioned by the high priest (5:28)

5:28* had been commanded not to teach in this (Jesus') name

5:28* had filled Jerusalem with his doctrine and had (seemingly) intended to bring Jesus' blood upon his accusers

5:29* believed that he ought to obey God rather than men

5:32* witness of God (and of His works)

5:33* Jewish leaders took counsel to slay him

5:34* put a little space from the Sanhedrin (for their deliberation)

5:40* called back before the council, beaten, commanded not to speak in the name of Jesus, and let go

160

PHILIP *(continued)*

Acts 5:41* departed from the council rejoicing that he was counted worthy to suffer shame for His name

5:42* daily in the temple and in every house, ceased not to teach and preach Jesus Christ

6: 2* called the multitude together and stated it was not reasonable that he should leave the Word of God and serve tables

6: 3* instructed that seven men of honest report be chosen to be appointed to serve tables

6: 4* determined to give himself continually to prayer and to the ministry of the Word

6: 6* the chosen seven were set before him, for whom he prayed and laid his hands on them

8: 1* remained in Jerusalem in the midst of great persecution

8:14* was in Jerusalem

8:14* hearing that Samaria had received the Word of God, sent Peter and John to Samaria

9:27* Saul (Paul) was brought to him by Barnabas and he was informed of Saul's (Paul's) conversion experience and his bold preaching at Damascus

9:28* was accompanied by Saul (Paul) in coming out and going out at Jerusalem

10:39* was witness of all things Jesus did both in the land of the Jews and in Jerusalem

10:41* a witness chosen before of God

10:41* ate and drank with Jesus after His resurrection

10:42* commanded of Jesus to preach unto the people, and testified that it was Jesus which was ordained of God to be the Judge of quick and dead

11: 1* was in Judea

11: 1* heard that the Gentiles had also received the Word of God

11:15* the Holy Ghost fell on him at the beginning (Pentecost)

13:31* saw Jesus many days

13:31* came up with Jesus from Galilee to Jerusalem

13:31* was His (Jesus') witness unto the people

15: 2* Paul, Barnabas, and others were sent by the church at Antioch to consult with him over the matter of circumcision

15: 4* received Paul, Barnabas, and the others from Antioch

15: 6* came together (with the elders) to consider the matter (of circumcision)

15: 8* given the Holy Ghost

Acts 15: 9* God made no difference between him and a Gentile

15:10* was not able to bear the yoke

15:22* acting with the elders, sent chosen men back to Antioch with Paul and Barnabas

15:23* acting with the elders and brethren, wrote letters of instruction to the Gentiles at Antioch, Syria, and Cilicia

15:24* gave no commandment that Gentile believers must be circumcised and keep the law

15:25* considered it good, being assembled, to send chosen men unto the believers

15:25* loved Barnabas and Paul

15:27* sent Judas and Silas to the Gentile believers

15:33* Judas (Barsabas) and Silas returned unto him

16: 4* with the elders, ordained decrees

16: 4* was at Jerusalem

Rom 16: 7* Andronicus and Junia were well known to him

1Cor 4: 9* Paul thought God had set him (and the apostles) forth last, as it were appointed to death

4: 9* made a spectacle unto the world, to the angels, and to men

4:10* a fool for Christ's sake

4:10* weak, despised

4:11* hungered, thirsted, was naked, was buffeted, and had no certain dwelling place

4:12* labored, working with his own hands

4:12* being reviled, he blessed; being persecuted, he suffered it; being defamed, he entreated (4:13)

4:13* made as the filth of the world, and the offscouring of all things

9: 5* had power to lead about a sister, a wife

15: 5* had seen the risen Lord

15: 7* the risen Lord was seen of him

15:11* preached

Rev 21:14* name inscribed in the twelve foundations of the new Jerusalem

21:14 an apostle of the Lamb

2. The husband of Herodias and brother of Herod Antipas.

Matt 14: 3 brother of Herod (Antipas) the tetrarch

14: 3 husband of Herodias

Mark 6:17 brother of Herod the king

6:17 husband of Herodias

6:17 Herodias, his wife, had married Herod the king

6:18 his wife (Herodias) was not the lawful wife of Herod (his brother)

Luke 3:19 husband of Herodias

3:19 brother of Herod

161

PHILIP *(continued)*
3. Another brother of Herod, Tetrarch of Ituraea, and of the region of Trachonitis.

Luke 3: 1 contemporary of Tiberius Caesar, and Pontius Pilate, Herod and Lysanias (tetrarchs) and Annas and Caiaphas (high priests) (3:2)
      3: 1 tetrarch of Ituraea and of the region of Trachonitis
      3: 1 brother of Herod

4. The evangelist, one of seven men of honest report, full of the Holy Ghost, chosen to serve tables as a deacon in the Jerusalem church, and received the laying on of hands by the apostles.

Acts 6: 3 of honest report
      6: 3 full of the Holy Ghost and wisdom
      6: 5 chosen to serve tables
      6: 6 was set before the apostles
      6: 6 apostles prayed and laid their hands on him
      8: 5 went to the city of Samaria and preached Christ unto them
      8: 6 people gave heed to his message
      8: 6 did miracles
      8: 7 cast out unclean spirits and healed many of diseases
      8:12 people believed his preaching concerning the kingdom of God
      8:13 did miracles and signs
      8:26 commanded by the angel of the Lord to go south unto the way that goeth down from Jerusalem unto Gaza
      8:27 arose and went
      8:29 told of the Spirit to go near and join himself to the chariot (of the eunuch)
      8:30 ran to the Ethiopian eunuch and hearing him read the prophet Esaias (Isaiah), asked him if he understood what he read
      8:31 was desired of the eunuch to come up (in the chariot) and to sit with him
      8:34 asked by the eunuch of whom the prophet spoke
      8:35 opened his mouth and preached unto him Jesus
      8:38 went down into the water and baptized the eunuch
      8:39 caught away by the Spirit of the Lord
      8:40 was found at Azotus, and passing through preached in all the cities
      8:40 came to Caesarea
      21: 8 visited by those of Paul's company (in his house)
      21: 8 the evangelist
      21: 8 lived in Caesarea
      21: 8 one of the seven (deacons)
      21: 8 Paul and his company abode with him
      21: 9 had four daughters (virgins) which prophesied
Acts 21:10 Paul and his company tarried many days with him

PHILOLOGUS [fil-ol'-o-gus = a lover of words]
A believer at Rome greeted by Paul.

Rom 16:15 saluted by Paul
      16:15 was with the saints

PHLEGON [fle'-gon = burning]
A Christian at Rome saluted by Paul.

Rom 16:14 saluted by Paul
      16:14 was with other brethren

PHYGELLUS [fi-jel'-lus = fugitive]
A man in Asia who turned away from Paul.

2Tim 1:15 lived in Asia
      1:15 turned away from Paul (along with Hermogenes)

PILATE [pi'-lut = armed with a spear]—see PONTIUS PILATE

PONTIUS PILATE [pon'-she-us; pi'-lut = of the sea; armed with a spear]
The Roman procurator (governor) over Judea, consented to the mob, and delivered Jesus to be crucified.

Matt 27: 2 governor
      27: 2 Jesus delivered unto him
      27:11 the governor
      27:11 inquired of Jesus as to who He was
      27:13 questioned Jesus
      27:14 marveled greatly at Jesus' silence
      27:15 the governor
      27:15 was wont to release unto the people a prisoner
      27:17 offered for release Jesus or Barabbas
      27:18 knew that for envy Jesus had been delivered
      27:19 was set down on the judgment seat
      27:19 asked by his wife to have nothing to do with Jesus
      27:21 the governor
      27:21 asked whom he should release unto the people
      27:22 asked leaders what to do with Jesus
      27:23 the governor
      27:23 asked what evil Jesus had done
      27:24 saw he could not prevail, washed his hands of the matter, and claimed he was innocent of the blood of Jesus
      27:26 released Barabbas
      27:26 scourged Jesus
      27:26 delivered Jesus to be crucified
      27:27 the governor
      27:58 begged by Joseph of Arimathea, for the body of Jesus
      27:58 commanded Jesus' body to be delivered (to Joseph of Arimathea)

PONTIUS PILATE(continued)

Matt 27:65   gave the chief priests and Pharisees a watch over the tomb of Jesus

28:14   the governor

Mark 15: 1   Jesus was delivered unto him

15: 2   questioned Jesus as to His identity

15: 4   questioned Jesus again

15: 5   marveled at Jesus' silence

15: 6   customarily released one prisoner at the feast

15: 9   asked the crowd if they desired the release of the "King of the Jews"

15:12   asked the multitude what to do with Jesus

15:14   asked what evil Jesus had done (to be worthy of death)

15:15   willing to content the people, released Barabbas

15:15   scourged Jesus and delivered Him to be crucified

15:43   was asked for the body of Jesus, by Joseph of Arimathea

15:44   marveled that Jesus was already dead

15:44   called the centurion and asked whether Jesus had been dead any time

15:45   knowing of Jesus' death at the hand of the centurion, gave Jesus' body to Joseph (of Arimathea)

Luke 3: 1   contemporary of Tiberius Caesar, and Herod, Philip and Lysanias (tetrarchs) and Annas and Caiaphas (high priests) (3:2)

3: 1   governor of Judea

13: 1   had mingled the blood of the Galileans with their sacrifices

20:20   had power and authority

20:20   was governor

23: 1   Jesus led unto him

23: 3   asked Jesus if He were the King of the Jews

23: 4   found no fault in Jesus

23: 6   asked if Jesus were a Galilean and then sent Him to Herod (23:7)

23:11   Jesus returned to him from Herod

23:12   he and Herod the same day were made friends whereas before they were at enmity

23:13   reported to the Jews that after examining Jesus he had found no fault in Him concerning their accusations (23:14)

23:15   had sent Jesus to Herod

23:15   declared that nothing worthy of death is done unto Him (or found in Him)

23:16   decided to chastise Jesus and release Him

23:17   of necessity, must release one (prisoner) at the feast

23:20   was willing to release Jesus

23:22   the third time confronted the crowd with the question as to the evil which Jesus had done

Luke 23:22   found no cause of death in Him

23:22   desired to chastise Jesus and to let Him go

23:23   allowed the voices of the crowd and the chief priests to prevail and gave sentence that it should be as they required (23:24)

23:25   released Barabbas, but delivered Jesus to the will of the crowd

23:38   wrote a superscription for Jesus' cross

23:52   the body of Jesus was begged of him (by Joseph of Arimathaea)

John 18:29   desired the nature of the accusation against Jesus

18:30   Jesus delivered unto him

18:31   told the Jews to take Jesus and judge Him according to their law

18:33   entered into the judgment hall again, called for Jesus, and asked Him if He were King of the Jews

18:35   not a Jew

18:35   Jesus delivered unto him

18:37   questioned Jesus again if He were a king

18:38   asked Jesus "What is truth?"

18:38   stated that he found no fault at all in Jesus

18:39   questioned the Jews if he should release Jesus according to the custom

19: 1   scourged Jesus

19: 4   went forth again, stating he had found no fault in Jesus

19: 5   concerning Jesus, stated, "Behold the man!"

19: 6   told the Jews to crucify Jesus, for he found no fault in Him

19: 8   was the more afraid

19: 9   went again into the judgment hall and asked Jesus whence He was

19:10   had power to crucify or release Jesus

19:11   had no power at all except it were given him from above

19:12   sought to release Jesus

19:13   brought Jesus forth and sat down in the judgment seat

19:14   told the Jews to behold their King

19:15   asked if he should crucify the Jews' King

19:16   delivered Jesus to be crucified

19:19   wrote a title concerning Jesus and put it on the cross

19:21   chided by the chief priests for what he had written

19:22   stood firm upon his decision

19:31   besought by the Jews to break the legs of those on the cross, and that they might be taken away

19:38   besought by Joseph of Arimathea for the body of Jesus and gave him leave

PONTIUS PILATE *(continued)*

Acts	3:13	the Jews had denied Jesus in his presence
	3:13	was determined to let Jesus go
	4:27	had gathered with others against Jesus (to do the predetermined will of God) (4:28)
	13:28	was desired of the people that Jesus should be slain
1Tim	6:13	was witness of a good confession from Jesus Christ

PORCIUS FESTUS [por'-she-us; fes'-tus = swinish; festival]
Succeeded Felix as governor, sat in judgment upon Paul, and granted Paul's appeal unto Caesar.

Acts	24:27	succeeded Felix (as governor?)
	25: 1	came into the province and after three days ascended from Caesarea to Jerusalem
	25: 2	was informed against Paul by the high priest and chief of the Jews
	25: 4	determined that Paul should be kept at Caesarea and he himself would depart shortly
	25: 5	offered that any who desired could go to Jerusalem with him to accuse Paul
	25: 6	tarried among them more than ten days and went down to Caesarea
	25: 6	sat on the judgment seat and commanded Paul to be brought
	25: 9	willing to do the Jews a pleasure, asked Paul if he were willing to go to Jerusalem to be judged by him
	25:10	very well knew Paul had done no wrong
	25:12	conferred with the council and granted Paul's appeal (unto Caesar)
	25:13	King Agrippa and Bernice came to Caesarea to salute him
	25:14	declared Paul's cause unto the king (Agrippa) (25:21)
	25:15	was at Jerusalem
	25:15	informed by the chief priests and elders concerning Paul
	25:15	desired of the Jews to have judgment against Paul
	25:16	declared the Roman law concerning capital punishment to the Jews
	25:17	without delay sat on the judgment seat and commanded (Paul) to be brought forth
	25:18	Paul's accusers brought no accusations as he had supposed they would
	25:20	doubting the manner of questions (placed against Paul) had asked him to go to Jerusalem to be judged
	25:21	commanded Paul to be kept till he might send him to Caesar

Acts	25:22	hearing Agrippa's desire to hear Paul, granted his wish
	25:23	at his commandment Paul was brought forth
	25:24	informed Agrippa concerning Paul
	25:24	had been dealt with by the Jews both at Jerusalem and (Caesarea) concerning Paul
	25:25	found Paul had committed nothing worthy of death and determined to send him to Augustus
	25:26	had no certain thing to write unto Augustus
	25:26	referred to Augustus as lord
	25:26	brought Paul before Agrippa for examination in order to have something to write to Augustus
	25:27	seemed unreasonable to him to send a prisoner and not signify the crimes laid against him
	26:24	told Paul with a loud voice that he was beside himself, and that much learning had made him mad
	26:25	noble
	26:30	the governor
	26:30	rose up, went aside and talked with the others, that Paul had done nothing worthy of death or of bonds (26:31)
	26:32	informed by Agrippa that Paul might have been set at liberty if he had not appealed unto Caesar

PRISCA ♀ [pris'-cah = ancient]—see PRISCILLA

PRISCILLA ♀ [pris-sil'-lah = ancient; little old woman]
Also Prisca, wife of Aquila, forced to leave Rome under an edict of Claudius, went to Corinth, along with her husband, who was a tentmaker by trade, and, with her husband, instructed Apollos more fully in the way of God.

Acts	18: 2	found by Paul, who came unto her and Aquila
	18: 2	wife of Aquila
	18: 2	lately come from Italy
	18: 3	Paul abode with her (and Aquila)
	18: 3	a tentmaker by occupation (as was Paul)
	18:18	sailed to Syria with Paul
	18:19	left at Ephesus by Paul
	18:26	hearing Apollos, took him unto herself (and Aquila), and expounded the way of God more perfectly
Rom	16: 3	was to be greeted (along with Aquila) by the Roman church for Paul
	16: 3	helper of Paul in Christ Jesus
	16: 4	for Paul's life had laid down her own neck
	16: 4	given thanks by Paul and all the churches of the Gentiles

PRISCILLA *(continued)*

Rom	16: 5	the church met in her (and Aquila's) house
1Cor	16:19	saluted the Corinthian church
	16:19	the church met in her house (and Aquila's)
2Tim	4:19	was to be saluted by Timothy, for Paul

PROCHORUS [prok'-o-rus = leader of the dance; leader of praise]
One of seven men of honest report, full of the Holy Ghost, chosen to serve tables as a deacon in the Jerusalem church, and received the laying on of hands by the apostles.

Acts	6: 3	of honest report
	6: 3	full of the Holy Ghost and wisdom
	6: 5	chosen to serve tables
	6: 6	was set before the apostles
	6: 6	apostles prayed and laid their hands on him

PUBLIUS [pub'-le-us = common]
The chief man of the island of Melita, received and lodged Paul, Aristarchus, and Luke, and his father was healed of a fever and a bloody flux by Paul.

Acts	28: 7	had possessions
	28: 7	the chief man of the island (Melita)
	28: 7	received Paul and Aristarchus (and Luke) and lodged them three days courteously
	28: 8	his father lay sick of a fever and of a bloody flux
	28: 8	his father was healed by Paul

PUDENS [pu'-denz = shamefaced]
A Christian friend of Paul at Rome, sent greetings to Timothy, and possibly the husband of Claudia.

2Tim	4:21	sent greetings to Timothy by Paul

Q

QUARTUS [quar'-tus = fourth]
A believer who sent greetings to the Roman Christians.

Rom	16:23	a (Christian) brother
	16:23	saluted the church at Rome

R

RACHAB ♀ [ra'-kab = broad]—see RAHAB

RACHEL ♀ [ra'-chel = a lamb or sheep]
Also Old Testament Rahel, younger sister of Leah, daughter of Laban, favorite wife and cousin of Jacob, and mother of Joseph and Benjamin.

Matt	2:18	personification of Israel

RAGAU [ra'-gaw = feed ye]
Son of Phalec, father of Saruch, and an ancestor of Jesus. (Possibly identical with Old Testament Reu)

Luke	3:35	father of Saruch
	3:35	son of Phalec

RAHAB ♀ [ra'-hab = wide]
Also Rachab, a harlot of Jericho who obtained the blessing of the Lord for her faith displayed by hiding the two Israeli spies, mother of Boaz by Salmon, and great-grandmother of David. (See also Josh 2,6)

Matt	1: 5	mother of Booz (Boaz) by Salmon
Heb	11:31	by faith perished not with them that believed not
	11:31	the harlot
	11:31	received the spies with peace
Jas	2:25	the harlot
	2:25	justified by works when she received the messengers and sent them out another way

REBECCA ♀ [re-bek'-kah = flattering; tying]
Old Testament Rebekah, daughter of Bethuel (nephew of Abraham), wife of Isaac, and mother of Jacob and Esau. (See also Gen 22—29, 35, 49)

Rom	9:10	conceived by Isaac
	9:12	told that the elder (son, Esau) would serve the younger (son, Jacob)

REUBEN [ru'-ben = behold a son]
One of the patriarchs, the firstborn of Jacob and Leah, and forfeited messianic lineage through immorality. (See also Gen 29—30, 35—37, 42—50; Ex 1, 6; Num 1, 26)

Matt	1: 2	begat by Jacob
John	4:12	drank of the well (Jacob's)
	4:12	a child of Jacob
	7: 8	begat by Jacob
	7: 8	one of the patriarchs
	7: 9	one of the patriarchs
	7: 9	moved with envy, sold Joseph into Egypt
	7:11	found no sustenance
	7:12	sent by Jacob to Egypt for corn
	7:13	on his second visit (to Egypt) Joseph was made known to him
	7:13	was made known unto Pharaoh
	7:15	went down into Egypt and died
	7:16	was carried into Sychem and was laid in the sepulcher that Abraham bought
Rev	7: 5	twelve thousand sealed of his tribe
	21:12	his name is inscribed upon the gates of the new Jerusalem
	21:12	a child of Israel (Jacob)

RHESA [re'-sah = head]
Son of Zerubbabel, father of Joanna, and an ancestor of Jesus.

Luke   3:27   father of Joanna
          3:27   son of Zorobabel

RHODA ♀ [ro'-dah = a rose]
A maid or servant in the house of Mary the mother of John Mark in Jerusalem, and failed to open the door for Simon Peter.

Acts   12:12   was present at the prayer meeting at the house of Mary (12:13)
       12:13   a damsel
       12:13   hearkened to the knock of (Simon) Peter at the door of the gate
       12:14   knew (Simon) Peter's voice
       12:14   opened not the gate for gladness, but ran in and told how (Simon) Peter stood before the gate
       12:15   the people thought her to be mad, but she constantly affirmed that it was even so (as she had stated)
       12:17   beckoned unto by Peter to hold her peace

ROBOAM [ro-bo'-am = enlargement of the people]
Old Testament Rehoboam, son of Solomon, father of Abia, and reigned as first king of Judah at the time of the division of the kingdom. (See also 1Kng 11—15; 2Chr 9—13)

Matt   1: 7   begotten of Solomon
       1: 7   begat Abia

RUFUS [ru'-fus = red]
1. Brother of Alexander, son of Simon the Cyrenian who was compelled to carry Jesus' cross. (Probably identical with #2)

Mark   15:21   son of Simon (a Cyrenian)
       15:21   brother of Alexander
       15:21   his father carried Jesus' cross

2. A Christian at Rome saluted by Paul. (Probably identical with #1)

Rom   16:13   saluted by Paul
      16:13   chosen in the Lord
      16:13   his mother also saluted by Paul

RUTH ♀ [rooth = friendship]
A Moabitess, daughter-in-law of Naomi, married Boaz the kinsman redeemer, bore Obed, and an ancestress of David. (See also Ruth 1—4)

Matt   1: 5   mother of Obed by Booz (Boaz)

S

SADOC [sa'-dok = righteous; just]
Son of Azor, father of Achim, and an ancestor of Jesus.

Matt   1:14   begotten of Azor
      1:14   begat Achim

SALA [sa'-lah = petition]
Old Testament Salah and Shelah, son of Arphaxad, father of Eber, and an ancestor of Jesus. (See also Gen 10, 11)

Luke   3:35   father of Heber
       3:35   son of Cainan (3:36)

SALATHIEL [sa-la'the-el = I have asked of God]
Also Old Testament Shealtiel, son or grandson of Jechonias, father of Zerubbabel, and an ancestor of Jesus. (See also Ezra 3, 5; Neh 12; Hag 1, 2)

Matt   1:12   begotten by Jechonias in Babylon
      1:12   begat Zorobabel
Luke   3:27   father of Zorobabel
       3:27   son of Neri

SALMON [sal'-mon = clothing; garment]
Also Old Testament Salma, son of Naasson, father of Boaz (by Rahab), and an ancestor of Jesus. (See also Ruth 4; 1Chr 2)

Matt   1: 4   begotten of Naasson
      1: 5   begat Booz (Boaz) of Rachab (Rahab)
Luke   3:32   father of Booz (Boaz)
       3:32   son of Naasson

SALOME ♀ [sa-lo'-me = peaceful]; Mother of James and John (apostles), and wife of Zebedee.

Matt   20:20   mother of Zebedee's children (James and John)
       20:20   had sons
       20:20   came to Jesus, worshiping Him and desiring a certain thing of Him
       20:21   asked that He grant that her two sons might sit, the one on His right hand and the other on His left in His kingdom
       27:55   beheld the crucifixion from afar off (27:56)
       27:55   followed Jesus from Galilee, ministering unto Him (27:56)
       27:56   mother of Zebedee's children (James and John)
Mark   15:40   looked on afar off (at the crucifixion of Jesus)
       15:41   followed Jesus when He was in Galilee, ministering unto Him
       16: 1   brought sweet spices to anoint Jesus (body)
       16: 2   very early the first day of the week, came to the sepulcher
       16: 3   questioned who should roll away the stone from the door of the sepulcher
       16: 4   looked and saw that the stone was rolled away
       16: 5   entered the sepulcher and saw a young man sitting clothed in a long white garment

SALOME *(continued)*
Mark 16: 5 was afraid
    16: 6 told to not be afraid but to behold the place where Jesus had been laid
    16: 7 instructed to go tell His disciples and Peter, that He goeth into Galilee and there they would see Him
    16: 8 quickly fled from the sepulcher for she trembled and was amazed
    16: 8 said nothing to anyone because of fear
Luke 23:49 observed the cross from afar

SAMSON [sam'-sun = distinguished; strong]
A Nazarite, of the tribe of Dan, a judge of Israel for twenty years, a man of riddles, and of enormous physical strength. (See also Judg 13—16)
Heb 11:32 acted by faith (11:34)
    11:39 had obtained a good report through faith
    11:39 received not the promise

SAMUEL [sam'-u-el = heard of God]
Son of Elkanah and Hannah, a Levite, the last judge of Israel and the first prophet, and anointed both Saul and David as king. (See also 1Sam 1—28)
Acts 3:24 a prophet who foretold of these days
    13:20 the prophet
Heb 11:32 acted by faith (11:34)
    11:39 had obtained a good report through faith
    11:39 received not the promise

SAPPHIRA ♀ [saf-fi'-rah = sapphire]
A participant at the Jerusalem church, along with her husband Ananias lied to the Holy Spirit concerning the sale of their property, and consequently was struck down in death.
Acts 5: 1 wife of Ananias
    5: 1 sold a possession with her husband and kept back part of the price (5:2)
    5: 2 was privy to the deal (along with her husband)
    5: 7 came in three hours after her husband's death, not knowing what was done
    5: 8 testified to the same figures of sale as had her husband concerning the price of the land
    5: 9 had agreed together (with her husband) to tempt the Spirit of the Lord
    5: 9 would be carried out by the same ones who had buried her husband
    5:10 fell down at his (Simon Peter's) feet and yielded up the ghost
    5:10 was found dead
    5:10 carried forth by the young men and buried by her husband

SARA ♀ [sa'-rah = princess]—see SARAH

SARAH ♀ [sa'-rah = princess]
Also Sara and Old Testament Sarai, originally Sarai, wife and half-sister of Abraham, name changed by the Lord to Sarah (Princess), and conceived and bare a son Issac at age ninety. (See also Gen 11—12, 16—25, 49)
Rom 4:19 her womb was dead
    9: 9 would have a son according to the promise
Gal 4:22 a freewoman, who bore Abraham a son
    4:30 freewoman
    4:30 mother of Issac (son of the freewoman)
    4:30 her son would be heir (but not with the son of the bondwoman)
    4:31 the free (woman)
Heb 11:11 through faith received strength to conceive seed
    11:11 delivered of a child when she was past age because she judged Him faithful who had promised
    11:13 died in faith, not having received the promises, but was persuaded of them and embraced them
    11:13 confessed that she was a stranger and pilgrim on the earth
    11:16 desired a better country
    11:16 God was not ashamed to be called her God
    11:16 God hath prepared for her a city
    11:39 had obtained a good report through faith
    11:39 received not the promise
1Pet 3: 6 obeyed Abraham calling him lord

SARUCH [sa'-ruk = intertwined]
Old Testament Serug, son of Ragau, father of Nachor, and an ancestor of Jesus. (See also Gen 11; 1Chr 1)
Luke 3:34 father of Nachor (3:35)
    3:35 son of Ragau

SAUL [sawl = asked; requested]
1. The apostle—see PAUL
2. Son of Cis (Kish), of the tribe of Benjamin, anointed by Samuel as first king of Israel, tall of stature, committed suicide at Gilboa, and was succeeded as king by David. (See also 1Sam 9—31; 2Sam 22; 1Chr 8—15)
Acts 13:21 God gave him as king to the nation of Israel
    13:21 the son of Cis
    13:21 of the tribe of Benjamin
    13:21 ruled forty years
    13:22 removed of the Lord

SCEVA [see'-vah = mind reader]
A Jew, chief priest at Ephesus; seven sons tried to exorcise evil spirits and being unsuccessful, were wounded and forced to flee.
Acts 19:14 had (at least) seven sons
    19:14 a Jew
    19:14 chief of the priests

SECUNDUS [se-cun'-dus = fortunate]
A Christian of Thessalonica who accompanied
Paul into Asia.

Acts 20: 4 of the Thessalonians
20: 4 accompanied Paul into Asia
20: 5 went before and tarried for Paul
(and Luke) at Troas
20: 6 abode seven days with Paul (and
Luke) at Troas
20:13 going before by ship, sailed unto
Assos
20:14 met Paul at Assos, took him in, and
came to Mitylene
20:15 sailed over against Chios, next day
arriving at Samos, tarried at
Trogyllium, and the next day came
to Miletus
20:34 Paul's hands had ministered unto
his necessities

SEM [sem = a name]
Old Testament Shem, son of Noah, elder brother
of Ham and Japheth, saved with his wife and
relatives in the ark, and received a blessing along
with Japheth for his actions concerning his father.
(See also Gen 5—11; 1Chr 1)

Luke 3:36 father of Arphaxad
3:36 son of Noe (Noah)

SEMEI [sem'-e-i = heard of Jehovah; guarded of
Jehovah]
Son of Joseph, father of Mattathias, and an ances-
tor of Jesus. (Possibly Old Testament Shimei)

Luke 3:26 father of Mattathias
3:26 son of Joseph

SERGIUS PAULUS [sur'-je-us; pawl'-us = earth-
born; little]
The Roman deputy or proconsul of Cyprus, heard
the Word of God from Paul and Barnabas who
were visiting as missionaries, and was converted.

Acts 13: 6 was on the isle of Paphos (13:7)
13: 7 was with Bar-jesus (Elymas)
13: 7 the deputy of the country
13: 7 a prudent man
13: 7 called for Barnabas and Saul
(Paul) and desired to hear the
Word of God
13: 8 Bar-jesus (Elymas) withstood Barnabas and Saul (Paul) seeking to
turn the deputy away from the faith
13: 8 the deputy
13:12 the deputy
13:12 observing the judgment of Bar-
jesus (Elymas), believed
13:12 was astonished at the doctrine of
the Lord

SETH [seth = compensation]
Also Old Testament Sheth, third son of Adam
and Eve, and younger brother of Cain and Abel
(among others). (See also Gen 4, 5)

Luke 3:38 father of Enos
3:38 son of Adam

SILAS (Silvanus) [si'-las = woody]
Also Silvanus, a missionary traveling companion
of Paul on the second missionary journey, and
imprisoned with Paul at Philippi. (Possibly identical with Tertius)

Acts 15:22 sent (along with Judas Barsabas)
to Antioch with Paul and Barnabas
15:22 a chosen man of the company (of
the Jerusalem church)
15:22 a chief man among the brethren
15:23 bearer of letters from the apostles,
elders, and brethren to the Gentile
brethren in Antioch, Syria, and
Cilicia
15:25 a chosen man, sent, with Barnabas
and Paul
15:27 sent by the Jerusalem council to
confirm by mouth the message of
the letter
15:30 dismissed, came to Antioch,
gathered the multitude together,
and delivered the epistle
15:32 a prophet
15:32 exhorted the brethren with many
words, and confirmed them
15:33 tarried a space and was let go in
peace
15:34 was pleased to abide still in Antioch
15:40 chosen by Paul, as his partner, and
departed (for a missionary journey)
15:41 accompanied Paul through Syria
and Cilicia
16: 1 came to Derbe and Lystra
16: 4 went through the cities delivering
the decrees that were ordained of
the apostles and elders which were
at Jerusalem
16: 6 had gone throughout Phrygia and
the region of Galatia
16: 6 forbidden of the Holy Ghost to
preach the Word in Asia
16: 7 came to Mysia and desired to go
into Bithynia, but not suffered of
the Spirit to do so
16: 8 passing by Mysia came down to
Troas
16:10 endeavored to go into Macedonia,
assured that the Lord had called
him to preach the gospel unto them
16:11 loosing from Troas, took a straight
course to Samothracia
16:11 the next day went on to Neapolis
16:12 went on to Philippi and abode there
certain days
16:13 on the Sabbath went out of the city
to a place of prayer and spoke unto
the women
16:14 heard by Lydia
16:15 constrained by Lydia to abide at
her house
16:16 met by a damsel possessed with a
spirit of divination as he went to
prayer
16:17 followed by a damsel possessed

SILAS *(continued)*

Acts 16:17 with a spirit of divination
Acts 16:17 claimed by one to be the servant of the most high God, which showed the way of salvation
16:19 caught and drawn into the marketplace unto the rulers
16:20 claimed as a Jew
16:20 brought before the magistrates, accused of exceedingly troubling the city and teaching customs not lawful for Romans to receive or to observe (16:21)
16:22 the multitude rose up against him, and he was commanded to be beaten
16:23 received many stripes and was cast into prison
16:24 was thrust into the inner prison by the jailer, and his feet were made fast in the stocks
16:25 at midnight prayed and sang praises unto God
16:25 heard by the (other) prisoners
16:26 his bands were loosed
16:28 remained in prison
16:30 brought out (of prison)
16:31 instructed the jailer in the way of salvation
16:32 spoke the Word of the Lord unto the jailer and to all in his house
16:33 his stripes were washed by the Philippian jailer
16:34 taken into the jailer's house and sat at meat
16:35 released by the magistrates (from prison) (16:36)
16:37 had been beaten, openly uncondemned, and cast into prison
16:37 a Roman
16:37 in prison with Paul
16:38 a Roman
16:39 besought, brought out of the prison, and desired to depart out of the city
16:40 went out of the prison, and entered into the house of Lydia
16:40 having seen the brethren comforted them and departed
17: 1 passed through Amphipolis and Apollonia and came to Thessalonica
17: 4 some Thessalonians consorted with him and Paul
17: 6 was not found in the house of Jason
17: 6 had turned the world upside down
17: 6 was come to Thessalonica
17: 7 had been received by Jason (in his house)
17: 7 accused of disloyalty to Caesar by saying there is another king (Jesus)
17: 9 had security taken of him and was let go

Acts 17:10 sent away by night into Berea
17:10 went into the synagogue (at Berea)
17:14 abode still in Berea
17:15 receiving a commandment from Paul to come to him with all speed, departed
17:16 Paul waited for him (and Timothy) at Athens
18: 5 was come from Macedonia
18:11 continued a year and six months (with Paul in the house of Justus)
18:18 sailed into Syria (with Paul)
18:19 came to Ephesus
18:21 sailed from Ephesus
18:22 landed at Caesarea
18:22 went down to Antioch
18:23 spent some time there (in Antioch), departed, and went over all the country of Galatia and Phrygia (with Paul)
19: 1 passed through the upper coasts and came to Ephesus
19:10 continued two years (with Paul in Asia)
2Cor 1:19 preached the Son of God, Jesus Christ, among the Corinthians
1:19 his preaching was not yea and nay, but in Him (Christ) was yea
1The 1: 1 mentioned, along with Timotheus, by Paul in greeting in book of 1 Thessalonians
1: 2 thanked God always for the Thessalonian church, mentioning them in his prayers
1: 5 gave the gospel not only in word, but in power, and in the Holy Spirit, and in much assurance
1: 5 his testimony was well known among the Thessalonian brethren (for good)
1: 6 the Thessalonian Christians became his followers (and the Lord's)
1: 9 people in Macedonia and Achaia knew of his good work with the Thessalonians
1:10 delivered from the wrath to come (by Christ Jesus)
2: 1 his work with the Thessalonians was not in vain
2: 2 suffered and was shamefully treated at Philippi
2: 2 was bold in God to speak the gospel of God unto the Thessalonians with much contention
2: 3 his exhortation was not of deceit, uncleanness, nor in guile
2: 4 spoke the gospel, of which he was put in trust
2: 4 sought not to please men, but God
2The 1: 1 mentioned, along with Timotheus, by Paul in greetings to the book of 2 Thessalonians
1Pet 5:12 helped Peter with manuscript of 1 Peter

SILAS *(continued)*
1Pet   5:12   a faithful brother to addressee of
              1 Peter

SILVANUS [sil-va'-nus = woody]—see SILAS

SIMEON [sim'-e-un = hearing]
1. the apostle—see SIMON PETER (?)
2. A just and devout man in Jerusalem, waited
for the consolation of Israel, would not see death
until he had seen the Messiah, and present at
Jesus' presentation at the temple.
Luke   2:25   lived in Jerusalem
       2:25   a just and devout man who waited
              for the consolation of Israel
       2:25   the Holy Ghost was upon him
       2:26   the Holy Ghost had revealed to
              him that he would not see death
              before he had seen the Christ
       2:27   came by the Spirit into the temple
       2:28   took Baby Jesus up in his arms and
              blessed God
       2:29   asked the Lord to let him now de-
              part in peace
       2:30   his eyes had seen the salvation of
              the Lord
       2:34   blessed Joseph, Mary, and Jesus
              and addressed Mary (2:35)
3. Son of Juda, father of Levi, and an ancestor of
Jesus.
Luke   3:29   father of Levi (3:30)
       3:30   son of Juda
4. The patriarch, second son of Jacob by Leah,
and forfeited messianic lineage through immoral-
ity. (See also Gen 49)
Matt   1: 2   begotten by Jacob
John   4:12   drank of the well (Jacob's)
       4:12   a child of Jacob
Acts   7: 8   begat by Jacob
       7: 8   one of the patriarchs
       7: 9   one of the patriarchs
       7: 9   moved with envy, sold Joseph into
              Egypt
       7:11   found no sustenance
       7:12   sent by Jacob to Egypt for corn
       7:13   on his second visit (to Egypt),
              Joseph was made known to him
       7:13   was made known unto Pharaoh
       7:15   went down into Egypt and died
       7:16   was carried into Sychem and was
              laid in the sepulcher that Abraham
              bought
Rev   7: 7   twelve thousand sealed of his tribe
      21:12   his name is inscribed upon the
              gates of the new Jerusalem
      21:12   a child of Israel (Jacob)
5. Niger [ni'-jur = black]
Surnamed Niger, a prophet and teacher in the
church at Antioch, and one of a group which
commissioned Barnabas and Paul to missionary
service.
Acts 13: 1   was in the church at Antioch
      13: 1   a prophet and teacher
      13: 1   called Niger

Acts 13: 2   ministered to the Lord and fasted
      13: 3   fasted, prayed, and laid his hands
              on Barnabas and Saul (Paul) and
              sent them away

SIMON [si'-mun = hearing]
1. Simon Peter
Also Bar-jesus, Cephas, Peter, Simeon (?), son of
Jonas, brother of Andrew, from Bethsaida, an
apostle of Jesus Christ, one of the twelve, a fisher-
man, married, lived at Capernaum, thrice denied
Jesus, the undesignated leader of the apostles, a
member of Jesus' inner circle with James and
John, given a new name Cephas by Jesus, apostle
to the circumcision (the Jews), and writer of the
New Testament epistles of 1 and 2 Peter.
Matt   4:18   seen (while fishing with Andrew)
              by Jesus at the Sea of Galilee
       4:18   fisherman
       4:18   brother of Andrew
       4:19   called by Jesus and straightway left
              his net and followed Him (4:20)
       8:14   visited at his house by Jesus
       8:14   had a wife
       8:15   his mother-in-law was healed by
              Jesus
       8:15   ministered unto by his wife's
              mother
       8:23* followed Jesus into a ship
       8:25* came to and awoke Jesus and asked
              Him to save the disciples, for they
              perished
       8:26* fearful
       8:26* of little faith
       8:27* marveled at Jesus
       9:10* sat at meat with Jesus along with
              publicans and sinners
       9:14* fasted not
       9:19* followed Jesus
       9:37* instructed to pray that the Lord
              would send forth laborers into His
              harvest (9:38)
      10: 1* was called unto Jesus
      10: 1   one of the twelve disciples (of Jesus)
      10: 1* given power to cast out unclean
              spirits
      10: 1* given power to heal all manner of
              sickness and disease
      10: 2   one of the twelve apostles
      10: 2   brother of Andrew (also an apostle)
      10: 5   one of the twelve (apostles)
      10: 5* commanded to go neither to the
              Gentiles, nor into any city of the
              Samaritans
      10: 6* sent forth by Jesus to the lost sheep
              of the house of Israel
      10: 7* commanded by Jesus to preach
              "the kingdom of heaven is at hand"
      10: 8* commanded to heal the sick,
              cleanse the lepers, raise the dead,
              cast out devils (demons)
      10: 8* had freely received
      10: 9* was to provide neither gold, nor
              silver, nor brass, nor scrip, neither

SIMON (continued)

two coats, neither shoes, nor staves (for himself) (10:10)

Matt 10:11* in every city or town, was to inquire who is worthy, and to abide with them

10:12* was to salute each house he entered

10:13* his peace was to come upon each worthy house, but return to him if unworthy

10:14* was to shake off the dust of his feet therein, when not received or heard by a house or city

10:16* sent forth (by Jesus) as a sheep in the midst of wolves

10:16* was to be wise as a serpent and harmless as a dove

10:17* would be delivered to the councils, scourged in synagogues, and brought before governors and kings for (Jesus') sake (10:18)

10:19* was to take no thought concerning what he would speak when delivered up, for the Spirit of his Father would speak in him (10:20)

12: 1* was an hungered and plucked corn in the field and ate

12: 2* accused by the Pharisees of acting unlawfully on the Sabbath day

12:49* called mother and brethren by Jesus

13:10* questioned Jesus about His use of parables

13:11* was given unto him to know the mysteries of the kingdom of Heaven

13:16* saw and heard (spiritually)

13:17* had seen and heard (spiritually)

13:18* had the parable of the sower explained by Jesus (13:23)

13:36* had the parable of the wheat and tares explained by Jesus (13:43)

13:51* claimed to have understood all these things (parables)

14:15* came to Jesus and requested Him to send the multitude away

14:16* instructed by Jesus to feed the multitude

14:17* requested by Jesus to bring the five loaves and two fishes to Him (14:18)

14:19* given the loaves blessed by Jesus

14:19* distributed the loaves to the multitude

14:20* took up of the fragments that remained twelve baskets full

14:22* constrained by Jesus to get into a ship and to go before Him unto the other side (of Sea of Galilee)

14:24* his ship was tossed with waves

14:25* approached by Jesus (walking on the sea)

14:26* saw Jesus walking on the water (Sea of Galilee) and was afraid

14:27* told by Jesus to be of good cheer and not be afraid

Matt 14:28 requested Jesus to allow him to walk on the water

14:29 bidden by Jesus, and walked on the water to go to Jesus

14:30 began to sink when fear overcame faith and asked Jesus to save him

14:31 caught by Jesus and chided for his doubting and lack of faith

14:32 got into the ship

14:33* being in the ship, worshiped Jesus, claiming Him to be the Son of God

14:34* came into the land of Gennesaret

15: 2* accused by the scribes and Pharisees of transgressing the tradition of the elders by not washing his hands when he ate bread

15:12* came to Jesus, informing Him that the Pharisees were offended at His saying

15:15 asked Jesus for explanation of a parable

15:16 asked by Jesus if he were without understanding also

15:23* came and besought Jesus to send away her that cried after him

15:32* was called (unto Jesus)

15:34* had seven loaves and a few little fishes

15:36* given the loaves and fishes (by Jesus)

15:36* gave the loaves and fishes to the multitude

15:37* took up of the broken meat that was left seven baskets full

16: 5* was come to the other side and had forgotten to take bread

16: 6* told to beware of the leaven of the Pharisees and Sadducees

16: 7* reasoned with other disciples over Jesus' words

16: 7* had taken no bread

16: 8* of little faith

16: 8* reasoned with the other disciples (concerning the lack of bread)

16: 9* took up baskets (of fragments)

16:10* took up baskets (of fragments)

16:11* did not understand Jesus' words concerning the leaven (doctrine) of the Pharisees and Sadducees

16:12* understood how that Jesus spoke not of bread, but of the doctrine of the Pharisees and Sadducees

16:13* was in Caesarea Philippi

16:13* answered Jesus' question concerning His identity (16:14)

16:15* questioned as to his view of Jesus' identity

16:16 claimed Jesus to be the Christ, the Son of the living God

16:17 blessed of Jesus for his answer and told that this knowledge had been revealed to him by the Father in Heaven

16:17 son of Jona

SIMON (continued)

Matt 16:18 Jesus called him Peter (a rock or stone)

16:19 would be given the keys to the kingdom of Heaven to bind and loose on earth and in Heaven

16:20* charged, by Jesus, to tell no man that He was Jesus the Christ

16:21* shown by Jesus the sufferings He must undergo

16:22 rebuked Jesus

16:23 refuted by Jesus as Satan

16:23 was an offense unto Jesus, for he savored not the things that be of God, but those that be of men

17: 1 taken up by Jesus into an high mountain apart

17: 2 witnessed the transfiguration of Jesus

17: 3 saw Moses and Elias talking with Jesus

17: 4 was present (at transfiguration of Jesus)

17: 4 desired to make tabernacles for Jesus, Elias, and Moses

17: 5 hearing the voice of the Lord out of a cloud, fell on his face and was sore afraid (17:6)

17: 7 touched by Jesus and told to arise and be not afraid

17: 8 lifted up his eyes and saw no man but Jesus

17: 9 coming down from the mountain, charged by Jesus to tell the vision to no man until He be risen from the dead

17:13 understood that Jesus spoke of John the Baptist

17:22* abode in Galilee

17:23* was exceedingly sorry

17:24* came to Capernaum

17:24 questioned by those that received tribute

17:25 was come into the house

17:25 questioned by Jesus concerning the paying of tribute (17:26)

17:27 given detailed instructions for paying the tribute for himself and Jesus

18: 1* asked Jesus who is the greatest in the kingdom of Heaven

18:21 spoke with Jesus concerning forgiving his brother who sins against him (18:22)

19:13* rebuked those who brought children to Jesus

19:14* rebuked, in turn, by Jesus

19:25* exceedingly amazed at Jesus' answer to the rich young ruler and asked who could be saved

19:27* had forsaken all and followed Jesus

19:27 asked Jesus what the disciples would receive since they had forsaken all and followed Jesus

19:28* had followed Jesus

Matt 19:28* promised by Jesus to sit upon the twelve thrones judging the twelve tribes of Israel

20:17* going up to Jerusalem, taken apart and foretold by Jesus of His betrayal, crucifixion, and resurrection (20:19)

20:24* was moved with indignation towards James and John because of their request of Jesus

20:29* departed from Jericho (for Jerusalem)

21: 1* arrived in Bethphage and Mount of Olives

21:20* saw the withered fig tree and marveled

24: 1* came to Jesus to show Him the buildings of the temple

24: 2* Jesus spoke to him of the coming destruction of the temple

24: 3* asked Jesus of the sign of His coming and of the end of the world

26: 8* was indignant at the actions of the woman

26:10* had troubled the woman

26:17* asked Jesus where he should prepare for Him the Passover

26:19* did as Jesus had appointed and made ready the Passover

26:20 celebrated Passover with Jesus and the rest of the twelve

26:22 asked Jesus if he were the one to betray Him

26:26* while eating (the Passover) was given the bread by Jesus

26:27* given the cup (by Jesus)

26:30* having sung an hymn, went out into the Mount of Olives

26:31* Jesus predicted that he would be offended because of Him

26:33 said he would never be offended because of Jesus

26:34 before the cock crew, would deny Jesus thrice

26:35* claimed he would never deny Jesus, even though it meant death

26:36* came with Jesus to Gethsemane

26:36* instructed to sit and pray

26:37 went with Jesus

26:38 told by Jesus to tarry and watch with Him

26:40* fell asleep in garden of Gethsemane

26:40 rebuked by Jesus

26:41* told by Jesus to watch and pray lest he enter into temptation

26:43* fell asleep again in the garden for his eyes were heavy

26:45* told to sleep on now and take his rest

26:46* told to arise and go (with Jesus)

26:51 was with Jesus

26:51 drew his sword, struck a servant of the high priest, and smote off his ear

SIMON *(continued)*

Matt 26:52 told to put away his sword
26:56* forsook Jesus and fled
26:58 followed Jesus afar off unto the palace of Caiaphas, and went in and sat with the servants to see the end
26:69 sitting without the palace, approached by a damsel who said he was with Jesus
26:70 first denial of Jesus
26:71 approached by another maid while on the porch, who accused him of being with Jesus
26:72 second denial of Jesus made with an oath
26:73 accused again of being one of them (disciples), for his speech betrayed him
26:74 third denial (made with cursing and swearing)
26:75 remembering the words of Jesus concerning his denial, went out and wept bitterly
28:13* would be accused of stealing Jesus' body by night
28:16* went into Galilee into the place (mountain) appointed
28:17* saw Jesus and worshiped Him
28:19* given the great commission (28:20)
28:20* Jesus would always be with him, even unto the end of the world

Mark 1:16 seen by Jesus casting a net into the sea
1:16 brother of Andrew
1:16 a fisherman
1:17 told by Jesus to follow Him and become a fisher of men
1:18 forsook his nets and followed Jesus
1:21 went into Capernaum with Jesus
1:29 had been at the synagogue at Capernaum
1:29 lived at Capernaum
1:29 he and his brother entered their house, along with Jesus, James, and John
1:30 had a wife
1:30 his wife's mother lay sick of a fever
1:31 his mother-in-law was healed by Jesus
1:31 ministered unto by his wife's mother
1:36 followed Jesus to His solitary place of prayer (1:37)
2:15 sat at meat with Jesus, Levi (Matthew), and many publicans and sinners
2:18 did not fast as the disciples of John (the Baptist) and Pharisees did
2:23 plucked ears of corn in the corn fields on the Sabbath day
3: 7 withdrew from the synagogue with Jesus to the sea
3:14* ordained by Jesus (to be with Him)

Mark 3:14* would be sent forth to preach (by Jesus)
3:15* would be given power by Jesus to heal sicknesses and to cast out devils (demons)
3:16 Jesus surnamed him Peter
3:16 a disciple of Jesus (one of the twelve)
3:20* could not eat bread with Jesus because of the multitude
4:10* asked Jesus about the parable of the sower
4:11* was given to know the mystery of the kingdom of God
4:33* had many parables taught him by Jesus
4:34* when alone, with the rest of the twelve, had all things expounded by Jesus
4:36* sent away the multitude
4:36* with the twelve, took Jesus to the other side of the sea
4:38* in fear, awakened Jesus in the midst of the storm
4:40* was fearful and had no faith
4:41* feared exceedingly
4:41* questioned among the other disciples as to what manner of man Jesus was that even the wind and the sea obey Him
5: 1* went with Jesus across the Sea of Galilee to the country of the Gadarenes
5:37 was allowed by Jesus to enter Jairus's house with Him
5:42 witnessed the raising of Jairus's daughter by Jesus
6: 1* followed Jesus into His own country
6: 7* sent forth two by two (by Jesus)
6: 7* given power over unclean spirits
6: 8* commanded to take nothing on his journey except a staff, and to be shod with sandals and only one coat (6:9)
6:12* went out and preached that men should repent
6:13* cast out many devils (demons) and anointed with oil many that were sick, and healed them
6:30* an apostle
6:30* gathered together unto Jesus to report what he had done and taught
6:31* had no leisure so much as to eat
6:32* departed privately with Jesus into a desert place by ship
6:36* asked Jesus to send away the multitude into the villages to buy themselves bread
6:37* told by Jesus to give food to the multitude
6:37* asked Jesus if he should go and buy bread to feed the people
6:38* when asked by Jesus the available

173

SIMON *(continued)*

provisions, reported five loaves and two fishes

Mark 6:39* made the people sit down by hundreds and by fifties (6:40)

6:41* given the food blessed by Jesus to distribute to the crowd

6:43* took up twelve baskets full of fragments and of the fishes

6:45* constrained by Jesus to get into the ship and go to the other side unto Bethsaida

6:47* was alone (with the other disciples) in the ship in the midst of the sea

6:48* toiled in rowing the ship for the winds were contrary

6:48* Jesus came unto him in about the fourth watch of the night walking upon the sea

6:49* saw Jesus walking upon the sea and cried out for he supposed it had been a spirit

6:50* saw Jesus and was troubled, but admonished by Him to fear not

6:51* was amazed beyond measure and wondered that the wind ceased as Jesus entered the ship

6:52* because of his hardened heart, had forgotten about the miracle of the loaves

6:53* came into the land of Gennesaret

6:54* got out of the ship

7: 5* walked not according to the traditions of the elders (ate bread with unwashed hands)

8: 5* informed Jesus of the seven loaves

8: 6* set the loaves before the people

8: 7* receiving the fishes blessed from Jesus, set them before the people

8: 8* gathered seven baskets of fragments

8:10* entered into a ship with Jesus and went into Dalmanutha

8:13* entering into the ship again with Jesus, departed to the other side

8:14* had forgotten to take bread, and had only one loaf in the ship

8:16* had no bread

8:17* having seen the miracles, still did not understand as his heart was possibly yet hardened

8:19* took up twelve baskets full of fragments at the feeding of the five thousand

8:20* took up seven baskets full of fragments at the feeding of the four thousand

8:27* went into the towns of Caesarea Philippi with Jesus

8:27* responded to Jesus' question concerning His identity with "John the Baptist, Elias, and one of the prophets" (8:28)

8:29 confirmed his belief that Jesus was the Christ

Mark 8:30* charged to tell no man that Jesus was the Christ

8:31* taught by Jesus of the things concerning Himself

8:32 began to rebuke Jesus

8:33 rebuked by Jesus and likened unto Satan

8:33 did not savor the things that were of God, but the things that were of men

9: 2 led up into a high mountain by Jesus

9: 2 witnessed the transfiguration of Jesus (9:8)

9: 4 Elias (Elijah) and Moses appeared to him and James and John at the transfiguration of Jesus

9: 5 desired to make tabernacles for Jesus, Moses, and Elijah

9: 6 knew not what to say for fear

9: 7 overshadowed by a cloud and heard the voice of God

9: 8 looked round about and saw no man but Jesus, James, and John

9: 9 forbidden to tell what he had seen until after the resurrection

9:10 questioned with James and John as to what the rising from the dead should mean

9:14* questioned by the scribes

9:30* passed through Galilee

9:32* did not understand the words of Jesus, but was afraid to ask

9:33* came to Capernaum

9:33* disputed with the other disciples on the way to Capernaum as to whom should be the greatest (9:34)

9:38* forbade a man from casting out devils (demons) in Jesus' name, because he did not follow him

10:13* rebuked those who brought young children to Jesus that He should touch them

10:14* rebuked, in turn, by Jesus

10:24* astonished at the words of Jesus concerning those with riches

10:26* astonished at Jesus' words

10:28* had left all and followed Jesus

10:32* went up to Jerusalem with Jesus and was amazed and afraid

10:41 was much displeased with James and John

10:46* went to Jericho

10:46* went out of Jericho with Jesus

11: 1* came nigh to Jerusalem, unto Bethphage and Bethany, at the Mount of Olives

11:11* went to Bethany with Jesus and stayed until the morrow (11:12)

11:14* heard Jesus curse the fig tree

11:15* returned to Jerusalem with Jesus

11:19* went out of Jerusalem

11:20* witnessed the fig tree dried up from the roots

11:21 called to Jesus' remembrance the

SIMON *(continued)*

Mark 11:27* curse of the fig tree and mentioned it to Jesus
Mark 11:27* came again to Jerusalem
13: 3* sat upon the Mount of Olives
13: 3 asked Jesus privately concerning the sign when all things shall be fulfilled (13:4)
13: 5 cautioned, by Jesus, to not be deceived
14:13 sent by Jesus to prepare the Passover (14:15)
14:17* in the evening of the first day of unleavened bread, went with Jesus to the upper room
14:18* sat and ate together with Jesus
14:19* began to be sorrowful over Jesus' statement of betrayal and to ask "Is it I?"
14:20* dipped with Jesus in the dish
14:22* ate the Passover with Jesus
14:23* drank of the communion cup
14:26* sung an hymn and went out to the Mount of Olives
14:29 confirmed that even though all others might be offended in Jesus, he would not
14:30 Jesus predicted that he would deny Him three times before the cock crow twice
14:31 exclaimed that even if it meant death, he would not deny Him
14:32* went to Gethsemane and was told to sit there while Jesus prayed
14:33 went apart with Jesus in the garden
14:34 asked by Jesus to tarry and watch
14:37 found sleeping by Jesus
14:37 asked by Jesus if he could not watch one hour
14:38 told to watch and pray lest he enter into temptation
14:40 found sleeping again by Jesus (for his eyes were heavy)
14:40 did not know what to answer Jesus
14:41 told by Jesus to sleep on and take his rest
14:42 told to rise and go
14:47 drew his sword and smote the servant of the high priest, cutting off his ear
14:50* forsook Jesus and fled
14:54 followed Jesus afar off even to the palace of the high priest
14:54 sat with the servants and warmed himself at the fire
14:66 was beneath in the palace
14:67 while warming himself, denied Jesus before the maid (14:68)
14:68 went out to the porch and heard the cock crow
14:69 denied Jesus again to a maid (14:70)
14:70 a Galilean
14:70 his speech was that of a Galilean

Mark 14:71 began to curse and swear in his third denial of Jesus
14:72 hearing the second crowing of the cock, recalled the words of Jesus
14:72 wept
16: 7 was to be told of Jesus' entrance into Galilee (after His resurrection)
16:10* mourned and wept
16:14* Jesus appeared unto him as he sat at meat (with the other disciples)
16:14* upbraided by Jesus for his unbelief and hardness of heart, because he believed not them which had seen Him after He was risen
16:15* commissioned to go into all the world and preach the gospel to every creature
16:20* went forth and preached everywhere, with signs following

Luke 4:31 lived in Capernaum
4:38 Jesus entered his house
4:38 had a wife
4:39 his mother-in-law was healed by Jesus
4:39 ministered unto by his wife's mother
5: 1 was on the lake of Gennesaret (Sea of Galilee) (5:3)
5: 2 a fisherman
5: 2 was washing the nets
5: 3 had a ship
5: 3 thrust his ship out from the land at Jesus' request
5: 5 had toiled all night and had taken nothing
5: 6 obeying Jesus, caught a great draught of fish
5: 7 filled the ship until it began to sink
5: 8 fell down at Jesus' feet asking the Lord to depart from him, for he was a sinful man
5: 9 was astonished at the draught of fishes which had been caught
5:10 partner with James and John
5:10 told by Jesus to fear not for from henceforth he would catch men
5:11 brought his ship to land
5:11 forsook all and followed Jesus
5:30* murmured against by scribes and Pharisees
5:30* ate and drank with publicans and sinners
5:33* ate and drank instead of fasting
6: 1* plucked ears of corn and ate (rubbing them in his hands) on the Sabbath
6: 2* claimed (by the Pharisees) to be doing that which was not lawful to do on the Sabbath days
6:13 chosen as one of the twelve (an apostle)
6:13* also called (named) an apostle
6:14 also named Peter by Jesus
6:14 brother of Andrew

SIMON (continued)

Luke 6:17* came down from the mountain with Jesus and stood in the plain

8: 1* went throughout every city and village with Jesus

8: 9* questioned Jesus concerning a parable

8:10* unto him it was given to know the mysteries of the kingdom of God

8:22* went into a ship with Jesus and launched forth for the other side

8:23* the boat, filled with water, put him in jeopardy

8:24* called Jesus Master

8:24* came to Jesus and awakened Him during the storm

8:25* asked by Jesus concerning his faith

8:25* was afraid and wondered concerning Jesus' power over the elements

8:26* arrived at the country of the Gadarenes (Gadara)

8:45 responded to Jesus' question as to who touched Him

8:51 suffered to go into Jairus's house with Jesus, alone with James and John and the father and mother of the maiden

8:55 witnessed the raising of Jairus's daughter from the dead by Jesus

9: 1* given power and authority over all devils (demons) and to cure diseases

9: 2* sent by Jesus to preach the kingdom of God and to heal the sick

9: 3* was to take neither staves, nor scrip, neither bread, neither money, neither have two coats

9: 4* was to abide in whatever house he entered

9: 6* went through the towns, preaching the gospel and healing everywhere

9:10* returned and told Jesus all he had done

9:10* went privately with Jesus into a desert place belonging to the city called Bethsaida

9:12* requested that Jesus send away the multitude, so that they might go into the towns and lodge and get victuals (food)

9:13* had only five loaves and two fishes, but was requested by Jesus to give food to the multitude

9:14* made the multitude sit down in companies by fifties (9:15)

9:16* gave the blessed loaves and fish unto the multitude

9:17* took up twelve baskets of fragments

9:18* was alone with Jesus (and the rest of the twelve)

9:18* in response to Jesus' question as to His identity, responded, "John the Baptist, Elias, and one of the prophets risen again" (9:19)

Luke 9:20* straitly charged and commanded to tell no man that He was the Christ (9:21)

9:20 in response to Jesus' question, answered that Jesus was "the Christ of God"

9:28 went up into a mountain to pray with Jesus

9:32 was heavy with sleep and upon awaking, saw Moses and Elias (Elijah) and the glory of Jesus

9:33 called Jesus Master

9:33 not knowing what he said, proposed that three tabernacles (booths) be made (for Jesus, Moses, and Elias)

9:34 feared as he was overshadowed and entered into a cloud

9:36 told no man in those days any of those things which he had seen at the transfiguration of Jesus

9:37 came down from the Mount of Transfiguration the next day

9:45* feared to ask Jesus concerning His teaching

9:46* reasoned with the other disciples as to which of them should be greatest

9:49* forbade a man from casting out devils (demons) in Jesus' name, because he followed not with the disciples

10:24* saw and heard what many prophets and kings had desired to experience

12: 1* warned by Jesus to beware of the leaven of the Pharisees

12: 4* friend of Jesus

12:41 asked Jesus if the parable of the servants had been given only to the disciples, or to the multitude

17: 5* asked Jesus to increase his faith

18:15* rebuked those who brought infants to Jesus

18:16* rebuked, in turn, by Jesus

18:28* had left all and followed Jesus

18:31* taken unto Jesus and instructed of things to come (18:33)

18:34* understood none of these teachings of Jesus

19:29* with Jesus came nigh to Bethphage and Bethany at the Mount of Olives

19:37* rejoiced and praised God with a loud voice (19:38)

22: 8 sent by Jesus along with John to prepare the Passover

22:13 went into the city, found it as Jesus had said, and made ready the Passover

22:14* sat down with Jesus (in the upper room for the Passover)

22:14* was called an apostle

22:15* Jesus truly desired his presence in eating the Passover

Luke 22:19* partook of the first Lord's Supper (22:20)

22:23* inquired among the disciples as to which of them would betray Jesus

22:24* a strife existed among him and the other disciples as to which one should be accounted the greatest

22:28* had continued with Jesus in His temptations

22:29* was appointed a kingdom (that he might eat and drink at Jesus' table in His kingdom and sit on thrones judging the twelve tribes of Israel) (22:30)

22:31 Satan had desired to have him, that he might sift him as wheat

22:32 Jesus had prayed for him that his faith not fail

22:32 when he was converted, he was to strengthen his brethren

22:33 told the Lord he was ready to go with Him to prison and to death

22:34 told by Jesus that before the cock crew, he would thrice deny knowing Him

22:35* had lacked nothing

22:36* told to prepare (for his new task)

22:39* followed Jesus to the Mount of Olives

22:40* told to pray that he enter not into temptation

22:45* found sleeping for sorrow (by Jesus)

22:46* told to rise and pray, lest he enter into temptation

22:49* perceiving the forthcoming events, asked Jesus if he should use his sword

22:50 smote Malchus, the servant of the high priest (with his sword) and cut off his right ear

22:54 followed Jesus afar off

22:55 sat down among those who had taken Jesus

22:57 first denial of Jesus

22:58 second denial of Jesus

22:59 confirmed as a Galilean

22:60 third denial of Jesus

22:60 immediately heard the cock crow

22:61 was looked upon by the Lord

22:61 remembering the words of Jesus concerning the denials, went out and wept bitterly (22:62)

24: 9* was told all things concerning the resurrection by Mary Magdalene, Joanna, Mary the mother of James, and the other women

24:10* an apostle

24:11 the words of the women seemed to him as idle tales and he believed them not

24:12 arose and ran to the sepulcher, stooped down, beheld the linen clothes laid by themselves and departed, wondering in himself at that which was come to pass

Luke 24:24 went to the sepulcher and found it even as the women had said, but saw not Jesus

24:33* being gathered together (with the other disciples), Cleopas found him and declared that the Lord was risen indeed and had appeared to Simon (24:34)

24:34 the risen Lord had appeared unto him

24:36* Jesus appeared unto him (after the resurrection), but he was terrified and affrighted, and supposed he had seen a spirit (24:37)

24:38* asked by Jesus why he was troubled and why thoughts arose in his heart

24:40* was shown Jesus' hands and feet

24:41* believed not yet for joy and wondered

24:42* gave Jesus a piece of a broiled fish and of an honeycomb

24:45* his understanding was opened by Jesus that he might understand the scriptures

24:46* was witness of these things (24:48)

24:49* told to tarry in Jerusalem until he was endued with power from on high

24:50* led by Jesus out as far as to Bethany and was blessed by Him

24:52* worshiped Jesus and returned to Jerusalem with great joy

24:53* was continually in the temple praising and blessing God

John 1:40 brother of Andrew

1:41 found by Andrew and told that he had found the Messiah

1:42 brought to Jesus by his brother Andrew

1:42 beheld by Jesus

1:42 son of Jona

1:42 given a new name, Cephas, meaning a stone (by Jesus)

1:44 of Bethsaida

2: 2* was called to the marriage in Cana of Galilee

2:11* believed on Jesus

2:12* went to Capernaum and continued there not many days

2:17* remembered that it was written of Him, "the zeal of thine house hath eaten me up"

2:22* after the resurrection, remembered Jesus' words and believed the scriptures and the words which Jesus had said

3:22* came into the land of Judea with Jesus and tarried there with Him

4: 2* did baptize

4: 8* had gone away unto the city to buy meat

SIMON *(continued)*

John 4:27* came unto Jesus and marveled that He talked with the Samaritan woman, yet did not question Jesus

4:31* called Jesus Master

4:31* implored Jesus to eat

4:33* questioned among the other disciples if Jesus had been brought food to eat

4:35* told to look on the fields for they are white already to harvest

4:38* had been sent to reap where he had not labored, and had entered into others' labors

6: 3* went up into a mountain and sat with Jesus

6: 8 brother of Andrew

6:10* instructed by Jesus to have the multitude sit down

6:11* distributed the loaves and fishes to the multitude

6:13* gathered twelve baskets of fragments

6:16* went down to the sea, entered a ship, and went toward Capernaum (6:17)

6:19* after rowing twenty-five to thirty furlongs, saw Jesus walking on the sea and was afraid

6:20* told to not be afraid

6:21* willingly received Him into the ship

6:22* was entered into the only boat there

6:22* was apart from Jesus in the boat alone (with the other disciples)

6:67* asked, by Jesus, if he would also go away

6:68 exclaimed that the Lord (Jesus) had the words of eternal life

6:69* believed and was sure that Jesus was the Christ, the Son of the living God

6:70* chosen as one of the twelve

9: 2* questioned Jesus concerning the man born blind

11: 8* called Jesus Master

11:11* friend of Lazarus

11:54* continued with Jesus at Ephraim

12:16* understood not, at first, the events of the triumphal entry of Jesus

12:16* after Jesus' glorification, remembered that these events had been written of Jesus, and had been done unto Him

13: 5* feet washed by Jesus

13: 8 exclaimed that Jesus should never wash his feet

13: 9 after an explanation, asked Jesus to wash not only his feet, but also his hands and head

13:12* had his feet washed by Jesus

13:13* called Jesus Master and Lord

13:14* had his feet washed by Jesus

13:14* told, by Jesus, to wash one another's feet

John 13:15* had been given an example that he should do as Jesus had done to him

13:18* was known and chosen of Jesus

13:21* when told that one of them would betray Jesus, looked on the others doubting of whom He spoke (13:22)

13:24 beckoned John to ask who it was that should betray Jesus

13:28* knew not for what intent Jesus spoke these words to Judas Iscariot

13:34* given a new commandment to love one another

13:34* loved of Jesus

13:35* love one for another was a mark that he was a true disciple of Jesus

13:36 could not follow Jesus now, but would follow Him afterwards

13:37 claimed that he would lay down his life for Jesus' sake

13:38 told by Jesus, that he would deny Him thrice before the cock crowed

14:25* was with Jesus

14:26* would be instructed by the Holy Spirit in all things

14:26* the words Jesus had spoken would be brought to his remembrance

14:27* Jesus' peace was given to him and left with him

14:31* was told to arise and go with Jesus

15: 3* is clean through the Word

15: 9* loved of Jesus

15:12* commanded to love one another

15:12* loved of Jesus

15:16* chosen of Jesus and ordained of Him to go and bring forth fruit, and that his fruit should remain

15:17* commanded to love one another

15:19* not of the world

15:19* chosen out of the world by Jesus

15:19* hated of the world

15:27* would bear witness, because he had been with Jesus from the beginning

16: 4* was with Jesus

16: 6* sorrow had filled his heart

16:12* could not bear the words of Jesus

16:22* presently had sorrow

16:24* had asked nothing of the Father in Jesus' name

16:27* loved of the Father

16:27* loved Jesus, and believed that He came from God

16:29* could now understand plainly Jesus' words

16:30* was sure that Jesus knew all things

16:30* believed that Jesus came forth from God

18: 1* went with Jesus over the brook Cedron and entered into a garden (Gethsemane)

18: 2* often resorted there with Jesus

18:10 smote the high priest's servant (Malchus) with the sword, cutting off his right ear

178

SIMON (*continued*)

John 18:11 Jesus instructed him to put away his sword

18:15 followed Jesus (to the trial)

18:16 stood at the door without (at the high priest's palace)

18:16 brought into the palace by John

18:17 made first denial (of Jesus) to the damsel that kept the door

18:18 stood with the servants and officers and warmed himself

18:25 stood and warmed himself

18:25 second denial of Jesus (that he was a disciple)

18:26 cut off the right ear of a servant (Malchus)

18:27 made the third denial, immediately after which the cock crew

20: 2 informed by Mary Magdalene that Jesus was taken out of the sepulcher

20: 3 went with John to the sepulcher

20: 4 was outrun by John, to the sepulcher

20: 6 coming after John, went into the sepulcher and saw the linen clothes and the napkin (20:7)

20: 9 as yet knew not the scripture that He must rise again from the dead

20:10 went away unto his own home

20:18* told by Mary Magdalene that she had seen the Lord and that He had spoken unto her

20:19* while assembled together (with the other disciples) with the doors shut for fear of the Jews, Jesus appeared in the midst

20:20* saw Jesus' hands and side and was glad

20:21* sent by Jesus and given His peace

20:22* breathed on by Jesus and received the Holy Ghost

20:25* told Thomas that he had seen the Lord

20:25* informed by Thomas that he would not believe without specific conditions being met

20:26* the doors being shut again, Jesus appeared the second time to him and the apostles

20:30* many other signs were done in his presence which are not written (in this book)

21: 1 saw Jesus at the Sea of Tiberias (Sea of Galilee) while with a group of the disciples (21:2)

21: 3 entering a ship, went fishing and caught nothing

21: 4 knew (recognized) not Jesus

21: 5 had no meat (had caught nothing)

21: 6 obeying Jesus' command, cast the net on the right side of the ship

21: 6 was not able to draw the net for the multitude of fishes

21: 7 hearing it was Jesus, girded his fisher's coat unto him (for he was naked) and cast himself into the sea

John 21: 9 coming to land, saw a fire of coals there, with fish and bread thereon

21:10 told by Jesus to bring of the fish which he had caught

21:11 drew the net to land, full of great fishes

21:12 told to come and dine

21:12 dared not ask who He was, knowing it was the Lord

21:13 given bread and fish by Jesus

21:14 third appearance of Jesus unto the disciples after His resurrection

21:15 had dined with Jesus

21:15 son of Jonas

21:15 asked by Jesus, if he loved Him more than these and answered, "Yea, Lord; thou knowest that I love thee"

21:15 told to feed Jesus' lambs

21:16 son of Jonas

21:16 asked the second time if he loved Jesus and answered that He knew that he loved Him

21:16 told to feed Jesus' sheep

21:17 son of Jonas

21:17 was asked the third time if he loved Jesus

21:17 was grieved because of Jesus' question

21:17 told to feed Jesus' sheep

21:18 when young girded himself and walked whither he would, but in old age would be carried where he would not, signifying by what death he should glorify God (21:19)

21:19 told to follow Jesus

21:20 turned and saw John following and asked Jesus what John's end would be (21:21)

21:22 rebuked by Jesus and told to follow Him

Acts 1: 2* had been given commandments by Jesus (through the Holy Ghost)

1: 2* chosen by Jesus

1: 3* was shown Jesus alive after His passion

1: 3* spoken to by Jesus of the things pertaining to the kingdom of God

1: 3* saw Jesus forty days

1: 4* commanded by Jesus not to depart from Jerusalem, but to wait for the promise of the Father

1: 5* would be baptized with the Holy Ghost

1: 6* questioned Jesus concerning the restoration of the kingdom to Israel

1: 7* was not to know the times or the seasons which the Father had put in His own power

1: 8* after receiving the Holy Spirit, would receive power and would be witness unto Jesus Christ through-

SIMON *(continued)*

out the earth

Acts
1: 9* beheld as Jesus was taken up into Heaven at His ascension

1:10* was joined by two men in white apparel while he looked steadfastly toward Heaven

1:11* a man of Galilee

1:11* was gazing up into Heaven

1:11* Jesus was taken up from him into Heaven

1:11* was told that Jesus would come in like manner as he had seen Him go into Heaven

1:12* returned to Jerusalem and went into an upper room (1:13)

1:14* continued in prayer and supplication with the women, Mary the mother of Jesus, and with His brethren

1:15 stood up in the midst of the disciples and spoke

1:15 persuaded the other apostles that another should be chosen to take the place of Judas Iscariot (1:22)

1:21* was with the Lord Jesus at various times

1:24* prayed concerning the ordination of one to be a witness of Jesus' resurrection

1:26* gave forth his lot (concerning Judas Iscariot's successor)

2: 1* present at the day of Pentecost

2: 2* while sitting in the house, cloven tongues like as of fire sat upon him, he was filled with the Holy Ghost, and spoke with other tongues (2:4)

2: 6 his speech confounded the multitude because every man heard in his own language

2: 7* a Galilean

2:13* mocked by some who claimed him as full of new wine

2:14* stood up with the other disciples and expounded to the multitude

2:15* was not drunk

2:32* was a witness to the resurrection of Jesus

2:37* asked by the multitude on the day of Pentecost what they should do

2:38 responded to the question of the multitude

2:40 testified and exhorted with many words

2:42* many continued steadfastly in his doctrine and fellowship

2:43* many wonders and signs were done by him

3: 1 went into the temple with John at the hour of prayer

3: 3 was asked an alms by the lame man at the gate of the temple

3: 4 fastened his eyes upon the lame man, instructing him to look at him

and John

Acts
3: 6 had no silver and gold

3: 6 gave unto the lame man such as he had

3: 6 commanded the lame man to rise up and walk

3: 7 took the lame man by the right hand and lifted him up

3: 8 entered into the temple with John and the formerly lame man

3:11 held by the formerly lame man in Solomon's porch

3:12 addressed the men of Israel concerning the healing of the lame man (3:26)

3:15 a witness of the resurrected (Jesus)

3:17 knew that through ignorance the men of Israel crucified Jesus

3:19 commanded people to repent and to be converted

4: 1 priests, captain of the temple, and the Sadducees laid hands on him (and John) and put him in hold (prison) overnight for preaching, through Jesus, the resurrection (4:3)

4: 7 set in the midst of the examining council and questioned concerning the healing of the lame man

4: 8 was filled with the Holy Ghost and spoke to the rulers and elders concerning Jesus Christ of Nazareth (4:12)

4:13 had boldness

4:13 an unlearned and ignorant man who had been with Jesus

4:15 commanded to go aside out of the council

4:16 had performed a notable miracle

4:18 commanded not to speak at all nor to teach in the name of Jesus (by the examining council)

4:20 could not but speak the things which he had seen and heard

4:21 being guiltless, was released

4:23 reported the words of the chief priest and elders to the believers

4:33* with great power gave witness of the resurrection of the Lord Jesus

4:33* great grace was upon him

4:35* the price of possessions sold by Christians was laid at his feet

4:35* distributed to every man (of the Christian community) as he had need

4:36* gave Joses a surname of Barnabas

4:37* Joses's money was laid at his feet

5: 2* the gift of Ananias and Sapphira was laid at his feet

5: 3 questioned Ananias as to his scheme of lying to the Holy Ghost (5:4)

5: 8 questioned Sapphira as to the price of the land which had been sold

SIMON *(continued)*

Acts 5: 9 questioned how Ananias and Sapphira had agreed together to tempt the Spirit of the Lord

5:10 Sapphira fell down (dead) at his feet

5:12* by his hands were many signs and wonders wrought among the people

5:12* was with one accord with the others in Solomon's porch

5:13* no man durst join himself to him (the apostles)

5:13* was magnified of the people

5:15 even his shadow falling upon the sick was desired

5:16* healed the multitude of sicknesses and unclean spirits

5:18* placed in the common prison by the high priest and Sadducees

5:19* released from prison by the angel of the Lord and told to go, stand and speak in the temple (5:20)

5:21* entered into the temple early in the morning and taught

5:22* was not found in the prison

5:25* was standing in the temple and teaching the people

5:26* brought without violence and set before the council (5:27)

5:27* questioned by the high priest (5:28)

5:28* had been commanded not to teach in this (Jesus') name

5:28* had filled Jerusalem with his doctrine and had (seemingly) intended to bring Jesus' blood upon his accusers

5:29* believed that he ought to obey God rather than men

5:32* witness of God (and of His works)

5:33* Jewish leaders took counsel to slay him

5:34* put a little space from the Sanhedrin (for their deliberation)

5:40* called back before the council, beaten, commanded not to speak in the name of Jesus, and let go

5:41* departed from the council rejoicing that he was counted worthy to suffer shame for His name

5:42* daily in the temple and in every house, ceased not to teach and preach Jesus Christ

6: 2* called the multitude together and stated it was not reasonable that he should leave the Word of God and serve tables

6: 3* instructed that seven men of honest report be chosen to be appointed to serve tables

6: 4* determined to give himself continually to prayer and to the ministry of the Word

6: 6* the chosen seven were set before

him, for whom he prayed and laid his hands on them

Acts 8: 1* remained in Jerusalem in the midst of great persecution

8:14 was in Jerusalem

8:14 sent (along with John) to Samaria by the other apostles

8:15 prayed for the Samaritans that they might receive the Holy Ghost

8:17 laid his hands on the Samaritans and they received the Holy Ghost

8:18 by the laying on of his hands, the Holy Ghost was given

8:18 was offered money by Simon (the sorcerer) for the ability to impart the Holy Ghost

8:20 condemned Simon (the sorcerer) for his wish to purchase the gift of God with money

8:23 perceived that Simon (the sorcerer) was in the gall of bitterness and in the bond of iniquity

8:24 besought by Simon (the sorcerer) to pray for him

8:25 testified and preached the Word of the Lord and returned to Jerusalem

8:25 preached the gospel in many villages of the Samaritans

9:27* Saul (Paul) was brought to him by Barnabas and he was informed of Saul's (Paul's) conversion experience and his bold preaching in Damascus

9:28* was accompanied by Saul (Paul) in coming in and going out at Jerusalem

9:32 went to the saints at Lydda

9:33 found a man (Aeneas) who had been sick in bed eight years of the palsy

9:34 healed Aeneas (of the palsy)

9:38 was in Lydda

9:38 two men sent to him from Joppa desired him that he delay not in coming to Joppa

9:39 arose and went with the men to Joppa and was brought into the upper chamber where Dorcas lay

9:39 was shown the coats and garments which Dorcas had made

9:40 put all the people out of the upper chamber, kneeled down and prayed

9:40 raised Dorcas from the dead

9:40 was seen by Dorcas at her resurrection

9:41 gave Dorcas his hand, lifted her up, called the saints and widows, and presented Dorcas alive

9:43 tarried many days in Joppa with one Simon a tanner

10: 5 was in Joppa

10: 5 surnamed Peter

10: 6 lodged with Simon the tanner

SIMON *(continued)*

Acts 10: 9   went up upon the housetop to pray about the sixth hour

10:10   became very hungry, and would have eaten, but fell into a trance

10:11   saw Heaven opened and a certain vessel descending upon him containing beasts, creeping things, and fowls

10:13   heard a voice telling him to rise, kill, and eat

10:14   said "no" to the Lord, for he had never eaten anything common or unclean

10:15   told not to call common those things that God had cleansed

10:16   had this experience repeated three times

10:17   doubted in himself what this vision should mean

10:18   surnamed Peter

10:18   the men, sent from Cornelius, asked if he were lodged at the house of Simon (a tanner)

10:19   thought on the vision

10:19   the Spirit informed him that three men sought for him

10:20   was instructed to arise, and get down and go with them, doubting nothing, for God had sent them

10:21   went down to the men (sent from Cornelius), identified himself, and asked the cause for their coming

10:22   God had warned Cornelius to send for him and to hear his words

10:23   called in the men sent from Cornelius, and lodged them

10:23   on the morrow went away with the men sent from Cornelius, and with certain brethren from Joppa

10:24   the next day entered into Caesarea

10:25   when coming in, was met by Cornelius who fell down at his feet

10:25   worshiped by Cornelius

10:26   took Cornelius up and told him to stand up, for he, himself, was also a (mere) man

10:27   talked with Cornelius and found many come together (at Cornelius's house)

10:28   a Jew

10:28   God had shown him that he should not call any man common or unclean

10:29   had come unto Cornelius without gainsaying

10:29   asked for what intent Cornelius had sent for him

10:32   was in Joppa

10:32   surnamed Peter

10:32   had lodged in the house of Simon (a tanner)

10:33   had done well in coming (to Cornelius)

Acts 10:34   perceived that God is no respecter of persons

10:39*   was witness of all things Jesus did both in the land of the Jews and in Jerusalem

10:41*   a witness chosen before of God

10:41*   ate and drank with Jesus after His resurrection

10:42*   commanded of Jesus to preach unto the people, and testified that it was Jesus which was ordained of God to be the Judge of quick and dead

10:44   spoke concerning Christ

10:45   had come to Caesarea with many of the circumcision

10:47   had received the Holy Ghost

10:48   commanded those upon whom the Holy Spirit had fallen, to be baptized in the name of the Lord

10:48   was prayed to tarry certain days by those of Cornelius's house

11: 1*   was in Judea

11: 1*   heard that the Gentiles had also received the Word of God

11: 2   went up to Jerusalem

11: 2   was contended with by them that were of the circumcision

11: 3   went in to uncircumcised men and ate with them

11: 4   rehearsed the matter from the beginning and expounded it to them that were of the circumcision

11: 5   was in Joppa praying

11: 5   in a trance saw a vision of a vessel let down from Heaven containing common and unclean creatures (11:6)

11: 7   heard a voice telling him to arise, slay, and eat

11: 8   said "no" to the Lord, for nothing common or unclean had ever entered his mouth

11: 9   told not to call common those things that God had cleansed

11:10   three times this vision was repeated unto him

11:11   was in the house (of Simon a tanner)

11:11   three men, sent from Caesarea unto him, came unto the house where he was

11:12   bade of the Spirit to go with the men from Caesarea, nothing doubting

11:12   was accompanied by six brethen (from Joppa) and entered Cornelius's house

11:13   was in Joppa

11:13   surnamed Peter

11:14   would tell Cornelius and all his house the words whereby they should be saved

11:15*   the Holy Ghost fell on him at the beginning (Pentecost)

SIMON (continued)

Acts 11:15 as he began to speak, the Holy Ghost fell on them (of Cornelius's house)

11:16 remembered the word of the Lord concerning the baptism with the Holy Ghost

11:17 had been given the gift (the Holy Ghost) when he had believed on the Lord Jesus Christ

11:17 was not one to withstand God

12: 3 King Herod proceeded to take him

12: 4 apprehended by Herod, put in prison, and delivered to four quaternions of soldiers

12: 5 was kept in prison

12: 5 prayer for him was made without ceasing of the church unto God

12: 6 was sleeping between two soldiers, bound with two chains

12: 7 the angel of the Lord came upon him and smote him on the side telling him to arise up quickly

12: 7 his chains fell off from his hands

12: 8 girded himself and put on his sandals, cast his garments about him, and followed the angel

12: 9 went out, following the angel, not believing it true, but thought it a vision

12:10 passed the first and second ward, the iron gate, and on through a street and the angel departed

12:11 coming to himself, knew of a surety that the Lord had sent His angel and delivered him out of the hand of Herod

12:11 was delivered from all the expectation of the people of the Jews

12:12 went to the house of Mary (mother of John Mark) where many were gathered together praying

12:13 knocked at the door of the gate

12:14 his voice was known by Rhoda

12:14 stood before the gate

12:15 some thought his angel was at the gate (instead of him)

12:16 continued knocking

12:16 was seen by those who had met for prayer

12:17 beckoning unto them to hold their peace, declared unto them how the Lord had brought him out of the prison

12:17 instructed that James and the brethren be told of these things

12:17 departed and went into another place

12:18 his absence caused no small stir among the soldiers

12:19 had been sought for by Herod and found not

13:31* saw Jesus many days

13:31* came up with Jesus from Galilee to Jerusalem

Acts 13:31* was His (Jesus') witness unto the people

15: 2* Paul, Barnabas, and others were sent by the church at Antioch to consult with him over the matter of circumcision

15: 4* received Paul, Barnabas, and the others from Antioch

15: 6* came together (with the elders) to consider the matter (of circumcision)

15: 7 God chose that by his mouth the Gentiles would hear the word of the gospel and believe

15: 8* given the Holy Ghost

15: 9* God made no difference between him and a Gentile

15:10* was not able to bear the yoke

15:22* acting with the elders, sent chosen men back to Antioch with Paul and Barnabas

15:23* acting with the elders and brethren, wrote letters of instruction to the Gentiles at Antioch, Syria, and Cilicia

15:24* gave no commandment that Gentile believers must be circumcised and keep the law

15:25* considered it good, being assembled, to send chosen men unto the believers

15:25* loved Barnabas and Paul

15:27* sent Judas and Silas to the Gentile believers

15:33* Judas (Barsabas) and Silas returned unto him

16: 4* with the elders, ordained decrees

16: 4* was at Jerusalem

16: 7* Andronicus and Junia were well known to him

1Cor 1:12 some of the Corinthian believers claimed to be (followers) of him

3:22 was the believers' (possession)

4: 1 the minister of Christ

4: 1 the steward of the mysteries of God

4: 9* Paul thought God had set him (the apostles) forth last, as it were appointed to death

4: 9* made a spectacle unto the world, to the angels, and to men

4:10* a fool for Christ's sake

4:10* weak, despised

4:11* hungered, thirsted, was naked, was buffeted, and had no certain dwelling place

4:12* labored, working with his own hands

4:12* being reviled, he blessed; being persecuted, he suffered it; being defamed, he entreated (9:13)

4:13* made as the filth of the world, and the offscouring of all things

9: 5 had power to lead about a sister, a

SIMON *(continued)*

wife

1Cor 9: 5 had a wife

15: 5 had seen the risen Lord

15: 7* the risen Lord was seen of him

15:11* preached

Gal 1:18 received a visit from Paul in Jerusalem

2: 7 gospel of the circumcision committed unto him as well as apostleship of the circumcision (2:8)

2: 9 perceived the grace given unto Paul and with James and John gave to Paul and Barnabas the right hand of fellowship

2: 9 sent to the circumcision

2:11 withstood, by Paul, face-to-face in Antioch for being inconsistent before the Gentiles

2:12 before had eaten with the Gentiles, but after certain came from James, withdrew and separated himself, fearing the circumcision (Jews)

2:14 a Jew, but living after the manner of Gentiles

2:14 was compelling the Gentiles to live as do the Jews

1Pet 1: 1 an apostle of Jesus Christ

1: 1 author of the book of 1 Peter

5: 1 exhorted the elders

5: 1 an elder

5: 1 a witness of the sufferings of Christ

5: 1 a partaker of the glory that shall be revealed

5:12 wrote 1 Peter with aid of Silvanus

2Pet 1: 1 author of 2 Peter

1: 1 a servant and an apostle of Jesus Christ

1:12 was not negligent in putting believers in remembrance of basic facts of the Christian life

1:13 was in the body

1:14 spoke of his impending death

1:16 eyewitness of the majesty of our Lord Jesus Christ

1:18 heard the voice of God the Father while with Jesus in the holy mount

3: 1 2 Peter was his second epistle (to these believers)

3: 1 stirred up the pure minds of the believers

3: 2 calls himself an apostle

3:15 Paul was his beloved brother (in Christ)

Rev 21:14* name inscribed in the twelve foundations of the new Jerusalem

21:14* an apostle of the Lamb

2. ZELOTES [ze-lo'-teze = a zealot]

Surnamed Zelotes, also called the Canaanite, and an apostle of Jesus Christ, one of the twelve.

Matt 8:23* followed Jesus into a ship

8:25* came to and awoke Jesus and asked Him to save the disciples, for they perished

Matt 8:26* fearful

8:26* of little faith

8:27* marveled at Jesus

9:10* sat at meat with Jesus, along with publicans and sinners

9:14* fasted not

9:19* followed Jesus

9:37* instructed to pray that the Lord would send forth laborers (9:38)

10: 1* was called unto Jesus

10: 1 was of the twelve disciples (of Jesus)

10: 1* given the power to cast out unclean spirits

10: 1* given power to heal all manner of sickness and disease

10: 2 one of the twelve apostles (10:4)

10: 4 the Canaanite

10: 5 one of the twelve (apostles)

10: 5* commanded to go neither to the Gentiles, nor into any city of the Samaritans

10: 6* sent forth by Jesus to the lost sheep of the house of Israel

10: 7* commanded by Jesus to preach "the kingdom of heaven is at hand"

10: 8* commanded to heal the sick, cleanse the lepers, raise the dead, cast out devils (demons)

10: 8* had freely received

10: 9* was to provide neither gold, nor silver, nor brass, nor scrip, neither two coats, neither shoes, nor staves (for himself) (10:10)

10:11* in every city or town, was to inquire who is worthy, and to abide with them

10:12* was to salute each house he entered

10:13* his peace was to come upon each worthy house, but return to him if unworthy

10:14* was to shake off the dust of his feet therein, when not received or heard by a house or city

10:16* sent forth (by Jesus) as a sheep in the midst of wolves

10:16* was to be wise as a serpent and harmless as a dove

10:17* would be delivered to the councils, scourged in synagogues, and brought before governors and kings for (Jesus') sake (10:18)

10:19* was to take no thought concerning what he would speak when delivered up, for the Spirit of his Father would speak in him (10:20)

12: 1* was an hungered and plucked corn in the field and ate

12: 2* accused by the Pharisees of acting unlawfully on the Sabbath day

12:49* called mother and brethren by Jesus

13:10* questioned Jesus about His use of parables

SIMON *(continued)*

Matt 13:11* was given unto him to know the mysteries of the kingdom of Heaven

13:16* saw and heard (spiritually)

13:17* had seen and heard (spiritually)

13:18* had the parable of the sower explained by Jesus (13:23)

13:36* had the parable of the wheat and tares explained by Jesus (13:43)

13:51* claimed to have understood all these things (parables)

14:15* came to Jesus and requested Him to send the multitude away

14:16* instructed by Jesus to feed the multitude

14:17* requested by Jesus to bring the five loaves and two fishes to Him (14:18)

14:19* given the loaves blessed by Jesus

14:19* distributed the loaves to the multitude

14:20* took up of the fragments that remained twelve baskets full

14:22* constrained by Jesus to get into a ship and to go before Him unto the other side (of the Sea of Galilee)

14:24* his ship was tossed with waves

14:25* approached by Jesus (walking on the sea)

14:26* saw Jesus walking on the water (Sea of Galilee) and was afraid

14:27* told by Jesus to be of good cheer and not be afraid

14:33* being in the ship, worshiped Jesus, claiming Him to be the Son of God

14:34* came into the land of Gennesaret

15: 2* accused by the scribes and Pharisees, of transgressing the tradition of the elders by not washing his hands when he ate bread

15:12* came to Jesus, informing Him that the Pharisees were offended at His saying

15:23* came and besought Jesus to send away her that cried after him

15:32* was called (unto Jesus)

15:34* had seven loaves and a few little fishes

15:36* given the loaves and fishes (by Jesus)

15:36* gave the loaves and fishes to the multitude

15:37* took up of the broken meat that was left seven baskets full

16: 5* was come to the other side and had forgotten to take bread

16: 6* told to beware of the leaven of the Pharisees and Sadducees

16: 7* reasoned with other disciples over Jesus' words

16: 7* had taken no bread

16: 8* of little faith

16: 8 reasoned with the other disciples (concerning the lack of bread)

Matt 16: 9* took up baskets (of fragments)

16:10* took up baskets (of fragments)

16:11* did not understand Jesus' words concerning the leaven (doctrine) of the Pharisees and Sadducees

16:12* understood how that Jesus spoke not of bread, but of the doctrine of the Pharisees and Sadducees

16:13* was in Caesarea Philippi

16:13* answered Jesus' question concerning His identity (16:14)

16:15* questioned as to his view of Jesus' identity

16:20* charged by Jesus to tell no man that He was Jesus the Christ

16:21* shown by Jesus the sufferings He must undergo

17:15* could not cure the lunatic boy (17:16)

17:19* asked Jesus why he could not cast out the devil (demon)

17:20* could not cast out the devil (demon) because of unbelief

17:22* abode in Galilee

17:23* was exceedingly sorry

17:24* came to Capernaum

18: 1* asked Jesus who is the greatest in the kingdom of Heaven

19:13* rebuked those who brought children to Jesus

19:14* rebuked, in turn, by Jesus

19:25* exceedingly amazed at Jesus' answer to the rich young ruler and asked who could be saved

19:27* had forsaken all and followed Jesus

19:28* had followed Jesus

19:28* promised by Jesus to sit upon the twelve thrones judging the twelve tribes of Israel

20:17* going up to Jerusalem, was taken apart and foretold by Jesus of His betrayal, crucifixion, and resurrection (20:19)

20:24* was moved with indignation towards James and John because of their request of Jesus

20:29* departed from Jericho (for Jerusalem)

21: 1* arrived in Bethphage and the Mount of Olives

21:20* saw the withered fig tree and marveled

24: 1* came to Jesus to show Him the buildings of the temple

24: 2* Jesus spoke to him of the coming destruction of the temple

24: 3* asked Jesus of the sign of His coming and of the end of the world

26: 8* was indignant at the actions of the woman

26:10* had troubled the woman

26:17* asked Jesus where he should prepare for Him the Passover

26:19* did as Jesus had appointed and

SIMON (continued)

		made ready the Passover
Matt	26:20	celebrated the Passover with Jesus and the rest of the twelve
	26:22	asked Jesus if he were the one to betray Him
	26:26*	while eating (the Passover) given the bread by Jesus
	26:27*	given the cup (by Jesus)
	26:30*	having sung an hymn, went out into the Mount of Olives
	26:31*	Jesus predicted that he would be offended because of Him
	26:35*	claimed he would never deny Jesus, even though it meant death
	26:36*	came with Jesus to Gethsemane
	26:36*	instructed to sit and pray
	26:38*	told by Jesus to tarry and watch with him
	26:40*	fell asleep in the garden of Gethsemane
	26:43*	fell asleep again in the garden (of Gethsemane)
	26:45*	told to sleep on now and take his rest
	26:46*	told to arise and go (with Jesus)
	26:56*	forsook Jesus and fled
	28:13*	would be accused of stealing Jesus' body by night
	28:16*	went into Galilee into the place (mountain) appointed
	28:17*	saw Jesus and worshiped Him
	28:19*	given the great commission (28:20)
	28:20*	Jesus would always be with him, even unto the end of the world
Mark	3:14*	ordained by Jesus (to be with Him)
	3:14*	would be sent forth to preach (by Jesus)
	3:15*	would be given power by Jesus to heal sicknesses and to cast out devils (demons)
	3:18	the Canaanite
	3:18	a disciple of Jesus (one of the twelve)
	3:20*	could not eat bread with Jesus because of the multitude
	4:10*	asked Jesus about the parable of the sower
	4:11*	was given to know the mystery of the kingdom of God
	4:33*	had many parables taught him by Jesus
	4:34*	when alone, with the rest of the twelve, had all things expounded by Jesus
	4:36*	sent away the multitude
	4:36*	with the twelve, took Jesus to the other side of the sea
	4:38*	in fear, awakened Jesus in the midst of the storm
	4:40*	was fearful and had no faith
	4:41*	feared exceedingly
	4:41*	questioned among the other disciples as to what manner of man

		Jesus was that even the wind and the sea obey Him
Mark	5: 1*	went with Jesus across the Sea of Galilee to the country of the Gadarenes
	6: 1*	followed Jesus into His own country
	6: 7*	sent forth two by two (by Jesus)
	6: 7*	given power over unclean spirits
	6: 8*	commanded to take nothing on his journey except a staff, and to be shod with sandals and only one coat (6:9)
	6:12*	went out, and preached that men should repent
	6:13*	cast out many devils (demons) and anointed with oil many that were sick, and healed them
	6:30*	an apostle
	6:30*	gathered together unto Jesus to report what he had done and taught
	6:31*	had no leisure so much as to eat
	6:32*	departed privately with Jesus into a desert place by ship
	6:36*	asked Jesus to send away the multitude into the villages to buy themselves bread
	6:37*	told by Jesus to give food to the multitude
	6:37	asked Jesus if he should go and buy bread to feed the people
	6:38*	when asked by Jesus the available provisions, reported five loaves and two fishes
	6:39*	made the people sit down by hundreds and by fifties (6:40)
	6:41*	given the blessed food by Jesus to distribute to the crowd
	6:43*	took up twelve baskets full of fragments and of the fishes
	6:45*	constrained by Jesus to get into the ship and go to the other side unto Bethsaida
	6:47*	was alone (with the other disciples) in the ship in the midst of the sea
	6:48*	toiled in rowing the ship for the winds were contrary
	6:48*	Jesus came unto him in about the fourth watch of the night walking upon the sea
	6:49*	saw Jesus walking upon the sea and cried out for he supposed it had been a spirit
	6:50*	saw Jesus and was troubled but admonished by Him to fear not
	6:51*	was amazed beyond measure and wondered that the wind ceased as Jesus entered the ship
	6:52*	because of his hardened heart, had forgotten about the miracle of the loaves
	6:53*	came into the land of Gennesaret
	6:54*	got out of the ship
	7: 5*	walked not according to the tradi-

SIMON *(continued)*

tions of the elders (ate bread with unwashed hands)

Mark 8: 5* informed Jesus of the seven loaves

8: 6* set the loaves before the people

8: 7* receiving the fishes blessed by Jesus, set them before the people

8: 8* gathered seven baskets of fragments

8:10* entered into a ship with Jesus and went into Dalmanutha

8:13* entering into the ship again with Jesus, departed to the other side

8:14* had forgotten to take bread, and had only one loaf in the ship

8:16* had no bread

8:17* having seen the miracles, still did not understand as his heart was possibly yet hardened

8:19* took up twelve baskets full of fragments at the feeding of the five thousand

8:20* took up seven baskets full of fragments at the feeding of the four thousand

8:27* went into the towns of Caesarea Philippi with Jesus

8:27* responded to Jesus' question concerning His identity with "John the Baptist, Elias, and one of the prophets" (8:28)

8:30* charged to tell no man that Jesus was the Christ

8:31* taught by Jesus of the things concerning Himself

9:14* questioned by the scribes

9:18* could not cast out a dumb spirit

9:30* passed through Galilee

9:32* did not understand the words of Jesus, but was afraid to ask

9:33* came to Capernaum

9:33* disputed with the other disciples on the way to Capernaum as to whom should be the greatest (9:34)

9:38* forbade a man from casting out devils (demons) in Jesus' name, because he did not follow him

10:13* rebuked those who brought young children to Jesus that He should touch them

10:14* rebuked, in turn, by Jesus

10:24* astonished at the words of Jesus concerning those with riches

10:26* astonished at Jesus' words

10:28* had left all and followed Jesus

10:32* went up to Jerusalem with Jesus and was amazed and afraid

10:41 was much displeased with James and John

10:46* went to Jericho

10:46* went out of Jericho with Jesus

11: 1* came nigh to Jerusalem, unto Bethphage and Bethany, at the Mount of Olives

Mark 11:11* went to Bethany with Jesus and stayed until the morrow (11:12)

11:14* heard Jesus curse the fig tree

11:15* returned to Jerusalem with Jesus

11:19* went out of Jerusalem

11:20* witnessed the fig tree dried up from the roots

11:27* came again to Jerusalem

14:17* in the evening of the first day of unleavened bread, went with Jesus to the upper room

14:18* sat and ate together with Jesus

14:19* began to be sorrowful over Jesus' statement of betrayal and to ask "Is it I?"

14:20* dipped with Jesus in the dish

14:22* ate the Passover with Jesus

14:23* drank of the communion cup

14:26* sung an hymn and went out to the Mount of Olives

14:31* exclaimed that even if it meant death, he would not deny Him

14:32* went to Gethsemane and was told to sit there while Jesus prayed

14:50* forsook Jesus and fled

16:10* mourned and wept

16:11* believed not Mary Magdalene's account

16:14* Jesus appeared unto him as he sat at meat (with the other disciples)

16:14* upbraided by Jesus for his unbelief and hardness of heart, because he believed not them which had seen Him after He was risen

16:15* commissioned to go into all the world and preach the gospel to every creature

16:20* went forth and preached everywhere, with signs following

Luke 6: 1* plucked ears of corn and ate (rubbing them in his hands) on the Sabbath

6: 2* claimed (by the Pharisees) to be doing that which was not lawful to do on the Sabbath days

6:13 chosen as one of the twelve

6:13* also called (named) an apostle

6:15 called Zelotes

6:15 an apostle

6:17* came down from the mountain with Jesus and stood in the plain

8: 1* went throughout every city and village with Jesus

8: 9* questioned Jesus concerning a parable

8:10* unto him it was given to know the mysteries of the kingdom of God

8:22* went into a ship with Jesus and launched forth for the other side

8:23* the boat, filled with water, put him in jeopardy

8:24* called Jesus Master

8:24* came to Jesus and awakened Him during the storm

SIMON *(continued)*

Luke 8:25* asked by Jesus concerning his faith
8:25* was afraid and wondered concerning Jesus' power over the elements
8:26* arrived at the country of the Gadarenes (Gadara)
9: 1* given power and authority over all devils (demons) and to cure diseases
9: 2* sent by Jesus to preach the kingdom of God and to heal the sick
9: 3* was to take neither staves, nor scrip, neither bread, neither money, neither have two coats
9: 4* was to abide in whatever house he entered
9: 6* went through the towns, preaching the gospel and healing everywhere
9:10* returned and told Jesus all he had done
9:10* went privately with Jesus into a desert place belonging to the city called Bethsaida
9:12* requested that Jesus send away the multitude, so that they might go into the towns and lodge and get victuals (food)
9:13* had only five loaves and two fishes, but was requested by Jesus to give food to the multitude
9:14* made the multitude sit down in companies by fifties (9:15)
9:16* gave the blessed loaves and fish unto the multitude
9:17* took up twelve baskets of fragments
9:18* was alone with Jesus (and the rest of the twelve)
9:18* in response to Jesus' question as to His identity, responded "John the Baptist, Elias, and one of the prophets risen again" (9:19)
9:20* straitly charged and commanded to tell no man that He was the Christ (9:21)
9:40* could not cast the spirit (demon) out of a boy
9:45* feared to ask Jesus concerning His teaching
9:46* reasoned with the other disciples as to which of them should be greatest
9:49* forbade a man from casting out devils (demons) in Jesus' name because he followed not with the disciples
10:24* saw and heard what many prophets and kings had desired to experience
12: 1* warned by Jesus to beware of the leaven of the Pharisees
12: 4* friend of Jesus
17: 5* asked Jesus to increase his faith
18:15* rebuked those who brought infants to Jesus
18:16* rebuked, in turn, by Jesus

Luke 18:28* had left all and followed Jesus
18:31* taken unto Jesus and instructed of things to come (18:33)
18:34* understood none of these teachings of Jesus
19:29* with Jesus, came nigh to Bethphage and Bethany at the Mount of Olives
19:37* rejoiced and praised God with a loud voice (19:38)
22:14* sat down with Jesus (in the upper room for the Passover)
22:14* was called an apostle
22:15* Jesus truly desired his presence in eating the Passover
22:19* partook of the first Lord's Supper (22:20)
22:23* inquired among the disciples as to which of them would betray Jesus
22:24* a strife existed among him and the other disciples as to which one should be accounted the greatest
22:28* had continued with Jesus in His temptations
22:29* was appointed a kingdom (that he might eat and drink at Jesus' table in His kingdom and sit on thrones judging the twelve tribes of Israel) (22:30)
22:35* had lacked nothing
22:36* told to prepare (for his new task)
22:39* followed Jesus to the Mount of Olives
22:40* told to pray that he enter not into temptation
22:45* found sleeping for sorrow (by Jesus)
22:46* told to rise and pray, lest he enter into temptation
22:49* perceiving the forthcoming events, asked Jesus if he should use his sword
24: 9* was told all things concerning the resurrection by Mary Magdalene, Joanna, Mary the mother of James, and the other women
24:10* an apostle
24:11* the words of the women seemed to him as idle tales and he believed them not
24:33* being gathered together (with the other disciples) Cleopas found him and declared that the Lord was risen indeed and had appeared to Simon (24:34)
24:36* Jesus appeared unto him (after the resurrection) but he was terrified and affrighted, and supposed that he had seen a spirit (24:37) ·
24:38* asked by Jesus why he was troubled and why thoughts arose in his heart
24:40* was shown Jesus' hands and feet
24:41* believed not yet for joy, and wondered

SIMON (*continued*)

Luke 24:42* gave Jesus a piece of a broiled fish and of an honeycomb

24:45* his understanding was opened by Jesus that he might understand the scriptures

24:46* was witness of these things (24:48)

24:49* told to tarry in Jerusalem until he was endued with power from on high

24:50* led by Jesus out as far as to Bethany and was blessed of Him

24:52* worshiped Jesus and returned to Jerusalem with great joy

24:53* was continually in the temple praising and blessing God

John 2: 2* was called to the marriage in Cana of Galilee

2:11* believed on Jesus

2:12* went to Capernaum and continued there not many days

2:17* remembered that it was written of Him, "the zeal of thine house hath eaten me up"

2:22* after the resurrection, remembered Jesus' words and believed the scriptures, and the words which Jesus had said

3:22* came into the land of Judea with Jesus and tarried there with Him

4: 2* did baptize

4: 8* had gone away unto the city to buy meat

4:27* came unto Jesus and marveled that He talked with the Samaritan woman, yet did not question Him

4:31* called Jesus Master

4:31* implored Jesus to eat

4:33* questioned among the disciples if Jesus had been brought food to eat

4:35* told to look on the fields for they are white already to harvest

4:38* had been sent to reap where he had not labored, and had entered into others' labors

6: 3* went up into a mountain and sat with Jesus

6:10* instructed by Jesus to have the multitude sit down

6:11* distributed the loaves and fishes to the multitude

6:13* gathered twelve baskets of fragments

6:16* went down to the sea, entered a ship, and went toward Capernaum (6:17)

6:19* after rowing twenty-five to thirty furlongs, saw Jesus walking on the sea and was afraid

6:20* told to not be afraid

6:21* willingly received Him into the ship

6:22* was entered into the only boat there

6:22* was apart from Jesus in the boat alone (with the other disciples)

John 6:67* asked, by Jesus, if he would also go away

6:69* believed and was sure that Jesus was the Christ, the Son of the living God

6:70* chosen as one of the twelve

9: 2* questioned Jesus concerning the man born blind

11: 8* called Jesus Master

11:11* friend of Lazarus

11:54* continued with Jesus at Ephraim

12:16* understood not, at first, the events of the triumphal entry of Jesus

12:16* after Jesus' glorification, remembered that these events had been written of Jesus, and had been done unto Him

13: 5* feet washed by Jesus

13:12* had his feet washed by Jesus

13:13* called Jesus Master and Lord

13:14* had his feet washed by Jesus

13:14* told by Jesus to wash one another's feet

13:15* had been given an example that he should do as Jesus had done to him

13:18* was known and chosen of Jesus

13:21* when told one of them would betray Jesus, looked on the others doubting of whom He spoke (13:22)

13:28* knew not for what intent Jesus spoke these words to Judas Iscariot

13:34* given a new commandent to love one another

13:34* loved of Jesus

13:35* love one to another was a mark that he was a true disciple of Jesus

14:25* was with Jesus

14:26* would be instructed by the Holy Spirit in all things

14:26* the words Jesus had spoken would be brought to his remembrance

14:27* Jesus' peace was given to him and left with him

14:31* was told to arise and go with Jesus

15: 3* is clean through the Word

15: 9* loved of Jesus

15:12* commanded to love one another

15:12* loved of Jesus

15:16* chosen of Jesus and ordained of Him to go and bring forth fruit, and that his fruit should remain

15:17* commanded to love one another

15:19* not of the world

15:19* chosen out of the world, by Jesus

15:19* hated of the world

15:27* would bear witness, because he had been with Jesus from the beginning

16: 4* was with Jesus

16: 6* sorrow had filled his heart

16:12* could not bear the words of Jesus

16:22* presently had sorrow

16:24* had asked nothing of the Father in Jesus' name

16:27* loved of the Father

SIMON (*continued*)

John 16:27* loved Jesus, and believed that He came from God
16:29* could now understand plainly Jesus' words
16:30* was sure that Jesus knew all things
16:30* believed that Jesus came forth from God
18: 1* went with Jesus over the brook Cedron and entered into a garden (Gethsemane)
18: 2* often resorted there with Jesus
20:18* told by Mary Magdalene that she had seen the Lord and that He had spoken unto her
20:19* while assembled together (with the other disciples) with the doors shut for fear of the Jews, Jesus appeared in the midst
20:20* saw Jesus' hands and side and was glad
20:21* sent by Jesus and given His peace
20:22* breathed on by Jesus and received the Holy Ghost
20:25* told Thomas that he had seen the Lord
20:25* informed by Thomas that he would not believe without specific conditions being met
20:26* the doors being shut again, Jesus appeared the second time to him and the apostles
20:30* many other signs were done in his presence which are not written (in this book)

Acts 1: 2* had been given commandments by Jesus (through the Holy Ghost)
1: 2* chosen by Jesus
1: 3* was shown Jesus alive after His passion
1: 3* spoken to by Jesus of the things pertaining to the kingdom of God
1: 3* saw Jesus forty days
1: 4* commanded, by Jesus, not to depart from Jerusalem, but to wait for the promise of the Father
1: 5* would be baptized with the Holy Ghost
1: 6* questioned Jesus concerning the restoration of the kingdom to Israel
1: 7* was not to know the times or the seasons which the Father had put in His own power
1: 8* after receiving the Holy Spirit, would receive power and would be witness unto Jesus Christ throughout the earth
1: 9* beheld as Jesus was taken up into Heaven at His ascension
1:10* was joined by two men in white apparel while he looked steadfastly toward Heaven
1:11* a man of Galilee
1:11* was gazing up into Heaven

Acts 1:11* Jesus was taken up from him into Heaven
1:11* was told that Jesus would come in like manner as he had seen Him go into Heaven
1:12* returned to Jerusalem and went into an upper room (1:13)
1:14* continued in prayer and supplication with the women, Mary the mother of Jesus, and with His brethren
1:21* was with the Lord Jesus at various times
1:24* prayed concerning the ordination of one to be a witness of Jesus' resurrection
1:26* gave forth his lot (concerning Judas Iscariot's successor)
2: 1* present at the day of Pentecost
2: 2* while sitting in the house, cloven tongues like as of fire sat upon him, and he was filled with the Holy Ghost and spoke with other tongues (2:4)
2: 6* his speech confounded the multitude because every man heard in his own language
2: 7* a Galilean
2:13* mocked by some who claimed him as full of new wine
2:14* stood with (Simon) Peter
2:15* was not drunk
2:32* was a witness to the resurrection of Jesus
2:37* asked by the multitude on the day of Pentecost what they should do
2:42* many continued steadfastly in his doctrine and fellowship
2:43* many wonders and signs were done by him
4:33* with great power gave witness of the resurrection of the Lord Jesus
4:33* great grace was upon him
4:35* the price of possessions sold by Christians was laid at his feet
4:35* distributed to every man (of the Christian community) as he had need
4:36* gave Joses a surname of Barnabas
4:37* Joses's money was laid at his feet
5: 2* the gift of Ananias and Sapphira was laid at his feet
5:12* by his hands were many signs and wonders wrought among the people
5:12* was with one accord with the others in Solomon's porch
5:13* no man durst join himself to him (the apostles)
5:13* was magnified of the people
5:16* healed the multitude of sicknesses and unclean spirits
5:18* placed in the common prison by the high priest and Sadducees

SIMON *(continued)*

Acts 5:19* released from prison by the angel of the Lord and told to go, stand, and speak in the temple (5:20)

5:21* entered into the temple early in the morning and taught

5:22* was not found in the prison

5:25* was standing in the temple and teaching the people

5:26* brought without violence and set before the council (5:27)

5:27* questioned by the high priest (5:28)

5:28* had been commanded not to teach in this (Jesus') name

5:28* had filled Jerusalem with his doctrine and had (seemingly) intended to bring Jesus' blood upon his accusers

5:29* believed that he ought to obey God rather than men

5:32* witness of God (and of His works)

5:33* Jewish leaders took counsel to slay him

5:34* put a little space from the Sanhedrin (for their deliberation)

5:40* called back before the council, beaten, commanded not to speak in the name of Jesus, and let go

5:41* departed from the council rejoicing that he was counted worthy to suffer shame for His name

5:42* daily in the temple and in every house, ceased not to teach and preach Jesus Christ

6: 2* called the multitude together and stated it was not reasonable that he should leave the Word of God and serve tables

6: 3* instructed that seven men of honest report be chosen to be appointed to serve tables

6: 4* determined to give himself continually to prayer and to the ministry of the Word

6: 6* the chosen seven were set before him, for whom he prayed and laid his hands on them

8: 1* remained in Jerusalem in the midst of great persecution

8:14* was in Jerusalem

8:14* hearing that Samaria had received the Word of God, sent Peter and John to Samaria

9:27* Saul (Paul) was brought to him by Barnabas and he was informed of Saul's (Paul's) conversion experience and his bold preaching at Damascus

9:28* was accompanied by Saul (Paul) in coming in and going out at Jerusalem

10:39* was witness of all things Jesus did both in the land of the Jews and in Jerusalem

Acts 10:41* a witness, chosen before of God

10:41* ate and drank with Jesus after His resurrection

10:42* commanded of Jesus to preach unto the people, and testified that it was Jesus which was ordained of God to be the Judge of quick and dead

11: 1* was in Judea

11: 1* heard that the Gentiles had also received the Word of God

11:15* the Holy Ghost fell on him at the beginning (Pentecost)

13:31* saw Jesus many days

13:31* came up with Jesus from Galilee to Jerusalem

13:31* was His (Jesus') witness unto the people

15: 2* Paul, Barnabas, and others were sent by the church at Antioch to consult with him over the matter of circumcision

15: 4* received Paul, Barnabas, and the others from Antioch

15: 6* came together (with the elders) to consider the matter (of circumcision)

15: 8* given the Holy Ghost

15: 9* God made no difference between him and a Gentile

15:10* was not able to bear the yoke

15:22* acting with the elders, sent chosen men back to Antioch with Paul and Barnabas

15:23* acting with the elders and brethren, wrote letters of instruction to the Gentiles at Antioch, Syria, and Cilicia

15:24* gave no commandment that Gentile believers must be circumcised and keep the law

15:25* considered it good, being assembled, to send chosen men unto the believers

15:25* loved Barnabas and Paul

15:27* sent Judas and Silas to the Gentile believers

15:33* Judas (Barsabas) and Silas returned unto him

16: 4* with the elders, ordained decrees

16: 4* was at Jerusalem

Rom 16: 7* Andronicus and Junia were well known to him

1Cor 4: 9* Paul thought God had set him (and the apostles) forth last, as it were appointed to death

4: 9* made a spectacle unto the world, to the angels, and to men

4:10* a fool for Christ's sake

4:10* weak, despised

4:11* hungered, thirsted, was naked, was buffeted, and had no certain dwelling place

4:12* labored, working with his own hands

191

SIMON *(continued)*

1Cor 4:12* being reviled, he blessed; being persecuted, he suffered it; being defamed, he entreated (4:13)
       4:13* made as the filth of the world and the offscouring of all things
       9: 5* had power to lead about a sister, a wife
      15: 5* had seen the risen Lord
      15: 7* the risen Lord was seen of him
      15:11* preached
Rev   21:14* name inscribed in the twelve foundations of the new Jerusalem
     21:14* an apostle of the Lamb

3. (Half)-brother of Jesus; son of Mary; and brother of James, Joses, and Juda.

Matt 12:46 a (half) brother of Jesus
     12:46 stood without, desiring to speak with Jesus
     12:46 had brothers
     12:47 had brothers
     12:47 stood without, desiring to speak with Jesus
     13:55 thought to be the brother of Jesus, James, Joses, and Judas
     13:55 assumed to be the son of Joseph and Mary
     13:56 had sisters
Mark   3:31 a brother of Jesus
      3:31 came with his brethren and his mother, stood without, and sent and called for Jesus
      3:32 sought Jesus
      3:32 had brethren
      6: 3 (half) brother of Jesus
      6: 3 brother of James, Joses, and Juda
      6: 3 son of Mary
      6: 3 had sisters
Luke   8:19 came to Jesus (along with his mother and his brethren)
      8:19 could not come at Jesus for the press (crowd)
      8:20 stood without desiring to see Jesus
      8:20 had brethren
John   2:12 went to Capernaum and continued there not many days
      7: 3 requested Jesus to depart and go into Judea, that His disciples also might see the works that He did
      7: 5 did not believe in Jesus
      7: 6 his time was always ready
      7: 7 cannot be hated of the world
      7:10 was gone up (to the feast)
Acts   1:14 was present in the upper room
      1:14 continued with one accord, in prayer and supplication, with the apostles, the women, his mother, and His brethren
      2: 1 present at the day of Pentecost
      2: 2 while sitting in the house, cloven tongues, like as of fire, sat upon him, he was filled with the Holy Ghost and spoke with other tongues (2:4)

1Cor 9: 5 had power to lead about a sister, a wife

4. A leper from Bethany in whose house Jesus was anointed with precious ointment of spikenard by Mary (sister of Martha and Lazarus).

Matt 26: 6 a leper
     26: 6 his house was in Bethany
     26: 6 visited by Jesus
     26: 6 a woman entered his house and poured a box of precious ointment on Jesus' head (26:7)
Mark 14: 3 lived in a house in Bethany
     14: 3 a leper
     14: 3 visited by Jesus (while he sat at meat)
     14: 3 a woman entered his house and poured ointment of spikenard on Jesus' head

5. A man of Cyrene compelled to carry Jesus' cross, and father of Alexander and Rufus.

Matt 27:32 from Cyrene
     27:32 compelled to carry Jesus' cross
Mark 15:21 a Cyrenian
     15:21 passing by, coming out of the country, was compelled to carry Jesus' cross
     15:21 father of Alexander and Rufus
Luke 23:26 a Cyrenian (who was coming out of the country)
     23:26 compelled to carry the cross after Jesus

6. A Pharisee in whose house Jesus' feet were washed with tears.

Luke   7:36 a Pharisee
      7:36 desired Jesus to eat with him
      7:36 Jesus visited his house and sat down to meat
      7:37 a woman (a sinner) visited Jesus at his home
      7:37 the Pharisee
      7:39 the Pharisee
      7:39 had bidden Jesus (to his house)
      7:39 thought that Jesus must not be a prophet, or He would have known the woman to be a sinner
      7:40 Jesus asked to speak with him
      7:40 called Jesus Master
      7:43 judged rightly, and correctly answered Jesus' question
      7:44 Jesus entered his house
      7:44 gave Jesus no water for His feet
      7:45 gave Jesus no kiss
      7:46 did not anoint Jesus' head with oil

7. Father of Judas Iscariot.

John   6:71 father of Judas Iscariot
     12: 4 father of Judas Iscariot
     13: 2 father of Judas Iscariot
     13:26 father of Judas Iscariot

8. A sorcerer of Samaria who offered money for the power to give the Holy Spirit by the laying on of his hands.

Acts   8: 9 a man

SIMON *(continued)*

Acts 8: 9 had used sorcery to bewitch the people of Samaria
 8: 9 gave out that he was some great one
 8:10 given heed by all from the least to the greatest
 8:10 considered by many as the "great power of God"
 8:11 had regard of the people because he had bewitched them with sorceries
 8:13 believed the message of Philip
 8:13 was baptized and continued with Philip
 8:13 beheld the miracles and signs which were done
 8:18 saw that through the laying on of apostles' hands, the Holy Ghost was given
 8:18 offered money to (Simon) Peter and John for power to lay hands on people that they might receive the Holy Ghost (8:19)
 8:20 condemned by (Simon) Peter for thinking the gift of God could be purchased with money
 8:21 had neither part nor lot in this matter for his heart was not right in the sight of God
 8:22 was wicked
 8:23 was in the gall of bitterness and in the bond of iniquity
 8:24 besought (Simon) Peter to pray for him

9. A tanner of Joppa with whom Peter lodged.

Acts 9:43 lived in Joppa
 9:43 (Simon) Peter tarried many days with him
 9:43 a tanner
 10: 6 a tanner
 10: 6 Simon Peter lodged with him
 10: 6 his house was by the sea side
 10:17 the men, sent from Cornelius, had made inquiry for his house and stood before the gate
 10:22 God had warned Cornelius to send for (Simon) Peter in his house
 10:32 lived in Joppa
 10:32 had lodged Simon Peter in his house by the sea side
 10:32 a tanner
 11:11 (Simon) Peter was in his house

10. the Canaanite [ca'na-an-ite = a trafficker]—see SIMON ZELOTES

SOLOMON [sol'-o-mun = peace]
Son of David and Bathsheba, last king of Israel prior to the division of the kingdom, wisdom exceeded that of all others, champion of the polygamists with seven hundred wives and three hundred concubines, reigned forty years and succeeded by his son Rehoboam. (See also 1Kng 1—14)

Matt 1: 6 begotten by David the king of her that had been the wife of Urias
 1: 7 begat Roboam
 6:29 in all his glory, was not arrayed like the lilies of the field
 12:42 queen of the south came from the uttermost part of the earth to hear his wisdom
 12:42 Christ is greater than he
Luke 11:31 had wisdom
 11:31 one greater than he had come
 12:27 in all his glory, was not arrayed like one of the lilies
John 10:23 a porch in the temple bore his name
Acts 3:11 a porch in the temple bore his name
 5:12 a porch in the temple bore his name
 7:47 built an house for God

SOPATER [so'-pa-tur = savior of his father]
A Christian brother from Berea who accompanied Paul into Asia. (May be identical with Sosipater)

Acts 20: 4 of Berea
 20: 4 accompanied Paul into Asia
 20: 5 went before and tarried for Paul (and Luke) at Troas
 20: 6 abode seven days with Paul (and Luke) at Troas
 20:13 going before by ship, sailed unto Assos
 20:14 met Paul at Assos, took him in, and came to Mitylene
 20:15 sailed over against Chios, next day arrived at Samos, tarried at Trogyllium, and the next day came to Miletus
 20:34 Paul's hands had ministered unto his necessities

SOSIPATER [so-sip'-a-tur = savior of his father]
A kinsman of Paul who saluted the church at Rome. (May be identical with Sopater)

Rom 16:21 kinsman of Paul (and Lucius and Jason)
 16:21 saluted the church at Rome

SOSTHENES [sos'-the-neze = savior of his nation]
Chief ruler of the synagogue at Corinth, beaten by the Greeks, and a Christian brother of Paul.

Acts 18:17 the chief ruler of the synagogue
 18:17 beaten before the judgment seat by the Greeks
1Cor 1: 1 (Christian) brother of Paul

STACHYS [sta'-kis = ear of corn]
A Roman Christian, beloved of Paul, and carrier of greetings.

Rom 16: 9 saluted by Paul
 16: 9 beloved of Paul

STEPHANAS [stef'-a-nas = crown]
A believer whose household was the first saved of Achaia, baptized by Paul, and supplied Paul's needs in lieu of the Corinthian church.

STEPHANUS *(continued)*

1Cor	1:16	his household baptized by Paul
	16:15	his house was the first fruits of Achaia
	16:15	of Achaia
	16:15	his house had addicted themselves to the ministry of the saints
	16:17	had gone to Paul (along with Fortunatus and Achaicus)
	16:17	supplied Paul's needs (which the Corinthian church had failed to do)
	16:18	had refreshed Paul's spirit and that of the Corinthian church

STEPHEN [ste'-ven = crown]
One of seven men of honest report, full of the Holy Ghost, chosen to serve tables as a deacon in the Jerusalem church, received the laying on of hands by the apostles, and the first martyr of the Christian church.

Acts	6: 3	of honest report
	6: 3	full of the Holy Ghost and wisdom
	6: 5	chosen to serve tables
	6: 5	a man full of faith and of the Holy Ghost
	6: 6	was set before the apostles
	6: 6	apostles prayed and laid their hands on him
	6: 8	full of faith and power
	6: 8	did great wonders and miracles among the people
	6: 9	certain of the synagogue arose who disputed with him
	6:10	his wisdom and the spirit by which he spoke were irresistible by his critics
	6:11	certain of the synagogue persuaded men to falsely accuse him of speaking blasphemy against Moses and against God
	6:12	was caught and brought to the council
	6:13	false witnesses testified that he ceased not to speak blasphemy
	6:15	his face was as the face of an angel
	7: 2	spoke of the Jews as brethren
	7: 2	claimed Abraham as father (of his lineage)
	7:11	claimed the patriarchs as fathers
	7:12	claimed the patriarchs as fathers
	7:15	claimed the patriarchs as fathers
	7:54	his hearers gnashed on him with their teeth
	7:55	full of the Holy Ghost
	7:55	looked up into Heaven, and saw the glory of God, and Jesus standing on the right hand of God
	7:56	saw the heavens opened and the Son of man standing on the right hand of God
	7:57	they ran upon him with one accord, and cast him out of the city, and stoned him (7:58)
	7:59	was stoned
	7:59	called upon God and the Lord Jesus to receive his spirit
	7:60	kneeled down and with a loud voice asked God not to lay this sin to the charge of these Jewish leaders
	7:60	fell asleep (died)
	8: 1	Saul (Paul) consented to his death
	8: 2	carried to his burial by devout men
	8: 2	great lamentation was made over him
	11:19	a persecution had risen about him
	22:20	his blood was shed
	22:20	a martyr
	22:20	Paul consented unto his death

SUSANNA ♀ [su-zan'-nah = lily]
Ministered unto the needs of Jesus of her own substance during His public ministry.

Luke	8: 2	had been healed of evil spirits and infirmities (8:3)
	8: 3	ministered unto Him of her substance

SYNTYCHE ♀ [sin'-ti-ke = fortunate]
A woman in the church at Philippi who evidently had a dispute or disagreement with another woman, Euodias, and encouraged by Paul to be of the same mind (agreement).

Phil	4: 2	besought (by Paul) to be of the same mind in the Lord with Euodias

T

TABITHA ♀ [tab'-ith-ah = gazelle; doe]——
see DORCAS

TERTIUS [tur'-she-us = third]
Paul's amanuensis or secretary who wrote Romans as Paul dictated the book. (Possibly identical with Silas)

Rom	16:22	wrote (transcribed) the epistle of Romans
	16:22	saluted the church at Rome in the Lord

TERTULLUS [tur-tul'-lus = third]
An orator who went to Caesarea with Ananias the high priest to accuse Paul before Felix.

Acts	24: 1	went to Caesarea with Ananias (the high priest)
	24: 1	an orator
	24: 1	informed the governor (Felix) against Paul
	24: 2	was called forth and accused Paul before Felix

TERTULLUS (*continued*)

Acts 24: 4 prayed that Felix would hear a few words
24: 5 accused Paul as being pestilent, a mover of sedition among all the Jews, a ringleader of the sect of the Nazarenes, and profaner of the temple (24:6)

THADDAEUS [thad-de'-us = breast; sucking plenty]
A surname of Lebbaeus, an apostle of Jesus Christ, and one of the twelve. (Possibly identical with Judas "Jude," and/or Judas "Juda" the half-brother of Jesus)

Matt 8:23* followed Jesus into a ship
8:25* came to and awoke Jesus and asked Him to save the disciples, for they perished
8:26* fearful
8:26* of little faith
8:27* marveled at Jesus
9:10* sat at meat with Jesus, along with publicans and sinners
9:14* fasted not
9:19* followed Jesus
9:37* instructed to pray that the Lord would send forth laborers into His harvest (9:38)
10: 1* was called unto Jesus
10: 1 one of the twelve disciples
10: 1* given power to cast out unclean spirits
10: 1* given power to heal all manner of sickness and disease
10: 2 one of the twelve apostles (10:3)
10: 3 surnamed Thaddaeus
10: 5 one of the twelve (apostles)
10: 5* commanded to go neither to the Gentiles, nor into any city of the Samaritans
10: 6* sent forth by Jesus to the lost sheep of the house of Israel
10: 7* commanded by Jesus to preach "the kingdom of heaven is at hand"
10: 8* commanded to heal the sick, cleanse the lepers, raise the dead, cast out devils (demons)
10: 8* had freely received
10: 9* was to provide neither gold, nor silver, nor brass, nor scrip, neither two coats, neither shoes, nor staves (for himself) (10:10)
10:11* in every city or town, was to inquire who is worthy, and to abide with them
10:12* was to salute each house he entered
10:13* his peace was to come upon each worthy house, but return to him if unworthy
10:14* was to shake off the dust of his feet therein, when not received or heard by a house or city
10:16* sent forth (by Jesus) as a sheep in the midst of wolves

Matt 10:16* was to be wise as a serpent and harmless as a dove
10:17* would be delivered to the councils, scourged in synagogues, and brought before governors and kings for Jesus' sake (10:18)
10:19* was to take no thought concerning what he would speak when delivered up, for the Spirit of his Father would speak in him (10:20)
12: 1* was an hungered and plucked corn in the field and ate
12: 2* accused by the Pharisees of acting unlawfully on the Sabbath day
12:49* called mother and brethren by Jesus
13:10* questioned Jesus about His use of parables
13:11* was given unto him to know the mysteries of the kingdom of Heaven
13:16* saw and heard (spiritually)
13:17* had seen and heard (spiritually)
13:18* had the parable of the sower explained by Jesus (13:23)
13:36* had the parable of the wheat and tares explained by Jesus (13:43)
13:51* claimed to have understood all these things (parables)
14:15* came to Jesus and requested Him to send the multitude away
14:16* instructed by Jesus to feed the multitude
14:17* requested by Jesus to bring the five loaves and two fishes to Him (14:18)
14:19* given the loaves blessed by Jesus
14:19* distributed the loaves to the multitude
14:20* took up of the fragments that remained twelve baskets full
14:22* constrained by Jesus to get into a ship and to go before Him unto the other side (of Sea of Galilee)
14:24* his ship was tossed with waves
14:25* approached by Jesus (walking on the sea)
14:26* saw Jesus walking on the water (Sea of Galilee) and was afraid
14:27* told by Jesus to be of good cheer and not be afraid
14:33* being in the ship, worshiped Jesus, claiming Him to be the Son of God
14:34* came into the land of Gennesaret
15: 2* accused by the scribes and Pharisees, of transgressing the tradition of the elders by not washing his hands when he ate bread
15:12* came to Jesus, informing Him that the Pharisees were offended at His saying
15:23* came and besought Jesus to send away her that cried after him
15:32* was called (unto Jesus)

195

THADDAEUS *(continued)*

Matt 15:34* had seven loaves and a few little
fishes
15:36* given the loaves and fishes (by
Jesus)
15:36* gave the loaves and fishes to the
multitude
15:37* took up of the broken meat that
was left seven baskets full
16: 5* was come to the other side and had
forgotten to take bread
16: 6* told to beware of the leaven of the
Pharisees and Sadducees
16: 7* reasoned with the other disciples
over Jesus' words
16: 7* had taken no bread
16: 8* of little faith
16: 8* reasoned with the other disciples
(concerning the lack of bread)
16: 9* took up baskets (of fragments)
16:10* took up baskets (of fragments)
16:11* did not understand Jesus' words
concerning the leaven (doctrine) of
the Pharisees and Sadducees
16:12* understood how that Jesus spoke
not of bread, but of the doctrine of
the Pharisees and Sadducees
16:13* was in Caesarea Philippi
16:13* answered Jesus' question concerning His identity (16:14)
16:15* questioned as to his view of Jesus'
identity
16:20* charged by Jesus to tell no man
that He was Jesus the Christ
16:21* shown by Jesus the sufferings He
must undergo
17:15* could not cure the lunatic boy
(17:16)
17:19* asked Jesus why he could not cast
out the devil (demon)
17:20* could not cast out the devil
(demon) because of unbelief
17:22* abode in Galilee
17:23* was exceedingly sorry
17:24* came to Capernaum
18: 1* asked Jesus who is the greatest in
the kingdom of Heaven
19:13* rebuked those who brought children to Jesus
19:14* rebuked, in turn, by Jesus
19:25* exceedingly amazed at Jesus' answer to the rich young ruler and
asked who could be saved
19:27* had forsaken all and followed Jesus
19:28* had followed Jesus
19:28* promised by Jesus to sit upon the
twelve thrones judging the twelve
tribes of Israel
20:17* going up to Jerusalem, was taken
apart and foretold by Jesus of His
betrayal, crucifixion, and resurrection (20:19)
20:24* was moved with indignation
towards James and John because

of their request of Jesus

Matt 20:29* departed from Jericho (for
Jerusalem)
21: 1* arrived in Bethphage and Mount
of Olives
21:20* saw the withered fig tree and marveled
24: 1* came to Jesus to show Him the
buildings of the temple
24: 2* Jesus spoke to him of the coming
destruction of the temple
24: 3* asked Jesus of the sign of His coming and of the end of the world
26: 8* was indignant at the actions of the
woman
26:10* had troubled the woman
26:17* asked Jesus where he should prepare for Him the Passover
26:19* did as Jesus had appointed and
made ready the Passover
26:20* celebrated Passover with Jesus and
the rest of the twelve
26:22* asked Jesus if he were the one to
betray Him
26:26* while eating (the Passover) was
given the bread by Jesus
26:27* was given the cup (by Jesus)
26:30* having sung an hymn went out into
the Mount of Olives
26:31* Jesus predicted that he would be
offended because of Him
26:35* claimed he would never deny Jesus,
even though it meant death
26:36* came with Jesus to Gethsemane
26:36* instructed to sit and pray
26:38* told by Jesus to tarry and watch
with Him
26:40* fell asleep in the garden of
Gethsemane
26:43* fell asleep again in the garden (of
Gethsemane)
26:45* told to sleep on now and take his
rest
26:46* told to arise and go (with Jesus)
26:56* forsook Jesus and fled
28:13* would be accused of stealing Jesus'
body by night
28:16* went into Galilee into the place
(mountain) appointed
28:17* saw Jesus and worshiped Him
28:19* given the great commission (28:20)
28:20* Jesus would always be with him,
even unto the end of the world
Mark 3:14* ordained by Jesus (to be with Him)
3:14* would be sent forth to preach (by
Jesus)
3:15* would be given power, by Jesus, to
heal sicknesses and to cast out devils (demons)
3:18 a disciple of Jesus (one of the
twelve)
3:20* could not eat bread with Jesus because of the multitude
4:10* asked Jesus about the parable of

196

the sower

Mark 4:11* was given to know the mystery of the kingdom of God

4:33* had many parables taught him by Jesus

4:34* when alone, with the rest of the twelve, had all things expounded by Jesus

4:36* sent away the multitude

4:36* with the twelve, took Jesus to the other side of the sea

4:38* in fear, awakened Jesus in the midst of the storm

4:40* was fearful and had no faith

4:41* feared exceedingly

4:41* questioned among the other disciples as to what manner of man Jesus was that even the wind and the sea obey Him

5: 1* went with Jesus across the Sea of Galilee to the country of the Gadarenes

6: 1* followed Jesus into His own country

6: 7* sent forth two by two (by Jesus)

6: 7* given power over unclean spirits

6: 8* commanded to take nothing on his journey except a staff, and to be shod with sandals and only one coat (6:9)

6:12* went out, and preached that men should repent

6:13* cast out many devils (demons) and anointed with oil many that were sick, and healed them

6:30* an apostle

6:30* gathered together unto Jesus to report what he had done and taught

6:31* had no leisure so much as to eat

6:32* departed privately with Jesus into a desert place by ship

6:36* asked Jesus to send away the multitude into the villages to buy themselves bread

6:37* told by Jesus to give food to the multitude

6:37* asked Jesus if he should go and buy bread to feed the people

6:38* when asked by Jesus the available provisions, reported five loaves and two fishes

6:39* made the people sit down by hundreds and by fifties (6:40)

6:41* given the food blessed by Jesus to distribute to the crowd

6:43* took up twelve baskets full of fragments and of the fishes

6:45* constrained by Jesus to get into the ship and go to the other side unto Bethsaida

6:47* was alone (with the other disciples) in the ship in the midst of the sea

6:48* toiled in rowing the ship for the winds were contrary

Mark 6:48* Jesus came unto him in about the fourth watch of the night walking upon the sea

6:49* saw Jesus walking upon the sea and cried out for he supposed it had been a spirit

6:50* saw Jesus and was troubled but admonished by Him to fear not

6:51* was amazed beyond measure and wondered that the wind ceased as Jesus entered the ship

6:52* because of his hardened heart had forgotten about the miracle of the loaves

6:53* came into the land of Gennesaret

6:54* got out of the ship

7: 5* walked not according to the traditions of the elders (ate bread with unwashed hands)

8: 5* informed Jesus of the seven loaves

8: 6* set the loaves before the people

8: 7* receiving the fishes blessed by Jesus, set them before the people

8: 8* gathered seven baskets of fragments

8:10* entered into a ship with Jesus and went into Dalmanutha

8:13* entering into the ship again with Jesus, departed to the other side

8:14* had forgotten to take bread, and had only one loaf in the ship

8:16* had no bread

8:17* having seen the miracles, still did not understand as his heart was possibly yet hardened

8:19* took up twelve baskets full of fragments at the feeding of the five thousand

8:20* took up seven baskets full of fragments at the feeding of the four thousand

8:27* went into the towns of Caesarea Philippi with Jesus

8:27* responded to Jesus' question concerning His identity with "John the Baptist, Elias, and one of the prophets" (8:28)

8:30* charged to tell no man that Jesus was the Christ

8:31* taught by Jesus of the things concerning Himself

9:14* questioned by the scribes

9:18* could not cast out a dumb spirit

9:30* passed through Galilee

9:32* did not understand the words of Jesus, but was afraid to ask

9:33* came to Capernaum

9:33* disputed with the other disciples on the way to Capernaum as to who should be the greatest (9:34)

9:38* forbade a man from casting out devils (demons) in Jesus' name, because he did not follow him

THADDAEUS *(continued)*

Mark 10:13* rebuked those who brought young children to Jesus that he should touch them

10:14* rebuked, in turn, by Jesus

10:24* astonished at the words of Jesus concerning those with riches

10:26* astonished at Jesus' words

10:28* had left all and followed Jesus

10:32* went up to Jerusalem with Jesus and was amazed and afraid

10:41 was much displeased with James and John

10:46* went to Jericho

10:46* went out of Jericho with Jesus

11: 1* came nigh to Jerusalem, unto Bethphage and Bethany, at the Mount of Olives

11:11* went to Bethany with Jesus and stayed until the morrow (11:12)

11:14* heard Jesus curse the fig tree

11:15* returned to Jerusalem with Jesus

11:19* went out of Jerusalem

11:20* witnessed the fig tree dried up from the roots

11:27* came again to Jerusalem

14:17* in the evening of the first day of unleavened bread, went with Jesus to the upper room

14:18* sat and ate together with Jesus

14:19* began to be sorrowful over Jesus' statement of betrayal and to ask "Is it I?"

14:20* dipped with Jesus in the dish

14:22* ate the Passover with Jesus

14:23* drank of the communion cup

14:26* sung an hymn and went out to the Mount of Olives

14:31* exclaimed that even if it meant death, he would not deny Him

14:32* went to Gethsemane and was told to sit there while Jesus prayed

14:50* forsook Jesus and fled

16:10* mourned and wept

16:11* believed not Mary Magdalene's account

16:14* Jesus appeared unto him as he sat at meat (with the other disciples)

16:14* upbraided by Jesus for his unbelief and hardness of heart, because he believed not them which had seen Him after He was risen

16:15* commissioned to go into all the world and preach the gospel to every creature

16:20* went forth and preached everywhere, with signs following

Luke 6: 1* plucked ears of corn and ate (rubbing them in his hands) on the Sabbath

6: 2* claimed (by the Pharisees) to be doing that which was not lawful to do on the Sabbath days

6:13 chosen as one of the twelve

Luke 6:13* also called (named) an apostle

6:16 an apostle

6:16 brother of James (probably son of Alphaeus)

6:17* came down from the mountain with Jesus and stood in the plain

8: 1* went throughout every city and village with Jesus

8: 9* questioned Jesus concerning a parable

8:10* unto him it is given to know the mysteries of the kingdom of God

8:22* went into a ship with Jesus and launched forth for the other side

8:23* the boat, filled with water, put him in jeopardy

8:24* called Jesus Master

8:24* came to Jesus and awakened Him during the storm

8:25* asked by Jesus concerning his faith

8:25* was afraid and wondered concerning Jesus' power over the elements

8:26* arrived at the country of the Gadarenes (Gadara)

9: 1* given power and authority over all devils (demons) and to cure diseases

9: 2* sent by Jesus to preach the kingdom of God and to heal the sick

9: 3* was to take neither staves, nor scrip, neither bread, neither money, neither have two coats

9: 4* was to abide in whatever house he entered

9: 6* went through the towns, preaching the gospel, and healing everywhere

9:10* returned and told Jesus all he had done

9:10* went privately with Jesus into a desert place belonging to the city called Bethsaida

9:12* requested that Jesus send away the multitude so that they might go into the towns and lodge and get victuals (food)

9:13* had only five loaves and two fishes, but was requested by Jesus to give food to the multitude

9:14* made the multitude sit down in companies by fifties (9:15)

9:16* gave the blessed loaves and fish unto the multitude

9:17* took up twelve baskets of fragments

9:18* was alone with Jesus (and the rest of the twelve)

9:18* in response to Jesus' question as to His identity, responded "John the Baptist, Elias, and one of the prophets risen again" (9:19)

9:20* straitly charged and commanded to tell no man that He was the Christ (9:21)

9:40* could not cast the spirit (demon) out of a boy

THADDAEUS *(continued)*

Luke   9:45* feared to ask Jesus concerning His teaching

        9:46* reasoned with the other disciples as to which of them should be greatest

        9:49* forbade a man from casting out devils (demons) in Jesus' name because he followed not with the disciples

     10:24* saw and heard what many prophets and kings had desired to experience

    12: 1* warned by Jesus to beware of the leaven of the Pharisees

    12: 4* friend of Jesus

    17: 5* asked Jesus to increase his faith

   18:15* rebuked those who brought infants to Jesus

   18:16* rebuked, in turn, by Jesus

   18:28* had left all and followed Jesus

   18:31* taken unto Jesus and instructed of things to come (18:33)

   18:34* understood none of these teachings of Jesus

   19:29* with Jesus, came nigh to Bethphage and Bethany at the Mount of Olives

   19:37* rejoiced and praised God with a loud voice (19:38)

   22:14* sat down with Jesus (in the upper room for the Passover)

   22:14* was called an apostle

   22:15* Jesus truly desired his presence in eating the Passover

   22:19* partook of the first Lord's Supper (22:20)

   22:23* inquired among the disciples as to which of them would betray Jesus

   22:24* a strife existed among him and the other disciples as to which one should be accounted the greatest

   22:28* had continued with Jesus in His temptations

   22:29* was appointed a kingdom (that he might eat and drink at Jesus' table in His kingdom and sit on thrones judging the twelve tribes of Israel) (22:30)

   22:35* had lacked nothing

   22:36* told to prepare (for his new task)

   22:39* followed Jesus to the Mount of Olives

   22:40* told to pray that he enter not into temptation

   22:45* found sleeping for sorrow (by Jesus)

   22:46* told to rise and pray, lest he enter into temptation

   22:49* perceiving the forthcoming events, asked Jesus if he should use his sword

   24: 9* was told all things concerning the resurrection by Mary Magdalene, Joanna, Mary the mother of James, and the other women

Luke 24:10* an apostle

   24:11* the words of the women seemed to him as idle tales and he believed them not

   24:33* being gathered together, (with the other disciples) Cleopas found him and declared that the Lord was risen indeed and had appeared to Simon (24:34)

   24:36* Jesus appeared unto him (after the resurrection) but he was terrified and affrighted and supposed he had seen a spirit (24:37)

   24:38* asked by Jesus why he was troubled and why thoughts arose in his heart

   24:40* was shown Jesus' hands and feet

   24:41* believed not yet for joy, and wondered

   24:42* gave Jesus a piece of a broiled fish and of an honeycomb

   24:45* his understanding was opened by Jesus that he might understand the scriptures

   24:46* was witness of these things (24:48)

   24:49* told to tarry in Jerusalem until he was endued with power from on high

   24:50* led by Jesus out as far as to Bethany and was blessed of Him

   24:52* worshiped Jesus and returned to Jerusalem with great joy

   24:53* was continually in the temple, praising and blessing God

John   2: 2* was called to the marriage in Cana of Galilee

    2:11* believed on Jesus

    2:12* went to Capernaum and continued there not many days

    2:17* remembered that it was written of Him, "the zeal of thine house hath eaten me up"

    2:22* after the resurrection, remembered Jesus' words and believed the scriptures and the words which Jesus had said

    3:22* came into the land of Judea with Jesus and tarried there with Him

    4: 2* did baptize

    4: 8* had gone away unto the city to buy meat

    4:27* came unto Jesus and marveled that He talked with the Samaritan woman, yet did not question Him

    4:31* called Jesus Master

    4:31* implored Jesus to eat

    4:33* questioned among the disciples if Jesus had been brought food to eat

    4:35* told to look on the fields for they are white already to harvest

    4:38* had been sent to reap where he had not labored and had entered into others' labors

    6: 3* went up into a mountain and sat

THADDAEUS *(continued)*

with Jesus

John 6:10* instructed by Jesus to have the multitude sit down

6:11* distributed the loaves and fishes to the multitude

6:13* gathered twelve baskets of fragments

6:16* went down to the sea, entered a ship, and went toward Capernaum (6:17)

6:19* after rowing twenty-five to thirty furlongs, saw Jesus walking on the sea and was afraid

6:20* told to not be afraid

6:21* willingly received Him into the ship

6:22* was entered into the only boat there

6:22* was apart from Jesus in the boat alone (with the other disciples)

6:67* asked, by Jesus, if he would also go away

6:69* believed and was sure that Jesus was the Christ, the Son of the living God

6:70* chosen as one of the twelve

9: 2* questioned Jesus concerning the man born blind

11: 8* called Jesus Master

11:11* friend of Lazarus

11:54* continued with Jesus at Ephraim

12:16* understood not at first, the events of the triumphal entry of Jesus

12:16* after Jesus' glorification, remembered that these events had been written of Jesus, and had been done unto Him

13: 5* feet washed by Jesus

13:12* had his feet washed by Jesus

13:13* called Jesus Master

13:14* had his feet washed by Jesus

13:14* told by Jesus to wash one another's feet

13:15* had been given an example that he should do as Jesus had done to him

13:18* was known and chosen of Jesus

13:21* when told that one of the disciples would betray Jesus, looked on the others doubting of whom He spoke (13:22)

13:28* knew not for what intent Jesus spoke these words to Judas Iscariot

13:34* given a new commandment to love one another

13:34* loved of Jesus

13:35* love one to another was a mark that he was a true disciple of Jesus

14:22 not Iscariot

14:22 asked Jesus how He would manifest Himself to the apostles, and yet not unto the world

14:25* was with Jesus

14:26* would be instructed by the Holy Spirit in all things

14:26* the words Jesus had spoken would

be brought to his remembrance

John 14:27* Jesus' peace was given to him and left with him

14:31* was told to arise and go with Jesus

15: 3* is clean through the Word

15: 9* loved of Jesus

15:12* commanded to love one another

15:12* loved of Jesus

15:16* chosen of Jesus and ordained of Him to go and bring forth fruit, and that his fruit should remain

15:17* commanded to love one another

15:19* not of the world

15:19* chosen out of the world by Jesus

15:19* hated of the world

15:27* would bear witness, because he had been with Jesus from the beginning

16: 4* was with Jesus

16: 6* sorrow had filled his heart

16:12* could not bear the words of Jesus

16:22* presently had sorrow

16:24* had asked nothing of the Father in Jesus' name

16:27* loved of the Father

16:27* loved Jesus, and believed that he came from God

16:29* could now understand plainly Jesus' words

16:30* was sure that Jesus knew all things

16:30* believed that Jesus came forth from God

18: 1* went with Jesus over the brook Cedron and entered into a garden (Gethsemane)

18: 2* often resorted there with Jesus

20:18* told by Mary Magdalene that she had seen the Lord and that He had spoken unto her

20:19* while assembled together (with the other disciples) with the doors shut for fear of the Jews, Jesus appeared in the midst

20:20* saw Jesus' hands and side and was glad

20:21* sent by Jesus and given His peace

20:22* breathed on by Jesus and received the Holy Ghost

20:25* told Thomas that he had seen the Lord

20:25* informed by Thomas that he would not believe without specific conditions being met

20:26* the doors being shut again, Jesus appeared the second time to him and the apostles

20:30* many other signs were done in his presence which are not written (in this book)

Acts 1: 2* had been given commandments by Jesus (through the Holy Ghost)

1: 2* chosen by Jesus

1: 3* was shown Jesus alive after His passion

1: 3* spoken to by Jesus of the things

THADDAEUS *(continued)*

Acts

pertaining to the kingdom of God
1: 3* saw Jesus forty days
1: 4* commanded by Jesus not to depart from Jerusalem, but to wait for the promise of the Father
1: 5* would be baptized with the Holy Ghost
1: 6* questioned Jesus concerning the restoration of the kingdom to Israel
1: 7* was not to know the times or the seasons which the Father had put in His own power
1: 8* after receiving the Holy Spirit, would receive power and would be witnesses unto Jesus Christ throughout the earth
1: 9* beheld as Jesus was taken up into Heaven at His ascension
1:10* was joined by two men in white apparel while he looked steadfastly toward Heaven
1:11* a man of Galilee
1:11* was gazing up into Heaven
1:11* Jesus was taken up from him into Heaven
1:11* was told that Jesus would come in like manner as he had seen Him go into Heaven
1:12* returned to Jerusalem and went into an upper room (1:13)
1:14* continued in prayer and supplication with the women, Mary the mother of Jesus, and with His brethren
1:21* was with the Lord Jesus at various times
1:24* prayed concerning the ordination of one to be a witness of Jesus' resurrection
1:26* gave forth his lot (concerning Judas Iscariot's successor)
2: 1* present at the day of Pentecost
2: 2* while sitting in the house, cloven tongues like as of fire sat upon him, he was filled with the Holy Ghost, and spoke with other tongues (2:4)
2: 6* his speech confounded the multitude because every man heard in his own language
2: 7* a Galilean
2:13* mocked by some who claimed him as full of new wine
2:14* stood with (Simon) Peter
2:15* was not drunk
2:32* was a witness to the resurrection of Jesus
2:37* asked by the multitude on the day of Pentecost what they should do
2:42* many continued steadfastly in his doctrine and fellowship
2:43* many wonders and signs were done by him
4:33* with great power gave witness of the resurrection of the Lord Jesus

Acts
4:33* great grace was upon him
4:35* the price of possessions sold by Christians was laid at his feet
4:35* distributed to every man (of the Christian community) as he had need
4:36* gave Joses a surname of Barnabas
4:37* Joses's money was laid at his feet
5: 2* the gift of Ananias and Sapphira was laid at his feet
5:12* by his hands were many signs and wonders wrought among the people
5:12* was with one accord with the others in Solomon's porch
5:13* no man durst join himself to him (the apostles)
5:13* was magnified of the people
5:16* healed the multitude of sicknesses and unclean spirits
5:18* placed in the common prison by the high priest and Sadducees
5:19* released from prison by the angel of the Lord and told to go, stand, and speak in the temple (5:20)
5:21* entered into the temple early in the morning and taught
5:22* was not found in the prison
5:25* was standing in the temple and teaching the people
5:26* brought without violence and set before the council (5:27)
5:27* questioned by the high priest (5:28)
5:28* had been commanded not to teach in this (Jesus') name
5:28* had filled Jerusalem with his doctrine and had (seemingly) intended to bring Jesus' blood upon his accusers
5:29* believed that he ought to obey God rather than men
5:32* witness of God (and of His works)
5:33* Jewish leaders took counsel to slay him
5:34* put a little space from the council (for their deliberation)
5:40* called back before the council, beaten, commanded not to speak in the name of Jesus, and let go
5:41* departed from the council rejoicing that he was counted worthy to suffer shame for His name
5:42* daily in the temple and in every house, ceased not to teach and preach Jesus Christ
6: 2* called the multitude together and stated it was not reasonable that he should leave the Word of God and serve tables
6: 3* instructed that seven men of honest report be chosen to be appointed to serve tables
6: 4* determined to give himself continually to prayer and to the ministry of the Word

THADDAEUS *(continued)*

Acts 6: 6* the chosen seven were set before
him, for whom he prayed and laid
his hands on them

8: 1* remained in Jerusalem in the midst
of great persecution

8:14* was in Jerusalem

8:14* hearing that Samaria had received
the Word of God, sent Peter and
John to Samaria

9:27* Saul (Paul) was brought to him by
Barnabas and he was informed of
Saul's (Paul's) conversion experi-
ence and his bold preaching at
Damascus

9:28* was accompanied by Saul (Paul)
in coming in and going out at
Jerusalem

10:39* was witness of all things Jesus did
both in the land of the Jews and in
Jerusalem

10:41* a witness, chosen before of God

10:41* ate and drank with Jesus after His
resurrection

10:42* commanded of Jesus to preach unto
the people, and testified that it was
Jesus which was ordained of God
to be the Judge of quick and dead

11: 1* was in Judea

11: 1* heard that the Gentiles had also
received the Word of God

11:15* the Holy Ghost fell on him at the
beginning (Pentecost)

13:31* saw Jesus many days

13:31* came up with Jesus from Galilee to
Jerusalem

13:31* was His (Jesus') witness unto the
people

15: 2* Paul, Barnabas, and others were
sent by the church at Antioch to
consult with him over the matter
of circumcision

15: 4* received Paul, Barnabas, and the
others from Antioch

15: 6* came together (with the elders) to
consider the matter (of circumcision)

15: 8* given the Holy Spirit

15: 9* God made no difference between
him and a Gentile

15:10* was not able to bear the yoke

15:22* acting with the elders, sent chosen
men back to Antioch with Paul and
Barnabas

15:23* acting with the elders and brethren,
wrote letters of instruction to the
Gentiles at Antioch, Syria, and
Cilicia

15:24* gave no commandment that Gentile believers must be circumcised
and keep the law

15:25* considered it good, being assembled, to send chosen men unto the
believers

Acts 15:25* loved Barnabas and Paul

15:27* sent Judas and Silas to the Gentile
believers

15:33* Judas (Barsabas) and Silas returned unto him

16: 4* with the elders, ordained decrees

16: 4* was at Jerusalem

Rom 16: 7* Andronicus and Junia were well
known to him

1Cor 4: 9* Paul thought God had set him (and
the apostles) forth last, as it were
appointed to death

4: 9* made a spectacle unto the world,
to the angels, and to men

4:10* a fool for Christ's sake

4:10* weak, despised

4:11* hungered, thirsted, was naked, was
buffeted, and had no certain dwelling place

4:12* labored, working with his own
hands

4:12* being reviled, he blessed; being
persecuted, he suffered it; being
defamed, he entreated (4:13)

4:13* made as the filth of the world, and
the offscouring of all things

9: 5* had power to lead about a sister, a
wife

1Cor 15: 5* had seen the risen Lord

15: 7* the risen Lord was seen of him

15:11* preached

Rev 21:14* name inscribed in the twelve foundations of the new Jerusalem

21:14* an apostle of the Lamb

THAMAR ♀ [tha'-mar = a palm tree]
Old Testament Tamar and mother of Phares and
Zara by Judas (her father-in-law). (See also Gen
38)

Matt 1: 3 mother of Phares and Zara by
Judas

THARA [tha'-rah = thou mayest breathe]
Old Testament Terah, son of Nachor, and father
of Abraham. (See also Gen 11)

Luke 3:34 father of Abraham
3:34 son of Nachor

THEOPHILUS [the-of'-il-us = loved of God]
The recipient of the Gospel of Luke and the Acts
of the apostles. (Possibly a nobleman or man of
high rank)

Luke 1: 3 most excellent (possibly a ruler)
1: 3 recipient of the Gospel of Luke
1: 4 had been instructed (concerning
Christ)

Acts 1: 1 recipient of the Book of the Acts

THEUDAS [thew'-das = the gift of God]
Referred to by Gamaliel as a haughty leader of
about four hundred men who led insurrection or
revolt; was slain and his work brought to nought.

Acts 5:36 boasted himself to be somebody

THEUDAS *(continued)*
Acts   5:36 about four hundred men joined themselves to him
         5:36 was slain

THOMAS [tom'-us = twin]
Called Didymus, an apostle of Jesus Christ, one of the twelve, absent at Jesus' first postresurrection appearance to the group, doubted, and later declared his belief and conviction after physical evidence was presented.

Matt   8:23* followed Jesus into a ship
        8:25* came to and awoke Jesus, and asked Him to save the disciples, for they perished
        8:26* fearful
        8:26* of little faith
        8:27* marveled at Jesus
        9:10* sat at meat with Jesus along with publicans and sinners
        9:14* fasted not
        9:19* followed Jesus
        9:37* instructed to pray that the Lord would send forth laborers into His harvest (9:38)
     10: 1* was called unto Jesus
     10: 1 one of the twelve disciples (of Jesus)
     10: 1* given power to cast out unclean spirits
     10: 1* given power to heal all manner of sickness and disease
     10: 2 one of the twelve apostles (10:3)
     10: 5 one of the twelve (apostles)
     10: 5* commanded to go neither to the Gentiles, nor into any city of the Samaritans
     10: 6* sent forth by Jesus to the lost sheep of the house of Israel
     10: 7* commanded by Jesus to preach "the kingdom of heaven is at hand"
     10: 8* commanded to heal the sick, cleanse the lepers, raise the dead, cast out devils (demons)
     10: 8* had freely received
     10: 9* was to provide neither gold, nor silver, nor brass, nor scrip, neither two coats, neither shoes, nor staves (for himself) (10:10)
    10:11* in every city or town was to inquire who is worthy, and to abide with them
    10:12* was to salute each house he entered
    10:13* his peace was to come upon each worthy house, but return to him if unworthy
    10:14* was to shake off the dust of his feet therein, when not received or heard by a house or city
    10:16* sent forth (by Jesus) as a sheep in the midst of wolves
    10:16* was to be wise as a serpent and harmless as a dove
    10:17* would be delivered to the councils, scourged in synagogues, and brought before governors and kings for (Jesus') sake (10:18)
Matt 10:19* was to take no thought concerning what he would speak when delivered up, for the Spirit of his Father would speak in him (10:20)
     12: 1* was an hungered and plucked corn in the field and ate
     12: 2* accused by the Pharisees of acting unlawfully on the Sabbath day
    12:49* called mother and brethren by Jesus
    13:10* questioned Jesus about His use of parables
    13:11* was given unto him to know the mysteries of the kingdom of Heaven
    13:16* saw and heard (spiritually)
    13:17* had seen and heard (spiritually)
    13:18* had the parable of the sower explained by Jesus (13:23)
    13:36* had the parable of the wheat and tares explained by Jesus (13:43)
    13:51* claimed to have understood all these things (parables)
    14:15* came to Jesus and requested Him to send the multitude away
    14:16* instructed by Jesus to feed the multitude
    14:17* requested by Jesus to bring the five loaves and two fishes to Him (14:18)
    14:19* given the loaves blessed by Jesus
    14:19* distributed the loaves to the multitude
    14:20* took up of the fragments that remained twelve baskets full
    14:22* constrained by Jesus to get into a ship and to go before Him unto the other side
    14:24* his ship was tossed with waves
    14:25* approached by Jesus (walking on the sea)
    14:26* saw Jesus walking on the water (Sea of Galilee) and was afraid
    14:27* told by Jesus to be of good cheer and not be afraid
    14:33* being in the ship, worshiped Jesus, claiming Him to be the Son of God
    14:34* came into the land of Gennesaret
    15: 2* accused by the scribes and Pharisees, of transgressing the tradition of the elders by not washing his hands when he ate bread
    15:12* came to Jesus, informing Him that the Pharisees were offended at His saying
    15:23* came and besought Jesus to send away her that cried after him
    15:32* was called (unto Jesus)
    15:34* had seven loaves and a few little fishes
    15:36* given the loaves and fishes (by Jesus)

THOMAS (continued)

Matt 15:36* gave the loaves and fishes to the multitude

15:37* took up of the broken meat that was left seven baskets full

16: 5* was come to the other side and had forgotten to take bread

16: 6* told to beware of the leaven of the Pharisees and Sadducees

16: 7* reasoned with the other disciples over Jesus' words

16: 7* had taken no bread

16: 8* of little faith

16: 8* reasoned with the other disciples (concerning the lack of bread)

16: 9* took up baskets (of fragments)

16:10* took up baskets (of fragments)

16:11* did not understand Jesus' words concerning the leaven (doctrine) of the Pharisees and Sadducees

16:12* understood how that Jesus spoke not of bread, but of the doctrine of the Pharisees and Sadducees

16:13* was in Caesarea Philippi

16:13* answered Jesus' question concerning His identity (16:14)

16:15* questioned as to his view of Jesus' identity

16:20* charged by Jesus to tell no man that He was Jesus the Christ

16:21* shown by Jesus the sufferings He must undergo

17:15* could not cure the lunatic boy (17:16)

17:19* asked Jesus why he could not cast out the devil (demon)

17:20* could not cast out the devil (demon) because of unbelief

17:22* abode in Galilee

17:23* was exceedingly sorry

17:24* came to Capernaum

18: 1* asked Jesus who is the greatest in the kingdom of Heaven

19:13* rebuked those who brought children to Jesus

19:14* rebuked, in turn, by Jesus

19:25* exceedingly amazed at Jesus' answer to the rich young ruler and asked who could be saved

19:27* had forsaken all and followed Jesus

19:28* had followed Jesus

19:28* promised by Jesus to sit upon the twelve thrones judging the twelve tribes of Israel

20:17* going up to Jerusalem, taken apart and foretold by Jesus of His betrayal, crucifixion, and resurrection (20:19)

20:24* was moved with indignation towards James and John because of their request of Jesus

20:29* departed from Jericho (for Jerusalem)

21: 1* arrived in Bethphage and Mount of Olives

Matt 21:20* saw the withered fig tree and marveled

24: 1* came to Jesus to show Him the buildings of the temple

24: 2* Jesus spoke to him of coming destruction of temple

24: 3* asked Jesus of the sign of His coming and of the end of the world

26: 8* was indignant at the actions of the woman

26:10* had troubled the woman

26:17* asked Jesus where he should prepare for Him the Passover

26:19* did as Jesus had appointed and made ready the Passover

26:20 celebrated the Passover with Jesus and the rest of the twelve

26:22 asked Jesus if he were the one to betray Him

26:26* while eating (the Passover) given the bread by Jesus

26:27* given the cup (by Jesus)

26:30* having sung an hymn, went out into the Mount of Olives

26:31* Jesus predicted that he would be offended because of Him

26:35* claimed he would never deny Jesus, even though it meant death

26:36* came with Jesus to Gethsemane

26:36* instructed to sit and pray

26:38* told by Jesus to tarry and watch with Him

26:40* fell asleep in the garden of Gethsemane

26:43* fell asleep again in the garden (of Gethsemane)

26:45* told to sleep on now and take his rest

26:46* told to arise and go (with Jesus)

26:56* forsook Jesus and fled

28:13* would be accused of stealing Jesus' body by night

28:16* went into Galilee into the place (mountain) appointed

28:17* saw Jesus and worshiped Him

28:19* given the great commission

28:20* Jesus would always be with him, even unto the end of the world

Mark 3:14* ordained by Jesus (to be with Him)

3:14* would be sent forth to preach (by Jesus)

3:15* would be given power by Jesus to heal sicknesses and to cast out devils (demons)

3:18 a disciple of Jesus (one of the twelve)

3:20* could not eat bread with Jesus because of the multitude

4:10* asked Jesus about the parable of the sower

4:11* was given to know the mystery of the kingdom of God

4:33* had many parables taught him by

THOMAS *(continued)*

Jesus

Mark 4:34* when alone, with the rest of the twelve, had all things expounded by Jesus

4:36* sent away the multitude

4:36* with the twelve, took Jesus to the other side of the sea

4:38* in fear, awakened Jesus in the midst of the storm

4:40* was fearful and had no faith

4:41* feared exceedingly

4:41* questioned among the other disciples as to what manner of man Jesus was that even the wind and the sea obey Him

5: 1* went with Jesus across the Sea of Galilee to the country of the Gadarenes

6: 1* followed Jesus into His own country

6: 7* sent forth two by two (by Jesus)

6: 7* given power over unclean spirits

6: 8* commanded to take nothing on his journey except a staff, and to be shod with sandals and only one coat (6:9)

6:12* went out and preached that men should repent

6:13* cast out many devils (demons) and anointed with oil many that were sick and healed them

6:30* an apostle

6:30* gathered together unto Jesus to report what he had done and taught

6:31* had no leisure so much as to eat

6:32* departed privately with Jesus into a desert place by ship

6:36* asked Jesus to send away the multitude into the villages to buy themselves bread

6:37* told by Jesus to give food to the multitude

6:37* asked Jesus if he should go and buy bread to feed the people

6:38* when asked by Jesus the available provisions, reported five loaves and two fishes

6:39* made the people sit down by hundreds and by fifties (6:40)

6:41* given the food blessed by Jesus to distribute to the crowd

6:43* took up twelve baskets full of fragments and of the fishes

6:45* constrained by Jesus to get into the ship and go to the other side unto Bethsaida

6:47* was alone (with the other disciples) in the ship in the midst of the sea

6:48* toiled in rowing the ship for the winds were contrary

6:48* Jesus came unto him in about the fourth watch of the night walking upon the sea

Mark 6:49* saw Jesus walking upon the sea and cried out for he supposed it had been a spirit

6:50* saw Jesus and was troubled, but admonished by Him to fear not

6:51* was amazed beyond measure and wondered that the wind ceased as Jesus entered the ship

6:52* because of his hardened heart, had forgotten about the miracle of the loaves

6:53* came into the land of Gennesaret

6:54* got out of the ship

7: 5* walked not according to the traditions of the elders (ate bread with unwashed hands)

8: 5* informed Jesus of the seven loaves

8: 6* set the loaves before the people

8: 7* receiving the fishes blessed by Jesus, set them before the people

8: 8* gathered seven baskets of fragments

8:10* entered into a ship with Jesus and went into Dalmanutha

8:13* entering into the ship again with Jesus, departed to the other side

8:14* had forgotten to take bread and had only one loaf in the ship

8:16* had no bread

8:17* having seen the miracles, still did not understand as his heart was possibly yet hardened

8:19* took up twelve baskets full of fragments at the feeding of the five thousand

8:20* took up seven baskets full of fragments at the feeding of the four thousand

8:27* went into the towns of Caesarea Philippi with Jesus

8:27* responded to Jesus' question concerning His identity with "John the Baptist, Elias, and one of the prophets" (8:28)

8:30* charged to tell no man that Jesus was the Christ

8:31* taught by Jesus of the things concerning Himself

9:14* questioned by the scribes

9:18* could not cast out a dumb spirit

9:30* passed through Galilee

9:32* did not understand the words of Jesus, but was afraid to ask

9:33* came to Capernaum

9:33* disputed with the other disciples on the way to Capernaum as to whom should be the greatest (9:34)

9:38* forbade a man from casting out devils (demons) in Jesus' name, because he did not follow him

10:13* rebuked those who brought young children to Jesus that He should touch them

10:14* rebuked, in turn, by Jesus

THOMAS (*continued*)

Mark 10:24* astonished at the words of Jesus concerning those with riches

10:26* astonished at Jesus' words

10:28* had left all and followed Jesus

10:32* went up to Jerusalem with Jesus and was amazed and afraid

10:41 was much displeased with James and John

10:46* went to Jericho

10:46* went out of Jericho with Jesus

11: 1* came nigh to Jerusalem, unto Bethphage and Bethany, at the Mount of Olives

11:11* went to Bethany with Jesus and stayed until the morrow (11:12)

11:14* heard Jesus curse the fig tree

11:15* returned to Jerusalem with Jesus

11:19* went out of Jerusalem

11:20* witnessed the fig tree dried up from the roots

11:27* came again to Jerusalem

14:17* in the evening of the first day of unleavened bread, went with Jesus to the upper room

14:18* sat and ate together with Jesus

14:19* began to be sorrowful over Jesus' statement of betrayal and to ask "Is it I?"

14:20* dipped with Jesus in the dish

14:22* ate the Passover with Jesus

14:23* drank of the communion cup

14:26* sung an hymn and went out to the Mount of Olives

14:31* exclaimed that even if it meant death, he would not deny Him

14:32* went to Gethsemane and was told to sit there while Jesus prayed

14:50* forsook Jesus and fled

16:10* mourned and wept

16:11* believed not Mary Magdalene's account

16:14* Jesus appeared unto him as he sat at meat (with the other disciples)

16:14* upbraided by Jesus for his unbelief and hardness of heart, because he believed not them which had seen Him after He was risen

16:15* commissioned to go into all the world and preach the gospel to every creature

16:20* went forth and preached everywhere, with signs following

Luke 6: 1* plucked ears of corn and ate (rubbing them in his hands) on the Sabbath

6: 2* claimed (by the Pharisees) to be doing that which was not lawful to do on the Sabbath day

6:13* chosen as one of the twelve

6:13* also called (named) an apostle

6:15 an apostle

6:17* came down from the mountain with Jesus and stood in the plain

Luke 8: 1* went throughout every city and village with Jesus

8: 9* questioned Jesus concerning a parable

8:10* unto him it is given to know the mysteries of the kingdom of God

8:22* went into a ship with Jesus and launched forth for the other side

8:23* the boat, filled with water, put him in jeopardy

8:24* called Jesus Master

8:24* came to Jesus and awakened Him during the storm

8:25* asked by Jesus concerning his faith

8:25* was afraid and wondered concerning Jesus' power over the elements

8:26* arrived at the country of the Gadarenes (Gadara)

9: 1* given power and authority over all devils (demons) and to cure diseases

9: 2* sent, by Jesus, to preach the kingdom of God and to heal the sick

9: 3* was to take neither staves, nor scrip, neither bread, neither money, neither have two coats

9: 4* was to abide in whatever house he entered

9: 6* went through the towns, preaching the gospel and healing everywhere

9:10* returned and told Jesus all he had done

9:10* went privately with Jesus into a desert place belonging to the city called Bethsaida

9:12* requested that Jesus send away the multitude, so that they might go into the towns and lodge and get victuals (food)

9:13* had only five loaves and two fishes, but was requested by Jesus to give food to the multitude

9:14* made the multitude sit down in companies by fifties (9:15)

9:16* gave the blessed loaves and fish unto the multitude

9:17* took up twelve baskets of fragments

9:18* was alone with Jesus (and the rest of the twelve)

9:18* in response to Jesus' question as to His identity, responded "John the Baptist, Elias, and one of the prophets risen again" (9:19)

9:20* was straitly charged and commanded to tell no man that He is the Christ (9:21)

9:40* could not cast the spirit (demon) out of a boy

9:45* feared to ask Jesus concerning His teaching

9:46* reasoned with the other disciples as to which of them should be greatest

9:49* forbade a man from casting out

THOMAS *(continued)*

Luke 10:24* saw and heard what many prophets and kings had desired to experience

12: 1* warned by Jesus to beware of the leaven of the Pharisees

12: 4* friend of Jesus

17: 5* asked Jesus to increase his faith

18:15* rebuked those who brought infants to Jesus

18:16* rebuked, in turn, by Jesus

18:28* had left all and followed Jesus

18:31* taken unto Jesus and instructed of things to come (18:33)

18:34* understood none of these teachings of Jesus

19:29* with Jesus came nigh to Bethphage and Bethany at the Mount of Olives

19:37* rejoiced and praised God with a loud voice (19:38)

22:14* sat down with Jesus (in the upper room for the Passover)

22:14* was called an apostle

22:15* Jesus truly desired his presence in eating the Passover

22:19* partook of the first Lord's Supper (22:20)

22:23* inquired among the disciples as to which of them would betray Jesus

22:24* a strife existed among him and the other disciples as to which one should be accounted the greatest

22:28* had continued with Jesus in His temptation

22:29* was appointed a kingdom (that he might eat and drink at Jesus' table in His kingdom and sit on thrones judging the twelve tribes of Israel) (22:30)

22:35* had lacked nothing

22:36* told to prepare (for his new task)

22:39* followed Jesus to the Mount of Olives

22:40* told to pray that he enter not into temptation

22:45* was found sleeping for sorrow (by Jesus)

22:46* told to rise and pray, lest he enter into temptation

22:49* perceiving the forthcoming events, asked Jesus if he should use his sword

24: 9* was told all things concerning the resurrection by Mary Magdalene, Joanna, Mary the mother of James, and the other women

24:10* an apostle

24:11* the words of the women seemed to him as idle tales and he believed them not

24:33* being gathered together (with the other disciples), Cleopas found him and declared that the Lord was risen indeed and had appeared to Simon (24:34)

Luke 24:38* asked by Jesus why he was troubled and why thoughts arose in his heart

24:40* was shown Jesus' hands and feet

24:41* believed not yet for joy and wondered

24:42* gave Jesus a piece of a broiled fish and of an honeycomb

24:45* his understanding was opened by Jesus that he might understand the scriptures

24:46* was witness of these things (24:48)

24:49* told to tarry in Jerusalem until he was endued with power from on high

24:50* led by Jesus out as far as to Bethany and was blessed of Him

24:52* worshiped Jesus and returned to Jerusalem with great joy

24:53* was continually in the temple praising and blessing God

John 2: 2* was called to the marriage in Cana in Galilee

2:11* believed on Jesus

2:12* went to Capernaum and continued there not many days

2:17* remembered that it was written of Him, "the zeal of thine house hath eaten me up"

2:22* after the resurrection, remembered Jesus' words and believed the scriptures had said, and the words which Jesus had said

3:22* came into the land of Judea with Jesus and tarried there with Him

4: 2* did baptize

4: 8* had gone away unto the city to buy meat

4:27* came unto Jesus and marveled that He talked with the Samaritan woman, yet held his peace

4:31* called Jesus Master

4:31* implored Jesus to eat

4:33* questioned among the disciples if Jesus had been brought food to eat

4:35* told to look on the fields for they are white already to harvest

4:38* had been sent to reap where he had not sown and had entered into others' labors

6: 3* went up into a mountain and sat with Jesus

6:10* instructed, by Jesus, to have the multitude sit down

6:11* distributed the loaves and fishes to the multitude

6:13* gathered twelve baskets of fragments

6:16* went down to the sea, entered a ship, and went toward Capernaum (6:17)

THOMAS *(continued)*

John 6:19* after rowing twenty-five to thirty furlongs, saw Jesus walking on the sea and was afraid

6:20* told to not be afraid

6:21* willingly received Him into the ship

6:22* was entered into the only boat there

6:22* was apart from Jesus in the boat alone (with the other disciples)

6:67* asked by Jesus if he would also go away

6:69* believed and was sure that Jesus was the Christ, the Son of the living God

6:70* chosen as one of the twelve

9: 2* questioned Jesus concerning the man born blind

11: 8* called Jesus Master

11:11* friend of Lazarus

11:16 called Didymus (meaning twin)

11:16 desired to go to Bethany and die (with Lazarus)

11:54* continued with Jesus at Ephraim

12:16* understood not, at first, the events of the triumphal entry of Jesus

12:16* after Jesus' glorification, remembered that these events had been written of Jesus, and had been done unto Him

13: 5* feet washed by Jesus

13:12* had his feet washed by Jesus

13:13* called Jesus Master and Lord

13:14* had his feet washed by Jesus

13:14* told by Jesus that he ought to wash one another's feet

13:15* had been given an example that he should do as Jesus had done to him

13:18* was known and chosen of Jesus

13:21* when told that one of them would betray Jesus, looked on the others, doubting of whom He spoke (13:22)

13:28* knew not for what intent Jesus spoke these words to Judas Iscariot

13:34* given a new commandment to love one another

13:34* loved of Jesus

13:35* love one to another was a mark that he was a true disciple of Jesus

14: 5* knew neither where the Lord was going nor the way (to His Father's house)

14:25* was with Jesus

14:26* would be instructed by the Holy Spirit in all things

14:26* the words Jesus had spoken would be brought to his remembrance

14:27* Jesus' peace was given to him and left with him

14:31* was told to arise and go with Jesus

15: 3* is clean through the Word

15: 9* loved of Jesus

15:12* commanded to love one another

15:12* loved of Jesus

John 15:16* chosen of Jesus and ordained of Him to go and bring forth fruit, and that his fruit should remain

15:17* commanded to love one another

15:19* not of the world

15:19* chosen out of the world by Jesus

15:19* hated of the world

15:27* would bear witness, because he had been with Jesus from the beginning

16: 4* was with Jesus

16: 6* sorrow had filled his heart

16:12* could not bear the words of Jesus

16:22* presently had sorrow

16:24* had asked nothing of the Father in Jesus' name

16:27* loved of the Father

16:27* loved Jesus and believed that He came from God

16:29* could now understand plainly Jesus' words

16:30* was sure that Jesus knew all things

16:30* believed that Jesus came forth from God

18: 1* went with Jesus over the brook Cedron and entered into a garden (Gethsemane)

18: 2* often resorted there with Jesus

20:18* told by Mary Magdalene that she had seen the Lord and that He had spoken unto her

20:24 one of the twelve (disciples)

20:24 called Didymus (meaning twin)

20:24 was not present with the others at Jesus' first appearance unto them

20:25 was told by the other disciples that they had seen the Lord

20:25 would not believe He had risen without certain specific conditions being met

20:26* the doors being shut again, Jesus appeared the second time to the entire group, he being present

20:27 told by Jesus to reach his finger and behold His hands, to reach his hand and thrust it into His side, and be not faithless, but believing

20:28 recognized Jesus as his Lord and God

20:29 because he had seen, he had believed

20:30* many other signs were done in his presence which are not written (in this book)

21: 1 saw Jesus at the Sea of Tiberias (Sea of Galilee) while with a group of disciples (21:2)

21: 2 called Didymus

21: 3 entering a ship, went fishing and caught nothing

21: 4 knew (recognized) not Jesus

21: 5 had no meat (had caught nothing)

21: 6 obeying Jesus' command, cast the net on the right side of the ship

21: 6 was not able to draw the net for

THOMAS *(continued)*

the multitude of fishes

John 21: 8 being not far from land, came in a little ship, dragging the net with fishes

21: 9 coming to land, saw a fire of coals with fish and bread thereon

21:10 told by Jesus to bring of the fish which he had caught

21:12 told to come and dine

21:12 dared not ask who He was, knowing it was the Lord

21:13 given bread and fish by Jesus

21:14 saw the resurrected Jesus

21:15 had dined with Jesus

Acts 1: 2* had been given commandments by Jesus (through the Holy Ghost)

1: 2* chosen by Jesus

1: 3* was shown Jesus alive after His passion

1: 3* spoken to by Jesus of the things pertaining to the kingdom of God

1: 3* saw Jesus forty days

1: 4* commanded, by Jesus, not to depart from Jerusalem, but to wait for the promise of the Father

1: 5* would be baptized with the Holy Spirit

1: 6* questioned Jesus concerning the restoration of the kingdom to Israel

1: 7* was not to know the times or the seasons which the Father had put in His own power

1: 8* after receiving the Holy Spirit, would receive power and would be witness unto Jesus Christ throughout the earth

1: 9* beheld as Jesus was taken up into Heaven at His ascension

1:10* was joined by two men in white apparel while he looked steadfastly toward Heaven

1:11* a man of Galilee

1:11* was gazing up into Heaven

1:11* Jesus was taken up from him into Heaven

1:11* was told that Jesus would come in like manner as he had seen Him go into Heaven

1:12* returned to Jerusalem and went into an upper room (1:13)

1:14* continued in prayer and supplication with the women, Mary the mother of Jesus, and with His brethren

1:21* was with the Lord Jesus at various times

1:24* prayed concerning the ordination of one to be a witness of Jesus' resurrection

1:26* gave forth his lot (concerning Judas Iscariot's successor)

2: 1* present at the day of Pentecost

2: 2* while sitting in the house, cloven tongues like as of fire sat upon him and he was filled with the Holy Ghost and spoke with other tongues (2:4)

Acts 2: 6* his speech confounded the multitude because every man heard in his own language

2: 7* a Galilean

2:13* mocked by some who claimed him as full of new wine

2:14* stood with (Simon) Peter

2:15* was not drunk

2:32* was a witness to the resurrection of Jesus

2:37* asked by the multitude on the day of Pentecost what they should do

2:42* many continued steadfastly in his doctrine and fellowship

2:43* many wonders and signs were done by him

4:33* with great power gave witness of the resurrection of the Lord Jesus

4:33* great grace was upon him

4:35* the price of possessions sold by Christians was laid at his feet

4:35* distributed to every man (of the Christian community) as he had need

4:36* gave Joses a surname of Barnabas

4:37* Joses's money was laid at his feet

5: 2* the gift of Ananias and Sapphira was laid at his feet

5:12* by his hands were many signs and wonders wrought among the people

5:12* was with one accord with the others in Solomon's porch

5:13* no man durst join himself to him (the apostles)

5:13* was magnified of the people

5:16* healed the multitude of sicknesses and unclean spirits

5:18* placed in the common prison by the high priest and Sadducees

5:19* released from prison by the angel of the Lord and told to go, stand, and speak in the temple (5:20)

5:21* entered into the temple early in the morning and taught

5:22* was not found in the prison

5:25* was standing in the temple and teaching the people

5:26* brought without violence and set before the council (5:27)

5:27* questioned by the high priest (5:28)

5:28* had been commanded not to teach in this (Jesus') name

5:28* had filled Jerusalem with his doctrine and had (seemingly) intended to bring Jesus' blood upon his accusers

5:29* believed that he ought to obey God rather than men

5:32* witness of God (and of His works)

THOMAS *(continued)*

Acts 5:33* Jewish leaders took counsel to slay him
5:34* put a little space from the Sanhedrin (for their deliberation)
5:40* called back before the council, beaten, commanded not to speak in the name of Jesus and let go
5:41* departed from the council rejoicing that he was counted worthy to suffer shame for His name
5:42* daily in the temple and in every house, ceased not to teach and preach Jesus Christ
6: 2* called the multitude together and stated it was not reasonable that he should leave the Word of God and serve tables
6: 3* instructed that seven men of honest report be chosen to be appointed to serve tables
6: 4* determined to give himself continually to prayer and to the ministry of the Word
6: 6* the chosen seven were set before him, for whom he prayed and laid his hands on them
8: 1* remained in Jerusalem in the midst of great persecution
8:14* was in Jerusalem
8:14* hearing that Samaria had received the Word of God, sent Peter and John to Samaria
9:27* Saul (Paul) was brought to him by Barnabas and he was informed of Saul's (Paul's) conversion experience and his bold preaching at Damascus
9:28* was accompanied by Saul (Paul) in coming in and going out at Jerusalem
10:39* was witness of all things Jesus did both in the land of the Jews and in Jerusalem
10:41* a witness chosen before of God
10:41* ate and drank with Jesus after His resurrection
10:42* commanded of Jesus to preach unto the people, and testified that it was Jesus which was ordained of God to be the Judge of quick and dead
11: 1* was in Judea
11: 1* heard that the Gentiles had also received the Word of God
11:15* the Holy Ghost fell on him at the beginning (Pentecost)
13:31* saw Jesus many days
13:31* came up with Jesus from Galilee to Jerusalem
13:31* was His (Jesus') witness unto the people
15: 2* Paul, Barnabas, and others were sent by the church at Antioch to consult with him over the matter

of circumcision

Acts 15: 4* received Paul, Barnabas, and the others from Antioch
15: 6* came together (with the elders) to consider the matter (of circumcision)
15: 8* given the Holy Ghost
15: 9* God made no difference between him and a Gentile
15:10* was not able to bear the yoke
15:22* acting with the elders, sent chosen men back to Antioch with Paul and Barnabas
15:23* acting with the elders and brethren, wrote letters of instruction to the Gentiles at Antioch, Syria, and Cilicia
15:24* gave no commandment that Gentile believers must be circumcised and keep the law
15:25* considered it good, being assembled, to send chosen men unto the believers
15:25* loved Barnabas and Paul
15:27* sent Judas and Silas to the Gentile believers
15:33* Judas (Barsabas) and Silas returned unto him
16: 4* with the elders, ordained decrees
16: 4* was at Jerusalem
Rom 16: 7* Andronicus and Junia were well known to him
1Cor 4: 9* Paul thought God had set him (and the apostles) forth last, as it were appointed to death
4: 9* made a spectacle unto the world, to the angels, and to men
4:10* a fool for Christ's sake
4:10* weak, despised
4:11* hungered, thirsted, was naked, was buffeted and had no certain dwelling place
4:12* labored, working with his own hands
4:12* being reviled, he blessed; being persecuted, he suffered it; being defamed, he entreated (4:13)
4:13* made as the filth of the world, and the offscouring of all things
9: 5* had power to lead about a sister, a wife
15: 5* had seen the risen Lord
15: 7* the risen Lord was seen of him
15:11* preached
Rev 21:14* name inscribed in the twelve foundations of the new Jerusalem
21:14* an apostle of the Lamb

TIBERIUS (Caesar) [ti-be'-re-us = from the Tiber]
A stepson of Augustus and an emperor of Rome whose full name was Tiberius Claudius Nero.

Matt 22:20 his image and superscription were on the penny (22:21)

TIBERIUS (continued)

Mark	12:14	received tribute
	12:16	image and superscription were on the (Roman) penny
	12:17	Jesus commanded that the people render to him the things that were his
Luke	3: 1	had reigned fifteen years
	3: 1	contemporary of Pontius Pilate, Herod, Philip, and Lysanias (tetrarchs) and Annas and Caiaphas (high priests) (3:2)
	20:22	received tribute
	20:24	his image and superscription were on the (Roman) penny
	20:25	those things which were his were to be rendered to him
	23: 2	some falsely claimed that Jesus had forbidden to give tribute to him
John	19:12	Pilate would not be his friend if he released Jesus
	19:12	was spoken against by those who made themselves a king
	19:15	claimed as the only king by the Jews
Acts	17: 7	Paul and Silas (and Timothy and Jason) were accused of disloyalty to his decrees
	17: 7	a king

TIMAEUS [ti-me'-us = highly prized]
Father of Bartimaeus.

Mark	10:46	father of Bartimaeus

TIMON [ti'-mon = honorable]
One of seven men of honest report, full of the Holy Ghost, chosen to serve tables as a deacon in the Jerusalem church, and received the laying on of hands by the apostles.

Acts	6: 3	of honest report
	6: 3	full of the Holy Ghost and wisdom
	6: 5	chosen to serve tables
	6: 6	was set before the apostles
	6: 6	apostles prayed and laid their hands on him

TIMOTHEUS [tim-o'-the-us = honored of God]
—see TIMOTHY

TIMOTHY [tim'-o-thy = honored of God]
Also Timotheus, a disciple of Lystra, son of a Greek father and a Jewish mother (Eunice), grandson of Lois, spiritual son and traveling companion of Paul, and recipient of 1 and 2 Timothy (while pastor at Ephesus).

Acts	16: 1	a disciple
	16: 1	was in Lystra
	16: 1	mother was a Jewess
	16: 1	father was a Greek
	16: 2	was well reported of by the brethren at Lystra and Iconium
	16: 3	Paul wanted him to travel with him
	16: 3	circumcised by Paul

Acts	16: 3	father was a Greek
	16: 4	went through the cities delivering the decrees that were ordained of the apostles and elders which were at Jerusalem
	16: 6	had gone throughout Phrygia and the region of Galatia
	16: 6	forbidden of the Holy Ghost to preach the word in Asia
	16: 7	came to Mysia and desired to go into Bithynia, but not suffered of the Spirit to do so
	16: 8	passing by Mysia came down to Troas
	16:10	endeavored to go into Macedonia, assured that the Lord had called him to preach the gospel unto them
	16:11	loosing from Troas, took a straight course to Samothracia
	16:11	the next day went on to Neapolis
	16:12	went on to Philippi and abode there certain days
	16:13	on the Sabbath went out of the city to a place of prayer and spoke unto the women
	16:14	heard by Lydia
	16:15	constrained by Lydia to abide at her house
	16:16	met by a damsel possessed with a spirit of divination as he went to prayer
	16:17	followed by a damsel possessed with a spirit of divination
	16:17	claimed by one to be the servant of the most high God, which showed unto us the way of salvation
	17: 1	passed through Amphipolis and Apollonia and came to Thessalonica
	17: 6	was not found in the house of Jason
	17: 6	had turned the world upside down
	17: 6	was come to Thessalonica
	17: 7	had been received of Jason (in his house)
	17: 7	accused of disloyalty to Caesar by saying there was another king
	17: 9	had security taken of him and was let go
	17:10	sent away by night to Berea
	17:10	went into the synagogue at Berea
	17:14	abode still in Berea
	17:15	receiving a commandment from Paul to come to him with all speed, departed
	17:16	Paul waited for him and Silas at Athens
	18: 5	was come from Macedonia
	18:11	continued a year and six months (with Paul in the house of Justus)
	18:18	sailed into Syria (with Paul)
	18:19	came to Ephesus
	18:21	sailed from Ephesus
	18:22	landed at Caesarea
	18:22	went down to Antioch

TIMOTHY *(continued)*

Acts	18:23	spent some time there (in Antioch), departed, and went over all the country of Galatia and Phrygia (with Paul)
	19: 1	passed through the upper coasts and came to Ephesus
	19:10	continued two years (with Paul in Asia)
	19:22	sent into Macedonia by Paul
	19:22	ministered unto Paul
	20: 4	accompanied Paul into Asia
	20: 5	went before and tarried for Paul (and Luke) at Troas
	20: 6	abode seven days with Paul (and Luke) at Troas
	20:13	going before by ship, sailed unto Assos
	20:14	met Paul at Assos, took him in, and came to Mitylene
	20:15	sailed over against Chios, the next day arrived at Samos, tarried at Trogyllium, and the next day came to Miletus
	20:34	Paul's hands had ministered unto his necessities
Rom	16:21	a workfellow of Paul
	16:21	saluted the church at Rome
1Cor	4:17	sent by Paul to the Corinthians to bring them in remembrance of Paul's ways
	4:17	the beloved (spiritual) son of Paul
	4:17	faithful in the Lord
	16:10	worked the work of the Lord
	16:11	was not to be despised, but conducted forth in peace unto Paul
	16:11	Paul looked for him to come with the brethren
2Cor	1: 1	(Christian) brother of Paul
	1:19	preached the Son of God, Jesus Christ, among the Corinthians
	1:19	his preaching was not yea and nay, but in Him (Christ) was yea
Phil	1: 1	the servant of Jesus Christ
	2:19	Paul trusted in the Lord Jesus to send him to report on the state of the Philippians
	2:20	was likeminded (as Paul) to naturally care for the state of the Philippian church
	2:22	as a son with the father, he had served with Paul in the gospel
	2:23	Paul hoped to send him to the Philippian church
	4:21	sent greetings to the church at Philippi (through Paul)
Col	1: 1	a Christian brother to Paul and the Colossians
	1: 2	mentioned by Paul in the greeting in the book of Colossians
1The	1: 1	mentioned, along with Silvanus, by Paul in greetings to the Thessalonians
	1: 2	thanked God always for the Thes-

		salonian church, mentioning them in his prayers
1The	1: 5	gave the gospel not only in word, but in power, and in the Holy Spirit, and in much assurance
	1: 5	his testimony was well known among the Thessalonian brethren for good
	1: 6	the Thessalonian Christians became his followers (and the Lord's)
	1: 7	people in Macedonia and Achaia knew of his good work with the Thessalonians (1:9)
	1:10	delivered from the wrath to come (by Christ Jesus)
	2: 3	his exhortation was not of deceit, uncleanness, nor in guile
	2: 4	spoke the gospel, of which he was allowed of God to be put in trust
	2: 4	sought not to please men, but God
	3: 2	sent by Paul to establish the Thessalonians and to comfort them concerning their faith
	3: 2	a Christian brother of Paul
	3: 2	a minister of God
	3: 2	fellow laborer, with Paul, in the gospel of Christ
	3: 6	took good tidings to Paul concerning the faith and charity of the Thessalonians
2The	1: 1	mentioned, along with Silvanus, by Paul in greetings to the Thessalonians
1Tim	1: 2	recipient of epistle of 1 Timothy
	1: 2	spiritual son of Paul
	1: 3	was in Ephesus and besought by Paul to remain there in order to charge the Ephesians to teach the faith
	1:18	charged, by Paul, to war a good warfare
	3: 1	given instruction, by Paul, concerning officers and duties in the church of God (3:13)
	4:12	was young
	4:14	had spiritual gift given him by prophecy with the laying on of hands of the presbytery
	6:12	professed a good profession before many witnesses
	6:20	charged, by Paul, to keep that which had been committed to his trust
2Tim	1: 2	recipient of epistle of 2 Timothy
	1: 2	dearly beloved (spiritual) son of Paul
	1: 3	remembered, by Paul, in prayer night and day
	1: 4	greatly desired to be seen by Paul
	1: 4	Paul was mindful of his tears
	1: 5	had unfeigned faith
	1: 5	his grandmother was Lois
	1: 5	his mother was Eunice
	1: 6	received a gift of God by the putting

on of Paul's hands

2Tim 1:13 witnessed Paul's sound teaching
1:14 encouraged, by Paul, to keep by the Holy Spirit that good thing which was committed unto him
2: 1 called (spiritual) son by Paul
2: 2 heard many things of Paul (among many witnesses) and was admonished to commit those things to faithful men
2: 3 admonished to endure hardness as a good soldier of Jesus Christ
2: 7 instructed to consider the words of Paul, and the Lord would give him understanding in all things
2:14 instructed, by Paul, to charge the Christians before God that they strive not about words to no profit
2:15 instructed to study to show himself approved, a workman that needeth not to be ashamed, rightly dividing the Word of truth
2:16 admonished to shun profane and vain babblings
2:22 instructed to flee youthful lusts, but to follow righteousness, faith, charity, and peace, and to be possessed of a pure heart
3: 5 warned, by Paul, to turn away from ungodly men
3:10 fully knew the doctrine, manner of life, purpose, faith, longsuffering, charity, patience, persecutions, and afflictions of Paul at Antioch, at Iconium, and at Lystra (3:11)
3:14 had learned many things of Paul
3:15 from a child had known the Holy Scriptures
4: 1 charged, by Paul, before God, to preach the Word, to be instant in season, out of season, to reprove, rebuke, and exhort with all longsuffering and doctrine (4:2)
4: 5 admonished by Paul to endure afflictions, to do the work of an evangelist, and to make full proof of his ministry
4: 9 requested by Paul, to diligently endeavor to come shortly to him
4:11 asked, by Paul, to bring Mark with him, to Paul
4:13 asked, by Paul, to bring his cloak (left at Troas with Carpus), his books, and especially the parchments
4:14 warned, by Paul, to beware of Alexander the coppersmith (4:15)
4:19 requested by Paul to salute Prisca, Aquila, and the household of Onesiphorus
4:21 diligently requested, by Paul, to come to him before winter
4:21 greetings sent to him by Eubulus, Pudens, Linus, Claudia, and all the brethren (by the hand of Paul in this epistle)

2Tim 4:22 given a benediction by Paul
Phle : 1 mentioned by Paul in greeting in the book of Philemon
: 1 Christian brother of Paul
: 1 dearly beloved and fellow laborer of Philemon
: 2 fellow soldier of Archippus
Heb 13:23 was set at liberty

TITUS [ti'-tus = nurse; rearer]

A Grecian traveling companion of Paul and his spiritual son, reported to Paul on the condition of the Corinthian church, ministered on Crete, and recipient of the book of Titus.

2Cor 2:13 a (Christian) brother of Paul
2:13 was not found by Paul (in Troas)
7: 6 comforted Paul by his coming
7: 7 was comforted in the Corinthians
7: 7 informed Paul of the Corinthians' condition
7:13 had joy
7:13 his spirit was refreshed (by the Corinthians)
7:14 Paul had boasted to him concerning the Corinthians (in truth)
7:15 his inward affection was more abundant toward the Corinthians
7:15 remembered the obedience of the Corinthians
7:15 had been received by the Corinthians with fear and trembling
8: 6 had begun work among the Corinthians
8:16 God had put an earnest care in his heart for the Corinthians
8:17 accepted exhortation
8:17 being more forward, of his own accord went unto the Corinthians
8:18 Paul sent Luke to accompany him
8:19 chosen of the church to travel with Paul (and possibly Luke)
8:20 avoided that any man should blame him in abundance (of grace) which he administered
8:21 provided for honest things, not only in the sight of the Lord, but also in the sight of men
8:23 partner and fellow helper of Paul concerning the Corinthian
9: 3 sent by Paul to the Corinthian church
9: 5 exhorted to go before (to Corinth) and make up the bounty (for the saints)
12:17 sent by Paul unto the Corinthians
12:18 desired of Paul (to be sent to the Corinthians)
12:18 Luke sent with him (by Paul, to the Corinthians)
12:18 made no gain of the Corinthians

TIMOTHY *(continued)*

2Cor	12:18	walked in the same spirit (as Paul)
	12:18	walked in the same steps (as Paul)
Gal	2: 1	taken to Jerusalem by Paul and Barnabas
	2: 3	was with Paul in Jerusalem
	2: 3	a Greek
	2: 3	was not compelled to be circumcised
2Tim	4:10	departed unto Dalmatia
Tit	1: 4	recipient of letter from Paul (epistle of Titus)
	1: 4	(spiritual) son of Paul after the common faith
	1: 5	left in Crete, by Paul, to set things in order to ordain elders in every city
	2: 1	admonished by Paul to speak things which become sound doctrine
	3:12	asked by Paul to meet him in Nicopolis and to bring Zenas and Apollos (3:13)

TROPHIMUS [trof'-im-us = a foster child; nutritious]
An Ephesian traveling companion of Paul whom he left sick at Miletus.

Acts	20: 4	of Asia
	20: 4	accompanied Paul into Asia
	20: 5	went before and tarried for Paul (and Luke) at Troas
	20: 6	abode seven days with Paul (and Luke) at Troas
	20:13	going before by ship, sailed unto Assos
	20:14	met Paul at Assos, took him in, and came to Mitylene
	20:15	sailed over against Chios, next day arrived at Samos, tarried at Trogyllium, and next day came to Miletus
	20:34	Paul's hands had ministered unto his necessities
	21:29	had been seen in Jerusalem with Paul
	21:29	an Ephesian
	21:29	people supposed he had been brought into the temple by Paul
2Tim	4:20	left sick at Miletus by Paul

TRYPHENA ♀ [tri-fe'-nah = luxurious]
A female believer in Rome, greeted by Paul, who labored much in the Lord.

Rom	16:12	saluted by Paul
	16:12	labored in the Lord

TRYPHOSA ♀ [tri-fo'-sah = luxuriating]
A female believer in Rome, greeted by Paul, who labored much in the Lord.

Rom	16:12	saluted by Paul
	16:12	labored in the Lord

TYCHICUS [tik'-ik-us = fortunate; fateful]
A beloved Christian brother and traveling companion of Paul who reported to the Ephesian church on the affairs of Paul.

Acts	20: 4	of Asia
	20: 4	accompanied Paul into Asia
	20: 5	went before, and tarried for Paul (and Luke) at Troas
	20: 6	abode seven days with Paul (and Luke) at Troas
	20:13	going before by ship, sailed unto Assos
	20:14	met Paul at Assos, took him in, and came to Mitylene
	20:15	sailed over against Chios, the next day arrived at Samos, tarried at Trogyllium, and the next day came to Miletus
	20:34	Paul's hands had ministered unto his necessities
Eph	6:21	a beloved brother (of Paul)
	6:21	a faithful minister in the Lord assigned to report to the Ephesian church on the affairs of Paul
Col	4: 7	reported (along with Onesimus) of Paul to the Colossians (4:8)
	4: 7	a beloved brother (of Paul) and a faithful minister and fellow servant in the Lord
	4: 8	sent (by Paul) to the Colossian church to learn of their estate (to be reported back to Paul) and to comfort their hearts
	4: 9	would make known unto the Colossians all things done by Paul
2Tim	4:12	sent, by Paul, to Ephesus
Tit	3:12	possibly sent by Paul to Titus

TYRANNUS [ti-ran'-nus = sovereign]
A man of Ephesus in whose school Paul reasoned daily for the space of two years.

Acts	19: 9	had a school in Ephesus
	19: 9	Paul disputed daily in his school (for two years) (19:10)

U

URBANE [ur'-bane = of the city; polite]
A Christian of Rome, a helper of Paul in Christ, who received greetings from Paul.

Rom	16: 9	saluted by Paul
	16: 9	Paul's helper in Christ

URIAS [u-ri'-as = Jehovah is light]
Old Testament Uriah, the Hittite, the former husband of Bathsheba, and a mighty warrior whom David had murdered. (See also 2Sam 11, 12)

Matt	1: 6	former husband of Solomon's mother

Z

ZABULON [zab'-u-lon = habitation; dwelling]
Old Testament Zebulun, one of the patriarchs, and the tenth son of Jacob by Leah (her sixth). (See also Gen 30, 46)

Matt	1: 2	begotten of Jacob
	1: 2	had brethren
John	4:12	drank of the well (Jacob's)
	4:12	a child of Jacob
Acts	7: 8	begotten of Jacob
	7: 8	one of the patriarchs
	7: 9	one of the patriarchs
	7: 9	moved with envy, sold Joseph into Egypt
	7:11	found no sustenance
	7:12	sent by Jacob to Egypt for corn
	7:13	on his second visit (to Egypt), Joseph was made known to him
	7:13	was made known unto Pharaoh
	7:15	went down into Egypt and died
	7:16	was carried into Sychem and was laid in the sepulcher that Abraham bought
Rev	7: 8	twelve thousand sealed of his tribe
	21:12	his name is inscribed upon the gates of the new Jerusalem
	21:12	a child of Israel (Jacob)

ZACCHAEUS [zak-ke'-us = pure]
A publican (tax collector) of Jericho who was short of stature, converted at the words of Jesus, and provided restitution for those he had defrauded.

Luke	19: 1	lived in Jericho (19:2)
	19: 2	a rich man
	19: 2	chief among the publicans
	19: 3	sought to see Jesus, but could not because of the press (crowd)
	19: 3	was little of stature
	19: 4	ran before and climbed up into a sycamore tree to see Jesus
	19: 5	Jesus saw him and told him to make haste and come down, for today He must abide at his house
	19: 6	made haste, came down, and received Jesus joyfully
	19: 7	a sinner
	19: 8	stood before the Lord declaring that he would give to the poor and make restitution
	19: 9	salvation came to his house
	19: 9	son of Abraham (of his lineage)

ZACHARIAS [zak-a-ri'-as = Jehovah is renowned]
Old Testament Zachariah, son of Berechias, slain by the Jews between the temple and the altar.

Matt	23:35	his blood would be upon the scribes and Pharisees
	23:35	son of Barachias
	23:35	slain between the temple and the altar

Luke	11:51	his blood would be required of this generation
	11:51	perished between the altar and the temple

2. Father of John the Baptist, husband of Elisabeth, a priest of the course of Abia, and a righteous man who walked blameless in all the commandments and ordinances of the Lord.

Luke	1: 5	lived in the days of Herod the king
	1: 5	a priest (of the course of Abia)
	1: 5	his wife (Elisabeth) was of the daughters of Aaron
	1: 6	a righteous man who walked blameless in all commandments and ordinances of the Lord
	1: 7	childless because his wife was barren
	1: 7	well stricken in years
	1: 8	executed the priest's office before God
	1: 9	his lot was to burn incense in the temple
	1:11	an angel of the Lord appeared unto him in the temple
	1:12	was troubled and feared at the presence of the angel
	1:13	told that his prayer was heard and that his wife would bear him a son to be named John
	1:18	questioned the angel's words because he and his wife were old
	1:19	Gabriel (an angel) was sent to speak to him
	1:20	would be dumb, and not able to speak until Gabriel's prediction was fulfilled (because of unbelief)
	1:21	tarried long in the temple
	1:22	upon his exit from the temple was unable to speak, but beckoned to the people
	1:22	remained speechless
	1:23	after his ministration was accomplished he departed to his own house
	1:24	his wife conceived
	1:39	lived in the hill country in a city in Juda
	1:40	Mary entered his house
	1:57	his wife brought forth a son
	1:59	his name originally given to his son by those present
	1:63	asking for a writing table, wrote that his son's name would be John
	1:64	immediately his mouth was opened, his tongue loosed, and he spoke and praised God
	1:67	father of John (the Baptist)
	1:67	was filled with the Holy Ghost
	1:67	prophesied
	1:76	prophesied that his son John would be called the prophet of the Highest
	3: 2	father of John (the Baptist)

ZARA [za'-rah = sprout (?)]

ZARA *(continued)*
Old Testament Zerah, son of Judas by Thamar, twin brother of Phares, and an ancestor of Jesus. (See also Gen 38, 46; Josh 7, 22; 1Chr 2, 9)

Matt   1: 3   begotten by Judas of Thamar
          1: 3   brother of Phares

ZEBEDEE [zeb'-e-dee = Jehovah is gift]
Father of James and John (apostles), husband of Salome, and a fisherman by trade.

Matt   4:21   father of James and John (apostles)
         4:21   was in a ship with James and John mending nets
         4:22   left by his sons to follow Jesus
       10: 2   father of James and John (apostles)
      20:20   his wife and sons came to Jesus to ask favor to have his sons sit on the right and left hand of Jesus in His kingdom (20:21)
      26:37   his two sons went with Jesus to garden of Gethsemane
      27:56   his wife beheld afar off the crucifixion of Jesus
      27:56   had children (James and John)
Mark   1:19   father of James and John (apostles)
         1:19   was in the ship with James, John, and hired servants (1:20)
         1:20   had hired servants
         1:20   was left by his sons to follow Jesus
         3:17   father of James and John (apostles)
Luke   5:10   father of James and John (apostles)
John   21: 2   had sons (who were with Jesus and other disciples)

ZENAS [ze'-nas = the gift of Zeus]
A believer and lawyer (interpreter of the Mosaic law) whom Paul requested Titus to send to him at Nicopolis.

Tit   3:13   a lawyer
      3:13   Paul asked Titus to bring him to Nicopolis to be with Paul

ZOROBABEL [zo-rob'-a-bel = born at Babylon; melted by Babylon]
Old Testament Zerubbabel, son of Salathiel, an ancestor of Jesus, and led a group of captives back from Babylon to Jerusalem to begin reconstruction of the temple and the city. (See also 1Chr 3; Ezra 2—5; Neh 12; Hag 1, 2; Zech 4)

Matt   1:12   begotten by Salathiel
         1:13   begat Abiud
Luke   3:27   father of Rhesa
         3:27   son of Salathiel